CURATING THE GREAT WAR

Curating the Great War explores the inception and subsequent development of museums of the Great War and the animating spirit which lay behind them.

The book approaches museums of the Great War as political entities, some more overtly than others, but all unable to escape from the politics of the war, its profound legacies and its enduring memory. Their changing configurations and content are explored as reflections of the social and political context in which they exist. Curating of the Great War has expanded beyond the walls of museum buildings, seeking public engagement, both direct and digital, and taking in whole landscapes. Recognizing this fact, the book examines these museums as standing at the nexus of historiography, museology, anthropology, archaeology, sociology and politics as well as being a *lieux de mémoire*. Their multi-vocal nature makes them a compelling subject for research and above all the book highlights that it is in these museums that we see the most complete fusion of the material culture of conflict with its historical, political and experiential context.

This book is an essential read for researchers of the reception of the Great War through material culture and museums.

Paul Cornish was, for 32 years, a curator at Imperial War Museums. He is co-editor of the Routledge series *Material Culture and Modern Conflict*.

Nicholas J. Saunders is Professor of Material Culture at Bristol University, UK, and co-director of the 'Great Arab Revolt Project'.

CURATING THE GREAT WAR

Edited by Paul Cornish and Nicholas J. Saunders

Routledge
Taylor & Francis Group

LONDON AND NEW YORK

Cover image: Stephen Dixon, Buttoncard, 2015. (© Stephen Dixon. Photographer Stephen Dixon. Medium: Real Photo Postcard, military buttons, thread. Dimensions: 14cms high x 9cms wide. Location: Private collection).

First published 2023
by Routledge
4 Park Square, Milton Park, Abingdon, Oxon OX14 4RN

and by Routledge
605 Third Avenue, New York, NY 10158

Routledge is an imprint of the Taylor & Francis Group, an informa business

British Library Cataloguing-in-Publication Data
A catalogue record for this book is available from the British Library

Library of Congress Cataloging-in-Publication Data
A catalog record has been requested for this book

ISBN: 978-1-032-20433-8 (hbk)
ISBN: 978-1-032-20269-3 (pbk)
ISBN: 978-1-003-26353-1 (ebk)

DOI: 10.4324/9781003263531

Typeset in Bembo Std
by KnowledgeWorks Global Ltd.

CONTENTS

FIGURES

CONTRIBUTORS

Martin Barry is a mature PhD student in the Archaeology and Anthropology Department at the University of Bristol. His research topic 'A Box of Conflict Memories – Materiality, Memory and Princess Mary's Gift Box 1914–1920' looks at the history and legacy of the Christmas tin given to soldiers from a material culture standpoint. He is also a part-time Assistant Teacher at the university, running seminars about Material Culture for undergraduate students. He has designed and curated a number of museum exhibitions about the First World War.

Isabelle Brandauer was born in Tyrol and holds a PhD in history from the University in Innsbruck. Her work and numerous publications have focused on the First World War in the region. In 2007–2010, she was scientific coordinator for the Bergisel Museum at the Tyrolean State Museum in Innsbruck. She is currently head of the Tirol Panorama with Kaiserjägermuseum in that city. In 2017–2019, she was coordinator for the Maximilian commemoration year 2019 on behalf of the state of Tyrol.

Ana Carden-Coyne is Director of the Centre for the Cultural History of War (CCHW) at the University of Manchester. Her publications include *Reconstructing the Body: Classicism, Modernism and the First World War* (Oxford University Press, 2009) and *The Politics of Wounds: Military Patients and Medical Power in the First World War* (Oxford University Press, 2014). For the First World War centenary she co-curated the exhibition *The Sensory War 1914–2014* with Manchester Art Gallery and the Whitworth Art Gallery and, for the Somme centenary, *Visions of the Front, 1916–18* (Whitworth Art Gallery).

Željko Cimprić is a co-founder and now retired curator of the award-winning Kobarid Museum (Kobariški Muzej) in the Soča Valley, Slovenia. As a historian of the Soča (Isonzo) Campaign of the First World War and a mountaineer, he became a co-founder of the Walk of Peace (Poti miru v Posočju) Foundation also in Kobarid.

Paul Cornish was, for 32 years, a curator at Imperial War Museums. He was part of the teams that created IWM London's permanent First and Second World War Galleries (2014 and 2021). In collaboration with Nicholas J. Saunders, he co-organized six IWM-based conferences on the material culture of conflict and co-edited the volumes *Contested Objects* (2009), *Bodies in Conflict* (2014), *Modern Conflict and the Senses* (2017) and *Conflict Landscapes* (2021). He is co-editor of the Routledge series *Material Culture and Modern Conflict*.

Philip W. Deans completed an undergraduate degree in Performing Arts at Canterbury Christ Church University in 2011, a postgraduate degree in Military History at the University of Chester in 2012 and a postgraduate degree in Museum Studies at Newcastle University in 2014. Following a hiatus from studying, he completed doctoral research at Newcastle University in 2021. A museum historian, Philip is currently a board member of the Museums and Galleries History Group and a visiting researcher at Newcastle University.

Dominiek Dendooven is a researcher and curator at In Flanders Fields Museum, Ieper, Belgium. Major exhibitions coordinated by him include *Man-Culture-War. Multicultural Aspects of the First World War* (2008) and *'Phoenix': Reconstructing Flanders Fields* (2020). He has published extensively on issues such as commemoration (*Menin Gate & Last Post. Ypres as Holy ground*, 2001/2014), the reconstruction of Ypres (*Ypres. War and Reconstruction*, 2020) and the non-European presence on the Western Front (*Asia in Flanders Fields. Indians and Chinese on the Western Front 1914–1920*, 2021).

Mark J.R. Dennis, MA FRHistS FSA, is curator at the Museum of Freemasonry in London. He has published chapters in books and catalogues including 'Contested Objects – material memories of the Great War' Routledge 2009 and 'The Material Culture of Freemasonry' in the Brill Handbook of Freemasonry 2014. He has designed and curated numerous exhibitions examining the material culture of freemasonry in the UK and elsewhere. He is currently a PhD candidate at the University of Bristol.

Stephen Dixon is Professor of Contemporary Crafts at Manchester School of Art. As an academic and researcher as well as a maker, Dixon's practice engages with the narrative and decorative traditions of ceramics and brings this rich visual vocabulary to bear on contemporary issues and contemporary experience. Recent work has focused on the commemorative potential of ceramics and has resulted in an increasing engagement with museums, archives and the public to explore memory and memorialization in the context of the centenary of the

Great War. His work features in numerous public collections, including the Museum of Arts & Design New York, the British Council, the Crafts Council and the V & A.

Siobhán Doyle completed a PhD in Museum Studies at Technological University Dublin in May 2020, funded by the Dean of the College of Arts & Tourism scholarship award. Siobhán's doctoral research concerns the material and visual culture of modern Ireland with a particular focus upon the role of exhibition display in representations of death and in commemorative narratives. Siobhán's research has been published by the European Remembrance and Solidarity Network in 2018 and Arms and Armour journal in 2019.

Dawid Kobiałka holds a doctorate from the Adam Mickiewicz University in Poznań and works at the Institute of Archaeology and Ethnology of the Polish Academy of Science in Warsaw. His research interests include public archaeology, heritage studies and archaeologies of the recent past.

Boštjan Kravanja is an assistant professor at the Department of Ethnology and Cultural Anthropology, University of Ljubljana, Slovenia. His research interests include anthropology of tourism, anthropology of space and place, political uses of religions and mythologies, sacred places and landscapes, experiential aspects of ethnographic fieldwork, aspects of South Asian tourism and different uses of heritage in the contemporary world. His regional interests lie in South Asia, Macedonia and Slovenia.

Alessandra Martina is a graduate of the University of Trieste, Italy. She is curator of the Museum of the Great War at Gorizia, where, among many other exhibitions, she co-created the Great War centenary exhibition: *Luoghi di pace dal fronte del sangue. Carso, Isonzo, Gorizia: cento anni fa campi di battaglia, oggi luoghi di pace e di incontro al centro dell'Europa.*

Kirstie Ross, currently Senior Curator Cultural Heritage at Tasmanian Museum and Art Gallery, has worked as a social history curator in museums in New Zealand and Australia since 2004. During the 2014–2018 centennial commemorations, she was the lead curator of Te Papa's Gallipoli: The scale of our war and also worked on smaller exhibitions and a number of digital projects related to New Zealand's wartime home front. With Kate Hunter, she has published on the material culture of the Great War and has an ongoing research interest in the history of social history in museums.

Nicholas J. Saunders is Professor of Material Culture at Bristol University, UK, and co-director of the 'Great Arab Revolt Project'. Between 1998 and 2004, he was British Academy Senior Research Fellow at University College London, making the first anthropological study of the material culture of the

First World War. He has undertaken research in France, Belgium, Bosnia, Jordan, Mexico, Peru and the Caribbean, and currently in Slovenia with the 'Soca/Isonzo Valley Conflict Landscapes Project'. He is also researching the First World War material culture of the Chinese Labour Corps on the Western Front. He has published widely on the anthropology and archaeology of modern conflict, including *Trench Art* (2003), *Matters of Conflict* (2004), *Killing Time: Archaeology and the First World War* (2007), *Desert Insurgency: Archaeology, T.E. Lawrence, and the Arab Revolt* (2020). With Paul Cornish, he has edited *Contested Objects* (2009), *Bodies in Conflict* (2014), *Modern Conflict and the Senses* (2017) and *Conflict Landscapes* (2021). He is co-editor of the Routledge series *Material Culture and Modern Conflict*.

Andrew Shapland is Sir Arthur Evans Curator of Bronze Age and Classical Greece, Department of Antiquities, Ashmolean Museum. He began researching the archaeology of the Macedonian Campaign while a curator at the British Museum and with Liana Stefani he co-edited *Archaeology Behind the Battle Lines: The Macedonian Campaign (1915–1919) and Its Legacy* (2017).

James Wallis is a Research Fellow at the University of Essex, an Honorary Research Fellow at the University of Exeter and a freelance contractor. He is currently involved with the 'Reflections on the Centenary of the First World War: Learning and Legacies for the Future' project, evaluating outcomes of the 2014–18 centennial commemorations across the UK. He is also an Associate for Imperial War Museums' Public Institute for the Understanding of War and Conflict. His interdisciplinary published work includes Commemorative Spaces of the First World War: Historical Geographies at the Centenary PRoutledge, 2017).

Thomas Weissbrich is Head of the Militaria Collection, Deutsches Historisches Museum, Berlin. A PhD in history and author of *The King's old clothes. The uniforms of Frederick II of Prussia as objects for collection, display and study*. In Günther, S. de and P. Zitzelsperger (eds), *Signs and Symbols. Dress at the Intersection between Image and Realia*. Berlin/Boston, 2018, pp 59–88.

Jennifer Wellington is a lecturer in modern history at University College Dublin. She received honours degrees in Law and English from the Australian National University. Following this she completed her PhD in history at Yale University, where her PhD thesis was awarded the Hans Gatzske Prize for Outstanding Dissertation in a field of European history. Her book, *Exhibiting War*, was published by Cambridge University Press in 2017. She is now researching the broader legal, social and cultural history of war trophies.

Jay Winter is the Charles J. Stille Professor of History Emeritus at Yale University. He is the author of, *inter alia, Sites of Memory, Sites of Mourning; Remembering War* and *War beyond words: Languages of remembrance from the Great War to the present.* In the field of public history, he was one of the founders of the Historial de la Grande Guerre at Péronne, France, and received an Emmy award for his 1997 television documentary *The Great War and the Shaping of the Twentieth Century.*

Bérénice Zunino is a lecturer at the University of Franche-Comté (Besançon). Her research interests focus on the cultural history of the First World War and visual studies in the German-speaking world during the first half of the twentieth century. In particular, she published in 2019: *Die Mobilmachung der Kinder im Ersten Weltkrieg. Kriegskultur und illustrierte Kriegskinderliteratur im Deutschen Kaiserreich (1911–1918).* Berlin, Peter Lang.

FOREWORD

Jay Winter

In Ljubljana's majestic castle, high above the city, there are photographs of Italian prisoners of war in the city after the Battle of Caporetto in 1917. Their faces bring home to casual visitors how close to the surface of collective and personal memory is the Great War. In many parts of Europe, we just have to brush aside other private or public representations of the past, in this case, the Habsburg past and the Yugoslav past, and there it is.

The Kodak revolution of the First World War is part of the reason why myriad traces of the war are within our reach. Soldiers took photographs all the time, whatever the rules of censorship said. This global archive of photography enables us to have what Emmanuel Levinas called a face-to-face encounter with the men and women of 1914–18. This encounter, he goes on, is asymmetrical, since we can see not just similarities between today and yesterday, but the alterity of the past.

This kind of encounter, with those whose history is both very close to ours and very far away, is part of the enduring attraction of the First World War to students, scholars, citizens and travellers alike. Everyone knows that the *First* World War, was just that, the first of the century. In most museums of the Great War, we are still a few steps away from the dark tourism of the Second World War. Ljubljana under the Habsburgs was not Ljubljana under the Nazis, the Italians or the Ustasha. The Italian prisoners in the photographs displayed in the castle were soldiers of Liberal, not fascist, Italy.

We historians and curators of exhibitions and museums on the Great War do not have to deal with the crimes of the Nazis, the Stalinists, or the Japanese military. It is clear, though, that much that happened during the war prepared the way for these criminals. There are Armenian genocide memorials and museums in many parts of the world. In Yerevan, Armenia, the Armenian Genocide

Museum-Institute opened in 1995. In Valence, where many Armenians found a home after 1915, there is an Armenian Heritage Centre. It opened in 2005 and has a permanent exhibition on the genocide and exile that followed.

In the world of the public history of the Great War, though, the story we tell is of a patriotic and not a criminal generation. In 1914, the vast majority believed that their country was in the right to go to war and that the war they fought was a defensive war, one they did not want, but could not avoid fighting. Herein lies the difference between the two world wars in many countries, especially Germany, Italy and Japan. In most other cases, families with photographs of relatives who served in 1914–18 on both sides are unequivocally proud of their ancestors.

That is one reason why the Great War is part of the family history of the whole of Europe, including the neutrals. Museums are spaces of family history, writ large, on the map of the nation or empire as a whole. In recent years, family history has grown in part due to the way the internet has opened up to anyone access to individual lives in documents and photographs. The European Union site *Europeana* has a very popular portal on the First World War.

In addition, the appeal of the history of the First World War has grown in Eastern Europe and elsewhere because to go back to 1918 is to return to the struggle for independence. This is true in Finland, Poland and the Baltic states. In the post-war years, Communists celebrated 1917, not 1914, and consequently from 1917 in Russia, and from 1945 to 1989 in Eastern Europe, the Great War was occluded, if not erased entirely, from the national narrative. Now after the fall of the Soviet empire, the Great War is back, and public interest in it has grown rapidly. There is a First World War Museum in Tsarkoye Selo, near the palace of Catherine the Great, not far from St Petersburg. In its displays are unusual items, including gas masks used for animals at the front.

Museums and exhibitions are important institutions in the British Commonwealth, as Jennifer Wellington shows in her contribution to this book. But outside of Europe and areas of white settlement, there are fewer museums specifically dedicated to telling the story of 1914–18. There is an Indian War Memorial Museum, built in 1919, in the Red Fort in Delhi. The troubled history of the British in India in particular in the Second World War and in its aftermath has complicated efforts either to probe the family history of or to commemorate publicly the war as a whole. Santanu Das has led the way in bringing not only Indians but all people of colour into the centre of the narrative of the war.[1] European museums gesture in this direction; in the future, non-European museums need to take the lead in this domain.

The global war has come to the stage during the centenary. South African artist William Kentridge's *Gesamtkunstwerk* 'The Head and the Load' was a stunning theatrical evocation of the barbarity of the war in Africa. For a very large public, his work opened up the world of war in Africa. It is to be hoped that others will take up his challenge and bring out in Africa other facets of the African story of the war. South Africans, seeking a museum specifically dedicated to the South African effort in the war, must go to Longueval on the

Somme, and there are still traces of the mentality of apartheid in some of the designs. Wisely the new South Africa has kept intact traces of the old South Africa, while creating a more rigorous narrative alongside it.

The Eurocentric bias of most work on curating exhibitions, war museums and other sites of memory of the Great War is built into the subject. And there are exceptions. One of the most penetrating essays in this book is Nicholas Saunders' account of literally digging up traces of the Hejaz Railway and the Arab Revolt. He is one of the founders of 'modern conflict archeology', and his reflections on material culture have informed the way we approach the remains of war. Kirstie Ross's essay on the hugely successful exhibition 'The Scale of War' at the Museum of New Zealand Te Papa Tongarewa (Te Papa) shows how indigenous cultural forms informed and enhanced the narrative of Gallipoli. The use of larger-than-life sculpture was particularly effective in enabling visitors to reflect on the larger-than-life narrative in which Gallipoli has been configured for over a century. In viewing this exhibition, I shared with many other people a visceral sense of what the word 'Great' meant in the term the Great War. It left the right impression that the war was huge and terrible and charged with emotion and significance. Here was an exhibition that honoured those who fought, without glorifying war.

National and regional viewpoints have changed over time. Just as historians of Europe have taken to writing their national histories from a global point of view,[2] so museums in Europe have led the way in going beyond a simply European narrative of the war. The variety and richness of interpretations and visual strategies of display in First World War museums is evident throughout this book, and so is the shift in perspective in many of them to a transnational approach.

Above all, what this book shows is the way those who design and develop war exhibitions and war museums today both draw on and move on from a substantial archive their predecessors have left behind. If past is prologue, then we can all look forward with a sense of excitement to the next phase of creative work in this field.

Notes

1 See Santanu Das (ed.), *Race, Empire and First World War Writing* (Cambridge: Cambridge University Press, 2011); and Das, *India, Empire, and First World War Culture: Writings, Images and Songs* (Cambridge: Cambridge University Press, 2018); and Das, *Sensing the Sepoy*, in N.J. Saunders and P Cornish (eds.), *Modern Conflict and the Senses* (London: Routledge, 2017:307–326).
2 Patrick Boucheron and Stéphane Gerson (eds.), *France in the World: A New Global History*. (New York: Other Press, 2017).

INTRODUCTION

Challenging perspectives on museums and the Great War

Paul Cornish

Curating

In the course of the conference that constituted the genesis of this book, my colleague Toby Haggith lamented the recent debasement of the term 'curating'.[1] In
the modern British-English idiom, a 'curator' was now apparently just someone
who picked or selected things – clothes, internet content, music, cocktails, or what
have you. This is paradoxical at a time when, as this book shows, curating is
taking a greater and more sophisticated variety of forms than ever before. Where,
formerly, curators were required to preserve, study, and interpret objects from
the past, they might now be expected – as this book amply proves – to undertake a variety of audience engagements (Brandauer, this volume), to participate
in the creation of new artefacts (Dixon, this volume), or even to curate whole
landscapes (Cimprić; Kravanja, this volume).

Curators have been described as 'authors who interpret the past by relating
space, objects and written text in distinct combinations' (Wallis and Taylor 2018:
102). This is certainly supported by what you will read in this book, but it has
not always been universally the case. In some museums, the role of the curator
(if defined as a collections-focused museum worker) is divorced from the interpretive, exhibition-making function; the latter being handled by an exhibitions
office or similar department. This was indeed the situation for much of my time
at Imperial War Museums (IWM), with curators only regaining a full part in
exhibition creation under the most recent Director General, Diane Lees.[2] In this
volume, however, it will be seen that the term curatorship will be used in its
broadest sense – encompassing the work archaeologists, politicians, artists, soldiers, and amateur enthusiasts alongside that of museum professionals (Kravanja;
Saunders; Shapland, this volume). As will be clear from the papers here, museums can only benefit from this sort of inclusivity and broadness of engagement.

DOI: 10.4324/9781003263531-1

In addition to being cross-disciplinary, this is also a consciously international volume. Traditions of curating and of interpreting the Great War vary greatly from country to country (Fleury 2014: 4–6) and while there has been some fruitful collaborative study in the field between scholars in France and Germany, more effort is required to connect anglophone curators with the wider museum family. Among other things, this volume might be seen as a step in that direction.

Museums are, in essence, public domain entrepots of material culture. Curators are the arbiters and mediators of this material culture; knowingly or unknowingly they are exposing, and indeed contributing to, the social lives of the artefacts that they curate. A material culture studies perspective is therefore very appropriate to the analysis of war museums and their work. This volume seeks to further and facilitate such research, being, as it is, the sixth in a series inspired by conferences on the material culture of conflict held at IWM London (Saunders 2004; Saunders and Cornish 2009; Cornish and Saunders 2014; Saunders and Cornish 2017; Saunders and Cornish 2021). Already, over recent years, a number of such studies have appeared, many of them benefitting from 'insider' information due to the authors being part of, or embedded in, the museum world (Cornish 2017; Cundy 2017; Wallis and Taylor 2018; Tomasiewicz 2020). This is a development to be encouraged, and one which contrasts favourably with the tendency of some scholars to impose philosophies and structures upon war museums and their exhibitions without engaging fully with the curators on the museological frontline (for instance, Lisle 2006; Emig 2007). I can offer an extreme example from personal experience. In 2015, a symposium on *The Redesign of the Imperial War Museum* was held just 40 minutes' walk from IWM London but with no invitation extended to any member of IWM staff (IIC). The reason given to a member of IWM's First World War Galleries team who did turn up was that the presence of 'practitioners' might 'stifle free debate'; moreover, they might not be capable of grasping the issues under discussion (Ian Kikuchi, pers. comm.).

One cannot dismiss out of hand the analyses arrived at by studies conducted on such an abstracted level – they may reveal deeply ingrained cultural and philosophical tendencies which are invisible to those unable to observe from such a detached standpoint. There is nothing wrong with keeping curators on their toes! However, as Esben Kjeldbaek has cogently argued, ideological critiques that focus on text and narrative, cannot, by themselves, 'describe a medium which, at the core, consists of authentic three-dimensional objects placed in a space' (Kjeldbaek 2001: 120). To this, I would add, from my own observation, that, as most studies of this type are seeking to comprehend (or often, in fact, to construct) an *institutional* philosophy, they grossly underestimate the agency of *individual* curators, exhibitions managers, and designers. Furthermore, the practicalities of exhibition-making have no place in these narratives. For example, my colleague who was the uninvited guest at the above conference noted down the following phrase used in the context of IWM's display of the so-called Néry Gun[3]: 'and here we see the turn to art at the moment of the battle itself, the need to aestheticize violence'. This 'need' was described in rather more bathetic terms

FIGURE 0.1   A major regeneration project. The author in the atrium of IWM London as the redevelopment that included new First World War galleries took shape. (© Author.)

by my colleague, who had himself created the gun's digital-label, as: 'having no photographs or film of the battle itself, I made do with a painting from the Illustrated London News' (Ian Kikuchi, pers. comm.). Exhibition content is as much a function of availability as it is of choice; sometimes curating an exhibition really is about 'making-do' (Barry; Wallis, this volume).

Above all, such studies pay scant attention to the twin tyrants under which every exhibition creator across the world suffers: budget and space. All curators have to make compromises in order to accommodate these two oppressors. The same rules apply whether one is working on a major regeneration project (Cornish 2017;Wallis and Taylor 2018; Dendooven, this volume) (Figure 0.1) or creating a temporary exhibition in a small provincial museum (Barry, this volume). Whether we are writing critiques of existing museums and exhibitions or attempting to lay down guidelines for how this might be undertaken in the future (see below), we can never allow ourselves to forget these fundamental limitations on curatorial freedom of action.

Curating the Great War

Museums of the Great War present a unique set of challenges to those who curate their content. These challenges differ from country to country, with the museology of the war mirroring local variations in public consciousness and memory of the conflict. The nature of the cultural heritage of the war, originally conditioned by whether the war was seen as a victory or a defeat, has usually undergone changes in the context of subsequent political and military developments; most notably fascism, communism, European unification and, above all, the Second World War (Deans; Martina; Weissbrich; Zunino, this volume). For some people, even though their territory was a Great War battlefield, the war itself, if recalled at all, has always been somebody else's war (Cimprić; Kobiałka, this volume). Contemporary attitudes to war museums are further influenced by the long period of post-1945 'peace' – in the sadly erroneous belief that war is an unnatural interruption of the 'normality' of peace (Cornish and Saunders 2021: xxix).

Many of these museums were created during the Great War or in its immediate aftermath. At the outset, therefore, they were recording something which was more current affairs than history and stocked with artefacts that most visitors would readily recognize. Today they all record and interpret events beyond living memory, but which nevertheless retain a strong hold on public consciousness in some places. This trajectory was not as inevitable as its temporal progression might suggest. Not many of the founders of those early war museums would have expected to see them still flourishing in the twenty-first century (Kavanagh 1994: 135). The fact that they still prosper is a testament to the enduring influence of the Great War on our understanding of our history. Unsurprisingly, therefore, the history of Great War museums mirrors, to a significant extent, the three historiographical configurations of the war identified by Winter and Prost (2005: 6–33). To create a full understanding of this process, it be might instructive to interpolate Esben Kjeldbaek's slightly provocative (but both persuasive and amusing to insiders) 'three generations' of museology – the 'personal', the 'educational', and the 'post-modern' – into these historiographical phases (Kjeldbaek 2001: 121). Kjeldbaek further suggests that these generations each conform to an Aristotelian mode of persuasion: successively, Ethos, Logos and Pathos (Kjeldbaek 2009: 387–388).

Great War museums are, of course, manifestations of the material culture of conflict in their own right. And despite the unique attributes of the 'war to end all war' that they were created to record, they frequently cannot altogether escape a broader material and historical context. The Historial de la Grande Guerre at Péronne and the Museo Storico Italiano della Guerra in Rovereto stand on the sites of medieval castles. The First World War section of the Musée de l'Armée at Les Invalides in Paris is locked in an unequal struggle for attention with galleries filled with the glorious uniforms of the First Empire. The Great War content of the German Army Museum in Dresden sits within the former barracks of the Royal Saxon Army, built with money exacted from France after the Franco-Prussian war. At the Bavarian Army Museum at Ingolstadt, the First World War display is housed in a nineteenth-century bastion of the former 'fortress-town'. It was of course the Great War that consigned both the Bavarian and Saxon armies to the history books. In Flanders Fields Museum sits within the reconstructed

Lakenhalle (Cloth Hall), which symbolizes both the medieval wealth of Flanders and the architectural riches of the town of Ieper prior to its wartime destruction. These museums are therefore part of multi-vocal landscapes – pieces of material culture on a broader artefactual (frequently conflict-related) canvas. In the case of In Flanders Fields an awareness of this circumstance has influenced both its exhibition programme and its recently redeveloped form (Chielens et al 2006; Saunders 2021: 9).

One thing that almost all Great War museums have in common is that they cannot escape being *lieux de mémoire* (Brandt 1994: 107–108; Whitmarsh 2001; Fleury 2014: 13). Indeed, in some cases, museums actually appeared before other forms of commemoration and memorialization had been erected (Cornish 2018: 226). The Imperial War Museum was first among such creations. Its founders were aware of the potential pecuniary advantages of making it part of a memorial (Cornish 2004: 42), but the foundering of plans for a lavish national memorial complex meant that the IWM was obliged to settle for preserving a 'record' of the British Empire's war effort, rather than attempting to memorialize those who had died (Wellington 2017: 281). A memorial role, albeit subsidiary, was, nevertheless, imposed upon the IWM from the outset – notably in King George V's speech at the opening in 1920 (Brandt 1994: 112).

Furthermore, those in charge have frequently co-opted the tropes and indeed the artefactual expressions of memorialization to maintain visitor footfall. This was equally true of object-focused Armistice Day activities in the 1930s (Cornish 2004: 46–47) and the installation of the poppy sculptures *Weeping Window* (IWM London) and *Wave* (IWM North) during the autumn of 2018 (1418Now). Certainly, the public need little encouragement to engage with the IWM on this basis. For example, during 2014, it became clear that many of IWM London's unprecedentedly large number of visitors were making a double pilgrimage, to see the new First World War Galleries and to view the original poppy installation, *Blood Swept Lands and Seas of Red*, at the Tower of London. This is just the British experience of course; other countries have followed different arcs of remembrance (Edwards 2000; Reynolds 2013: 283–418; Osborne 2018), but the names alone of various museums make clear their link with memorialization. The Australian War Memorial and the Mémorial de Verdun are perhaps the most strident examples and, although not a national memorial, the name of the Historial was coined to combine History and Memorial (Reynolds 2013: 398). An urge to memorialize lay at the heart of the construction of Freemason's Hall in London (Dennis, this volume). In more recent times, In Flanders Fields Museum has adopted a consciously commemorative posture (Dendooven, this volume).

This public imposition of a commemorative or memorial function on war museums should remind us that, when visiting a First (or indeed Second) World War exhibition, visitors will bring along their own agendas and preconceptions (Winter and Prost 2005: 188). At one extreme, these may relate to fairly widespread and firmly established public memories of the war, such as those found in Britain (Todman 2005; Wilson 2013). This peculiar interpretation of the war and its concomitant public expectations in terms of museum content are not limited to Britain itself, being exported to such places as the Historial or In Flanders Fields by their many British visitors. At the other extreme of public memory lie places like Russia, Poland, and Slovenia, where, despite the presence of the Great War heritage, public understanding of the conflict has historically been limited and overlaid with more urgent political considerations (Cornish and Saunders 2019: xviii; Cimprić; Kobiałka; Kravanja, this volume). This legacy, combined with the decades of turmoil and bloodshed which the Great War might be said to have unleashed upon eastern Europe (Gerwarth 2016), means that the heritage and memory of the war can be contentious issues there (Reynolds 2013: 392–398).

All museums of the Great War are likely to face criticism from informed visitors who feel that their particular area of interest or knowledge does not receive sufficient coverage. This is inevitable as exhibition creators must start from a position of creating a coherent narrative, rather than cobbling together a compendium of stories that can only ever be subjective and partial. IWM London's First World War Galleries had scarcely opened before the Director General received representations from highly placed people in Australia regarding the fact that no specific mention was made of Sir John Monash, commander of the Australian Corps on the Western Front from May 1918. This might seem extraordinary in the context of an exhibition that was intended to explain a whole World War at a time when actual knowledge of things as basic as who fought on what side was dwindling (Cornish 2017: 16). However, Monash remains a totemic figure in Australia, one of the legacies, no doubt, of Australian War Memorial founder Charles Bean's establishment of a link between the Great War and Australian nationhood (Wellington, this volume). No historian denies Monash's qualities as a commander. Indeed, he would doubtless feature in any list of the top ten *Corps* commanders of the war – but how many people, in Australia or anywhere else, could even *name* nine other formation commanders of the same rank? A similar complaint, made to me personally, reflects issues raised by Doyle in this volume. A very persistent visitor interrupted a gallery tour that I was giving, to loudly bewail the lack of specific mention of 36th Ulster Division's action on the 'first day of the Somme'.

Complaints of greater significance and concern came from individuals and groups eager to see proportionate representation of non-white participants in the war. During the creation of the exhibition, we had been very aware of the need to maintain diversity in our content and equally conscious of the fact that the war could be cast as a global conflict, as achieved with great success in Hew Strachan's short history *The First World War* (Strachan 2003).[4] But the practicalities of space and visitor dwell-time meant that, inexorably, the Western Front and British Home Front imposed themselves as the centre of gravity of a narrative that strove to answer four 'big questions' (Cornish 2017: 16). This had the unfortunate side-effect of pushing theatres like the Middle East and Africa (where most soldiers of colour – at least those fielded by the British Empire – fought) to the margins. The curator's role here, post-opening, was to engage with sometimes angry stakeholders and, even when subjected to verbal abuse, to try to comprehend the deeply rooted historical injustice and neglect (see, for instance, Barrett 2014; Olusoga 2014; Smith 2014; Mathieu 2018) that constituted the fundamental problem.[5] Nevertheless, to fully represent the global and multi-ethnic nature of the conflict, we would have had to have created a very different exhibition right from the outset. IWM's exhibition teams took this lesson on board, and it informed the process of creating IWM London's new Second World War Galleries (2016–2021). The First World War galleries did make use of public evaluation (Cornish 2017: 16), but during the Second World War Galleries project curators engaged directly with their potential audience in a series of professionally moderated events, while the design of the exhibition was still in progress.

War museums as political entities

Museums then are political spaces, whether they like it or not. Those who set out to curate the Great War need to be aware of this and of the backstory of the institutions in which they work. A museum 'will always carry with it the legacy of its origins, for better or worse' (Barrett 2012: 112). If commemoration was a key element in the founding principles of most 'commemoration was a political act; it could not be neutral' (Winter 1995: 82). Some First World War museums have historically espoused avowedly nationalistic or militaristic principles (Martina; Weissbrich, this volume). The Australian War Memorial is inextricably linked with Australian conceptions of nationhood (Wellington, this volume). More recent times have witnessed the welcome establishment of war museums with strongly internationalist outlooks, notably the Historial de la Grande Guerre (1992) and In Flanders Fields Museum (1996).

Curators these days are also only too aware that their interpretation of history might be seized upon by others as a weapon in 'culture wars'. There are famous examples linked to Second World War bombing exhibits at the US National Air and Space Museum (Lisle 2006) and the Canadian War Museum (Dean 2009), where exhibitions were actually altered under pressure from veterans and politicians who supported (or exploited) their concerns. More recently, Poland has witnessed the shameful revision – by the diktat of central government – of the entire internationalist conception of the Museum of the Second World War in Gdansk (*The Guardian* 2019), in favour of a narrative of Polish exceptionalism.

Britain is evidently no longer immune to such developments, as shown by recent threats by its Minister of Culture to defund museums for 'taking acts motivated by activism or politics' (UK Government). At about the same time IWM received a communication from a *Daily Telegraph* journalist demanding, under Britain's Freedom of Information Act, to see any memoranda relating to changes to the museum's treatment of Winston Churchill, in the wake of the recent Black Lives Matter protests. Traditionally Freedom of Information has been the standby of lazy journalists hoping to manufacture a story by sending an annual enquiry asking how many items a given museum has lost or had stolen in the preceding year. The fact that it is now (albeit with a complete lack of understanding of how history is 'done' in museums) being weaponized in this way is telling.

At the time of writing, I have the feeling that these will just be the opening skirmishes of a culture war that will apply the same pressures to British curators as their counterparts across the Atlantic or in Poland have had to face. Can the historiography of the First World War hope to be immune from being hijacked in this way? In one sense, it might be protected by the curious and uniquely British engagement with the war that makes it mainstream, and completely acceptable, to suggest that the war was a futile endeavour, a 'defeat round whose neck some-one had hung a victory medal', according to former Poet Laureate Ted Hughes. It is equally acceptable to condemn British generals and war leaders and, indeed, to question the causes of the war and Britain's motivation for participating in it (see Todman 2005: 73–152). IWM London's First World War galleries adopted a perspective that was at odds with this conception (Cornish 2017: 18–22, 26). Perhaps surprisingly, they have escaped attack in the media for this departure from this deep-seated Anglocentric vision of the Great War. However, central to the incipient British culture war is Britain's colonial history. It is in this con-text that museum representations of the Great War may find themselves drawn into this faux conflict of ideas (Figure 0.2).

FIGURE 0.2 Representatives of the multi-ethnic French Army in miniature at IWM London. These dolls were purchased for the museum during the First World War at the famous Parisian toyshop *Au Nain Bleu*. (© Author.)

Perhaps curators should draw strength from these developments however, as attacks from pressure groups, and even governments, show the importance accorded to museum exhibitions and their power to shape public understanding of history. There are countless examples of historians publishing controversial research, with the First World War being at the forefront of such historiography (for example, Taylor 1966; Ferguson 1998; Zuber 2002; Clark 2012). But for them, the only outcome of the controversy is a rise in book sales. Imagine the fuss if a museum took one such text and used it – without further context or qualification – as the sole basis of an exhibition? Likewise, imagine the rage of Britain's print-media and (at time of writing) of the Culture Secretary himself, if IWM's First or Second World War galleries, or the Churchill War Rooms, followed Dan Todman's lead in his justly lauded Second World War history *Britain's War* in identifying Churchill as 'even by the standards of his time' a 'savage racist' (Todman 2016: 55).

Limitations: The need to attract an audience

However, before curators run away with the idea of themselves as all-powerful arbiters of the public understanding of history, they need to remember limitations that they all have to work within. As already mentioned, the availability of budget and space circumscribes every curatorial activity, from collecting, to public engagement, to exhibition creation. Further compromises are necessary in the last of these roles, when the ideas and requirements of project managers, designers, AV contractors, marketing departments, and others have to be taken into account. The need to attract sufficient footfall to maintain the financial viability of their museum is also a factor for many. Sometimes these considerations will clash with the ambitions of history/object focused curators. While this can be annoying to them, it has to be admitted that sometimes curators need to be saved from themselves; with less curatorial 'purity' frequently making for a better exhibition. It would be tempting to suggest that this is a universal rule, applying to all exhibitions, although there is at least one major exception in the world of Great War museums.

The Historial de la Grande Guerre offers an example of an exhibition created in a different way, with academics presented with a tabula rasa on which to create a museum and research centre, largely unencumbered by commercial considerations. It can claim to have set new standards in its informed, culturally anchored treatment of the Great War (Winter and Prost 2005: 186–188; Reynolds 2013: 398–399; Fleury 2014: 9). The Historial manifests an austere, although not (to me at least) unattractive, attitude to how war museums should comport themselves. Eschewing any attempt at 'pseudo-realism' it places visitors in a silent space, devoid of 'artificial triggers of emotion or thought' and designed to encourage reflection (Winter and Prost 2005: 187; Winter 2010: 10). However, while this deeply considered museological approach might attract many – and the Historial does claim a respectable attendance of circa 80,000 visitors per annum – it will almost certainly not serve to attract the crowds that a national museum like IWM London needs. In order to find the half of its income that is not provided by grant-in-aid from the government, IWM aims to exceed a million visitors per annum at its Lambeth Road site. No one has yet been brave or reckless enough to suggest that this might be achieved by spurning the 'wow factor' in exhibition design, so AV presentations, music, and soundscapes all have their place, insofar as exhibition budgets permit.

The immersive museum is an Anglo-Saxon concept, essentially dating from the 1980s (Fleury 2014: 5), but was probably an idea already possessed of a theoretical existence, which was awaiting the technology (and funds) to make it a reality (Cundy 2017: 368). The concept took off in the UK after the huge success of the York Archaeological Trust's Jorvik Viking Centre, which opened in 1984. It has subsequently been employed to interpret the Great War in a number of museums (Miles 2017: 78–83); most frequently in the form of immersive 'trenches' (Fleury 2014: 12–13). In 1990, IWM London's newly opened First World War gallery incorporated a 'Trench Experience', complete with Jorvik-style mannequins, sounds, and smells. This was a counterpart to IWM's already extant (and frankly appalling) 'Blitz Experience' (Cundy 2017: 368–369; Tomasiewicz 2020: 227–228). These, 'Experiences' are now gone, although evidently mourned by the generation of visitors who experienced them as school-children (Cornish 2017: 24).

This sort of sensorial experience can be very good at bringing archaeology to life, as the founders of the Jorvik Centre realized, and as would be clear to anyone who has seen the spectacular 2013 re-display of the Mary Rose at Portsmouth. However, it is easy to see limitations in its application in war museums. Dan Todman acutely described IWM London's Trench Experience as 'a version of the past which cannot be allowed to be accurate' (Todman 2005: 217). It seems to be the case that, for war museums, the choice with this sort of 'experience' lies between the bland (Cornish 2017: 23–24) and something that pushes the boundaries of good taste. There are, nevertheless, other ways of making a gallery into a sensory experience. Soundscapes, lighting, and AV content can all play their part if the gallery space is of the, nowadays preferred, 'black-box' configuration (Cornish 2017: 22–23; Miles 2017: 79–80). There might even be an imaginative leap of the type that produced Te Papa's astonishing Gallipoli: The Scale of Our War exhibition, which was dominated by gigantic dioramas, with mannequins 2.4 times life size (Ross, this volume). Given that most people visit museums as a leisure activity, rather than for self-improvement or education, these attention-grabbing exhibition techniques should not be sniffed at if combined (as in all the examples mentioned here) with a sound grasp of history and an understanding that original objects remain absolutely fundamental to what a museum does.[6] And when artefacts are lacking, this sort of approach offers the possibility of creating awareness of history that might otherwise be hidden; witness, for instance John Akomfrah's visually stunning multi-screen installation *Mimesis: African Soldier*, which was exhibited at IWM London in 2018–2019 (IWM)

As well as striving to attract visitors, curators need to take care not to actively repel them. It would be easy to fill any Great War gallery with such an array of horrific images as to terrify children and nauseate adult visitors. Imagine the content of Ernst Friedrich's International Anti-War Museum (Weissbrich, this volume) mediated by the full panoply of modern display technology. Only those with prurient or voyeuristic intent would willingly visit such a gallery, so it would defeat its own purpose. This does not mean that curators should shy away from representing the horrors of war however, and most contemporary Great War exhibitions do so. Here material culture can come to the curator's aid, as the objects themselves bespeak their terrible purposes or fates. Witness, for instance, the gruesome (yet extraordinarily diverse) array of trench knives and clubs, or the frighteningly rudimentary gas masks, found in IWM's galleries (Cornish 2017: 25); or the awful assemblage of primitive prostheses (arranged in near-human form) at the Musée de la Grande Guerre at Meaux.

Limitations: Curator culture

Curators must accept that, ultimately, their museums 'never describe war; they only tell us about its footprints on the map of our own lives' (Winter 2013 23). They can only do their best to weave together objects and fragments of personal experiences to interpret history, as it inexorably recedes from the consciousness of an ever-evolving audience. It is therefore essential that curators stay aware of the cultural milieu in which they themselves are obliged to operate – not merely with regard to the outward expression of their role in exhibition-making, but in understanding the potential limitations imposed by their own backgrounds. My example here is curating in Britain. Other countries have different experiences, often enjoying closer links between the museum and academic worlds. However, given the character of the world of public history in general, I suspect that the same issues might be in play, to some extent, worldwide.

In the course of my 38 years in museums, curating became increasingly professionalized. In the British Museum of the 1980s, traces were still to be found of the gentleman-curator, who might have stepped from the pages of Angus Wilson or Anthony Powell. While this might suggest exclusivity, curators in those days were actually drawn from a reasonably wide cross section of society. National museum curators were civil servants, recruited through the Civil Service Commission. To become the lowest grade of curator (Grade G), one technically needed only a handful of 'O-Level' exam passes. Post-graduate qualifications in Museum Studies were rare among curators at that time, although the University of Leicester had commenced its pioneering courses in the field as early as 1966.

In more recent times, Museum Studies qualifications have come to be seen as an essential entry in the CV of anyone hoping to make a career as a curator. This new generation of curators brought fresh thinking the museum world, reflecting the 'New Museology' (Vergo 1989) developed since the '80s and the rise of 'Public History' (Cauvin 2018). This has naturally created a generation of curators who pay greater attention than did their forebears to the methodology and philosophy of interpretation. However, recent discussions with my (much younger) colleagues identified a major downside to this development, in that it severely circumscribes diversity. Those who feel able to take a post-graduate course and, as is common these days, to work as volunteers to gain experience, are almost entirely drawn from what, for want of a better descriptor, we must call the well-off 'white middle-class'. In Britain, the financial privations which must be undergone at this 'early career' stage are by no means compensated for by expected earnings. Curator's salaries – never generous – dwindled steadily against those on offer in the private sector following the 'untying' of museum staff from the Civil Service pay structure in 1997. It is hard to think of any way in which this sad state of affairs can be addressed without spending serious money – something that no museum has, or is likely to be given, particularly in the wake (as I write) of the 2020–2022 COVID pandemic.

Curators themselves might have little or no say in recruitment or salary provisions; but it is incumbent upon them to be aware of these imperfect circumstances and to try to understand their own cultural preconceptions. It hardly needs to be said that they should seek to create exhibitions that are inclusive and have diverse voices, but also give a balanced and accessible interpretation of history. In 1915, the President of Britain's Museum's Association identified the need to respond to 'the clamouring voices of the present' (Wellington 2017: 30). Curators of the Great War today are still faced with this task. But what is the best way of achieving it?

Tasks for Great War curators

Don't limit your audience!

First of all, I would suggest that curators seek to make their exhibitions accessible and attractive to the widest possible audience – or at least those of an age to understand the fundamental issues. This is by no means a universally held view in museums, where audience segmentation techniques are often used to identify and focus on groups most likely to make a visit and (most importantly) spend their money. One can't help but feel that chasing a particular audience undermines the basic mission that any war museum should be pursuing. Furthermore, I have my doubts about the process by which the segmentation is achieved, having, aged 60, taken the test used by IWM and found that it identified me as a 'thrill seeker' (and therefore not among IWM's chief target audience). I recall that my colleagues and I were amused when a curator on the British Museum's 2014 *Germany: Memories of a Nation* exhibition told us that their target audience was 'British people'. In retrospect however, perhaps it's not so daft to aspire to such a broad spectrum of visitors.

While I cannot speak for war museums as a whole, I have detected in IWM in recent years a sort of panic that a young twenty-first century audience will not be able or willing to engage with the museum's subject matter. This has mani-fested itself in an obsession with dealing with current affairs, such as the refugee crisis or the war in Syria, frequently via artistic or journalistic engagements (as the museum has next to no collections to represent these events). This seems to me to be extraordinary, at a time when certain British political figures feel able to claim that a Europe of competitive nation-states is a better and more 'natural' state of affairs than a united Europe. After all, about 90 per cent of IWM's collec-tions could be mobilized to disprove such historically illiterate notions. In short, the history of twentieth-century conflict actually *is* current affairs. Curators in war museums would surely be failing if they failed to drive home the horrors spawned by division and rivalry. This is especially important in the context of the long era of peace which those of us in the western world have been fortunate enough to experience. It is up to war museums to give their visitors an under-standing of the terrible realities of loss, occupation, devastation, and genocide. When history is being hi-jacked and *Pathos* is cynically exploited to trample down *Logos*, curators should aim to restore the balance.

Don't be squeamish!

At the most basic level, it behoves curators to ensure that their institutions do not shy away from the very nature of their callings as war museums. There have long been those within these institutions who deplore their subject matter and wish they were something else – a 'museum of war and peace' or a museum of 'social history' (Tomasiewicz 2020: 213).[7] Anchoring the history and the objects exhibited in human experience is never a bad thing. However, I am sure that, in more than one institution, 'peopling' exhibitions (Tomasiewicz 2020: 213–214) and suggesting that they are primarily there to tell personal 'stories' is used as a way of evading a more direct engagement with difficult subject matter. Indeed, I would go further and assert that claiming to tell 'people's stories' is fundamen-tally dishonest. No museum of this type has access to material that can represent the whole life and experience of any given person. Generally, it will possess only items related to the brief period when that person was at war. It cannot attempt to give a full picture of these people's lives, let alone penetrate their inner life. In my view, the true aim of 'peopling' galleries should be as a means of engaging the visitor; personal experiences (fragmentary and partial as they might be) are great for adding 'colour' and 'chiaroscuro' and encouraging empathy. However, per-sonal experience should never be deployed divorced from the context of a cogent narrative – there is no point in hearing about an experience without knowing why the person was undergoing it.

Mind your language!

If curators of the Great War are to face the fact that representing a ghastly and bloody conflict is their task, they should take care with the language that they

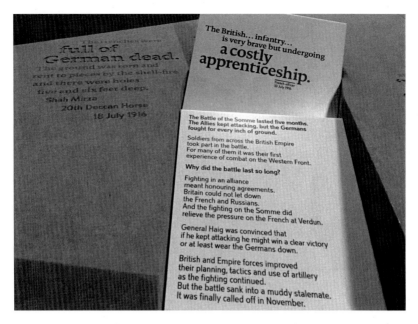

The British... infantry... is very brave but undergoing a costly apprenticeship.

French officer
10 July 1916

full of German dead. The ground was torn and rent to pieces by the shell-fire and there were holes five and six feet deep.

Shah Mirza
20th Deccan Horse
18 July 1916

The Battle of the Somme lasted five months. The Allies kept attacking, but the Germans fought for every inch of ground.

Soldiers from across the British Empire took part in the battle. For many of them it was their first experience of combat on the Western Front.

Why did the battle last so long?

Fighting in an alliance meant honouring agreements. Britain could not let down the French and Russians. And the fighting on the Somme did relieve the pressure on the French at Verdun.

General Haig was convinced that if he kept attacking he might win a clear victory or at least wear the Germans down.

British and Empire forces improved their planning, tactics and use of artillery as the fighting continued. But the battle sank into a muddy stalemate. It was finally called off in November.

FIGURE 0.3 Two uses of text in IWM London's First World War Galleries. A 'chapter' panel sits alongside a contemporary quotation debossed in glass-reinforced concrete. (© Author.)

employ. Most people outside the museum world would be amazed at the amount of time and effort expended on writing and editing exhibition text. For example, the text for IWM London's First World War Galleries underwent months of revisions and edits before it was considered sufficiently engaging, clear, and concise (Figure 0.3). Curators have to attempt the difficult feat of making exhibition text immediately engaging, readily comprehendible and accurate, all within a very limited word-allowance. After all, as everyone who works in museums is aware: 'an exhibition is not a book'. The language used is vitally important. To maximize accessibility, it needs to conform to a relatively low reading-age. It is encouraging that, given the nature of the subject matter, most modern-day curators of Great War exhibitions seem eager to avoid being too detached in their text-writing style. Furthermore, they eschew 'antagonistic' language, largely in favour of a 'cosmopolitan' approach (Berger 2020). The next step should surely be that advocated by Dominiek Dendooven in his afterword to this volume, with curators seeking to take an *agonistic* stance in their text (see also Berger 2020). This approach offers a win-win in simultaneously avoiding the harmful 'othering' of antagonism and the potentially unreflective detachment of cosmopolitanism. Agonism seeks to create a passionate and dialogic engagement with the past. What better way could there be to attract the younger audience that so many war museums fear being spurned by?

Accept help – it's free!

In Europe and elsewhere across the world – for instance at the Australian War Memorial – there has traditionally been a stronger link between academic study of the history of the Great War than in British institutions. However, this is not to say that British curators cannot access the support of the academic community. My example of poor academic engagement above happily represents an exception rather than the norm. University academics gave generously of their time to provide an Advisory Board for IWM's First World War Galleries project and, at time of writing, are performing the same valuable role for the Second World War Galleries project. Given the emphasis that universities place on the 'impact' of their work, recruiting these scholars proved easy. The benefit was enormous, with these historians not only adding their authority to IWM's exhibition narrative, but frequently helping to find ways to explain complicated matters in ways that were both accessible and accurate. Such collaborations are not necessarily limited to huge capital projects like the regeneration of IWM London, as Barry and Carden-Coyne (this volume) show. In future curators should look to make such partnerships international. Obstacles of language (both linguistic and museological) would have to be overcome, but there would much to be gained by a more general mutual understanding of the varying historiography and museology that applies to the Great War (see Fleury 2014).

Conclusion

Chief among the insights gained from such an international perspective (and one that should be reinforced by this book) is that while there are many 'wrong' ways of curating the Great War (now largely consigned to museological history, thankfully), there is no single 'right' way. To take just four institutions within a 200-mile geographical radius: IWM London, In Flanders Fields, the Historial, and the gloriously object-rich Musée de la Grande Guerre at Meaux; all offer completely different visitor experiences, while offering historically sound interpretations of the same subject matter. Museological evolution, like biological evolution, does not just run in a straight line, its many branches all have the potential to end in a viable organism.

What all such institutions have in common are collections of original artefacts capable of speaking eloquently and with surprising immediacy (Cornish 2017: 24–25; Doyle, this volume) about the events of a century ago. It bears repeating that curators both interpret and contribute to the rich social lives of these objects. It is essential that, as they undertake this important task, these curators strive to understand their audience, their own limitations, but also their power to influence. While an institution like In Flanders Fields Museum might consciously seek to promote peace (Dendooven, this volume), I would suggest that the vast, resonant, not to say downright exciting, range of artefacts available to curators of Great War collections will, if properly exhibited and interpreted, guarantee that *any* Great War exhibition will constitute a powerful argument in favour of avoiding a similar catastrophe. Curators of such exhibitions will always have to work within certain restrictions, whether spatial, financial, or commercial, but this should not deter them from their overriding mission – to let the material culture speak.

Notes

1 The IWM Institute/University of Bristol conference 'Curating the Great War' was held at IWM London on 13–14 September 2018.
2 Frankly, it was my own frustrated curatorial impulse to 'interpret' that encouraged me to make the leap into the field of material culture studies.
3 A Thirteen-Pounder field gun damaged in a skirmish in 1914, during which three members of the Royal Horse Artillery won the Victoria Cross.
4 Incidentally, Sir Hew Strachan chaired the Academic Advisory Board which oversaw the content of the galleries. Unfortunately, another influential book, David Olusoga's *The World's War*, was not published until the design process was complete (Olusoga 2014).
5 Sad to relate, it would appear that attempts to improve inclusivity also draw angry responses (see Dendooven, this volume).
6 An exception that might prove or disprove this rule is M9, at Mestre in Italy, a museum without objects.
7 And we should deplore any attempt to divide history into categories like 'social', 'military', or 'political'. This outmoded concept looks ever more outdated at a time when cross-disciplinary approaches to all forms of social science are in the ascendant.

References

1418Now https://www.1418now.org.uk/commissions/poppies/locations/#main
Barrett, J. (2012) *Museums and the Public Sphere*. Chichester: John Wiley & Sons.
Barrett, M. (2014) 'White graves' and Natives: The Imperial War Graves Commission in East and West Africa, 1918–1939. In P. Cornish and N.J. Saunders (eds.), *Bodies in Conflict*, pp 80–90. London: Routledge.
Berger, S. (2020) Is the Memory of War in Contemporary Europe Enhancing Historical Dialogue? In E. Barkan, C. Goschler and J.E. Waller (eds.), *Historical Dialogue and the Prevention of Mass Atrocities*, pp 151–178. London: Routledge.
Brandt, S. (1994) The memory makers: Museums and exhibitions of the First World War. *History and Memory* 6 (1):95–122.
Cauvin, T. (2018) The rise of public history: An international perspective. *Historia Critica* 68:3–26.
Chielens, P., D. Dendooven and H. Decoodt (eds.) (2006) *De Laatste Getuige*. Tielt: Lanoo.
Clark, C. (2012) *The Sleepwalkers: How Europe Went to War in 1914*. United Kingdom: Penguin Books Limited.
Cornish, P. (2004) Sacred Relics: Objects in the Imperial War Museum 1917–39. In N.J. Saunders (ed.), *Matters of Conflict*, pp 35–50. London: Routledge.
———. (2017). Sensing War: Concept and Space in the Imperial War Museum's First World War Galleries. In N.J. Saunders and P. Cornish (eds.), *Modern Conflict and the Senses*, pp 13–28. London: Routledge.

Cornish, P. (2018) Afterword: The Mobilization of Memory 1917–2014. In J. Wallis and D.C. Harvey (eds.), *Commemorative Spaces of the First World War*, pp 101–114. London: Routledge.

Cornish, P. and N.J. Saunders (eds.) (2014) *Bodies in Conflict*. London: Routledge.

————. (2019) Preface. In U. Košir, M. Črešnar and D. Mlekuž (eds.), *Rediscovering the Great War: Archaeology and Enduring Legacies on the Soča and Eastern Fronts*, pp xxix–xxxi. London: Routledge.

————. (2021) Introduction. In N.J. Saunders and P. Cornish (eds.), *Conflict Landscapes: Materiality and Meaning in Contested Places*, pp xxvii–xxxiv. London: Routledge.

Cundy, A. (2017). War Memory and the Senses in the Imperial War Museum London, 1920–2014. In N.J. Saunders and P. Cornish (eds.), *Modern Conflict and the Senses*, pp 361–374. London: Routledge.

Dean, D. (2009) Museums as conflict zones: The Canadian War Museum and Bomber Command. *Museum and Society* 7 (1):1–15.

Edwards, P. (2000) Mort Pour la France. Conflict and commemoration in France after the First World War. *University of Sussex Journal of Contemporary History* 1:1–11.

Emig, R. (2007) Institutionalising Violence, Destruction and Suffering. Pitfalls, Paradoxes and Possibilities of War Museums in Britain. *Journal for the Study of British Cultures* 14 (1):52–64.

Ferguson, N. (1998). *The Pity of War*. London: Penguin.

Fleury, C. (2014). Muséographie(s) Comparée(s) de la Grande Guerre en 2013. *In Situ* 25:2–25.

Gerwarth, R. (2016) *The Vanquished*. London: Allen Lane.

IIC Conference: The Redesign of the Imperial War Museum (London): Memory and History Reconsidered. https://www.iiconservation.org/node/5533

IWM John Akomfrah on Mimesis: African Soldier https://www.iwm.org.uk/history/John%20Akomfrah%20on%20Mimesis%3A%20African%20Soldier

Kavanagh, G. (1994) *Museums and the First World War: A Social History*. Leicester: Leicester University Press.

Kjeldbaek, E. (2001) Post-modernism and the three generations of museums. *Nordisk Museologi* 2001 (1–2):119–126.

————. (2009) How Museums Speak. In E. Kjeldbaek (ed.), *The Power of the Object: Museums and World War II*, pp 362–392. Edinburgh: MuseumsEtc.

Lisle, D. (2006) Sublime lessons: Education and ambivalence in War Exhibitions. *Millenium – Journal of International Studies* 34:841–862.

Mathieu, S.-J. (2018) L'Union fait la force: Black soldiers in the Great War. *First World War Studies* 9 (2):230–244.

Miles, S. (2017) Sensorial Engagement in Tourism Experiences on the Western Front. In N.J. Saunders and P. Cornish (eds.), *Modern Conflict and the Senses*, pp 76–92. London: Routledge.

Olusoga, D. (2014) *The World's War*. London: Head of Zeus.

Osborne, B. (2018) Reflecting on the Great War 1914–2019. In J. Wallis and D.C. Harvey (eds.), *Commemorative Spaces of the First World War*, pp 209–224. London: Routledge.

Reynolds, D. (2013) *The Long Shadow*. London: Simon & Schuster

Saunders, N.J. (ed.) (2004) *Matters of Conflict*. London: Routledge.

————. (2021) The Dead and Their Spaces: Origins and Meanings in Modern Conflict Landscapes. In N.J. Saunders and P. Cornish (eds.), *Conflict Landscapes: Materiality and Meaning in Contested Places*, pp 3–33. London: Routledge.

Saunders, N. and P. Cornish (eds.) (2009) *Contested Objects*. London: Routledge.

_____. (2017) *Modern Conflict and the Senses*. London: Routledge.

_____.(2021) *Conflict Landscapes: Materiality and Meaning in Contested Places*. London: Routledge.

Smith, R. (2014) The Black Male Body in the White Imagination During the First World War. In P. Cornish and N.J. Saunders (eds.), *Bodies in Conflict*, pp 39–52. London: Routledge.

Strachan, H. (2003) *The First World War*. London: Simon & Schuster

Taylor, A.J.P. (1966) *The First World War: An Illustrated History*. London: Penguin.

The Guardian, 17 September 2019 https://www.theguardian.com/commentisfree/2019/sep/17/populist-rewriting-polish-history-museum-poland-gdansk

Todman, D. (2005). *The Great War: Myth and Memory*. London: Hambledon

_____. (2016) *Britain's War. Volume 1: Into Battle*. London: Allen Lane.

Tomasiewicz, K. (2020) We Are a Social History, Not a Military History Museum. In K. Hill (ed.), *Museums, Modernity and Conflict: Museums and Collections in and of War Since the Nineteenth Century*, pp 213–234. London: Routledge.

UK Government. (2020) Letter from Culture Secretary, 22 September 2020 https://www.gov.uk/government/publications/letter-from-culture-secretary-on-hm-government-position-on-contested-heritage

Vergo, P. (1989) *New Museology*. London: Reaktion Books.

Wallis, J. and J. Taylor. (2018) The Art of War Display: Imperial War Museum's First World War Galleries, 2014. In J. Wallis and D.C. Harvey (eds.), *Commemorative Spaces of the First World War*, pp 101–114. London: Routledge.

Wellington, J. (2017) *Exhibiting War: The Great War, Museums, and Memory in Britain, Canada and Australia*. Cambridge: Cambridge University Press.

Whitmarsh, A. (2001) 'We will remember them'. Memory and commemoration in War Museums. *Journal of Conservation and Museum Studies* 7:1–15.

Winter, J. (1995) *Sites of Memory, Sites of Mourning*. Cambridge: Cambridge University Press

_____. (2010) Designing a War Museum: Some Reflections on Representations of War and Combat. In E. Anderson, A. Maddrell, and K. McLoughlin (eds.), *Memory, Mourning, Landscape*, pp 1–19. Leiden: Brill.

_____. (2013) Museums and the Representation of War. In, W. Muchitsch (ed.) *Does War Belong in Museums?* Bielefeld: Transcript Verlag.

Winter, J. and A. Prost. (2005) *The Great War in History*. Cambridge: Cambridge University Press.

Wilson, R. (2013) *Cultural Heritage of the Great War in Britain*. Farnham: Ashgate

Zuber, T. (2002). *Inventing the Schlieffen Plan: German War Planning 1871–1914*. Oxford: Oxford University Press.

PART I

Museums, Identities and the Politics of Memory

1

FROM ONE WAR TO ANOTHER

German army museums and exhibitions on the First World War, 1914–1940

Thomas Weissbrich

On 23 August 1939, *The Battle of Tannenberg* exhibition opened in the Berlin *Zeughaus* (arsenal), the then leading German army museum. The historical background was the 25th anniversary of this battle fought in East Prussia at the end of August 1914, the 'greatest victory of the World War' according to the exhibition guide (Staatliches Zeughaus 1939: 4). From an operational-point of view, this superlative is indeed justified. But what use is the memory of a victory if the overall war ended in defeat?

Exhibitions on the First World War are closely linked to the history of military museums: The Great War was the first conflict which was accompanied by exhibitions from its beginning and which, after its end, underwent further museumization that continues to this day (Horne 2016). Of course, the paths were very different for winners and losers. In Great Britain and France, the museum exhibitions set up soon after the war met with a broad national consensus on remembrance. Germany, on the other hand, was far from this: for more than 10 years during the Weimar Republic, exhibitions and other media fought over the interpretation of the World War. As various research projects in recent years have shown, the Nazis above all used the topic of the war and its consequences for mental mobilization (Beil 2005; Beil 2010; Krumeich 2010; Krumeich 2015).

This chapter outlines what museumization and the associated interpretations of the First World War in Germany from 1914 to 1940, spanning from the German Empire to the Weimar Republic and the Nazi regime, looked like. In terms of museum history, the Berlin *Zeughaus*, which was initially the Royal Prussian Army Museum and later the leading army museum of the Nazi regime, is the focus of attention (Andrews 2014; Müller 1994; Rudolph and Goebel 2014; Weissbrich 2016a). In terms of the history of museum objects, attention is focused on a specific group of items that play an important role in this process. These include trophies in the form of conquered or captured enemy guns and flags.

DOI: 10.4324/9781003263531-3

1914–1918: War exhibitions and belief in victory

As a variant of history museums, army museums in Germany were already established in the late nineteenth century (Hacker and Vining 2007: 36–38). The initiative for their foundation was mostly taken by rulers and high-ranking officers who, in times of social and political change, wanted to legitimize themselves by depicting historical deeds of war. Pieces of armour and uniforms, weapons and equipment and other things conveyed splendour and glory, arranged chronologically and systematically. After the foundation of the German Empire in 1871, no national army museum was established. Instead, in accordance with the federal structure of the Empire, each of the four kingdoms – Prussia, Saxony, Württemberg and Bavaria – had a museum focusing on the history of its army.

In the Kingdom of Prussia, Wilhelm I had the Berlin *Zeughaus*, which served as an armoury, converted into an army museum open to the public (Müller 1994). The inscription placed above the entrance as early as the start of the eighteenth century, according to which 'spoils of war and trophies' were to serve as recognition of 'acts of arms', thus acquired a contemporary meaning. Opened in 1883, the museum combined a Hall of Fame glorifying the Hohenzollern kings and their army commanders in sculptures and frescoes with an exhibition on the history of the Brandenburg-Prussian Army. The Hall of Fame lived off the mutual relationship between two kinds of objects (Königliche Zeughaus Verwaltung 1914): on the one hand the pieces of Prussian origin, on the other the conquered or captured pieces of the opposing armies. The climax of the storytelling was the victory over France in 1871, which had played a decisive role in the foundation of the Empire.

While the glorious past had previously been conjured up in German army museums, this changed at the beginning of the war in August 1914: now current exhibitions appeared in the museums. They presented exhibitions of trophies to illustrate the achievements of the German army at home and to convey certainty of victory in a conflict the rulers declared a war of defence. This confidence, especially in the Kingdom of Prussia, was fed by the historical parallels drawn with the Franco-Prussian War of 1870–1871. The first military trophies captured by Prussian troops on the Eastern and Western fronts were publicly displayed in Berlin on 2 September 1914, the *Sedantag* (Day of Sedan), commemorating the victory over the French Emperor Napoleon III in 1870. Special items of booty were repeatedly displayed here, including British field guns, Russian machine guns and French regimental flags and finally, in March 1918, a British tank. In the courtyard and in the Hall of Fame of the Berlin *Zeughaus*, an exhibition was created under the command of Colonel Gustav von Neumann-Cosel and the civilian director Dr. Julius Binder. It would be constantly updated in the following years (Figure 1.1). The exhibited items came from collection points at the front. Captured enemy objects dominated: They were intended to emphasize Germany's military and moral superiority and strength as well as the inferiority and underhandedness of its enemies.

FIGURE 1.1   French and Russian flag trophies in the Hall of Fame of the Berlin Zeughaus, c. 1914. (© Deutsches Historisches Museum.)

Parallel to the exhibitions accompanying the war, systematic collections were created, both public and private (Brandt 1994). They were intended not only to document the events, but also, in the understanding of the time, to be monuments and serve for patriotic education, research and historiography (Lange 2003 8). The idea of an 'Imperial War Museum' (Lange 2010) was aimed at future memory. In April 1916, Berlin Museum Director Ludwig Justi came up with the plan. As a central museum, the Berlin Museum was intended to overcome German particularism and establish a national identity. The project was to be realized after the victorious end of the war, and the temporary exhibitions were to become permanent.

War exhibitions were not only held in the established army museums, which were subordinate to the war ministries. In the course of the conflict, which also had an increasingly negative impact on the civilian population economically, the governments developed a new model of exhibitions: The *German War Exhibition* was created in 1916 in cooperation between the Prussian War Ministry and the Central Committee of the Red Cross (Lange 2003). For four months at a time, similarly conceived exhibitions with around 500 exhibits were on show in major cities such as Berlin, Dresden, Stuttgart and Frankfurt (Main), mainly featuring guns and vehicles, rifles and equipment captured from the enemy armies. A new element was scenes re-enacted with life-size figurines such as 'Russian camp group singing and dancing to the balalaika', 'Gurkhas and Sikhs sneaking through a wire entanglement' and a reconstructed, accessible trench. Catalogues and postcard series were published to accompany the exhibitions, and 'explosives' could also be purchased as souvenirs (Anon 1916: 6). The exhibitions were intended to make the population aware of 'the severity of the still raging battles (…) by glimpsing the bellicose tools of our opponents'. They were also supposed to 'spark a feeling of gratitude towards our good troops' who would bravely protect the homeland (Anon 1916: 67). Visitors to the exhibitions were encouraged to *Durchhalten* (hold fast), to use the contemporary watchword. An appeal was made to their willingness to continue supporting the war effort through donations and loans.

The deeper infantry and artillery sank into trench warfare, the more hopes were raised by the newly created air force (Lange 2003: 35–40). The air force was the subject of the large *Spoils of the German Air War* exhibition, which was shown from February 1917 to September 1918 in Berlin, Dresden, Munich and Dortmund. To demonstrate the success of the aircraft, enemy aeroplanes, engines, instruments, weapons and ammunition were all presented. The catalogue declared 'that despite our strong numerical inferiority, we are absolutely superior to our enemies in the air, just as we are on land' (Anon 1918: 20). Such war exhibitions, which mainly showed booty, together with other propagandistic media, helped to maintain the belief in the victory of the army among large swathes of the population. The signing of the armistice at Compiègne on 11 November 1918, which was tantamount to surrender, therefore came as a complete and inexplicable surprise for the vast majority of Germans (Gross 2018: 132–134).

1918–1931: Controversial interpretations of the war

The November Revolution emerged from the collapse of the German army, the centuries-old monarchy abdicated, and the Republic was proclaimed. However, the responsible military officers, among them Field Marshal Paul von Hindenburg, did not admit that the army had been defeated militarily. The stab-in-the-back myth (*Dolchstoßlegende*), which maintained that the army had remained undefeated in the field, was born (Krumeich 2001; Schivelbusch 2001: 198–208). According to the various versions of this conspiracy theory, the culprits for the defeat were socialists, communists and social democrats, who sabotaged the necessary supply of the army at home, demoralized the population and thus brought down the army 'from behind'. The impression of the undefeated army was reinforced on 10 December 1918, when the Prussian regiments returning from the front marched through the garlanded Brandenburg Gate, where the Social Democratic President of the Republic, Friedrich Ebert, welcomed them to the cheers of Berliners.

In addition to the defeat, which was not understood or accepted by many, came the Treaty of Versailles. The territorial cessions, disarmament regulations and reparation payments demanded in the agreement were perceived as unfair; and not only in nationalist circles. The War Guilt Clause, which placed the blame for the war solely on Germany and its allies, was a particular cause for continuing indignation. As a reaction, the war guilt myth (*Kriegsunschuldslegende*) arose, which rejected German guilt as a malicious construction of the victors (Kolb 2005: 101). With left- and right-wing political positions radicalizing each other, Weimar politics and culture did not succeed in mental demobilization; the war continued in the minds of many (Mommsen 1997).

In post-war Germany, the army museums fell into a crisis of meaning. As a former site of the Hohenzollern military glory, the Berlin *Zeughaus* seemed anachronistic. The World War was removed from the exhibition. The Imperial Government paid little attention to the museum after it had been withdrawn from the Prussian War Ministry and placed under the Ministry of Science, Culture and National Education. The Peace Treaty signed in June 1919 had a direct effect on the museum's collections, as German weapons had to be rendered inoperable or scrapped as part of the demilitarization process. Among the 'reparations', Article 245 demanded the return of the booty gained in the war in France as well as the booty from the Franco-Prussian War of 1870–1871, including the 56 colours and standards from the surrender of the fortress of Metz. This demand is revealing with regard to France's need to avenge this defeat, still perceived as a national disgrace after almost half a century (Schivelbusch 2001: 120–139). Their 'reconquest' had to be all the more painfully felt in Germany, however, because the army was considered to be undefeated. In protest against the peace treaty, a group of German soldiers who felt their honour had been violated stole seven flags and burned them publicly (Weissbrich 2016b: 45–47). By 1923, some 2,500 military objects had been returned from Berlin to France, and the other army museums were also affected by this reclamation process (Müller 1994: 204). The *Zeughaus* management kept the memory of this loss alive by means of simple staging: In the courtyard, 41 empty pedestals with photos of the returned guns were left standing, thus referring accusingly to the Treaty of Versailles (Beil 2004: 228–232; Post 1933: 5–6).

At the same time, the museum acquired royal Prussian heritage,when it took over valuable orders and decorations from the stock of the General Order Commission, which had been dissolved. Republican politicians had no need for awards. Furthermore, the plan, repeatedly expressed during the war, to turn the army museums and their collections into war memorials, remained on the table. The deliberate lack of a state policy for museumization encouraged the ideological instrumentalization of the Great War by both the political right and left. Museum Director Binder tried to give the institution a new direction as a historical weapons museum. Criticism of this course first came from the conservative, nationalist side, which spoke of a 'disfigurement of the Hall of Fame' (Müller 1994: 206). Nevertheless, over the years, the *Zeughaus* became an important memorial for monarchists and conservatives, especially when the display case with the imperial mementoes was still on display. The institution was also criticized by pacifists. Ernst Friedrich provocatively proposed the rededication of the building: 'There could be no better way to commemorate and honour

FIGURE 1.2 'A beautiful symbol of peace in the Berlin Anti-War Museum', postcard, c. 1930. (© Private collection.)

the completely uselessly fallen, or more correctly, murdered 'heroes', than to convert the Berlin Zeughaus (…) for the establishment of an anti-war museum' (Friedrich n.d.: 4).

Friedrich was also one of the first to exhibit the war again after the war: In 1925, he opened his *International Anti-War Museum* in Berlin (Beil 2004: 239–258) (Figure 1.2). In just a few square meters, the exhibition demonstrated the horrors of war, evoked by photographs of facial injuries and mass graves or graphics by Käthe Kollwitz and Otto Dix. The curator thus challenged the glorifying concept of army museums and denounced the contempt for humanity and the irresponsibility of the military leadership.

Another interpretation of the First World War was offered by the Red Front Fighters' Federation, the combat unit of the German Communist Party (Beil 2004: 258–275). From 1926 to 1928, on the anniversary of the beginning of the war, the Federation commemorated the 'Imperialist war' with exhibitions dominated by photos and documents, thus warning against capitalism and militarism. In view of such left-wing activism and the break with traditional depictions of war and heroes, conservative and nationalist circles began to use exhibitions for their own purposes in the late 1920s (Beil 2004: 275–299). They worked with terms that in their opinion were not given enough attention: honour and memory. At least, these were the catchwords of *The German Front*, a travelling exhibition that had been successful since 1930. Its main exhibits were large dioramas of Verdun, Arras-Loretto, the Vosges and Ypres. The curator, Gustav Seyferle, formulated his mission in the declamatory sentence, 'Dishonourable is the nation that forgets its heroes' (Seyferle 1931: 2).

In fact, the Weimar governments had a hard time remembering the Great War and its approximately 1.9 million victims. Two irreconcilable views clashed. Some were in favour of an admonishing commemoration, emphasizing the horrors of war, while others wanted to underscore sacrifice and heroism. Since 1921, the *Volksbund Deutsche Kriegsgräberfürsorge* (German War Graves Commission) was committed to legally establishing the *Volkstrauertag* (People's Commemoration Day) as a day of celebration and remembrance for those who died in the war. This initiative repeatedly failed in parliament (Brandt 2000: 147–152). Nor could the governments decide to realize a national 'Imperial memorial'. All the same, after years of discussion, a project of the Free State of Prussia did come to fruition: In 1931, at the suggestion of the Social Democratic Prime Minister of Prussia Otto Braun, the *Neue Wache* (New Guardhouse) in Berlin, located next to the *Zeughaus*, was converted into a 'memorial for the fallen of the World War' (Demps 2011: 76–102).

To contextualize this confused and politically contentious state of affairs, it is instructive to compare it with the situation in victorious France. In Paris on 11 November 1920, the body of an unnamed soldier from the Battle of Verdun was buried under the *Arc de Triomphe*, thus creating the 'tomb of the unknown soldier' (Inglis 1994). Two years later, the government declared the day an official holiday. From then on, rituals performed in public offered the relatives of the approximately 1.4 million dead the opportunity to express their grief. The official museumization of the Great War also began quickly in France. At the Paris *Musée de l'Armée*, the special exhibition set up during the war was transferred to the permanent exhibition and now formed the final section of a narrative that began with the Middle Ages (Lagrange 2014). The two halls dedicated to the World War were named after the famous Marshals Philippe Pétain and Ferdinand Foch (Musée de l'Armée 1939: 25–27). Prominent World War exhibits were also placed in other parts of the museum. Of particular importance were the German flags captured in 1914/1915 as well as the French flags, lost in the Franco-Prussian War, repatriated from Berlin. Paraded through Paris at the Victory Parade on 11 November 1920, they were subsequently exhibited in the flag hall (Musée de l'Armée 1939: 30). Finally, one of the museum's striking large objects was the Compiègne Wagon, the train carriage where the armistice was signed in 1918.

The defence of the Republic, culminating in the victory over the German Empire, gave meaning to the victims of the Great War and was also portrayed as historical compensation for the defeat suffered in the Franco-Prussian War. France's losses had been enormous, but public commemoration of the war was not a contested process. Mourning and national pride went side by side with a deep wish that such trauma should never be repeated. This 'social pacification' is borne out by the behaviour of those who might be considered the most deeply concerned. In contrast to their counterparts in the defeated countries, French veterans' organizations adopted a strong anti-war stance (Prost 1992).

1931–1932: The return of the war to the museum

In Germany, the state museumization of the World War did not begin until the early 1930s, and the Berlin *Zeughaus* was one of the first museums to take up the subject again in 1931. The exhibition emphasized the historical significance of the place as a memorial. It also made direct reference to the Treaty of Versailles:

> As the largest Prussian weapons collection and guardian of the mementoes and trophies of the Prussian Army, the Zeughaus, remembering its venerable tradition, has made it its first task to prepare a site worthy of the tremendous events of the World War, a difficult, in some respects almost impossible task. After all, being rendered defenceless by the dictates of a hard peace, unmeasured booty was snatched from us, just as they demanded the shameful destruction of our own proud arms
>
> *(Post 1933: 3)*

Given that the *Zeughaus* operated under the aegis of the Social Democrat controlled Prussian government, the approach taken by the museum bears out the fact that hatred of the 1919 peace settlement was not limited to nationalist politicians.

Direct or indirect references to the returned objects, as the gun display in the courtyard had already offered since 1921, or to demilitarization, ran through the exhibition. In the vestibule two Fokker aircraft were installed; each was linked to a wartime air-ace, in one case Manfred von Richthofen, in the other Oswald Boelcke. They recalled the air force, but also made the visitor think about the present, when there was no air force any more due to the armament restrictions. In the courtyard of the *Zeughaus*, there were German field guns and trench mortars. The exhibition guide pointed out that they had had to be rendered unusable (Post 1933: 6).

The presentation of the exhibits was directly linked to the exhibition set up before 1914, which showed historical epochs as well as developments in the history of weapons and uniforms. An arrangement of uniforms illustrated the 'unequal balance of power' of the opponents in the war, namely 'four against eight' (Post 1933: 8–9) (Figure 1.3): While the uniforms of the four allies Germany, Austria, Turkey and Bulgaria hung in a display cabinet, they were facing 'the enormous phalanx of our main opponents (...) in the order of their entry into the war: Russia, Serbia, France, Belgium, England, Italy, Romania and the United States of North America'. In the middle of the room stood the figure of a German storm trooper with a gas mask, designated as 'the unknown soldier' (Post 1933: 9). While heroism and bravery were evident here, the exhibition of small arms spread over several rooms emphasized the technical superiority of the Germans but avoided references to the military and political circumstances of the war. The museum thus left the explanation of the defeat to its visitors, for which many probably invoked the widespread stab-in-the-back myth.

FIGURE 1.3 The World War Section on the upper floor of the Berlin Zeughaus, c. 1932. (© Deutsches Historisches Museum.)

Outside Prussia, too, the World War returned to army museums: In July 1932, a 'World War Section' tailored to the Württemberg regiments, including a room of honour for the fallen, opened in the Stuttgart Army Museum. Work began at the Munich Army Museum on a 'World War Section' to supplement the existing exhibition on the Bavarian army – including objects that were hidden and escaped the restitution claims of the Treaty of Versailles (Beil 2004: 232).

1934–1940: War memory and war preparation

After the Nazi election victory in January 1933, the army museums soon received new state attention. The military historian and museum employee, Werner Hahlweg, described their social task: 'They are monuments to military greatness, national and military educational institutions and places of research' (Hahlweg 1937a: 272). Their special function was 'to provide a worthy memorial to the achievements of the combatants of the World War, and moreover to make the people aware of the fateful significance of the Great War' (Hahlweg 1937a: 272).

Far more so than the other parties of the Weimar Republic, the Nazi Movement had recognized and used the memories of the World War as a politically relevant topic at an early stage, contributing to its rise from a small Munich splinter party to a large people's party (Krumeich 2015). The Nazi version of the stab-in-the-back myth identified the culprits for the defeat as the 'November Criminals' – the representatives of the November Revolution of 1918 – as well as Jews and Marxists. The so-called 'ignoble peace' of Versailles was denounced; war guilt was denied. Adolf Hitler himself called the World War 'the greatest and most unforgettable time' of his life and used his image as a simple frontline soldier and bearer of the Iron Cross and the Wound Badge again and again (Hitler 1925: 179). The Nazis succeeded in building on existing conservative and nationalist views and thus gained approval.

The army museums were of special interest to the new government as places of remembrance. They were not to display a self-contained, dormant past, but to have an effect on the present and the future and play an important role in military education. They aimed to train society in the spirit of the bellicose Nazi ideology. A theoretical study of the contents, organization and didactics of army museums began in specialist journals (Hahlweg 1935). New military museums were established: As early as February 1934 the *Historisches Militär Museum* opened in Koblenz, three months later the *Badisches Armee Museum* opened in Karlsruhe. In 1937, there were museums in the nine major former states that focused on the respective military tradition. This was in addition to garrison and regiment museums and the militaria sections in general and local history museums (Hahlweg 1937a: 272–278). In most of these exhibitions, the Great War occupied a prominent place.

In the ensemble of Nazi army museums, the Berlin *Zeughaus* took the leading role: In August 1933, the long-time director, the Jewish art historian Julius Binder, was dismissed. His successor was a First World War veteran; Rear Admiral Hermann Lorey took up his post on 1 August 1934, the 20th anniversary of the mobilization of 1914. Only a few months later, in January 1935, the *Zeughaus* became a memorial to Field Marshal Hindenburg, who had died on 2 August 1934 and who had been revered by many since 1914 as the 'victor of Tannenberg'. He died in office, as President of Germany. Hitler, who now assumed complete power by combining the offices of President and Chancellor, had his predecessor's death mask exhibited in the middle of the Hall of Fame.

The main task of the new museum director was 'to prepare a worthy site in the Zeughaus for the great events of the World War' (Hahlweg 1937b: 134). To this end, targeted acquisitions, transfers from government agencies and private donations expanded the collection. The substantive concept for the exhibition was developed by museum staff together with the Army Archive and the Research Institute for War and Army History in Potsdam. The new World War section clearly stood out from the previous design due to its historical division according to events of the war years. It took up almost half of the area of the ground floor. The war was depicted as a complex military event. Sequences with documents and maps showing its course alternated with sequences with uniforms, weapons, equipment, awards and models. Sober scenography and didactic elements made the presentation appear objective.

The opening took place during the Olympic Games on the historic date of 1 August 1936. The very first room answered the question of war guilt: 'The assassination of the heir to the Austrian throne on 28 June 1914 was the cause of the

World War' (Hahlweg 1937b: 137). As the official museum guide said, the aim of the exhibition was to keep alive the memory of the 'invincible spirit of the front' that had prevented the invasion of Germany by its enemies (Post 1936: 28). This struggle was also illustrated by world maps entitled 'War of the World against Us', which listed the annually increasing number of opponents of the Central Powers (Hahlweg 1937b: 137). Behind these remarks was the encirclement thesis perpetuated by the Supreme Army Command from the beginning of the World War onwards and the self-defence thesis closely related to it, which was intended to justify German actions. In the Nazi version, this became the 'struggle for existence and defence against an overpowering, hateful enemy' (Beil 2004: 320). Meanwhile, the Nazi regime used the Olympic Games as propaganda to prove the 'German love of peace' (Skor 2011: 321).

Several special exhibits supplemented the new permanent exhibition. Exhibitions about the booty that General Field Marshal Blücher had brought back in 1814 from the campaign against Napoleon (in 1934) or on the 250th birthday of the so-called Soldier King Friedrich Wilhelm I (in 1938) drew a connection between Prussia and National Socialism. Between 1934 and 1939, the ten-part exhibition series, *The World War in Pictures*, dealt with the great battles of the World War, with the focus in each case on operational aspects. In 1936, on the occasion of the events of 20 years before, *The Battle of Verdun* was displayed. The last passage of the exhibition guide shows how the nine months of battles, which were costly for all sides, were interpreted as a success: 'Despite everything, this shattering conclusion is brightly outshone by the successes achieved beforehand and the heroism of the German front-line soldier demonstrated in all the hard fights' (Staatliches Zeughaus 1936: 19).

On a national level, the *Zeughaus* had free discretion to interpret the World War. Other exhibitions and collections, such as the Anti-War Museum, had been closed or destroyed. On an international level, the museum offered the German counterpart to the French and British army museums, the *Musée de l'Armée* and the Imperial War Museum. The revisionist and heroicizing museum presentation of the World War was embedded in a wider media context, which included publications on military history, literature and films. Parallel to the museumization and medialization of the Great War, the Nazi government ignored the Treaty of Versailles: In March 1935 Adolf Hitler reintroduced general conscription, in March 1936 the newly created *Wehrmacht* occupied the demilitarized Rhineland and in January 1937 Hitler finally unilaterally terminated the Treaty of Versailles.

1940: Military revenge

The already-mentioned *Tannenberg* exhibition was the last exhibition of the Berlin *Zeughaus* on the First World War. Nine days after its opening on 23 August 1939, the Second World War began with the *Wehrmacht*'s invasion of Poland. From then on, the Nazi regime used the *Zeughaus* to directly portray itself and its power. On 10 March 1940, Hitler held his first 'Day of Commemoration of

Heroes' (*Heldengedenktag*) speech in the *Zeughaus*, thus linking the 'heroes' of the First World War with those of the current conflict. The Supreme Commander established a link from the early modern period to the present:

> From the hallowed halls of the building in which we find ourselves, the witnesses of an incomparable glorious past speak to us. The past was won and sealed with the blood of countless German heroes. We would have no right to enter this hall were it not for the sacred resolution in our hearts to be no less brave than those before us who carried these weapons and wore these decorations and uniforms.
>
> *(Domarius 1965: 1478)*

This speech was not only heard in the museum but also broadcast on the radio and printed in the newspaper. Hitler laid a wreath for the fallen of the First World War in the New Guardhouse central memorial.

Driven by the Nazi regime, the military revision of the First World War peace settlements began with the Battle of France, which lasted only a few weeks. On 14 June 1940, *Wehrmacht* soldiers entered Paris and occupied the capital, which had remained the unattained goal in the First World War. The following day, in a matter of hours, they took the fortifications of Verdun, which had been fought over bitterly for nine months in 1916 (Voigt 2016). After the military victory, a symbolic act was to eclipse the Armistice of Compiègne. On 22 June, the French delegation had to sign the armistice agreement, now dictated by Germany and tantamount to surrender, in the same railway carriage. In the view of the Nazis, the shame and disgrace of the Treaty of Versailles, which had arisen from the Armistice of 1918, was thus erased.

The triumph, described by the press as 'the most glorious victory in German history', required public celebration (VB 1940a). A victory parade took place in Berlin on 18 July. In his speech, propaganda minister Dr. Joseph Goebbels drew comparisons with the year 1918, and the *Völkischer Beobachter* newspaper commented with reference to the veterans:

This day also erases the last traces of bitterness in the minds of those who are not returning home for the first time after heroic struggle. They had already marched in here in 1918, but were mocked and ridiculed by an unleashed underworld. They were even insulted by the praise of those November criminals who, in their worthlessness, took pleasure in welcoming the army that they themselves had brought down behind its back (VB 1940b).

The booty of the Battle of France was not carried along on the parade. However, the museumization of the campaign began only a few weeks later in the army museums. Shortly before the beginning of the Second World War, they had already been instructed to take immediate initiatives to acquire items to exhibit in the event of a conflict (Müller 1994: 24). As in the First World War, this was the responsibility of so-called *Sammeloffiziere* (Collecting Officers).[1] The Berlin *Zeughaus* presented the new spoils of war in the exhibition *From the*

FIGURE 1.4 Exhibition on French and Polish spoils of war in the courtyard of the Berlin Zeughaus, 1940. (© Deutsches Historisches Museum.)

Western Wall into France (Figure 1.4): Enemy weapons, uniforms and equipment came from the battlefields. But the focus was on early modern cannon: eight bronze, artistically crafted gun barrels from a series, which had been cast in Berlin at the beginning of the eighteenth century. Emperor Napoleon I had them brought to Paris as booty in 1806 (Pommier 2011). Another historical gun was placed in front of the building: *Valerie*, a huge French fortress gun that had been captured by Prussian troops in 1871 and returned to Paris under the Treaty of Versailles.

After the occupation of Paris, Hitler had ordered 'the military property stolen from German lands since the French Revolution to be returned to the homeland' (Anon n.d. (1941): 4). Museum director Lorey had the *Musée de l'Armée*'s collections examined and some 2,000 objects transported to Berlin, including pieces returned to France after 1918 and 14 German military flags captured by French troops during the First World War. This was in direct reaction to the restitution claims of the Treaty of Versailles. Moreover, hundreds of early modern and medieval small arms and pieces of armour, which had been allegedly or actually confiscated by Napoleon I after the defeat of the Prussian Army in 1806, were also returned. In this way, not only was the museumization of the German defeat of 1918 eradicated, but the traces of earlier defeats were also erased.

As a sign of victory, Hitler had another museum object brought to Berlin: the Compiègne Wagon. On the 'Day of Commemoration of Heroes' in 1941, the train carriage was drawn as a victory trophy from the Brandenburg Gate to the *Lustgarten*.

Exhibited in the park near the *Zeughaus*, the wagon could be viewed on '*Wehrmacht* Day', 24 March 1941. In his 'Day of Commemoration' speech, Hitler made direct reference to the First World War (Hirschfeld 2010: 46–47). He interpreted the victory of the *Wehrmacht* as compensation for the defeat of 1918, giving meaning for the victims of the Great War. But even more: 'Perhaps it was also out of this powerful awareness that the German people today succeeded in doing such infinitely great things. It feels like the execution of the will of their brave ancestors' (Bouhler 1943: 432).

After the summer of 1941, the First World War quickly lost its significance as a historical and mental point of reference, and the exhibitions in the Berlin *Zeughaus* turned to a new theme. From May to June 1942, the exhibition *The Soviet Paradise* was shown in the *Lustgarten*. The Nazi regime wanted to use this exhibition to expose the purported nature of its main ideological opponent and legitimize the war of extermination against it (Tymkiw 2018: 200–219). Following this, the exhibition *Fighting in Central Russia*, which opened in March 1943 in the *Zeughaus*, took up current events of the War. Further exhibitions were planned, but were never to be realized (Rudolph and Goebel 2014: 151). At the end of 1943, British air raids severely damaged the *Zeughaus*, the roof truss was destroyed by fire, as was the depot. Nevertheless, the museum was the only one in Berlin, to remain open until September 1944. Subsequently the building was fought over by the Waffen-SS and the Red Army at the end of April 1945, and reduced to ruins (Figure 1.5). After the unconditional surrender of Germany, the Allied Command decided on 18 October 1945 to liquidate the 'Zeughaus War Museum in Berlin, which is a symbol of German militarism and a collection of war trophies acquired through robbery and looting'

FIGURE 1.5 'In destroyed Berlin – Monument of honesty with arsenal', postcard, c. 1946. (© Private collection.)

(Müller 1994: 230). The other German army museums were also looted or destroyed at the end of the War and were dissolved on 13 May 1946 by Control Council Directive No. 30. Only scattered remains of their extensive collections on the First World War remained.

Mission accomplished?

In the German Empire, the numerous exhibitions on war and spoils from 1914 to 1918 made the people believe in the victory of their army to the last. This illusion was shattered by the signing of the Armistice. Collapse and defeat hit an almost completely unprepared society. Conspiracy theories of having been 'stabbed in the back' were used by many as an explanation. The associated skepticism towards the Weimar Republic was mixed with indignation about the Treaty of Versailles, which was perceived as humiliating. Torn by ideological controversies, society found no common memory and interpretation of the lost war. This 'crisis of meaning' was reflected in the *Zeughaus* and other museums.

The Nazi regime, by contrast, had no doubts about how the war should be treated in museums. They had long used already existing and widespread conservative and nationalist ideas for their interpretation of the Great War. On the one hand, they praised the bravery and heroism of the German soldiers, on the other they complained about the injustice and disgrace of the armistice and Peace Treaty. The pattern of museumization of the war that they promoted was not aimed at presenting a closed past. Instead, the Nazis instrumentalized it as an energy source for the militaristic mobilization of society. The more the exhibitions emphasized the achievements and sacrifices, the more unjust the defeat seemed to appear. The more unjust the defeat, the more revisionist measures seemed justified. The trophies of the World War, which were charged with emotion, were almost ideal objects for this purpose: As prizes of war, they were considered the epitomes of repeatedly invoked military achievements. Their loss turned them into phantom objects, exemplifying the shame of the defeat allegedly suffered as a result of the 'stab in the back' and the humiliation of the Peace Treaty. This ambivalence is also inherent, under different auspices, in the French handling of German booty.

In the Nazi narrative, the victory over France in 1940 was the conclusion of the First World War. It erased the shame of November 1918 and restored honour. The victory and its propagated historical dimension were made visible to the public by returning the booty to its original location, the Berlin *Zeughaus*. This was not only a symbolic, ritual act, it was also Nazi self-therapy. But the plans of the Nazi regime did not stop there. The victory in the West was only the starting point for the reorganization of Europe under German tutelage and the launching of a great war of conquest and annihilation in the East: a war that was to culminate in the destruction of the *Zeughaus* and the end of its existence as a museum.

Note

1 In the First and Second World Wars, objects of note were sifted from the general booty by Collecting Officers who then took care of their transport to the various museums.

References

Andrews, M.-L. (2014) *'Memory of a Nation': Making and re-making history in the Berlin Zeughaus.* PhD Thesis, University of Sydney.

Anon. (1916) *Deutsche Kriegsausstellungen 1916.* Berlin: Klasing & Co.

———. (1918) *Offizieller Führer durch die Deutsche Luftkriegsbeute-Ausstellung Dortmund-Fredenbaum.* Berlin: Braunbeck.

———. (n.d. [1941]) *Liste der 1940 aus Frankreich zurückgeführten militärischen Gegenstände.*

Beil, C. (2004) *Der ausgestellte Krieg. Präsentationen des Ersten Weltkriegs 1914–1939.* Tübingen: Tübinger Vereinigung für Volkskunde.

———. (2005) Das mobilisierte Gedächtnis. Kriegsausstellungen in der Zwischenkriegszeit in Deutschland. In G. Korff (ed.), *KriegsVolksKunde. Zur Erfahrungsbindung durch Symbolbildung*, pp 87–115. Tübingen: Tübinger Vereinigung für Volkskunde.

———. (2010) Kriegsausstellungen während des Nationalsozialismus. In G. Krumeich (ed.), *Nationalsozialismus und Erster Weltkrieg*, pp 97–109. Essen: Klartext.

Bouhler, P. (ed.) (1943) *Der großdeutsche Freiheitskampf. Reden Adolf Hitlers.* München: Franz Eher Nachfolger.

Brandt, S. (1994) The memory makers: Museums and exhibitions of the First World War. *History & Memory* 6:95–122.

———. (2000) *Vom Kriegsschauplatz zum Gedächtnisraum: Die Westfront 1914–1940.* Baden-Baden: Nomos.

Demps, L. (2011) Die Neue Wache. *Vom königlichen Wachhaus zur Zentralen Gedenkstätte.* Berlin: Verlag für Berlin-Brandenburg.

Domarius, M. (1965) *Hitler. Reden und Proklamationen 1932–1945*, Vol 2.1. München: Süddeutscher Verlag.

Friedrich, E. (n.d.) *Das Anti-Kriegsmuseum.*

Gross, G.P. (2018) *Das Ende des Ersten Weltkriegs und die Dolchstoßlegende.* Stuttgart: Reclam.

Hacker, B.C. and M. Vining. (2007) Towards a history of military museums. In R. D. Smith (ed.), *ICOMAM 50. Papers on arms and military history 1957–2007*, pp 32–51. Leeds: Basiliscoe Press.

Hahlweg, W. (1935) Die Heeresmuseen. Wesen und Aufgaben. *Museumskunde* 7:59–71.

———. (1937a) Heeresmuseen. In H. Franke (ed.), *Handbuch der neuzeitlichen Wehrwissenschaften*, Bd. 2, pp 271–278. Das Heer, Berlin/Leipzig: De Gruyter & Co.

———. (1937b) Die Weltkriegsabteilung im Staatlichen Zeughaus zu Berlin. *Museumskunde* 9:134–138.

Hirschfeld, G. (2010) Der Führer spricht. Der Erste Weltkrieg in den Reden Adolf Hitlers. In G. Krumeich (ed.), *Nationalsozialismus und Erster Weltkrieg*, pp 35–51. Essen: Klartext.

Hitler, A. (1925) *Mein Kampf. Bd. 1. Eine Abrechnung.* München: Franz Eher Nachfolger.

Horne, J. (2016) Von Museen im Weltkrieg zu Weltkriegsmuseen. In C. Kott and B. Savoy (eds.), *Mars and Museum. Europäische Museen im Ersten Weltkrieg*, pp 33–52. Köln: Böhlau.

Inglis, K.S. (1994) Grabmäler für Unbekannte Soldaten. In R. Rother (ed.), *Die letzten Tage der Menschheit. Bilder des Ersten Weltkrieges*, pp 409–422. Berlin: Ars Nicolai.

Kolb, E. (2005) *Der Frieden von Versailles.* München: C. H. Beck.

Königliche Zeughaus Verwaltung (ed.) (1914) Das Königliche Zeughaus. *Führer durch die Ruhmeshalle und die Sammlungen.* Berlin: Julius Bard.

Krumeich, G. (2001) Die Dolchstoß-Legende. In E. Francois and H. Schulze (eds.), *Deutsche Erinnerungsorte,* 1, pp 585–599. München: C. H. Beck.

———— (ed.). (2010) *Nationalsozialismus und Erster Weltkrieg.* Essen: Klartext.

————. (2015) Wie die Nazis den Ersten Weltkrieg gewannen. Politische und kulturelle Ansätze. In G. Krumeich (ed.), *Deutschland, Frankreich und der Krieg. Historische Studien zu Politik, Militär und Kultur,* pp 302–316. Essen: Klartext.

————. (2018) Die unbewältigte Niederlage. *Das Trauma des Ersten Weltkrieges und die Weimarer Republik.* Freiburg: Herder.

Lagrange, F. (2014) La Grande Guerre au Musée de l'Armée. In Musée de l'Armée (ed.), *Vu du front. Représenter la Grande Guerre,* pp 136–140. Paris: Somogy.

Lange, B. (2003) Einen Krieg ausstellen. *Die "Deutsche Kriegsausstellung" 1916 in Berlin.* Berlin: Verbrecher-Verlag.

Lange, B. (2010) Das Kapitel "Reichskriegsmuseum". Plan eines idealen Themenmuseums. *Jahrbuch der Berliner Museen* 52:99–105.

Mommsen, H. (1997) Militär und Militarisierung in Deutschland 1914 bis 1938. In U. Frevert (ed.), *Militär und Gesellschaft im 19. und 20. Jahrhundert,* pp 265–276. Stuttgart: Klett-Cotta.

Müller, H. (1994) Das Berliner Zeughaus. *Vom Arsenal zum Museum.* Berlin: Brandenburgisches Verlags-Haus.

Musée de l'Armée (ed.) (1939) *Les Invalides et le Musée de l'Armée. Guide officiel.* Paris: Musée de l'Armée.

Pommier, C. (2011) Les canons prussiens de la batterie triomphale. *Revue de la Société des Amis du Musée de l'Armée* 142:60–70.

Post, P. (1933) Der Weltkrieg im Zeughaus. *Amtlicher Führer.* Berlin: Staatliche Museen.

————. (1936) Das Zeughaus. *Kurzer Gesamtführer. Amtlicher Führer.* Berlin: Bruno Schmidt.

Prost, A. (1992) *In the Wake of War. 'Les Ancienes Combattants' and French Society.* Providence/Oxford: Berg.

Rudolph, J. and B. Goebel. (2014) Krieg im Museum – Museum im Krieg. Das Berliner Zeughaus im Nationalsozialismus. *Landesgeschichtliche Vereinigung für die Mark Brandenburg e.V., Mitteilungsblatt* 115:131–161.

Schivelbusch, W. (2001) *The Culture of Defeat. National Trauma, Mourning, and Recovery.* New York: Picador.

Seyferle, G. (1931) Die Deutsche Front. *Eine Heldenehrung.* Chemnitz: Chemnitzer Tageblatt.

Skor, H. (2011) "Brücken über den Rhein". *Frankreich in der Wahrnehmung und Propaganda des Dritten Reichs, 1933–1939.* Essen: Klartext.

Staatliches Zeughaus (ed.) (1936) Der Weltkrieg in Bildern. *Gedächtnisschau 1916–1936. V. Der Kampf um Verdun, Amtlicher Wegweiser.* Berlin: Staatliche Museen.

————. (ed.) (1939) *Der Weltkrieg in Bildern. X. Die Schlacht bei Tannenberg. Amtlicher Wegweiser.* Berlin: Staatliche Museen.

Tymkiw, M. (2018) *Nazi Exhibition Design and Modernism.* Minneapolis/London: University of Minnesota Press.

VB. (1940a) *Völkischer Beobachter,* 189, 7 July.

————. (1940b) *Völkischer Beobachter,* 200, 18 July.

Voigt, D. (2016) Der Krieg, Verdun und die Nationalsozialisten. In M. Hörter and D. Voigt (eds.), *Verdun 1916. Eine Schlacht verändert die Welt*, pp 157–166. Münster: Aschendorffsche Verlagsbuchhandlung.

Weissbrich, T. (2016a) Die Weltkriege im Museum. Das Berliner Zeughaus 1934–1945. In T. Baensch, K. Kratz-Kessemeier and D. Wimmer (eds.), *Museen im Nationalsozialismus. Akteure – Orte – Politik*, pp 277–291. Köln: Böhlau.

———. (2016b) Rally Round the Flag: French and German Colours and Standards, 1870 to 1920. In K. Tetteris (ed.), *The vexillological seminar. In hoc signo vinces*, pp 41–47. Stockholm: Armémuseum.

2

THE GREAT WAR IN FRENCH MUSEUMS 1914–2018

Bérénice Zunino

It was the campaigns of Napoleon that first prompted the emergence across Europe of 'heritage awareness' (Savoy 2003: 146). But, in the case of France itself, the French Revolution had already raised the question of the destruction, seizure and preservation of works of art to an extent previously unknown. A further threshold in the involvement of cultural property in hostilities was crossed when the unprecedented violence of the First World War struck France. The Great War had a number of impacts on the history of cultural heritage on French soil, both in terms of destruction and in the creation of new war collections (Granger 2013; Savoy and Kott 2016; Ypersele 2013). In addition to the cultural property directly impacted by war in regions crossed by the front line, France, like other European countries, saw the creation of new provisions aimed at documenting the hostilities and mobilizing civilian support. Still today, the Great War remains strongly anchored in French local and family memories (Offenstadt 2010), and the centenary of the hostilities has once again shown the keen interest of the French in this conflict. This paper aims to examine the ideological and memorial challenges that the Great War has represented, and which it continues to represent, for French museums from the start of the conflict to the commemoration of its centenary in 2014–2018.

The history of museums and artistic heritage during and after the First World War remains, in France, a relatively unexplored field of research. Despite the development of cultural history in the 1980s, the concept of museums and collections as vectors of war culture between 1914 and 1918 did not immediately attract the attention of researchers (Maingon 2016). Finally, however, the new perspectives opened up by the concept of *lieux de mémoire* and, more recently, the emergence of Material Culture Studies and of a history of museums and museography have encouraged interdisciplinary engagements between historians, art-historians, curators and archaeologists in studying the fate of museums and

DOI: 10.4324/9781003263531-4

collections during and after the Great War, whether from a national (Bollard-Raineau and Kott 2014; Nivet 2013; Nivet and Lewuillon 2017; Tillier 2019), international (Saunders and Cornish 2009; Savoy and Kott 2016) or transnational (Meyer and Savoy 2014) perspective.

In a country like France, where the memory of the First World War is still strong, the heritage destroyed and created by that conflict has been the object of conflicted memories, which have seen a long evolution from 1914 until the centenary commemorations of 2014–2018. Here, I focus on three key moments in the French history of the museumization of the Great War: the origins of the war's artistic heritage and the creation of new collections during the conflict itself; the museography of the Great War in the principal French museums from the second half of the twentieth century until today; and finally the significant contribution of French museums to the commemorative activities of the centenary.

The museum at war

When considering the cultural heritage of the Great War, it is important to distinguish the fate of cultural property during hostilities – whether it has been the subject of conservation measures or destruction by the enemy – from objects 'produced and bequeathed by war' (Cappronnier et al 2014). The inexorable logic of Total War ensured that French cultural heritage, in common with that of other European countries enduring an enemy presence, became a strategic and ideological issue and, as a result, simultaneously a target of destruction and an object of covetousness. Faced with threats of intentional destruction in regions close to the front or damage during the bombing of French cities, public authorities took initiatives to preserve museum collections. In this iconoclastic war, they also set out to organize exhibitions, with the dual intention of denouncing this destruction while patriotically acclaiming French heritage.

In parallel with this official management of French works of art, the Great War aroused an unprecedented enthusiasm for war objects. Public and private collections reflected the previously unheard-of level of involvement of the whole of society in this mass war. Even in the immediate vicinity of the front line, soldiers paid special attention to war objects. As a result, these collections nowadays carry ideological and memorial burdens, since they signify the mobilization or remobilization of French society during the war, as much as they bear witness to attempts to ensure its long-term memory.

The burning and bombing of monuments, the looting of museums and the destruction of libraries and archives were all witnessed as the German Army made its initial advance in the West in 1914. Faced with the shock of going to war, the French authorities were aware of the increased need to preserve and conserve the country's monumental, artistic and archival heritage. In 1914, however, there was no plan to rescue French museums. It was not until August 1917 that the Service for the Protection and Evacuation of Works of Art and

Monuments was created (Désiré 2017: 89). Witnessing the August 1914 advance of German troops through Belgium, the French Administration of Fine Arts could do no more than recommend to the cities of Northeast France that they ensure the protection of their museums. The most worrying case was that of the Palais des Beaux-Arts in Lille, which housed very rich collections. These were safeguarded in basements or, in the case of the most precious works of art, such as *La Tête de cire*, walled-up.

But such precautions proved difficult to take; first due to a lack of human and financial resources in the context of general mobilization, secondly because drastic measures might undermine the morale of the French civilian population (Bollard-Raineau and Kott 2014). Some museums were closed and requisitioned for military purposes, the museum of Douai, for example, was transformed into a hospital. The collections of other museums in regions close to the front line are either stored in basements to try to shelter them from bombardment, or evacuated, as at Dunkirk, Boulogne-sur-Mer and Bergues. Other museums were purely and simply destroyed, as at Arras in July 1915 or at Péronne in July 1916. Plundered and entirely destroyed by the Germans, the Alfred-Danicourt museum of Péronne, which housed numismatic and glyptic archaeological collections as well as gold smithery, was reopened during the interwar period. Part of its collections had been cleverly concealed by the curator during the war; the remainder was reconstituted thanks to war reparations (De Sousa 2014). In the occupied zones of the North and the East of France, museums were placed under the direction of the *Kunstschutz*, the German service for the preservation of artistic heritage. But they did not find themselves protected by this. They became places of deposit for German *objets d'art* or were seized or requisitioned in support of the German war effort (Kott 2006).

Impacted by the fighting and coveted by the enemy, French museums took on political and ideological significance during the Great War. The looting of works of art perpetrated in Belgium and France offered the French the opportunity to reactivate the stereotype of the German thief and pillager of museums, previously employed during the Franco-Prussian War of 1870–1871. The damaged artistic heritage itself became the object of patriotic exhibitions which sought to denounce German 'barbarism'. In this cultural war, French museums symbolized 'civilization' and the universality allegedly embodied in French culture. As the home to collections tracing the history of humanity, the *Louvre* was used as a veritable political instrument between 1914 and 1918. Art historian Robert de La Sizeranne even pronounced it to be the embodiment of the 'moral force' of France (Maingon 2016: 16). Although it was closed in 1914 for a period of five years and partially emptied of its works (Figures 2.1 and 2.2), the *Louvre* contributed, thanks to works of art retained in Paris during the war, to the development of several patriotic exhibitions. These included 'War Art', 'Paintings of Glory' and 'Work by soldiers', which were organized by the periodical *Pays de France* and presented at the *Jeu de Paume* in 1915 (ibid.: 88; Saunders 2003:175).

FIGURE 2.1 The Louvre museum during the Great War. The Grande Galerie, with paintings removed. (© gallica.bnf.fr.)

FIGURE 2.2 The exterior of the Louvre in 1918, with sandbags placed to protect the antiquities from bomb blasts. (© gallica.bnf.fr.)

On 24 November 1916, the French capital witnessed the opening, by the President of the Republic at the *Petit Palais*, of a 'Museum of German Atrocities', also known as the 'Exhibition of German Vandalism'. This exhibition pursued the triple objective of showing the resistance and heroism of soldiers in their fight to protect French territory, accusing the enemy and remobilizing public support following the costly victory of the Battle of Verdun. According to Claire Maingon, the 300 or so pieces from the devastated regions exhibited there were literally imbued with the character of 'martyred' works, being presented in a sort of museographic 'cemetery' (Maingon 2014). The remnants of art objects collected from the ten Departments along the front line – hands and heads of statues, ruins, charred saints, silverware distorted by fire, damaged liturgical objects – rubbed shoulders with purely symbolic objects intended to add weight to the indictment against the destructive madness of German troops. These included shrapnel from Verdun or rubble from the fire at the cathedral in Reims, a symbol par excellence of German 'barbarism'.

To these categories of objects were added works of art saved by the French authorities; for example intact woodwork from the choir of Verdun cathedral dating from the eighteenth century. This museum initiative even prompted restorations. One such case is a Rubens painting 'The Adoration of the Magi', which had been damaged in the bombing of the Saint-Gervais-Saint-Protais cathedral in Soissons. These patriotic exhibitions all lent themselves to affirming the moral and cultural superiority of France over the brutality and the lack of · culture of the Germanic peoples.

Beyond these diverse cultural properties, which found their place in patriotic exhibitions, in France as well as other belligerent countries, the Great War generated new conflict-related material culture of its own. This social and anthropological phenomenon goes hand in hand with the need to legitimize the conflict and then, after 1918, to give meaning to the victims and the suffering caused by these four years of war (Saunders 2012). As symbolic appropriations of the war, this type of object appears both behind the frontline and in the rear.

The most notable phenomenon is known as 'artisanat des tranchées', 'Schützengraben-Handwerk' or 'trench art'. Through personal initiative, combatants reclaimed the very weapons and projectiles that had been produced to eliminate them and remade them. The term 'trench art' covers a vast field, which comprises not only objects made by soldiers at the Front, but items created in prison camps and hospitals, or those produced in the rear, for sale to civilians. The field is further enlarged, and indeed confused, by post-war artefacts, produced for sale to collectors or souvenir-hungry battlefield tourists (Saunders 2003: 143–156; Tillier 2019: 26–27). During the war itself, however, there was plainly a desire on the part of the combatants, to recover and conserve and transform these objects, in order to transmit their experience from the front to those around them and to future generations. In fact, the term 'museum' is frequently found used as a metaphor to designate collections of such artefacts in the wartime correspondence of French soldiers (ibid.: 17).

A different, but related, phenomenon manifested itself on the Home Front. The creation of what are known as 'collections de guerre' testifies to the enthusiasm of civilians and cultural institutions for war memorabilia between 1914 and 1918. Even if this phenomenon did not, in France, reach the pitch that it attained in Germany at the time (see, for example, Brandt 2004a), it was characterized by a strong dynamic in collecting traces of the war. Printed matter, postcards, posters, photographic material, personal letters, children's books, ration cards and all such objects became worthy of interest to make the experience of war more acceptable, to contribute to the cultural mobilization of French civilians and to bear witness to everyday life during the conflict for generations to come.

In France, large collections were formed at the initiative of public institutions, although these remained isolated enterprises (Didier 2008). Among them, we can cite the decisive role played in the collection of printed matter – in accordance with traditional French centralism – by the National Library of France. The Edouard Herriot collection, held by the Lyon Municipal Library, also represents a major public involvement in securing such material, being one of the largest public collections in France, with 20,000 objects and documents. But the most impressive 'collection de guerre' stemmed from the private initiative of an industrialist couple, Louise and Henri Leblanc. From 1914, supported by French parliamentarians and with the help of auxiliaries, they gathered all kinds of documents and objects relating to the conflict, before donating them to the French State in August 1917. Supplemented by official and private donations, this immense collection contains over 100,000 volumes of printed matter, 9,000 archive files, 10,000 maps and aerial photographs and 15,000 posters in many languages. It gave rise, in 1919, to the creation of the *Bibliothèque-Musée de la Guerre*, which in 1987 became the *Musée d'histoire contemporaine/Bibliothèque de documentation internationale contemporaine*. In 2018, it was relaunched as *La Contemporaine*. Before the Great War entered national military museums and regional history museums, these war collections represented, along with trench art, the first attempt to preserve the memory of the conflict through its material culture.

War memories at the museum

In victorious countries, both in England and in France, war collections enjoyed lasting success during the interwar period. Memorials, museums and war collections there embodied 'material representations of memory' (Saunders 2012: 284) of the conflict. In France, the Great War sparked an unprecedented wave of memorialization during the interwar period. For the first time, thanks to a 1913 law on historic monuments, the French authorities endeavoured to conserve sites of memory, battlefields, fortifications and French and German shelters. These foundations of war tourism and, above all, the 'collections de guerre' (the latter soon transformed into museums and libraries), retained a strongly nationalist dimension. Their main object was the glorification of the army and the celebration of the heroism of the *Poilus*. Against such a background, relations between French and German museums remain strained and burdened by Germanophobic stereotypes. A tentative cooperation is detectable from 1926, thanks to the mediation of the International Museums Office. This took place in the context of the Locarno Treaties of that year, wherein Germany normalized its relations with France and other signatories (Kott 2013). During the period 1939–1945, French museum collections were once again threatened by bombing and occupation by German troops. In safekeeping at the Château de Vincennes, near Paris, the collections of the War Museum were damaged by an outbreak of fire in 1944 (Didier 2008). In various museums and archives, significant losses were lamented, the most famous of which remains the fate of the original of the Treaty of Versailles, taken to the Reich Chancellery in June 1940 and probably destroyed at the end of the war.

After the turmoil of the Second World War, representations of the Great War in French museums underwent various changes up to the beginning of the twenty-first century. Depending on their status and their mission, these museums paid varying levels of attention to historiographical developments. At a time when witnesses and direct actors in the conflict still occupied an important place in French society, museums devoted to the conflict were founded thanks to networks of veterans. Thus, the Verdun Memorial, founded in 1967 on the initiative of the veteran Maurice Genevoix, was intended to commemorate the combat experience of Verdun, mainly from the French point of view. The Memorial continues to this day to depend upon the National Memorial Committee of Verdun (a non-profit association regulated by the French Associations Law of 1901).

However, the Memorial and its interpretation centre were renovated and enlarged between 2013 and 2016. They now present the battle from a Franco-German perspective and have acquired an immersive museography (audiovisual devices; reconstruction of a shell hole). This is something that is rare enough in French museums to be worthy of highlighting. The public is made aware of the Memorial's direct environment since the battlefield can be seen from the museum's terrace.[1] Of similar vintage is the *Musée de la Caverne du Dragon* on the Chemin des Dames, which opened in 1969, under the aegis of *le Souvenir français*, a commemorative organization founded in the wake of the Franco-Prussian War. This museum was completely refurbished in 1999 thanks to local Government funding (conseil général de l'Aisne) (Hardier 2004).

Other regional museums devoted to the Great War, being more recently conceived, were in a position to take greater account of current trends in historiography from the moment of their creation (Fleury 2014). This was certainly the case with the two main museums specially dedicated to the First World War, the *Historial de la Grande Guerre* in Péronne on the Somme and the *Musée de la Grande Guerre du pays de Meaux* on the Marne. These two institutions have integrated cultural and European dimensions of war into their museography. Both are located on the former front line and were created thanks to the support of local authorities. Unlike national army museums, their collections not only include military equipment but also many everyday objects. While the collections of the *Historial* were constituted from objects bought on the commercial market (patriotic crockery, toys, postcards, etc.) (Brandt 2004b; Fontaine et al 2008; Wahnich and Tisseron 2001), the museum at Meaux was created from the collection of Jean-Pierre Vernet (uniforms, trench art, artillery pieces, newspapers, etc.) (Anon. 2012).

Inaugurated in 1992, the *Historial*, endowed with an international scientific committee (which included among others Stéphane Audoin-Rouzeau, Jean-Jacques Becker, John Horne, Gerd Krumeich and Jay Winter), is both a museum and an international research centre. In a comparative approach, this museum offers visitors a cultural and social history of the Great War through the perspectives of the three combatants on the Somme: Germany, France and Great Britain. From a collection of everyday objects and works of art, the *Historial* highlights the similarities and differences in national perceptions of this 'total war' and expounds people's wartime experiences, both at the Front and in the rear. Without having recourse to the sort of immersive museography popular in Anglophone museums, the *Historial* places individual experiences of the war at the core of its offer, by opting for a scenography that encourages distancing and comparison.

The treatment of the military clothing and equipment illustrates this choice: arranged horizontally on the ground in 'Fosses', the uniforms evoke the inert bodies of combatants from the various belligerent nations. The pre-war period, the origins and the geopolitical and sociocultural consequences of the First World War are also discussed. The *Historial* was renovated just before the start of the centenary of the Great War, but maintained this unique anthropological and comparative approach. Like many territorial museums, the *Historial* also strives to enhance the battlefields near the museum; the nearby Thiepval Memorial's interpretation centre is directly dependent upon the *Historial*. More aestheticized, the Museum of the Great War in the Pays de Meaux is also firmly embedded in a heritage landscape. Panoramic windows connect the visitor with the exterior topography, over which the First Battle of the Marne unfolded. The inclusion of immersive content within the building is scheduled to be reinforced with exterior elements, including a trench constructed in the museum grounds and battles re-enactments with period uniforms.

The centenary at the museum

More than a hundred years after it outbreak, exhibitions devoted to the First World War still embody important memory issues in France. The intensive commemorative period of 2014–2018, which, in the context of museums, might be considered to have begun as early as 2012, imparted significant impetus to the activities of French Great War museums. To anticipate public demand and implement the centennial commemorative programme, a public interest group, the *Mission du centenaire*, was created in 2012 by the French government.[2]

Throughout the commemorative period, and until mid-2019, it fulfilled three main functions: coordinating French public and private initiatives that contributed to the centenary, organizing an official commemorative programme and furnishing the general public with information about these events and about the First World War in general. Directed by Joseph Zimet, the Centenary Mission was supported by an international and multidisciplinary scientific council which brought together historians representing various historiographical trends, as well as Great War specialists from other disciplines. Among them, we can mention Stéphane Audoin-Rouzeau, Annette Becker, Laurence Campa, Rémy Cazals, Robert Frank, John Horne, Gerd Krumeich, André Loez, Nicolas Offenstadt, Antoine Prost, Hew Strachan, Laurent Veyssière and Jay Winter.

French museums were heavily involved in these commemorations. From 2013 to 2018, no less than 1,474 exhibitions devoted to the Great War were certified and/or subsidized by the *Mission du centenaire*.[3] These exhibitions presented major variations in size, budget and attendance; and they did not all benefit from the same level of historical support. Some were organized by large national institutions, others by more modest establishments. Some were mounted in Paris, others in the regions (Zunino, 2022. Their distribution throughout France confirms that the memory of the First World War is still strong in France today.

Although Paris and its region, the Ile-de-France, hosted 15% of the exhibitions, museum activity between 2012 and 2018 was characterized by a strong national dynamic. This extended beyond the obvious presumption that interest would be concentrated in regions that had been directly affected by the hostilities. Thus, Departments which had been in direct contact with the front, which had been in the 'Zone of the Armies', or had been under German occupation, actually hosted just 30% of the total number of exhibitions. The centenary years of the beginning and end of the conflict turned out to be the most prolific with, respectively, 35% of the exhibitions organized in 2014 and 31% in 2018. During the years 2015–2017, museum activity on French territory was characterized by a more strongly regional dynamic, in accordance with a commemorative schedule drawn up by the Centennial Mission. At the Chemin des Dames for example, where the so-called Nivelle offensive (Second Battle of the Aisne) took place from 16 April 1917, the centenary year of 2017 actually became the chief commemorative season of the centenary. Among the many initiatives, the *Chemin des Dames 1917–2017* cultural project, presented at the *Caverne du Dragon* from 16 April to 30 September 2017, represented the cornerstone. It threw a spotlight on the failure of the French offensive and highlighted the traces of the fighting on the landscape that are still visible today.[4]

Thus, throughout the centenary quinquennium, France witnessed the birth of a large number of exhibitions, right across the country, marked by a local memory of the war. But there was noticeable variation in how thoroughly these exhibitions disseminated the fruits of recent research on the Great War. From the beginning of the centenary a strong interest in cultural and social history was notable, with emphasis on the experience of combatants and civilians (essentially

French ones) through stories of personal trajectories, the links between the front and the rear and the cultural manifestations of wartime. As the commemorative years progressed, however, there was an increase in the number of exhibitions, often endowed with a large budget and an international scientific committee, which tried to make the general public aware of the global history of the war, the other European fighting fronts, the non-European fronts and its impact on the colonial empires. In fact, there is a striking contrast between the 'Franco-French' character of many local initiatives and the efforts at internationalization made, especially from 2017, by large public museums.

In the many local and regional commemorative initiatives, the Great War was mainly presented from a French perspective. Organized in collaboration with municipal or Departmental archives, numerous local initiatives, in municipalities right across the country, favoured an approach based on local or regional history. These exhibitions were devoted to the daily lives of civilians (including women and children) and combatants from the city or region in which the exhibitions were mounted, often to commemorate the start of the war. For example, the Departmental Archives of Morbihan organized an exhibition on 'The Morbihannais in the 14–18 War'. Also in Brittany, the Nantes History Museum, in partnership with the local municipal archives, focused its exhibition on the cultural mobilization and the Great War experiences of Nantes children.[5] This drew upon wartime Nantes public school activity reports, children's homework and drawings, photographs, posters, postcards and other products of war culture.

In addition, numerous small exhibitions organized in 2018 by municipalities throughout France revealed that the *Poilu* is still a figure that the French identify with to this day. The titles of these cultural events speak for themselves: *En mémoire des poilus de 14–18* (Biarritz, Pyrénées-Atlantiques), *A nos Poilus!* (Ecomuseum of the Pays de la Cerise in Fougerolles, Haute-Saône), *A nos poilus, morts pour la France* (Cahuzac-sur-Vère Town Hall, Tarn.). This uninhibited celebration of the sacrifices of the combatants of the Great War, which would be unthinkable in other Continental European countries – especially in Germany, because of the subsequent exploitation of the figure of the *Frontkämpfer* by the Nazis – clearly shows the significance of the memory of the First World War in France and its strong local roots.

By contrast, large-scale exhibitions organized by public institutions, which led the way in delivering the centenary dynamic at a national level, broadened their approaches to a European, even global, perspective of war. The attempt to build, little by little, a European memory of the conflict was in fact one of the stated objectives of the Centenary Mission from its inception.[6] From 2012 to 2018, these exhibitions highlighted the Europeanization and progressive internationalization of the conflict – an emphasis not generally found in the majority of cultural events organized during the centenary. Mainly mounted in the French capital, they are also characterized by a strong interdisciplinary ethos, in which the history of art and visual studies in general occupied an important place.

Such is the case of the large exhibition which inaugurated the cycle of cultural events of the centenary. *1917*, which opened in 2012 at the *Centre Pompidou-Metz*, was organized in partnership with *La Contemporaine*, ECPAD and the *Musée de l'Armée*. Its scientific council brought together art historians (Philippe Dagen and Jean-Jacques Lebel), film historians (Laurent Véray) and literature specialists (Laurence Campa, Edouard Graham). Mounted in one of the regions most affected by the battles of the Great War, it focused on the year of the conflict which represented a pivotal point, both for the evolution of the war and for the emergence, from Western Europe to Russia, of the artistic avant-garde.

Likewise, *Vu du front. Représenter la Grande Guerre (La Contemporaine/Musée de l'Armée*, Paris, 2014) contributed to a better understanding of the processes of image production and of the international circulation of images during the First World War. Renouncing a strictly French and Eurocentric point of view, it focused on the producers and distributors of images from different fronts (land, air, sea) from a tri-national perspective (Germany, France, Great Britain) and looked at the circulation and dissemination of these images in the rest of the world, primarily in the United States. The fact that it placed these cultural productions in the context of pre-1914 history (the Boer Wars, the Russo-Japanese War, the Balkan Wars) reinforced its innovative character (Romanovski 2014). Focusing on the last days of peace in the summer of 1914 and on the outbreak of the conflict, the *Eté 14. Les derniers jours de l'ancien monde (Bibliothèque nationale de France*, Paris, 2014) was also characterized by a perspective at once European, international and global (Manfrin and Veyssière 2014).

The Franco-German dimension of the conflict was particularly to the forefront in French responses to its centenary. This provided a foundation for intense international scientific cooperation at the museum level. The centenary saw the creation of the *Historial franco-allemand de la Grande Guerre*, at Hartmannswillerkopf, a spur of the Vosges Mountains in Alsace that was bitterly contested in 1915. Inaugurated on 3 August 2017, it was the first bilateral institution devoted to the Great War with a joint Franco-German scientific council, co-chaired by Nicolas Offenstadt from France and Gerd Krumeich from Germany. The latter historian, also a member of the Scientific Council of the *Historial de la Grande Guerre* in Péronne, was closely associated with the design of several other French exhibitions with a Franco-German dimension, including *Jours de guerre et de paix. Regard franco-allemand sur l'art de 1910 à 1930* at Reims in 2014 and *Eté 1914: Nancy et la Lorraine dans la guerre* at Nancy in 2014.

Addressed during 2015–2016, on the occasion of its centenary, the genocide of the Armenians represented another museum theme that enabled the opening-up of the centenary to a European and global history of the Great War. Once again the French capital was to play the decisive part in addressing new historiographical trends and presenting them to the general public through exhibitions. For example, *Le génocide des Arméniens de l'Empire ottoman. Stigmatiser, Détruire, Exclure*, mounted by the Shoah Memorial in Paris in 2015, was a landmark exhibition, which sought to familiarize the French public with this tragic episode. Finally, by way of closing the cycle of centennial exhibitions, *A l'Est, la guerre sans fin 1918–1923* represented an effort towards the chronological and geographic decompartmentalization of the Great War, focusing, as it did, on the new conflicts, spawned by upheaval of 1914–1918, endured by the peoples of central and eastern Europe and the Levant from 1918 to 1923 (Lagrange and Bertrand 2018).

These multiple cultural initiatives show the importance of the centenary of the First World War in France. The year 2014 saw a significant increase in the number of museum visitors: for that year alone, the *Historial de la Grande Guerre* recorded 113,659 admissions while the museum at Meaux welcomed 133,000 visitors, an increase of 40% compared to 2013.[7] The *1917* exhibition in Metz received 219,071 visitors in 2012[8]; *Vu du front* had 38,977 in 2014[9] and *A l'Est, la guerre sans fin 1918–1923* received 56,079 in 2018.[10] Beyond these bare figures, it is not easy to assess the reception of these exhibitions by the public, inasmuch as they are largely influenced by other frameworks of perception than historiographical issues. The multiple types of appropriation and interpretation vary according to the personal backgrounds and expectations of visitors and to their prior knowledge of the Great War (Antichan and Teboul 2016). In the case of the *Vu du front* exhibition, for example, some visitors thought they detected a patriotic message in the way that elements of the national heritage were displayed, while others saw it as a pacifist and Europeanist message (ibid.: 34).

Conclusion

For France and the French, it is clear that the Great War initiated a vast and enduring process of patrimonialization, in the course of which its material culture became part of France's national cultural heritage. The impressive extent of – and enthusiastic public reaction to – the response of French museums to the centenary shows that the war and its material culture retain an important place in local and national memories, even after the passage of 100 years. For long the vectors of nationalism and Germanophobic stereotypes, museums and exhibitions devoted to the First World War are today increasingly engaging with current research trends and historiography. They are thus able to make an important contribution to efforts to build a memory of the Great War that is not just French, but also European.

Notes

1 https://memorial-verdun.fr/museecollections.
2 See the official *Mission du centenaire* site: https://www.centenaire.org/fr; also its objectives and timetable, as delivered to the President of the Republic by Joseph Zimet in September 2011: http://centenaire.org/sites/default/files/references-files/rapport_jz.pdf.
3 Estimates made on the basis of files listing exhibitions registered with Centennial Mission and data available on its site which lists and maps the exhibitions by year in the Centennial agenda: http://centenaire.org/fr/agenda.

4 https://www.chemindesdames.fr/fr/le-musee/expositions-et-actualites/chemin-des-dames-1917-2017.
5 http://www.chateaunantes.fr/fr/evenement/lecole-de-la-guerre-1914-1918.
6 See the September 2011 report of Joseph Zimet to the President of the Republic: http://centenaire.org/sites/default/files/references-files/rapport_jz.pdf.
7 https://www.courrier-picard.fr/art/10329/article/2017-02-11/lhistorial-de-peronne-est-il-trop-elitiste https://www.museedelagrandeguerre.eu/uploads/docs/RAPPORT_DACTIVITE_2014.pdf.
8 https://www.centrepompidou-metz.fr/sites/default/files/issuu/rapport_dactivite_2012.pdf.
9 https://musee-armee.fr/fileadmin/user_upload/Documents/Rapports-Activites/MA_Rapport-Activite-2014.pdf.
10 https://musee-armee.fr/fileadmin/user_upload/Documents/Rapports-Activites/MA_Rapport-Activite-2018.pdf.

References

Anon. (2012) *Le Musée de la Grande Guerre. Pays de Meaux. Un nouveau regard 14/18*. Paris: Editons France loisirs.

Antichan, S. and J. Teboul. (2016) Faire l'expérience de l'histoire? Retour sur les appropriations sociales des expositions du centenaire de la Première Guerre mondiale. *Matériaux pour l'histoire de notre temps* 121–122:32–39.

Bollard-Raineau, I. and C. Kott. (eds.) (2014) *Sauve qui peut. Des archéologues et musées mobilisés, 1914–1918*. Douai: Forum antique de Bavay et Musée de la Chartreuse de Douai.

Brandt, S. (2004a) *Nagelfiguren:* nailing patriotism in Germany 1914–18. In N.J. Saunders (ed.), *Matters of Conflict: Material culture, memory and the First World War*, pp 62–71. London: Routledge.

———. (2004b) The Historial de la Grande Guerre in Péronne, France. A Museum at the Former First World War Battlefield. *Museum International* 223 (56–3):46–52.

Cappronnier, J.-C., E. Marguin-Hamon and P. Smith. (2014) Le Patrimoine de la Grande Guerre. *In Situ. Revue des patrimoines* 25. Consulté le 02 mai 2019: http://journals.openedition.org/insitu/11683

De Sousa, D. (2014) L'incroyable destin des collections du musée Alfred-Danicourt de Péronne. *In Situ. Revue des patrimoines* 25. Consulté le 18 décembre 2019: http://journals.openedition.org/insitu/11479

Désiré, G. (ed.) (2017) *Une expérience du chaos: destructions, spoliations et sauvetages d'archives, 1789–1945*. Rennes/Paris: Presses universitaires de Rennes/Archives nationales.

Didier, C. (ed.). (2008) *Orages de papier. 1914–1918. Les collections de guerre des bibliothèques*. Paris: Somogy.

Fleury, C. (2014) Muséographie(s) comparée(s) de la Grande Guerre en 2013. Allemagne–Belgique–France–Royaume-Uni. *In Situ. Revue des patrimoines* 25. Consulté le 16 décembre 2019: http://journals.openedition.org/insitu/11559

Fontaine, C., A. Becker, S. Audoin-Rouzeau and M.-P. Prévost-Bault. (2008) *Les collections de l'Historial de la Grande Guerre*. Paris: Somogy.

Granger, C. (2013) La protection des collections des musées nationaux durant la Première Guerre mondiale. In P. Nivet (ed.), *Guerre et patrimoine artistique à l'époque contemporaine*, pp 247–260. Amiens: Ancrage.

Hardier, T. (2004) La Caverne du Dragon. In N. Offenstadt (ed.), *Le Chemin des Dames. De l'évènement à la mémoire*, pp 402–409. Paris: Stock.

Kott, C. (2006) *Préserver l'art de l'ennemi? Le patrimoine artistique en Belgique et en France.* Brussels: Peter Lang.

———. (2013) Un Locarno des musées? Les relations franco-allemandes en matière de muséographie dans l'entre-deux-guerres. In B. Tillier, D. Vezyroglou, and C. Wermester (eds.), *Actes de colloque/L'art allemand en France, 1919–1939. Diffusion, réception, transferts.* EA 4100 HiCSA (Histoire culturelle et sociale de l'art, université Paris 1-Panthéon Sorbonne): http://hicsa.univ-paris1.fr/page.php?r=18&id=394&lang=fr

Lagrange, F. and C. Bertrand (eds.) (2018) *A l'Est, la guerre sans fin 1918–1923.* Paris: Gallimard.

Maingon, C. (2014) L'instrumentalisation du patrimoine blessé. Paris, 1916: l'Exposition d'œuvres d'art mutilées ou provenant des régions dévastées par l'ennemi au Petit Palais. *In Situ. Revue des patrimoines* 23. Consulté le 01 mai 2019: http://journals.openedition.org/insitu/10960

———. (2016) *Le musée invisible. Le Louvre et la Grande Guerre, 1914–1921.* Mont-Saint-Aignan/Paris: Presses universitaires de Rouen et du Havre/Musée du Louvre éditions.

Manfrin, F. and L. Veyssière (eds.) (2014) *Eté 14. Les derniers jours de l'ancien monde.* Paris: Beaux livres.

Meyer, A. and B. Savoy (eds.) (2014) *The Museum Is Open. Towards a Transnational History of Museums 1750–1940.* Berlin: de Gruyter.

Nivet, P. (ed.). (2013) *Guerre et patrimoine artistique à l'époque contemporaine.* Amiens: Ancrage.

Nivet, P. and S. Lewuillon (eds.) (2017) *La Grande Guerre des archéologues.* Dijon: Editions universitaires de Dijon.

Offenstadt, N. (2010) *14-18 aujourd'hui. La Grande Guerre dans la France contemporaine.* Paris: Odile Jacob.

Romanovski, W. (ed.) (2014) *Vu du front. Représenter la Grande Guerre.* Paris: Somogy.

Saunders, N.J. (2003) *Trench Art: Materialities and Memories of War.* Oxford: Berg.

———. (2012) Objets de guerre. In S. Audoin-Rouzeau and J.-J. Becker (eds.), *Encyclopédie de la Grande Guerre 1914–1918*, pp 283–293. Paris: Perrin, vol. 2.

Saunders, N.J. and P. Cornish (eds.) (2009) *Contested Objects: Material Memories of the Great War.* London: Routledge.

Savoy, B. (2003) *Patrimoine annexé: les biens culturels saisis par la France en Allemagne autour de 1800.* Paris: Editions de la Maison des Sciences de l'Homme, vol. 1.

Savoy, B. and C. Kott (eds.) (2016) *Mars & Museum. Europäische Museen im Ersten Weltkrieg.* Cologne: Böhlau.

Tillier, B. (2019) *Déjouer la guerre? Une histoire de l'art des tranchées (1914–1918).* Strasbourg: Presses universitaires de Strasbourg.

Wahnich, S. and A. Tisseron. (2001) 'Disposer des corps' ou mettre la guerre au musée. L'historial de Péronne, un musée d'histoire européenne de la guerre de 1914–1918. *Tumultes* 16: 55–81.

Ypersele van, L. (2013) Patrimoine et propagande. Le cas de la destruction de Louvain en août 1914. In P. Nivet (ed.), *Guerre et patrimoine artistique à l'époque contemporaine*, pp 111–126. Amiens: Ancrage.

Zunino, B. (2022) La dynamique muséale du Centenaire: retour sur les expositions consacrées à la Grande Guerre. In N. Patin and A. Weinrich (eds.) *Quel Bilan scientifique du Centenaire de 1914–18?*, pp 303–333. Paris: Sorbonne Université Presses.

3

CURATING ON THE FRONTIER

The Museum of the Great War in Gorizia, Italy

Alessandra Martina

After the outbreak of war between Italy and Austria on 23 May 1915, and the opening of the Isonzo/Soča front, the city of Gorizia found itself in the war zone and directly in the line of fire. Its inhabitants experienced a foretaste of the Second World War, following which the international border cut straight through houses, separating not only buildings, gardens and cemeteries, but families and relationships as well. Subsequently, during the post-1945 era, citizens from both sides of the border worked hard to go beyond that line known as the 'iron curtain' – a psychological as well as a political border. Due to good relationships between the inhabitants and local authorities on both sides from the 1960s onwards, the border had been demolished step by step long before its actual suppression after Slovenia's independence in 1991 and its 2004 accession to the European Union.

War and ethnicity

A few words are necessary to explain the particular situation of Gorizia at the beginning of twentieth century. It was the capital of the County of Gorizia and Gradisca, one of the 17 Lands of the Habsburg Monarchy, and included in the Austrian Littoral together with Trieste and Istria. The county extended for 2,900 square kilometres (from the mountain region of Julian Alps to the Adriatic Sea) and had 250,000 inhabitants, of whom 154,564 were Slovenes, 90,146 Italians, and about 4,500 Germans, with the remainder belonging to other nationalities. Also residing in the city were 10,800 foreigners, almost all of whom were Italian workers who had emigrated from the Kingdom of Italy in order to find jobs and better pay. At that time, the city counted almost 30,000 inhabitants speaking Italian, Friulian, Slovenian, and German (DH 1980: 38; Medeot 1981: 12; Kalc 2013). In August 1914, thousands of them wearing Austro-Hungarian uniform set

DOI: 10.4324/9781003263531-5

off towards Serbia and Galicia. Some others, ardent Italian patriots, deserted and fled to Italy where in 1915 they enlisted in the Italian army.[1]

Just after the conquest of the city by the Italian army in August 1916, the military authority which took control declared the real intention of the new-comers, reporting to the High Command that 'now the province annexed to the Homeland no longer fears the Slavs, and, by provident and shrewd action, shall soon be made Italian' (ASPG 1917). At the end of the war, when the county was definitively annexed to the Kingdom of Italy, one of the main goals of the new rulers was to render this territory completely Italian. To achieve this purpose, museums would need to play a part (Martina 2018).

The Museum of the Redemption

A regional museum had existed in Gorizia since 1861 dealing with the cultural history of the territory (Sgubin 2007). In 1924, a completely new arrangement was set up, under the name of *Museo della redenzione* (The Museum of the Redemption) (Figure 3.1), in which actually only four rooms were dedicated to the First World War, while the other rooms had been set aside as an ethnographic museum, which presented a partial (in both senses) view of the history of Gorizia and its territory over the previous centuries, taking into account only the Italian component of the province (Martina ibid.). The whole museum was arranged so as to prove the 'Italian' origin of the territory, with references to Imperial Roman dominance and the 'Latin' or Italian origin of elements of the region's culture. In this context, great emphasis was placed upon the short period of Venetian suzerainty in 1508–1509. Nothing was said about more than 400 years of Habsburg rule and the presence of the multicultural identity that characterized

FIGURE 3.1 1924 Museum of the Redemption. Main hall. (© ERPAC – Fototeca dei Musei Provinciali di Gorizia.)

it in Gorizia. The museum's purpose was clearly to record the sacrifice and the suffering both of Italian soldiers and Gorizia's inhabitants, and at the same time to make the inhabitants aware of the positive effects derived from being part of the Italian kingdom.

There was no mention of the tens of thousands of men from the County of Gorizia who had recently served in Austro-Hungarian uniform. Conversely, great attention was devoted to the history of Italian Irredentism and its local exponents, as well as to the small group of men who fled to Italy in order to join the Italian Army, with special attention given to those who perished during the war. The war was then presented as a matter between Italy and Austria. In this way, the museum exalted Italian soldiers as heroes who gave their life to fulfil the Italian Risorgimento with the conquest of the 'unredeemed' territories. Moreover, the museum was also intended to record the sacrifice of the inhabitants of Gorizia and to justify the enormous losses and destruction suffered by the city. In any event, it was a home-made museum displaying a host of war relics, photographs, flags, newspapers, and written material together with artefacts coming from other museums in Gorizia that had survived the conflict. The leading theme for all was the confirmation of the 'Italianness' of Gorizia.

Fascism at the museum

During the late 1920s and 1930s, collecting artefacts continued and was augmented by donations from the city's citizens. A reorganization of the museum then became necessary, dividing the war related collection from other objects for which another venue would be established under the name of Museum of History and Art (Bozzi 1938; Anon 1939a; Anon 1939b). A group of experts formed of civilians and soldiers was set up to reorganize the museum in accordance with the Fascist regime's directions for celebrating the twentieth anniversary of Italy's victory (Baioni 2006). Also, and especially from the 1930s onwards, the old battlefields of the Great War saw ever larger numbers of visitors. Many organized tours were set up every year involving veterans and families of the fallen. The new museum now called *Museo della guerra e della redenzione* (Museum of the War and of the Redemption) became a stage of this tour of remembrance (Figure 3.2). The key concepts of the new museum were heroism and general sacrifice, and conversely, no space was given to personal mourning. It evoked a sort of retrospective consent for the war, bound up with the subsequent triumph of Fascism and current efforts to expand Italy's colonial empire (Maggiarotti 1927: 39, quoted in Daffara 1998).

Celestino Petrone, a Roman rationalist architect, creator of many war memorials in Italy, designed the new permanent exhibition where the visitors were immersed in an atmosphere which exalted the war, patriotism, and heroism. Scenographic innovations such as a walk-through trench that gave visitors the illusion that they were experiencing real life at the front. A careful use of lights and other architectural solutions came directly from the great exhibition about

FIGURE 3.2 The new rationalist style display in 1938, with the museum then named 'Museum of the War and of the Redemption'. (© ERPAC – Fototeca dei Musei Provinciali di Gorizia.)

the fascist revolution that had taken place in Rome in 1932 and were now set up in this new museum that had to promote national values (Martina ibid.).

As in the 1924 museum, this new one's representation of the war was preceded by a broad survey of the history of the region, beginning in prehistoric times. It displayed documents and artefacts whose primary purpose was to emphasize the superiority of Italian civilization. Then followed the description of the war, especially of the battles on the Isonzo/Soča front. A special emphasis was given to the sixth battle with the conquest of Gorizia by the Italian army in August 1916 (Figure 3.3). The chronology extended beyond the end of the war, with the

FIGURE 3.3 Room dedicated to the military events that preceded the sixth battle on the Isonzo Front. (1938). (© ERPAC – Fototeca dei Musei Provinciali di Gorizia.)

FIGURE 3.4 Room dedicated volunteers from Gorizia who died for the Italian irre-dentist cause. (© ERPAC – Fototeca dei Musei Provinciali di Gorizia.)

last room dedicated to the 'Fascist revolution' and to the conquest of East African colonies (Sema 2002). There were no references to embarrassing aspects such as the Italian defeat at Kobarid/Caporetto and its consequences or to the global dimension of the conflict. Other themes such as that of the memory of volunteers from Gorizia who perished during the war were transferred almost without change from the 1924 museum (Figure 3.4).

A new world and a new border

After the Second World War further changes took place. The first step was to get rid of every symbol of the Fascist regime. Moreover, the museum found itself in a rather embarrassing situation because it mainly based itself on the military victory that brought about the conquest of Gorizia and the annexation of a large territory of the valleys of the Isonzo/Soča and Vipava rivers. Now, following 20 years of Fascist repression, and violent occupations by, successively, Nazi Germany and Yugoslav partisans, most of the surrounding region and portions of Gorizia itself were consigned to Communist Yugoslavia; although the borders were not settled until 1947. A new approach was necessary. It began with changing the name and the venue of the old museum. The name was changed to 'Museum of the 1915–1918 war' as a section of the *Musei Provinciali* (Provincial museums) (Figure 3.5). Then the exhibition was transferred to the ground floor of the Palazzo Attems and the description of warfare on the Isonzo/Soča front became the single aim of the exhibition, with every reference to the history of the territory before and after the Great War eliminated.

Except for these changes, the itinerary of the visit was similar to that of the 1938 museum. However, special attention was, for the first time, given to the

FIGURE 3.5 Room dedicated to the Austro-Hungarian Army in the renamed 'Museum of the War 1915–1918' in the second post-war period. (1958). (© ERPAC – Fototeca dei Musei Provinciali di Gorizia.)

Austro-Hungarian army while the display in two rooms of many postcards relating to war propaganda printed in many of the belligerent states made the visitors conscious of the range of the nations involved in the war. Another section was dedicated to Red Cross nurses while a US volunteer uniform recognized Italy's new 'American friends'. The museum now fully displayed items from many private collectors; any type of material being now accepted and put into the exhibition without modifying the approach adopted by the museum that sought to represent the First World War as a paradigm of the long-lasting suffering caused by all wars (Sema 2002).

The Museum of the Great War today

A calamitous flood in October 1983 seriously damaged the exhibition rooms. This forced the staff of the museum to undertake restoration of material and a reorganization of the display by a scientific approach according to new historical research, not only in the military field but, also, and especially rewardingly, in the social aspects of a global war (Figure 3.6). This gave, for example, the opportunity to eliminate the long-standing stereotype of the 'redemption' of Gorizia. The revised itinerary describes the war as it was seen and experienced by millions of young men wearing different uniforms yet enduring the same sufferings and sacrifices. Everyday life in the trenches is a fundamental theme of this exhibition, which tells about daily life during the excited moments of an attack as well as during the long waits in-between. The first part of the itinerary documents 30 months of trench warfare on the Carso plateau and around Gorizia, when the city found itself on the front line.

FIGURE 3.6 Room dedicated to 'Total War' in the current display. (2020). (© ERPAC – Fototeca dei Musei Provinciali di Gorizia.)

The first image to greet today's museum visitors is a full-scale three-dimensional scene. It is the reconstruction of a devastated trench, which might have been found in any of the battlefields of the Great War, where two soldiers, one in Italian uniform, the other an Austro-Hungarian, lie dead (Figure 3.7). This realistic scene represents the central emotive theme of the museum and reminds the visitor of the fate of millions of soldiers; it conveys the horror of the war and at the same time opens up the museum to a dialogue with visitors, inviting them to reflect that any war is first and foremost about death. At the same time, it emphasizes the importance of peace and cooperation between peoples who had once been parties to the conflict (Fabi 2002).

FIGURE 3.7 Diorama representing the consequences of the war in the current display. (2020). (© ERPAC – Fototeca dei Musei Provinciali di Gorizia.)

The effects of the war for Gorizia are displayed in another room where the ravages are depicted in photos. Documents and other artefacts represent everyday life of a city under siege, bombarded by opposing armies; the taking of the city by the Italian army in August 1916, and the return of Austro-Hungarian troops immediately after the last battle on Isonzo/Soča front. The displays also focus on how the inhabitants who decided to remain in the city lived in a place where everything was lacking, terrified by continuous bombardment, forced to inhabit cellars, or deported to refugee camps in either Austria-Hungary or Italy, depending on the colour of the uniform of the occupying forces.

The itinerary then reflects on broader aspects of the war, such as propaganda, desertion, and prisoners. Then there is a description of the shift of the war front from the Isonzo/Soča to the Piave river, and the 1918 Austro-Hungarian occupation of the Veneto. At the end of the itinerary is a map of the Europe that resulted from the peace treaties. The visitor-journey concludes with a look at the history of the museum itself.

The fundamental concept of this exhibition can be found in the words of the poet Giuseppe Ungaretti, who wrote during his 1966 visit to Gorizia and the places where he had served during the First World War: 'The name of Gorizia ... is not the name of a victory – for victories on this earth are a sacrilegious illusion – but rather the name of a common suffering, ours and that of those standing on the other side who were known as the enemy but whom we, even though we loyally and blindly performed our duty, in our hearts thought of as our brothers' (Anon. 1996).

Final considerations

For those living in the region today, curating the 'Great War' means:

- Encouraging the study and the understanding of the history of modern war and 'wartime experience' by providing for didactic activities not only within the museum, but also at the sites where the battles were fought. The teaching of 'open-air' activities thus completes the museum's exposition and helps us to understand the conditions that soldiers of the Great War were forced to endure and at the same time to make clear the concept of static trench warfare, especially in the southern section of Isonzo/Soča front.
- Playing an active role in promoting local history that avoids localism and which, by contrast, situates micro-history within the context of global history. Offering a range of other activities such as conferences, presentation of literary works, and the mounting of temporary exhibitions.
- Collaboration with others whose work focuses on the region: associations, scientific institutions, collectors, with the aim of creating a network of historical disciplines and interests.
- There is still much to do, but the work is of fundamental importance for a small museum in a border region. By extending our curatorial remit beyond the walls of the museum, we have adopted what we consider to be the

optimal course for reconciling our twin duties, to maintain the memory of the Great War and, simultaneously, to safeguard and promote the unique landscape of the former frontline.

Note

1 It is difficult to calculate the exact number. It can be taken as reliable that several hundred Austrian-Italians from the Littoral deserted to be enrolled in the Italian Army (but not all who deserted were then enrolled), while 60,000–70,000 served in the Austro-Hungarian army.

References

Anon. (1939a) *Il museo della Guerra e della Redenzione di Gorizia.* Gorizia: Tipografia G. Iucchi.

———. (1939b) *Museo di Storia e d'Arte della Provincia di Gorizia – Borgo Castello.* Gorizia: Tipografia G. Iucchi.

———. (1996) Editorial. *Iniziativa Isontina* 28:40.

ASPG. (1917) Archivio Storico Provinciale Gorizia (ASPG), Archivio Documenti di Storia Patria (ADSP), b.9, fasc. 32/02, prot. n. 45, *Relazione sull'istituzione e sull'attività dell'Amministrazione provinciale, del Monte di Pietà ed unitavi Cassa di Risparmio e dell' Istituto provinciale di Credito Ipotecario,* 28 marzo 1917. Typescript. Gorizia: l'Amministrazione Provinciale.

Baioni, M. (2006) *Risorgimento in camicia nera: studi, istituzioni, musei nell'Italia fascista.* Torino: Comitato di Torino dell'Istituto per la storia del Risorgimento italiano.

Bozzi, C.L. (1938) Il Museo della Guerra e della Redenzione di Gorizia, *'La Panarie', Udine* 83:291–294.

Daffara, S. (1998) Nel marmo e nel bronzo. I monumenti ai caduti dal compianto alla celebrazione. In, 1918. *La guerra nella testa. Arte popolare, esperienze, memoria nel primo conflitto mondiale,* pp 61–72. (Catalogue of the exhibition at the Musei Provinciali di Gorizia 1998-1999.) Trieste: LINT Editoriale Associati.

DH (1980) *Die Habsburgermonarchie 1848–1918,* vol. III/1. Wien. Österreichischen Akademie der Wissenschaften.

Fabi, L. (2002) Museo, territorio, guerra e società. In *Guida al museo della grande guerra. Per non dimenticare,* pp 39–53. Gorizia: Musei Provinciali di Gorizia.

Kalc, A. (2013) Cenni sullo sviluppo della popolazione della principesca contea di Gorizia e Gradisca nell'ottocento e fino alla grande guerra. In, *Letture di un territorio. La Provincia di Gorizia e Gradisca: autonomia e governo 1861–1914,* pp 27–50. Gorizia: Musei Provinciali di Gorizia.

Maggiarotti, L.A. (1927) L'espressione del dolore nella pittura bellica. *Esercito e Nazione* 1:39.

Martina, A. (2018) Od Muzeja odrešitve do Muzeja velike vojne v Gorici. *Goriški Letnik* 42:265–276.

Medeot, C. (1981) *Ordinamento della Contea, in I cattolici isontini nel XX secolo, I, Dalla fine dell'800 al 1918.* Gorizia: Casse rurali ed artigiane della contea di Gorizia.

Sema, A. (2002) Storia di un museo isontino. In, *Guida al museo della grande guerra. Per non dimenticare,* p 1334. Gorizia: Provincia di Gorizia.

Sgubin, R. (2007) Alle origini dei Musei Provinciali di Gorizia: preistoria di un'istituzione singolare. In A. Delneri and R. Sgubin (eds.), *La pinacoteca dei Musei Provinciali di Gorizia,* pp 11–23. Vicenza: Terra Ferma.

4

CURATING DOMINION NARRATIVES OF THE GREAT WAR

Jennifer Wellington

The Great War can be imagined not only as an outbreak of mass violence but also an outbreak of mass collection. Long before the outcome of the war was clear, large-scale and systematic efforts to collect, exhibit, and memorialize it had begun. Both during and after the war, exhibitions were mounted that purported to convey to a home audience a visceral sense of what the war was really like. Exhibitions of the First World War staged by the Dominions of Australia, Canada, and New Zealand actively sought to present themselves as displaying authentic war images and artefacts. But from the very beginning, exhibitions were curated and shaped for a host of reasons besides what it was really like. Dominion war exhibitions aimed to construct narratives supporting specific political and cultural projects. These narratives contrasted with central British efforts. Imperial efforts tended, of necessity, to the broad and cosmopolitan, even initially focused on Allied and neutral audiences before turning to domestic persuasion as the war progressed. By contrast, Dominion curation buttressed narratives of Dominion valour, contribution, and national individuation as new 'martial nations' within the Imperial family. A common expression of this in Dominion propaganda was the desire to establish the contributions of each Dominion as particular, unique, and valued. These Dominion narratives had a dual aim: to persuade the British metropole, that Dominion forces were making an important, distinctive contribution; and to encourage Dominion populations to continue prosecuting the war.

This chapter will examine how the Dominions of Australia, Canada, and New Zealand presented their contribution to the war to the public in Britain by amassing and displaying art, trophies, and photography, and the varying ways these collections were used, or neglected, in presenting the war to Dominion audiences after the war. During the war, Dominion collecting varied somewhat in scale and timing, but operated in the same framework. All the Dominions

DOI: 10.4324/9781003263531-6

fought in the same war, within the same Imperial structure and Imperial propaganda context, and with the same initial project of laying claim to their part
of the Imperial story (and booty pile). After the end of the war, the trajectories
of the Dominions diverged. The narratives emerging from Dominion wartime
propaganda were institutionalized in war museums and exhibitions. The forms
this took were shaped by their particular circumstances. In Australia, the record
of national achievement presented in the new Australian War Museum[1] was frozen in the moment of victory. In Canada, the frenetic activity of the war years
slowed dramatically afterwards, in the context of a divided national narrative and
the absence of key figures. In New Zealand, efforts were muted and localized.

Schemes for collecting, curating, and exhibiting the war were inextricably
linked with wider programmes of Imperial and Dominion propaganda. They
did not, however, spring into existence fully formed at the beginning of the
hostilities. From the beginning, soldiers collected battlefield souvenirs, and purchased or created personal keepsakes, such as soldier-made 'trench art' fashioned
from the detritus of the battlefield. As one soldier in Britain's 37th Division
observed: 'this war will undoubtedly go down to posterity as the "War of
Souvenirs". The souvenir habit is, I suppose latent in all of us, and it only needed
a really good war like this to bring it bubbling to the surface' (Cornish 2009: 11).
In searching for, as Tim Cook puts it, 'singular objects that best represented
experiences', they concretized those wartime experiences and declared their
status as participants in significant, historic events (Cook 2012: 212). People at
home were also eager to see such objects, which seemingly embodied the vital
terror and pathos of the war.

In the first two years of the war, numerous museums, galleries, local councils,
and charitable groups autonomously collected and displayed war-related objects
and artworks. The President of the Museums Association, F.A. Bather, laid out
some of the motivations behind doing so in a July 1915 address to museum curators, arguing that during the war museums must exhibit 'the clamouring voices
of the present' and 'convey some idea of our Fleet, of our Armies in their various
fields, and of the Red Cross' (Bather 1915: 5). Numerous exhibitions staged in
1915 and 1916 were already attempting to do this: in the summer of 1915, for
example, a war exhibition including 'a number of relics from the battlefield',
the 'rusty metal work of the first bomb dropped on Southend', 'German proc-
lamations issued in Flanders', and 'a miniature munition factory' was organized
by the London County Council at the Prince's Skating Club, Knightsbridge
(Anon. 1915c: 3). In January 1915, the Museum of the Royal United Services
Institution had displayed the 'first field-gun captured from the Germans by the
1st Battalion of the Lincolnshire Regiment, and three head-dresses from captured German troops', and in February 1915, the Science Museum in South
Kensington mounted a two-room exhibition of war technologies (Anon. 1915a:
24; Anon. 1915b: 274).

It was in this context that state-sponsored efforts to curate the Great War
began and, over time, took over. This was not a simple top-down imposition:

independent community groups and commercial bodies were also often those demanding greater state involvement. As John Horne observes, as a liberal democracy, support for Britain's war 'came from persuasion – and self-persuasion – much more than from coercion' (Horne 1997: 195). Accordingly, the British effort in collection was rooted in, and initially led by, civil society, the ad-hoc efforts of a freshly mobilized citizen soldiery, and popular interest. Official propaganda efforts were born into a receptive environment and developed in stages over the course of the war. Such British efforts began with the establishment of the War Propaganda Unit, or 'Wellington House', in 1914. At that time, it was tasked with the dissemination of official propaganda to foreign – and especially neutral – countries (Harries and Harries 1983: 5). Before 1917, where the government directly engaged in domestic propaganda, it promoted specific campaigns, such as recruitment, war loans, and industrialization (Horne 1997: 198). The state gradually began to assert more control over representations of war, appointing official artists to paint and draw the conflict from 1916, and banning personal cameras from the Western Front and appointing official photographers to take photographs for an official pool of images which were then used by the illustrated press (Wellington 2017: 38–46). Public museums were closed as a war measure in 1916, reducing the depiction of war in established institutions (Kavanagh 1994: 36–51). By 1917, growing war weariness prompted the government to commence a 'broad-fronted campaign to sustain civilian morale for outright military victory', sponsoring fundraising campaigns, exhibitions, and lectures at home and producing visual and print propaganda from the front (Gregory 2008: 213). The same year, the National War Aims Committee was formed, tasked with organizing domestic propaganda campaigns and local events, and Wellington House was moved and expanded into a full government Department of Information (Monger 2012). The proposal for a National War Museum, approved by the War Cabinet in March 1917, was a civilly initiated, governmentally adopted outgrowth of this multi-pronged propaganda effort.

Dominion efforts to represent their respective war experiences, therefore, did not emerge in a vacuum: they were often echoing developments in the Imperial machine and always accommodating themselves within it. British propaganda was organized from an imperial perspective, producing a wealth of materials depicting a pan-empire war effort with troops from all over the globe. By contrast, the Dominions wanted to emphasize their bit of the story, *their* contribution to the war effort, both for domestic consumption and to advertise to the metropolitan population their contribution to that imperial effort. Contrary to contemporary narratives, the Dominions' nascent nationalism was not extra-imperial: as Mark Sheftall observes, the national war experience came to be seen as 'a rite of passage in which the Dominions' costly contribution to Allied victory helped solidify their identity as nations, rather than colonies, loyal to, but not subordinate to, the British Motherland' (Sheftall 2009: 5). Thus, both promoting themselves on the metropolitan stage *and* creating new national historical records were crucial components of Dominion efforts at curating the Great War. As Anna Maguire notes of New Zealand soldiers on leave in London during the war, Dominion agents operated as 'both insiders and outsiders in the imperial capital', pursuing Imperial and national war aims at the same time (Maguire 2016: 295).

The organizer of the Canadian War Records Office singularly embodied this duality. Businessman Max Aitken, from 1917 titled Lord Beaverbrook, had moved from his native Canada to London before the war and become a member of Parliament. During the war, he acted as an agent for both the Canadian and British governments and their war efforts, heading amongst many agencies the Canadian War Records Office, the Canadian War Memorials Fund, the (British) War Office Cinematograph Committee, and from 1918, the British Ministry of Information. Throughout all this manoeuvring in both nations' political spheres, he energetically drew on his political, journalistic, and military contacts (as well as his own personal wealth) to conduct 'a relentless campaign to extol the heroic deeds of Canadians in France' (Cook 2003: 268).

Photographic records were central in both the public conception of how to understand the war, and official efforts to promulgate their vision of war across Britain and the Dominions. Unsurprisingly, a large part of this campaign to extol Canada's achievements focused on the creation and dissemination of a photographic record of Canadians at war. Thus, within a month of Britain appointing its first official photographer in early 1916, Aitken had successfully lobbied for Canada to be able to appoint their own (Carmichael 1989: 17). E.H. Knoebel worked as Canada's official photographer in France between April 1916 and resigning due to ill health in August, when Ivor Castle and William Rider-Rider replaced him (Cook 2003: 283; Robertson 1978: 42). Photographs produced by these official photographers were displayed in a series of exhibitions in Britain, France, the United States, and Canada in the last two years of the war. These exhibitions actively manipulated audience desire for a window into the war in order to create national propaganda within an Imperial context. They emphasized the importance of Canada's contribution to the war and of Canada's significance within the Empire. Three different Canadian exhibitions toured numerous British towns and cities in 1917 and 1918, depicting war scenes and acts of Canadian valour for large crowds.

The first series of photographs, featuring enlarged prints depicting the Battle of the Somme, was shown at the Grafton Galleries in London at the end of 1916 and then toured numerous British provincial towns through 1917 and 1918 (LAC RG 9 III-D-1 4746, 4729, and 4731; LAC RG 37 D 366). The Canadian War Records Office, which underwrote the exhibition, saw it as part of a multifaceted project of promoting Canadian influence in Britain. This project also included staffing a production office through which flowed 'all recent scenes of Canadian activity at the front or in England' to the illustrated press (LAC RG 9 III-D-1 4746). Both the success of the exhibition and the compilation of an extensive Canadian war photograph collection served to promote and solidify Canada's national identity and stature within the empire. Hundreds of thousands of people saw a replica of this first Canadian official war photograph exhibition when it toured Canadian cities and also visited the United States (LAC RG 9 III-D-1 4746).

Canada's second photograph exhibition was an even more popularly successful expression of the ideas of Canadian connection to the Empire, investment in the war, and importance to securing victory (LAC RG 37 D 370). This exhibition, mounted initially at the Grafton Galleries in London from July to September 1917, primarily depicted the Canadian victory at Vimy Ridge in April 1917. London newspapers reported that attendance records were being 'created daily' by crowds 'anxious to get a photographic impression of the grim realities of war', and the exhibition's organizers reported large crowds to the Canadian government (Anon. 1917c). A replica of the exhibition was exhibited in Paris and then sent to tour Canada (BBK/E/2/9 Memorandum; LAC RG 9 III-D-1 4746 175 5: 21).

With such efforts the Canadian government used the spectacle of the photograph exhibition as a means of publicizing its contribution to the Imperial war effort, as well as supporting its claims to a significant role in the British Empire, all the while claiming to be doing no such thing. The Canadian General Turner, opening the second Canadian exhibition of war photos in 1917, echoed this affectation: Canada, he stated, 'in taking part in the world-war, desired thanks from nobody. They were doing their little bit as members of the British Empire, and they hoped to be long spared to be part and parcel of it' (Anon. 1917b: 9). That he was introducing an exhibition exclusively devoted to Canada's 'little bit', and showcasing spectacular images aiming to announce its drama and worth to thousands, was presumably to ensure that everyone knew exactly what the Canadians were not to be thanked for.

The centrepiece of the exhibition, Ivor Castle's huge image 'The Taking of Vimy Ridge', emphasized Canada's heroic contribution to the Imperial war effort. This 'largest photograph in the world' was enlarged to 11 feet high by 20 feet long and described in the exhibition catalogue as 'an impression, nay, indeed a reality, of the splendid horror snatched by the photographer, in a fraction of a second, from the clutching of Death' (Robertson 1978: 44).[2] It was 'taken in profile from the flank, and the clouds of smoke represented bursts of German shells above our men. In the distance they would see a tank at work, while in the foreground were a number of casualties' (Anon. 1917b: 9; Anon. 1917c). It was in fact a composite of two photographs, with explosions and heroically fallen Canadian bodies deliberately added to the scene (Brandon 2011: 115). It was also one notable exception to the embargo on photographic depictions of Allied dead (Keshen 1996: 36; Saunders 2001: 40). However, the inclusion of Canadian dead in 'The Taking of Vimy Ridge' was no realist expression of the cost or futility of war. Rather, it was an attempt to make the photograph fit conventions of traditional battle painting and thus conform to social expectations of the necessity of heroic sacrifice in the course of securing a glorious victory. In this case, the dead made a noble sacrifice in the course of the Canadian victory at Vimy Ridge in April 1917, an event later depicted as a national coming of age. This exceptional depiction of the dead was rooted entirely in its nature as a deliberately constructed narrative. Images of the dead that lay more troublingly outside of the official narrative of military glory were generally, and remarkably effectively, suppressed (Taylor 1991: 44).

Australian efforts at recording and publicizing their contribution to the war via photography soon followed Canada's. The English press photographer Herbert Baldwin began photographing the activities of Australian troops on the Western Front in November 1916. After he was discharged ill in mid-1917, two further Australian photographers were appointed: Hubert Wilkins and Frank Hurley. Like Canada, Australia had established (in their case in early 1917) an official War Records Section, headed by Captain J.L. Treloar, tasked with collecting records of Australia's involvement in the conflict. Also like Canada, this 'complete system of record collection' was the brainchild of one man wielding outsize influence: Charles Bean, Australia's official war correspondent. Bean also conceived of and successfully lobbied for an Australian war museum and edited Australia's 12-volume official history of the war, and writing six volumes himself (AWM 38 3DRL 6673/362).

Bean impressed upon the Australian collecting effort a particularly strong concern for posterity from the outset. This had a marked bearing on Australian photography. Bean in fact believed that the aims of creating *publicity* and collecting a comprehensive *record* of Australians in the war were incompatible. Unlike the Canadians' embrace of Castle's photo composites (Jolly 2003: 161), Bean felt that posterity demanded different approaches than propaganda: 'The photographer who had been trained for publicity work could not be induced to throw his heart into obtaining pictures which would not immediately interest the newspapers, however invaluable they were for Australian records' (AWM 38 3DRL 6673/362). This attitude led to some conflict with the Australian official photographer Frank Hurley, who successfully appealed to Bean's superiors to be permitted his flamboyantly dramatic photomontages in exhibitions during the war (Jolly 1999). In the end, Bean's influence was to ensure that Australian photographers both produced photographs designed for immediate propaganda use and at the same time collected images intended primarily for post-war museum or archival use.

A heavier emphasis on posterity however in no way detracted from a central narrative of the heroism and battle-christening of the Australian nation. When Australia's own war exhibition opened in London's Grafton Galleries in May 1918, it gave an exposition of valour and national coming-of-age just as heroic as the Canadians'. Regardless of any misgivings he may have had over Hurley's curation, Bean wrote an essay for the exhibition's official catalogue expounding the significance of 'Australia's Effort in the War', both physical and financial: 'Since the opening of the war Australia has mobilised, enlisted, or trained [...] one-twelfth of the population [...] The equipment, transport and maintenance of the forces abroad and had home has been organised and paid for by Australia alone' (Bean in Anon. 1918a: 5). As Robert Dixon notes, this can be seen as an exercise in 'guided spectatorship', in which 'the principal pedagogic thrust of the essay is to remind the British public of the relative enormity of Australia's commitment to the imperial war effort' (Dixon 2012: 49–50).

This story spanned the theatres of the war. On the western front, Australians going into battle were depicted in a number of Hurley's composites. The largest picture, titled 'The Raid', was made from 12 negatives, measured about 21 feet by 15 feet (6.4 metres by 4.5 metres), and depicted soldiers heading into action against an exciting – and 'real' – backdrop of explosions and new military technology[3] (Figure 4.1). This motif of drama and excitement was further elaborated in numerous images of the Middle Eastern theatre. Hurley had gone to Palestine in 1918 and photographed a 'programme of stunts which I require doing' with Australian troops, including a 'battery going into action, machine-gun drill and ambulance turnout' and two regiments re-enacting 'their famous charge at Beersheba'.[4] The images he created of 'stunts', 'action', and picturesque settings were highly romanticized and especially glamorized the Australian Light Horse (ALH) and the Australian Flying Corps (AFC). Hurley's diary entries on the exhibition record the multimedia presentation of these materials, as well as audience responses to them: a military band played throughout the day, and Hurley

FIGURE 4.1 Frank Hurley, 'An episode after the Battle of Zonnebeke' or 'The Raid', from Hurley, 'Exhibition of war photographs' 1917–1918. (Mitchell Library, State Library of New South Wales, FL10890624.)

noted that colour slides of scenes 'on the Western Front, Flanders, and also in Palestine' 'elicit applause at every showing'[5]. These colour images were projected onto a screen at intervals, and *The Times* described them as follows:

> The deep colour of the East comes out with rich effect. The marble glory of the Mosque of Omar is conveyed as vividly as the hue of the wild purple iris of Palestine or that anemone which brightens the road to Jerusalem. Many who will never visit them can gather a true notion of the Judean hills from these pictures.
>
> *(Anon. 1918b: 6)*

These spectacular images of the Middle Eastern exotic (laden with biblical and crusader resonances) and Australian daring aimed to show the British public the value of the Australian contribution to the war (Lee 2008; Wellington 2018) (Figure 4.2). They wove the Australian forces into a narrative not just of the Great War, but also into a long-established series of tropes about the romance of Empire. By asserting the value of Australia's contributions and couching them in the cliches of the outback horseman and self-reliant 'digger', the exhibition laid claim to a distinctly Australian part in the sweep of Imperial history: Australia was not merely an offshoot of the Imperial family, but a crucial part of the fabric of Empire.

Compared to Canada's and Australia's energetic self-promotion, New Zealand's attempts to officially record their own war experiences were belated and more muted. One driver of this was an aversion to expense: initially turning down an offer to share a photographer with the Australians on cost grounds, the New Zealand government entered into a purchase agreement with the War Office Cinematographic Committee for film footage of New Zealanders.

FIGURE 4.2 Frank Hurley, 'The advance through the desert with the ALH. in Palestine' from Hurley, 'Exhibition of war photographs' 1917–1918. (Mitchell Library, State Library of New South Wales, FL10890633.)

However, British photographers were stretched too thin to be able to supply New Zealand material. New Zealand eventually appointed an official photographer in March 1917, when the War Office approved Henry Armytage Sanders to work in France (Pugsley 1995: 20). His first photographs arrived in London in late May 1917 before being sent on to New Zealand; the first official photos to appear in the New Zealand press were part of a double page spread in an *Auckland Weekly News* supplement on 23 August 1917 (Anon. 1917d: 38–39). This slow start and modest resourcing led to a relative dearth of specifically New Zealand imagery circulating during the war.

New Zealand also set up a War Records Section and commenced securing an official artistic record of the war substantially later than Canada and Australia (Hutchison 2020: 519). As Caroline Lord observes, 'New Zealand's First World War art program was born out of embarrassment' (Lord 2020: 474). Canada and Australia had both begun efforts to secure a national artistic record by 1916; New Zealand took no action until February 1918. At this point, the Commander of the New Zealand Division on the Western Front issued an order intended to locate artists already serving in the New Zealand forces. New Zealand's first official war artist, Lance Corporal Nugent Welch, was thus seconded from the New Zealand Rifle Brigade and sent to the Western Front in May 1918 (Anon. 1918c: 4; Anon. 1918d: 5; Lord 2020: 474). In the end, due in large part to funding limitations, the scheme appointed mostly artists who happened to already be serving with the New Zealand forces (Hutchison 2020: 523–524). Brigadier-General Richardson, the officer directing the artists' scheme, was by July 1918 envisaging that these artworks would form a part of a future national war museum, to be heralded by a London exhibition of New Zealand artworks and other artefacts (Lord 2020: 474). Although the artists were given a wide degree of freedom over the subject matter of their artworks, they were also tasked with 'producing images that would appeal to the commemorative needs of the New Zealand public as well as promoting New Zealand's war effort internationally' (Lord 2020: 475). The Armistice in November 1918 followed unexpectedly soon, however. In the context of national demobilization, New Zealand's artists were put under pressure to finish their work quickly. The New Zealand paintings were never displayed as a full collection in the immediate post-war period (Hutchison 2020: 529).

By contrast, the Canadian official art scheme, the Canadian War Memorials Fund, was started in November 1916. As with the Canadian photographic effort, Max Aitken, Lord Beaverbrook was instrumental in establishing it. The fund aimed to 'perpetuate the memory of Canadians taking part in this War by oil paintings and the erection of suitable monuments distributed throughout the Dominion' (Letter 1917 BBK/E/2/9). At the suggestion of his friend, the press baron Harold Harmsworth, Lord Rothermere, this war art project was registered as a charity under the War Charities Act, in order to avoid the need for government approval of the scheme. (British authorities had initially frustrated Australian and Canadian attempts to commission their own war artists.) The Fund would be administered through the Canadian War Records Office and funded by its

commercial activities, enabling Beaverbrook and Rothermere to retain ownership and control over the collection (Tippett 1984: 24–25). Beaverbrook oversaw
the commissioning of artists in Britain, and Sir Edmund Walker, an influential
Toronto banker and art collector, and Eric Brown, Director of Canada's National
Gallery, oversaw operations in Canada: both 'home' and 'front' in the Canadian
war effort were to be depicted (Brandon 1998).

This was nation building on an aestheticized grand scale, intended to commemorate Canadian achievements 'in a permanent artistic form of unprecedented magnitude' (Memorandum 1917 BBK/E/2/9). Art was wanted 'to teach
posterity of the glorious part of the race' and to ensure knowledge of the British
Empire and Canada's role in it in perpetuity (LAC RG 9 III-D-1 4746 175 5).
Canada's worth in this reckoning consisted in being part of a glorious and
timeless Empire, and in playing a significant role in helping to make the British
Empire great. Consequently, though the foreword to the catalogue of the 1919
Canadian War Memorials Exhibition could claim that 'artists were selected in
the most catholic spirit, to represent every school and group, from the most
academic and traditional to the most revolutionary and advanced', Beaverbrook's
first concern was with the documentation of Canadian heroism (Anon. 1919nd: 6).
So, while the Canadian collection includes a number of modernist paintings, the
Canadian War Records Office (CWRO) also commissioned a number of large
traditional canvases of specific events, selected after the fact, the commission
being 'entrusted to the artist whose past achievement pointed most clearly to his
ability to do full justice to his task' (ibid.).

Indeed, the first artist hired by the CWRO was Richard Jack, who was hired
to complete one painting of the second Battle of Ypres (Jack 1917). Subject selection carried with it a nation-building imperative. The Canadian Home front was
thoroughly documented as a means of celebrating the wider Canadian effort.
Walker, for example, suggested that lumbering in the east in winter might make
a good 'war subject' (Walker to Brown 1918: MS 1 24). Canada's official art programme portrayed the war as a national (as well as 'imperial') project that went
beyond the troops at the front and included the experiences of millions at home.

Unlike Canada's, Australia's war art programme focused on the front to the
near exclusion of home. Moreover, the Australian approach to war art, from
the beginning, prized creating a historical record above any artistic concerns.
The ubiquitous Charles Bean, at that point Australia's official war correspondent,
wrote to Senator Pearce, the defence minister, in September 1916 arguing for the
appointment of artists based on their first-hand experience of the war (AWM 93
12/12/1 (2)). He suggested that soldier-artist contributors to the Anzac Book –
a collection of soldier art, humour, and writing from the Gallipoli campaign
Bean had edited and published in 1916 – might be asked 'if they care to turn
out one historical picture each of what they actually saw (or know for certain
to be accurate)' (AWM 93 12/12/1 (2); Hutchison 2015). Actual experience or
knowledge was, in Bean's view, crucial to the authenticity and the accuracy of
the artist's work. This attitude emphasized the role of art as another form of

historical record. Bean advanced these ideas at the same time as proposals for an Australian War Records Section were being formed. Andrew Fisher, Australia's High Commissioner to London, cabled Prime Minister Billy Hughes in early February 1917 that he considered that the 'nucleus' of a War Record Office 'should be set up as has already been done by Canada for purpose of Collection of historical material, photographs, sketches, trophies, etc. of Australia's part in the War' (AWM 93 12/12/1). As part of this, soldier-artists 'might each paint pictures of Australian Troops in action as seen by them' (AWM 93 12/12/1).

In accordance with this scheme, five artists who were already serving soldiers in the Australian Imperial Force, George Benson, Frank Crozier, Will Longstaff, Louis McCubbin, and James F. Scott, were chosen by Bean to create drawings and paintings for the Australian War Records Section. In doing so, they remained within the armed forces and, subject to its discipline, were not permitted to undertake any other work other than their war records work, the artistic product of which was made property of the Australian Government (AWM 38 3DRL 6673/286). A second set of artists, including the cartoonist Will Dyson, and the landscape painters Arthur Streeton and George Lambert, were given temporary officer commissions in order to go to the front. They were hired by the Australian High Commission in London with Bean advising, and thus connected to, if not formally a part of, the Australian War Records Section.

Overall, the intention of the Australian war art scheme was to adorn and illustrate Australian achievements in a historical record whose narrative was set and interpreted by commissioning officials. Compared to the Canadian scheme, Bean's programme left a high degree of selective editorial power in the hands of Australian officials. In general, the idea was not to employ the artists and then ask them to undertake the depiction of specific subjects, as was the case with the Canadian War Memorials Fund. Rather, Bean proposed that the Government might let selected artists know that, if they created a work of a given subject, *and* a committee decided that it was of 'a good standard', the Government 'would be prepared to consider the purchase of such pictures for the nation' (AWM 38 3DRL 6673/286). For Bean, personal war experience may have been necessary, but neither it nor artistic talent sufficed to guarantee that an artist's personal interpretation merited inclusion in a national collection. Art as record was again the priority: Bean proposed that the 'Committee' charged with selecting artworks should include 'one person who is an artist' and *also* 'one who has a knowledge of the historical value of these sketches, (who must have some knowledge of the events and places recorded)' (AWM 93 12/12/1 (1)).

To sufficiently illustrate events that Bean, now in the role of official historian, considered to be important, a large proportion of the Australian war art collection was in fact commissioned *after* the war to populate the new Australian War Museum. The War Museum Art Committee controlled not only the subject matter but also design of commissioned works: the artist charged with illustrating a given subject had to first submit to the Committee a cartoon outline of the art-work's composition, and if the Committee did not like it, the artwork could be rejected at this stage. Further, the Committee could reject the final product if it did not conform to their expectations (AWM 170 4/1). The art was envisioned as hanging among artefacts of war and serving a narrative of Australian exploits in the future national war museum. In this way, the Australian official war art collection differed markedly from the Canadian War Memorials Fund, which envisioned its collection as hanging in an independent, purpose-built war art gallery. This extraordinary degree of control produced a collection of war art that served as a visual companion to an official, romantic, heroic vision of the 'birth of the nation'.

George Lambert, for example, provided a number of battle paintings on a grand scale, all featuring the Australians bravely charging into battle: *The Charge of the Australian Light Horse at Beersheba, 1917* (1920), *Anzac, the Landing 1915* (1920–22), and *The charge of the 3rd Light Horse Brigade at the Nek, 7 August 1915* (1924). These were imaginative *reconstructions* rather than first-hand depictions in any real sense, prompted by wider editorial concerns, drawing on items loaned from the war museum and topographical sketches made on the battlefields years after the fact. Lambert's *Landing* at Anzac Cove also proffers a sanitized version of the events of 25 April 1915: the confusion and chaos of the day are invisible – all we see are Australians wearing determined expressions climbing ever upward – and the dead and wounded, while painted into the scene, are aesthetically arranged, bloodless, and intact of limb. The collection was not intended to form a catholic artistic record of the war and did not stand separately from the narrative of the Australian War Museum. Rather, a remarkably traditional and stylistically and thematically uniform collection served to tell a very specific story of Australia's experience of the war and of what it meant for Australia and Australia's place in the Empire.

Objects captured or collected on the battlefield were also seized upon as a means of telling the Dominions' war stories. War trophies, or objects (especially weapons) wrested from the enemy, were collected and concentrated behind the lines according to a centralized Imperial system, then shipped to an Imperial depot in London. Dominion claims to trophies were weighed at the War Office (Overseas Military Forces of Canada 1918: 97). Within the War Office, the War Trophies Sub-Committee was established to oversee the collection and distribution of all trophies captured by the Imperial armies fighting in the war. This included, from early 1917, allocating guns to the National (later Imperial) War Museum, which was assumed to have first pick of all Imperial trophies for its collections. The Dominions, and especially Canada and Australia, objected: trophies were seen as key elements in realizing their ambitions to have collections of objects and documentation that would relate their national experiences and affirm their distinctive character as a vital part of the Imperial story. An Australian Department of Defence cable to the Secretary of State for the Colonies argued that Australia should have first refusal of any trophies captured by Australians, explicitly to allow the development of the Australian narrative:

> Another viewpoint is that Britain already has a history and traditions and relics and trophies extending back for centuries and the present war however great is only adding to a long record and collection whereas Australia has none here other than what she draws from the mother country. A nation is built upon pride of race and now that Australia is making history of her own she requires every possible relic associated with this to help educate her children in that national spirit thereby ensuring her loyal adherence to and defence of the Empire of which she forms part.
>
> *(AWM 38 3DRL 6673/364)*

Likewise, reports from the Canadian War Records Office, overseen by the ever-present Lord Beaverbrook, asserted repeatedly that their primary aim was the creation of a permanent record of Canada's achievements. The Canadian War Records Office was vital, they argued in a memorandum addressed to the Overseas Military Forces of Canada in an attempt to preserve as many records as possible, as '[i]n the years following the war Canadians will expect to be told what Canadians have done in the war. They will want the younger generation to be taught the glory of Canada' (LAC RG 9 III-D-1 4746 175 5). Objects for exhibition formed part of a larger planned museum preservation and exhibition project: Sir Arthur Doughty, Canada's Dominion Archivist, pushed from 1915 for a collection of trophies and other 'memorials of this momentous event' and 'our ancestral heritage' to be created as an extension of the collection of artefacts pertaining to Canadian history he was already overseeing in his role at the Public Archives (Doughty 1916: 474).

During the war, thanks to its relative proximity, Canada had the most significant programme of exhibition. Having gained permission from the War Office, Canadian officials continued to collect war trophies and began ship them to Canada for exhibition. In October 1917, the government staged its first successful show in aid of the Red Cross, in Halifax, Nova Scotia (PANS MG 20 321). Further exhibitions of war trophies, drawing millions of spectators, followed across Canada and the United States in 1918 and into 1919 (Wellington 2017: 166–179). Australia exhibited some trophies it had collected in Australia House in London in 1918 (Figure 4.3) and established a separate store for Australian trophies at Millwall Docks in May that year, but it was not until after the war that large shipments of these trophies began to arrive in Australia.

With the end of the war, the status of collections inevitably changed, not least because they were no longer witnesses to narratives of contemporaneous feats of arms, but rather memory objects. For Australia, the end of the war brought Australians at home their first chance to directly experience the bulk of the collection laid up by Bean and Treloar to form their memory of the conflict: ships full of artefacts began to sail back to Australia, most arriving during 1919.

FIGURE 4.3 A view of a portion of the exhibits at the Australian War Museum, in Australia House, London, 1918. Unknown photographer. (© Australian War Memorial, D00258.)

These objects, along with collections of paintings, films, and photographs of the war discussed above, would form the nucleus of an Australian War Museum. Its organizers had very high hopes for it: in a memorandum written in early 1918, Charles Bean already clearly envisaged the War Museum as part of a project of building the great cultural institutions of a proud nation: 'Australia will unquestionably need her own national museum, her national gallery, and her national library in future, in which the history of her race will be preserved and illustrated, just as the history of the A.I.F. will be preserved in the War Museum Gallery and Library' (Bean Memorandum AWM 93 12/12/1).

The Australian War Museum opened in its first iteration in Melbourne in 1922. Over the next three years, it received over 780,000 visitors, and after it was moved to Sydney in 1925, it attracted over 10,000 on its first weekend. Staff kept meticulous attendance figures, and repeatedly and consciously compared themselves to the Imperial War Museum, creating tables demonstrating the Australian museum's greater popularity (AWM 265 17/2/2). The museum was designed and overseen down to its minutiae by Bean and John Treloar (Treloar, having overseen the Australian War Records Section during the war, had afterwards became the museum's Director).[6] Their vision was museum as rhetoric: the museum was constructed to express and impress upon the viewer the singularity of the Australian character and the value of Australia's achievements. The illustrated guidebook and the exhibition arrangement guided the visitor through a carefully designed narrative of Australia's involvement in the war; a large fold-out floor plan and explanatory essay further expanded 'the spatial and narrative logic of the exhibition' (Dixon 2012: 59). Visitors moved through a series of 'courts'. In the wording of the contemporary reports, 'weapons, munitions, pictures, photographs, models of battlefields, and all the flotsam and jetsam of war from all fronts' were in each court; each illustrated a particular Australian battle or campaign (Anon. 1922: 5).

The exposition was ordered chronologically and framed as a passage from heroic defeat at Gallipoli to a series of Australian victories in 1918. The stations of the museum closed with the opportunity to view 'important Australian Relics' and to examine a series of models of campaigns or battles in which Australians had fought in France in 1918 (AWM J292). The presentation was consistently victory-heavy: nine of the 21 campaign display cases were devoted to the successes of 1918 (Melrose 2005: 353). Australia was told of its 'coming of age as a nation – an armed nation – within the imperial federation' and offered a multitude of images or exhibits imputing its victory to the superior moral character of the Allied and especially the Australian forces (Dixon 2012: 61). Indeed, upon entering the Exhibition, Bean's guidebook fastened visitors' eyes on the bronze of a shirtless, muscled Anzac on Gallipoli, eyes staring determinedly into the distance while hefting petrol cans filled with water, a vision of physical perfection evincing a casual adaptability (and glossing over the inadequate rations and dysentery common in the real campaign).

During the war, influential Canadians had been amassing official war collections with similar motivations and aspirations to Bean and Treloar. Beaverbrook in particular made use of his various British and Canadian political and military connections to garner support for his projects, while Doughty's ideas of constructing a permanent record of Canada's war experience readily fell in with Beaverbrook's schemes. Canadian exhibitions had started to tour Canada, the United States in Britain during the war, and did not stop immediately with the armistice. Exhibitions of Canadian war trophies, war photographs and war art were mounted in London in 1919 (Anon. 1919a; Anon. 1919b). In Canada, 'hundreds of captured German guns, aircraft, and small arms were put on display in what was the best-attended building' during the 1919 Canadian National Exhibition (Graves 1985: 5; Vance 1995). Numerous local organizations requested trophies for events like annual fairs and exhibitions, and 125 small trophy displays were dispatched across the Dominion in the 'Peace Summer' of 1919. These peacetime exhibitions of war trophies and technologies emphasized Allied technological superiority and military dominance as a way of asserting that victory made the sacrifices of the war years worthwhile and legitimating the war. Canada, like Britain, also held aircraft displays (AIR 2/4427, AIR 2/4428; Soye 2009).

But while numerous Canadian bodies both collected and exhibited highly successfully during the war, the project of building a more permanent museum of record around this collection fell into abeyance for some time afterwards. Almost immediately after the Armistice, in December 1918, at the request of the minister of Militia and Defence, an Order-in-Council had created the Commission on War Records and Trophies, and in 1919 that commission was asked to collect and care for all material appropriate for a National War Memorial (Bernier 2005: 59–60). However, a museum-memorial on Australian lines did not eventuate. One reason was that the Canadians' collecting efforts were run by influential people split between Canada and the Imperial centre. Beaverbrook, who had been so central to Canada's propaganda and collecting interests, remained in Britain, where his business interests primarily lay, becoming involved with the Imperial War Museum.

Another cause was the competing demands of other nation-building projects on those who remained in (or returned to) Canada. The new Canadian National Gallery consumed the attentions of Edmund Walker and Eric Brown, who had assisted in collecting Canada's war art; and Doughty was busy running the National Archives, as well as overseeing the distribution of war trophies. The deaths of Edmund Walker in 1924 and Doughty in 1936 may also have deprived the museum project of protagonists in the inter-war period. Finally, the political realities of post-war Canada played a part. French-Canadians regarded the war with ambivalence, undermining its utility as unifying national vision (Courtois and Veyssière 2015; Djebabla 2014). And in 1921, the Union government of Sir Robert Borden that had governed Canada throughout the war was defeated soundly by William Lyon Mackenzie-King, marking a division between the post-war and wartime political establishments. Plans for a national war memorial museum as a government priority faded, and trophies were distributed across the country. 'Libraries and Archives Canada' now holds metres of files of municipalities writing to request trophies, often citing their superior contribution or sacrifice as compared to their neighbouring towns or cities.

Canada's war collection remained in storage as an Annexe to the National Archives in Ottawa. It was not until 1935, when only one of the original members of the Commission remained, that an Order-in-Council was issued stating that 'ministers are of the opinion that the time [had] now come when adequate provision should be made for the proper accommodation, cataloguing and care of those trophies which it is considered should be retained for Museum purposes' (LAC RG 24 E-1-C 17664 045-6 1). The Annexe of the National Archives began – slowly – to be prepared for exhibition. The Canadian war museum finally opened in 1942.

The development of a New Zealand war collection into a national war museum began late, and its momentum was checked by the unexpected rapidity of Allied victory. During the war, the question of a New Zealand collection to record the war received some attention at home and at the front. Brigadier-General Richardson, the director of the war artists' scheme, had also advocated for a broader scheme of records collection with the goal of creating a New Zealand War Museum (Ross 2017: 236–237). Although approved in June 1917, the New Zealand War Records Section was not operational for some months after that (Anon. 1917e: 7). At home, Dr Allan Thompson, Director of the Dominion Museum in Wellington, argued for collecting materials for display in a national war museum as early as 1917, explicitly referencing his difficulties unearthing materials related to the 'Maori Wars'. The records of the 'heroes of today', he averred, ought to be collected 'while the fighting is still going on, instead of leaving it to future generations to send out a search party' (Anon. 1917a: 6; Ross 2017). He began appealing to families of medal winners for portrait photographs that year, and by 1921 the Dominion Museum had received around 1,100 photographs (Ross 2018). Although some of these were hung in the Dominion Museum in 1918, they were never displayed in the war museum he had envisaged.

New Zealand's efforts were still gathering steam in 1918, when the Armistice arrived. As Caroline Lord observes, '[o]ne of the main reasons behind the collapse of the war museum project and the post-war decline of the war art collection was simply that the war ended before the project could be fully organised and completed' (Lord 2020: 480). The men working on these collecting schemes overseas were demobilized, and the War Records section 'gradually disestablished over the following months' (Lord 2020: 480). The items collected abroad were shipped back to New Zealand and crammed into limited storage space in the Dominion Museum, which, overloaded, in turn forwarded items to other institutions (Anon. 1919c: 8). In the early 1920s, New Zealand's government was facing economic difficulties and was wary of expenditure. While Richardson continued to advocate for a national war museum, and the government appointed a War Museum Provisional Committee in September 1919 to deal with issues connected to the 'proposed National War Museum' and an embryonic collection 'donated by the Imperial Military and Museum authorities', funding was never forthcoming, and the museum never eventuated (Anon. 1919e: 9).

The first purpose-built museum intended to commemorate the war was, as a result, a local rather than national endeavour. And even this project was somewhat opportunistic: Auckland's existing museum of natural history and ethnography needed new premises, and when building them was delayed until after the war, the museum's organizers 'did not want the proposed memorial for the Auckland district competing for available funds, so proposed that the two be combined' (Anon. 1919d: 5; Rankin 2006: 57). The Auckland Museum energetically pursued its own aims from 1918, with the museum's curator, F. Cheesman, writing to the Minister for Internal Affairs, that 'while fully admitting the necessity of a central collection at Wellington [...] a good local collection at Auckland was also necessary', and upon not receiving a reply rapidly enough, further pressed those claims to the Minster of Defence (AM MUS 1995-41).

The museum also sought donations from the public and in 1921–1922 recorded donations of items such as German food coupons, revolvers, and rifles, a 'Prussian helmet taken after the last assault on Fort Vaux, Verdun', and a small collection courtesy of a Captain R.G. Sellar including a 'Turkish soldier's letter', 'meat tickets issued at Bagdad', 'order of the day issued prior to the final advance

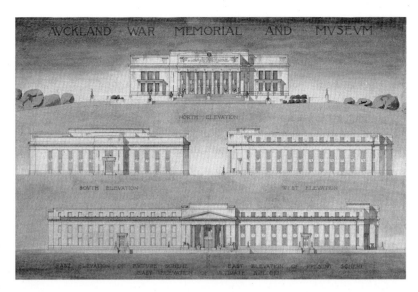

FIGURE 4.4 Original design for the Auckland Memorial and Museum. (Auckland Museum.)

in Mesopotamia', and 'Turkish soldier's identity disc' (Auckland Institute and Museum, 1922: 25–26). Although graced with a design intended to give it, in the competition-winning architect's words, the 'quiet dignity and subtle refinement necessary for the memorial purpose' it was an imperfect realization of the idea of a museum-memorial (AM MUS-2009-20-1-9) (Figure 4.4). When it opened in 1929, most of the new Auckland War Memorial Museum was devoted to its traditional collections, and the 'memorial sanctuary was situated on the top floor with a Hall of War Trophies alongside it, the military artefacts it housed given New Zealand significance only by their proximity to the Roll of Honour inscribed on the sanctuary walls' (Rankin 2006: 58). Its success as a memorial was contested, with the Returned Soldiers' Association, for example, protesting that the building was only 'to a small extent [a] war memorial' (Anon. 1928: 7).[7]

The Dominions of Canada, Australia, and New Zealand collected and exhibited representations and objects of war during the Great War and in the years afterwards. During the war, these collecting efforts operated within the same imperial bureaucratic and propaganda framework and evidenced similar desires to promote the importance of each Dominion's discrete contribution to the war effort. Photographs were used to convey in the popular press and in exhibitions the immediate drama and danger of the ongoing war and to encourage commitment to the continued prosecution of the conflict. Souvenirs, technology, and captured weaponry embodied the terror and triumph of the war (and the necessity of continuing to fight it) for curious audiences at home in an even more visceral manner. At the same time, official war art was commissioned with a slightly different goal: to record the efforts of the nation for posterity, narrating this story for presumably proud and curious future generations. However, these national schemes varied in scale, monetary support, editorial style, and timing and diverged after the war.

In post-war Australia, the narratives of valour and victory emerging from wartime propaganda quickly solidified in institutional form, as wartime collections were concentrated in the hands of the newly formed Australian War Memorial Museum, energetically stewarded by a number of the same the men engaged in amassing these collections during the war. In its final form, this museum also became the national war memorial, thus lending its collections greater, and symbolically outsized, significance. In Canada, the comprehensive and energetic collecting and exhibiting activities of the war years slowed dramatically after 1919, with key figures divided between Canada and the metropole, and the nation politically divided over the war's meaning. The grand museum of war art planned during the war never eventuated, and the expected Canadian War Museum did not open until 1942, in an annex of the National Archives. Smaller New Zealand's collecting bodies and official war art and photography schemes began later in the war and were always less well resourced, and consequently incomplete and more muted. In a post-war environment of financial constraint, no single national body became the repository for New Zealand's war collections, and even projects designed specifically to exhibit and memorialize the war like Auckland's War Memorial Museum were simultaneously civic projects aimed at promoting local histories, ethnography, and municipal pride.

In the divergent post-war trajectories of these Dominions' efforts to collect and curate the Great War, we see prefigured the varying memory cultures surrounding the war in Canada, New Zealand, and Australia today. In Canada, popular opinion in French Canada meant a post-war consensus on the meaning of the war remained elusive, while war museum projects stalled amidst other cultural and political projects. In New Zealand, the strength of local commemorations was not buttressed by the presence of a national institution devoted to asserting a narrative of the nation's war. In Australia, a centralized effort saw the prompt post-war creation of a national museum as national war memorial. It is notable that it is in Australia that the memory of the First World War is so strikingly central to modern identity and politics and distorts contemporary funding decisions about the cultural landscape: in 2021, controversy is presently raging at the Australian government's decision to dedicate 500 million Australian dollars to a massive expansion of the Australian War Memorial, while at the same time, numerous precious items in the underfunded National Archives of Australia are in danger of perishing.

Notes

1 The museum was not designated a national memorial until 1925. The subsequent name, Australian War Memorial, dates from the opening of the museum on its current site in Canberra in 1941.

2 Although my analysis focusses on the more 'spectacular' images in this exhibition, one of its other features was a number of photographs of German prisoners, also taken by Castle as another visual measure of Canadian success at Vimy. For an analysis of these, see Stokes (2017).

3 Frank Hurley, diary entry for 25 May 1918 (Dixon and Lee 2011: 104).

4 Frank Hurley, diary entries for 5 and 7 February 1918 (Dixon and Lee 2011: 94).

5 Frank Hurley, diary entry for 25 May 1918 (Dixon and Lee 2011: 104). See also Anon 6 (1918).

6 It was partially possible to create such a coherent vision because only a handful of people – predominantly Bean and Treloar – designed the narrative of the exhibition. Treloar, who found delegating difficult, personally wrote all of the 'tickets' or captions for each item in the museum. He also decided what artefacts to include in the exhibition and supervised the layout of the museum. Bean wrote the guidebook, which museum visitors could use to direct them through the exhibition (AWM 38 3DRL 6673/712).

7 For a more positive view, see R.A. Falla, director of the Canterbury Museum (Falla 1938).

References

Archival Sources

Auckland Museum (AM)

Auckland Institute and Museum, *Annual Report of the Auckland Institute and Museum for 1921–1922* (Auckland: Wilson & Horton, 1922).

MUS 1995-41 Auckland Museum. Correspondence War Trophies. Memorandum from F. Cheesman to C. J. Parr M.P., Auckland, 12 September 1919.

MUS+-2009-20-1-9. Grierson, Aimer & Draffin, Auckland War Memorial Museum Library.

Australian War Memorial (AWM)

AWM 38 3 DRL 6673/712.

AWM 38 3DRL 6673/712. Bean, C. E. W. MS of Short Guide to the AWM and covering letters, dated 1922.

AWM 38 3DRL 6673/362. Bean, C. E. W. The Australian War Records.

AWM 38 3DRL 6673/286. Bean art: artists: war art files. Australian Imperial Force Orders by General Sir W R Birdwood. Headquarters, Australian Imperial Force, In the Field, 26 February 1918.

AWM 38 3DRL 6673/364. Cable despatched to the Secretary of State for the Colonies from the Secretary of Defence, Melbourne, Quoted in Copy of Cable from Secretary of Defence Melbourne to Administrative Headquarters AIF London, 3 March 1918.

AWM 93 12/12/1. Bean, C. E. W. Memorandum. The Australian War Records. An account of the present development overseas and suggestions of course necessary to be taken at the end of the War, 33.

AWM 93 12/12/1 (1) Letter, Bean to H. C. Smart, 6 February 1917.

AWM 93 12/12/1 (2) Letter, Bean to Senator Pearce, 16 September 1916.

AWM 93 12/12/1 War Museum – General File. Cablegram, High Commissioner, London, to Prime Minister Billy Hughes, 8 February 1917.

AWM 170 4/1. Template agreement between Commonwealth of Australia and war artists, 1921_. (Filed 1921.) Art Committee Meetings, Agenda and Minutes, February 1921–July 1927 and February 1941.

AWM 265 17/2/2: Attendances.
AWM J292. Layout of Melbourne Exhibition and suggested circulation route.

Library and Archives Canada (LAC)

LAC RG 9 III-D-1 Vol. 4746 Folder 175 Folder 5. Reports. Origin of Records. 1915 to 1918. Report, Canadian War Records to Robert Borden.
LAC RG 9 III-D-1 Vol. 4729. Folder 131 File 4. Photographs Exhibition Correspondence.
LAC RG 9 III-D-1 Vol. 4731. Department of National Defence. Photographs. Folder 136 File 8. Photographs. Sales 1st Exhibition.
LAC RG 24 National Defence Series E-1-C, Vol 17664, File 045-6, Vol. 1.
LAC RG 37 D 366: Public Archives and National Library. War Trophies. Memoranda 1–4. Folder. 1A.
LAC. RG 37 D 370: Public Archives and National Library. War Trophies. Memoranda 14–16 Duplicates.
Overseas Military Forces of Canada, *Report of the Ministry* (London: Printed by the Authority of the Minister, Overseas Military Forces of Canada, 1918), 97.

Parliamentary Archives (UK)

BBK/E/2/9 General correspondence and memoranda war cinematograph committee. 27 August–31 October 1917. Letter, Beaverbrook, Canadian War Records Office to Sir Edward Kemp, Minister of Militia, 6 September 1917.
BBK/E/2/9 General correspondence and memoranda war cinematograph committee. 27 August–31 October 1917. Memorandum. Canadian War Memorials Fund. History and Objects. Beaverbrook Papers.

Sir Edmund Walker Papers, Thomas Fisher Rare Book Library, University of Toronto

MS 1 Box 24. Out Correspondence 1917–1919. Letter Walker to Brown, 18 October 1918.

Public Archives of Nova Scotia (PANS)

MG 20 Vol. 321. Canadian Red Cross Society, Transcripts of the history of the Red Cross in Nova Scotia During World War I. Typescript headed "Business and Advisory".

National Archives (UK)

AIR 2/4427 RAF Aerial Pageant – 1921 and AIR 2/4428 RAF Aerial Pageant – 1922.

Catalogues, periodicals, and posters

Anon. (1919) *A Catalogue of War Trophies, Relics and Souvenirs collected for the Canadian War Museum. Illustrating the Campaigns in France and Belgium of the Canadian Corps of the British Expeditionary Force. Commanded by Lieut.-Gen. Sir A. W. Currie, K.C.B., G.C.M.G.* (London).
———. (1915a) Museum of the Royal United Services Institution. *Museums Journal*, 14 January: 242.
———. (1915b) *Museums Journal* 14 February: 274.

_____ (1915c) A War Exhibition. *The Times* 28 June: 3.

_____. (1917a) Ambitious Scheme. A National Historical Collection. *Evening Post* 10 March: 6.

_____. (1917b) Vimy Ridge Pictures. The Second Canadian Exhibition. *The Times* 17 July: 9.

_____. (1917c) Grafton Gallery Crush. *Huge Crowds View Wonderful Firing-Line Pictures. Sunday Pictorial.* 22 July.

_____. (1917d) New Zealanders in France: Interesting glimpses of the life of our boys in the war zone. *Auckland Weekly News* 23 August: 38–39.

_____. (1917e) Historical Records. N.Z.E.F. War Section. *Evening Post.* 29 November: 7.

_____. (1918a) *Catalogue of Australian Official War Pictures and Photographs. Grafton Galleries, Grafton Street, London, W. London*: Australian Commonwealth Office: 5.

_____. (1918b) Colour Photographs. Capt. Hurley's Work in Palestine. *The Times* 6 June: 9.

_____. (1918c) War Pictures. Chance for New Zealand Artists. *Dominion* 18 June: 4.

_____. (1918d) War Pictures For National Collection. *New Zealand Times* 18 June: 5.

_____. (1919nd) *The Canadian War Memorials. Under Direction Canadian War Records Office.* Toronto Exhibition.

_____. (1919a) *Catalogue. Canadian War Memorials Exhibition Royal Academy, Piccadilly, W.*

_____. (1919b) *Wonderful Exhibition of Huge Canadian Victory Photographs in Colour. Grafton Galleries off Bond Street, W.* Art.IWM PST 13729.

_____. (1919c) A War Museum. More Accommodation Required. Wellington's War Collection. *Dominion* 12 March: 8.

_____. (1919d) Auckland's War Memorial. Museum in the Domain. And Waterfront Monument. Total Cost of £100,000. *Auckland Star* 27 June: 5.

_____. (1919e) War Trophies. Collection for a Museum. *Evening Post* 4 October: 9.

_____. (1922) Inanimate Witnesses. Australian Bravery in the War. Remarkable Museum Collection. *The Mercury* (Hobart). 25 April: 5.

_____. (1928) Auckland Museum. Only Partly War Memorial. *Waikato Times* 3 October: 7.

Bather, F.A. (1915) Address to the Museums Association on 'Museums and the War. *Museums Journal* 15: 2–10, p. 5.

Doughty, A.G. 1916. Canada's Record of the War. *University Magazine* 15, December: 474.

Falla, R.A. (1938) Functions of Museums. Appropriateness of War Memorials. Address by Mr. R. A. Falla. *Press*, 11 April: 4.

Jack, R. (1917) *The Second Battle of Ypres, 22 April to 25 May 1915*. Oil on canvas, 371.5 × 589 cm, CWM 19710261-0161, Beaverbrook Collection of War Art, Canadian War Museum.

Secondary Sources

Bernier, S. (2005) A brief history of Canadian forces military museums from 1919 to 2004 – Part 1. *Canadian Military Journal* 6:59–60.

Brandon, L. (1998) The Canadian War Memorial that Never Was. *Canadian Military History* 7 (4):45–54.

_____. (2011) Words and pictures: Writing atrocity into Canada's First World War official photographs. *The Journal of Canadian Art History/Annales d'Histoire de l'Art Canadien* 31:122–123.

Carmichael, J. (1989) *First World War Photographers*. London: Routledge.

Cook, T. (2003) Documenting war and forging reputations: Sir Max Aitken and the Canadian War Records Office in the First World War. *War in History* 10 (3):265–295.

———. (2012) 'Tokens of Fritz': Canadian soldiers and the art of souveneering in the Great War. *War & Society* 31 (3):211–226.

Cornish, P. (2009) 'Just a boyish habit' …? British and commonwealth war trophies in the First World War. In N. J. Saunders and P. Cornish (eds.), *Contested Objects: Material memories of the Great War*, pp 11–26 New York: Routledge.

Courtois, C.-P. and L. Veyssière (eds.) (2015) *Le Québec dans la grande guerre: engagements, refus, héritages*. Septentrion: Québec.

Dixon, R. (2012) *Photography, early cinema and colonial modernity*. London: Anthem Press

Dixon, R. and C. Lee (eds.) (2011) *The Diaries of Frank Hurley 1912–1941*. London, New York: Anthem Press.

Djebabla, M. (2014) Historiographie francophone de la Première Guerre mondiale: écrire la Grande Guerre de 1914–1918 en français au Canada et au Québec. *The Canadian Historical Review* 95 (3):407–417.

Graves, D.E. (1985) Booty! The story of Canada's world war one trophy collection. *Arms Collecting* 23 (1):3–10.

Gregory, A. (2008) *The Last Great War: British Society and the First World War*. Cambridge: Cambridge University Press.

Harries, M. and S. Harries. (1983) *The War Artists: British Official War Art of the Twentieth Century*. London: Michael Joseph in Association with the Imperial War Museum and the Tate Gallery.

Horne, J. (1997) Remobilizing for 'total war': France and Britain, 1917–1918. In J. Horne (ed.), *State, Society, and Mobilization in Europe during the First World War*, pp 195–211 Cambridge: Cambridge University Press.

Hutchison, M. (2015) 'Accurate the Point of Mania': Eyewitness testimony and memory making in Australia's Official Paintings of the First World War. *Australian Historical Studies* 46 (1):27–44.

———. (2020) Dominion imaginings: Commemorating WWI in Australian, Canadian and New Zealand Official painting. *Journal of Australian Studies* 44 (4):515–534.

Jolly, M. (1999) Australian First World War photography. Frank Hurley and Charles Bean. *History of Photography* 23 (2):141–148.

———. (2003) Composite propaganda photographs during the First World War. *History of Photography* 27 (2):154–165.

Kavanagh, G. (1994) *Museums and the First World War*. Leicester: Leicester University Press.

Keshen, J.A. (1996) *Propaganda and Censorship During Canada's Great War*. Edmonton: University of Alberta Press.

Lee, C. (2008) 'War is not a Christian Mission': Racial invasion and religious crusade in H. S. Gullett's Official History of the Australian Imperial Force in Sinai and Palestine. *Journal of the Association for the Study of Australian Literature* 7:85–96.

Lord, C. (2020) Artwork, artefact or archive? The evolution of New Zealand's official First World War art collection. *Journal of Australian Studies* 44 (4):473–491

Maguire, A. (2016) Looking for home? New Zealand soldiers visiting London during the First World War. *The London Journal* 41 (3):281–298.

Melrose, C. (2005) *'A praise that never ages': The Australian War Memorial and the 'national' interpretation of the First World War, 1922–35*. Unpublished PhD Thesis, The University of Queensland.

Monger, D. (2012) *Patriotism and Propaganda in First Word War Britain: The National War Aims Committee and Civilian Morale*. Liverpool: Liverpool University Press.

Pugsley, C. (1995) 'Who is Sanders?' New Zealand's official cameraman on the Western Front 1917–1919. *Stout Centre Review* 5 (1):19–22

Rankin, R. (2006) War museums in the British Dominions: conceptualising Imperial allegiance and colonial autonomy. *New Zealand Sociology* 21 (1):49–67.

Robertson, P. (1978) Canadian photojournalism during the First World War. *History of Photography* 2 (1): 37–52.

Ross, K. (2017) 'More the books can tell': Museums, Artefacts and the History of the Great War. In K. Pickles, L. Fraser and M. Hill (eds.), *History Making a Difference: New Approaches from Aotearoa*, pp 224–248. Newcastle upon Tyne: Cambridge Scholars Publishing.

———. (2018) 'We are sending you a 'home portrait': The Dominion Museum's Collection of Photographs of New Zealand's Medal Winners. New Zealand WW100, https://ww100.govt.nz/great-war-medal-winner-portaits#_edn4.

Saunders, N.J. (2001) Matter and Memory in the Landscapes of Conflict: The Western Front 1914–1919. In B. Bender and M. Winer (eds.), *Contested Landscapes: Movement, Exile and Place*, pp 37–54. Oxford and New York: Berg.

Sheftall, M.D. (2009) *Altered Memories of the Great War: Divergent Narratives of Britain, Australia, New Zealand and Canada.* London and New York: I. B. Tauris.

Soye, E.P. (2009) *Canadian War Trophies: Arthur Doughty and German aircraft allocated to Canada after the First World War.* Unpublished M.A. Thesis, Royal Military College, Canada.

Stokes, C.-J. (2017) Beyond 'The Taking of Vimy Ridge': The war photographs of William Ivor Castle. *Journal of Military and Strategic Studies* 18 (2):179–205.

Taylor, J. (1991) *War Photography: Realism in the British Press.* London: Routledge.

Tippett, M. (1984) *Art at the Service of War: Canada, Art, and the Great War.* Toronto: University of Toronto Press

Vance, J.F. (1995) Tangible demonstrations of a Great Victory: War trophies in Canada. *Material History Review 42/Revue d'histoire de la culture materielle* 42:47–56.

Wellington, J. (2017) *Exhibiting War: The Great War, Museums and Memory in Britain, Canada, and Australia.* Cambridge: Cambridge University Press

———. (2018) Imagined Landscapes in Palestine During the Great War. In J. Clarke and J. Horne (eds.), *Militarized Cultural Encounters in the Long Nineteenth Century. Making War, Mapping Europe*, pp 249–270. London: Palgrave.

5

CURATING THE GREAT WAR AT THE IMPERIAL WAR MUSEUM DURING THE SECOND WORLD WAR

Philip W. Deans

Introduction

This chapter investigates the approach to the curation of the Great War at the Imperial War Museum (IWM[1]) during the Second World War. It challenges assumptions that the years 1939–1945 were quiet for the institution. These assumptions have likely been ingrained by the institution's necessary withdrawal from public gaze along with the other national museums and galleries during the conflict (Standing Commission on Museums and Galleries 1948: 4). On the contrary, however, the Second World War was a busy time for the IWM: a time of institutional mistakes, learning, innovation and reinvention. Aside from helping national and local government provide the public with wartime facilities (ibid.: 17), the institution took evasive curatorial action not only to preserve its collection from the threat posed by aerial bombardment, but also to preserve its cultural relevancy from the threat posed by altered public perspective and opinion in the post-war era. The institution also enabled public understanding about the national situation through organizing a wartime exhibition.

The curation of the Great War is historicized in this chapter. As a result, curatorial work has been treated quite broadly, aligned with how such work would have been understood at the time. Today, museum curators, particularly from large museums, tend to be specialist workers rather than generalists (Burcaw 1997: 45–46). But before the Second World War, this was not normally the case. The curator – the first museal profession to be established – originally had a very broad remit of activities. As the International Council of Museums' *Key Concepts of Museology* states: 'For a long time the curator was in charge of all tasks directly relating to the objects in the collection, that is their preservation, research and communication' (Desvallées and Mairesse 2010: 68). After the expansion of museal workforces during the 1960s, however, these tasks began being undertaken

DOI: 10.4324/9781003263531-7

by specialist staff more focused on museum management, conservation, design or education (Murdoch 1994: 142; Boylan 2006: 417; Wilkinson 2014).

Accordingly, this chapter examines the work by the then curatorial team to protect the collection and present and reposition it towards the institution's public offer after the conflict. This involves considering activities which would not necessarily fall within a curatorial role today but did at the time (Plenderleith 1934; Plenderleith 1937; North, Davidson and Swinton 1941; Lewis 1989: 53–54). But first, it is important to understand how the institution operated hitherto, highlighting the significance of the period under consideration.

Institutional Context

IWM is synonymous today with representations of the Great War, now known as the First World War, which contribute to its remit of covering armed conflict from 1914 to the present. In doing so, it focuses on representing the United Kingdom, former empire and Commonwealth forces (Taylor 2009: 54, 80). The institution's mission today is to be 'a global authority on conflict and its impact on people's lives' and to be 'a leader in developing and communicating a deeper understanding of the causes, course and consequences of war' (IWM 2020: 4). This has not always been the case, however. From the IWM's founding in 1917 to the 1939 onset of the Second World War, the Great War was the institution's sole focus as a museum of what Wells (1914) optimistically called the 'war to end all war'. This was based on the erroneous belief that it would be the last such conflict before an everlasting utopian peace prevailed (Budgen 2018). Such aspirations became deeply embodied in the IWM's mindset during the succeeding two decades. King George V's speech at the museum's opening ceremony on 9 June 1920 expressed that future visitors would 'look back upon war, its instruments, and its organisation, as belonging to a dead past' (Wellington 2017: 242). The IWM earnestly promoted this view. Indeed, in 1938, the museum's Director-General and Curator at the time, Leslie Ripley Bradley, an officer veteran of the Great War, lamented that the museum's mission had been intended to 'make an historical record of the "war to end all war", and not the first in a series of world wars, each more terrible than the last' (IWM EN1/1/REP/032a: 1).

The precise way this message was interpreted depended on the historical moment. Informed by Stuart Hall's (2013: 10) proposition that 'meaning does not inhere in things [...]. It is constructed', this argument derives from a supposition propounded by Sue Malvern (2000: 181) about the cultural significance constructed around the 'war to end all war' rhetoric during the interwar years:

> The sentiment was sometimes used as a rationale to strengthen resolve during the war. Just after 1918, it could reinforce a mood of national mourning but it could also make criticism of the war seem like a dishonouring of the dead. By the mid-1930s, the statement might have been read as a powerful desire to avoid another war.

Indicators of this evolving significance can be perceived at the IWM over its formative years.

During the Great War, alongside establishing its collection, the IWM held various temporary exhibitions across London before obtaining permanent accommodation. Their aim was to fillip the British war effort (Kavanagh 1994: 142; Mercer 2013: 333–336) and encourage an Allied victory over the Central Powers (Cundy 2015: 250–253). The idea of the 'war to end all war' therefore had been deployed by the museum during 1917 and 1918 as a rallying cry or call for action. This view accords with that of Harries and Harries (1983: 118) that the institution's foundation comprised an 'element [...] in Lloyd George's reorganisation of propaganda and his effort to combat war-weariness'.

After the war, the IWM underwent a commemorative turn. Established formally at The Crystal Palace in Sydenham during 1920, the institution began to solemnly lionize the war dead whose stories it exhibited, and to sanctify their sacrifice (Malvern 2000: 185; Cundy 2015: 254–256). This built on earlier framings of the collection made between 1917 and 1918 that saw a variety of objects revered as 'sacred relics' (Cornish 2004: 46). Accordingly, they acquired commemorative dimensions alongside historical and technical ones, which Cundy (2017a: 265) calls their 'hybrid' quality. Thus the sacralization of the relics of a recent, but hopefully 'dead' past was deployed by the institution following the armistice as treatment for grief. The museum's move to the Imperial Institute in South Kensington during 1924 saw this hybridity increase, stimulated by cramped conditions that limited the material which could be displayed (Cundy 2015: 256–259; Cundy 2017a: 265).

The rise of Fascism and Nazism in the 1930s prompted the IWM to shift again by augmenting its commemorative message with warnings against renewed hostilities in Europe. Following a second relocation to the former Bethlem Royal Hospital building, Southwark (Cooke and Jenkins 2001), the institution's exhibitions, became more cautionary, with messages overtly framing war and armed conflict as folly (Malvern 2000: 192). This change was also articulated by the Director-General in the 1938 annual report, where he stated that the museum's mission was 'to show the futility of war, and that its heroism is bought at all too dear a cost' (IWM EN1/1/REP/032a: 1).

As another war loomed, therefore, the concept of the 'war to end all war' had been deployed in an admonitory capacity by the IWM. Indeed, from this point up until the wartime, reinvention over 1939–1945, it can be conceived that the IWM became somewhat akin to an early peace museum, which Joyce Apsel (2016: 12) describes as 'exhibiting the human costs of war through artefacts, including weapons and uniforms, and through photographs, drawings, and letters'.

Safeguarding Artefacts from the Great War

The earliest curatorial activity undertaken at the IWM in preparation for the Second World War was protecting its existing Great War collection. As the threat of another conflict loomed, previously unparalleled measures were taken by London's national museums and galleries. The first meeting to consider the issue was held as early as December 1933 (IWM EN2/1/CON/004: 1). That same year Hitler had been appointed Chancellor of Germany, and shortly thereafter he withdrew Germany from the League of Nations and the Disarmament Conference. As a proactive measure, it stands in sharp contrast with the much slower response by Britain overall to this emerging threat (Gibbs 1976: 84–85). As the international situation deteriorated over the 1930s, the effect of air warfare became ever more apparent through the Spanish Civil War; British museum curators even visited the warzone so they could see how Spanish curators dealt with the aerial threat (Pearson 2017: 63). The dangers posed by air raids on the United Kingdom had become horrifyingly clear (Romero Salvadó 2013: 31–32).

Preparations by London's national museums and galleries, eventually with the Standing Commission on Museums and Galleries[2], formulated common and individual policies to safeguard collections in the event of war (Pearson 2017: 61). For the IWM, these included evacuation and *in situ* protection measures (IWM EN1/1/REP/032b). The former involved moving certain collection items to country houses, confirmed by 1939 as Colworth House near Sharnbrook, Bedfordshire, owned by Henry Ludwig Mond, 2nd Baron Melchett; Penn House near Amersham, Buckinghamshire, owned by Francis Curzon, 5th Earl Howe; and Ramster Hall near Chiddingfold, Surrey, owned by Florence Priscilla Norman, Lady Norman (IWM EN2/1/MUS/002/3a). The latter involved strengthening the institution's building and constructing a strong room in the basement. A staff shelter was also constructed (IWM EN1/1/REP/032b; IWM EN2/1/MUS/002/16). All three houses were the property of families closely connected to the museum. Lord Melchett's father had been the driving force behind its creation, while Earl Howe and Lady Norman both served as Trustees.

Between 1933 and 1939, the IWM's decision-making on evacuation became informed by practical and ideological considerations. The former was straightforward, in that large, bulky and/or heavy objects, including tanks, naval guns and aircraft were difficult if not impossible to move. As the Director-General, Leslie Bradley, informed the Parliamentary Committee of Public Accounts after the conflict: 'we had to leave them there, whatever happened to them, in the war. They are too heavy to move' (Committee of Public Accounts 1957: 17).

The latter, by contrast, involved judgements about the collection's importance. As early as 1933, there appears to have been a view that the Imperial War Museum should not be evacuated at the expense of impeding the 'older' national museum and galleries' evacuations (IWM EN1/1/REP/032b: 1). The exact reason for this view may never be fully understood. One justification given was that its collections did not have the same cultural value or significance as those of older institutions (ibid.). This problematic assessment goes against modern and, to an extent, historical museum ethos (Markham 1938; Museums Association 2015: 7). It also raises questions about the institution's sincerity and commitment towards its earlier framing of such objects as 'sacred relics'. On war's outbreak, three object categories were created for the collection: those to be evacuated, which comprised artworks and photograph albums (IWM EN2/1/MUS/002/3b; IWM EN2/1/MUS/002/3c); those that could be moved but considered ineligible for evacuation, which went into the strong room; and the immovable objects, which were protected by sandbags and other barriers (IWM EN1/1/REP/032b). These safeguarding policies became active on 23 August 1939.This followed a pre-emptive decision by the Home Secretary who instructed the capital's national museums and galleries to close and execute their emergency plans (Pearson 2017: 64) (Figure 5.1).

Bradley reflected critically on this strategy after the Second World War, due to various difficulties that necessitated revising the safeguarding policies. His first criticism concerned the country houses which, while safely situated away

FIGURE 5.1 A barrage balloon is erected over the Imperial War Museum in anticipation of the air war that would take place above London. (© IWM Q64060.)

from potential bombing targets, were inconvenient or unsafe for storage. This arose during one post-war meeting at the Ministry of Works on safeguarding the London national museum and gallery collections in the event of war with the Soviet Union. Bradley agreed with Sir John Forsdyke, Director of the British Museum and Trustee of the Imperial War Museum, that 'Country houses provided the worst type of storage' (IWM EN2/1/GOV/111a: 2). In a separate memorandum, he condemned this form of emergency storage due to their difficulty of access and inappropriate environmental conditions (Ambrose and Paine 2018: 260–263). Furthermore, there was a risk of fire in these elderly and often still-inhabited houses.

Moreover, while owners willingly looked after so–called 'valuable' material, the same could not be said for large or less aesthetically pleasing items (IWM EN2/1/GOV/111b; see McCamley 2003 for a multi-institutional perspective). Penn House clearly shows the problems with such locations. From mid-1940, the entire deposited collection had to be relocated because of inappropriate conditions that pertained there through the owner's absence (see Deans 2019). Nevertheless, the owners of country houses often welcomed such uses, especially as it avoided far rougher treatment if requisitioned by the military – treatment that saw many demolished during and after the war (Robinson 2014: 7–9).

Bradley also criticized the initial decision to retain the majority of moveable items at the institution. While the war caused no fatalities there, some objects were lost and the building damaged by bombs and rockets. This confounded Bradley's pre-war expectations that IWM's collection might survive some damage to the building. As he later wrote: 'Experience in the recent war shows that only the toughest objects, guns, tanks, etc., can be left at the museum during war-time with any confidence. [...] In the event of another war we shall aim at almost total evacuation' (IWM EN2/1/GOV/111b: 1). On 31 January 1941, for example, the IWM's Naval Gallery received a direct hit. Alongside the destruction of many expensive ship models and other material that had remained there, the institution lost the world's last surviving Short Seaplane. Flown at the Battle of Jutland during the Great War, it made naval history by making the first ever aerial sighting of an enemy battle fleet (IWM EN2/1/ACC/004/7a) (Figures 5.2 and 5.3).

As the Blitz intensified, the IWM adjusted its safeguarding policy. The limited evacuation programme was replaced by a reactive strategy deployed on an as-and-when-necessary basis. Some items were temporarily accepted by more safely located institutions, while others were sent on nationwide tours. Further objects were also sent to country houses, under a commercial arrangement made with their lessors by the Ministry of Works (IWM EN1/1/REP/032b: 6–7). One of the last components to be evacuated was the library, as it had been intended that the reference departments would be retained as long as possible during hostilities. The holdings had been required for consultation by the general public and the government (ibid.: 5). Eventually this policy became unsustainable, and so, during June 1941, the library was evacuated to Barnstaple (ibid.: 7). With its departure, virtually everything which could be evacuated had been.

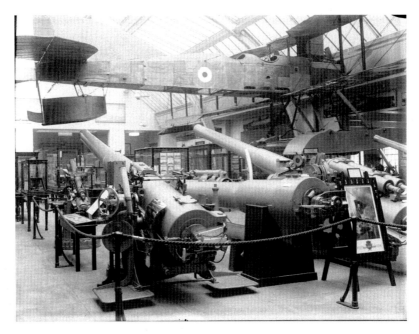

FIGURE 5.2 The Imperial War Museum's Naval Gallery in 1937. (© IWM Q61183.)

FIGURE 5.3 The same Naval Gallery following its direct hit on 31 January 1941. (© IWM MH127.)

Exhibiting Artefacts from the Great War

The outbreak of war saw the government enforce a wide-ranging closure of cultural and leisure venues, driven by a fear of blackout violation and the presumed dangers of holding large gatherings when there was a threat of air-attack. When the feared knock-out blow from the air failed to materialize, the Museums Association[3] saw opportunities for museums and galleries to develop their role in society unhindered by peacetime constraints. It therefore launched a successful campaign with the Standing Commission on Museums and Galleries which saw the government reverse its policy – on the proviso that no irregular expense be incurred or evacuated material be returned. Through this, the Board of Trustees of the IWM saw an opportunity for some limited reopening (IWM EN1/1/COB/049/4: 3). They therefore authorized Bradley to seek permission from the local authority, Southwark Borough Council, to reopen (IWM EN2/1/MUS/003/1ba). This was granted on 11 December 1939 (IWM EN2/1/MUS/003/1bb) following consultation and negotiations between council officials and the Metropolitan Police Service (TNA MEPO 2/3489).

On being granted this opportunity the IWM curated a special exhibition in the Naval, Army and Picture Galleries on the ground floor. Opening in January 1940, admittance was limited to 200 people at any one time, Monday–Saturday, in daylight hours (IWM EN2/1/MUS/003/1bb). This extended as the days got longer (IWM EN1/1/REP/032b: 9), eventually including Sundays (IWM EN2/1/MUS/003/1bc). All other spaces in the building were off-limits, although the reference departments on the second floor remained accessible by appointment (Blaikley 1940: 8). The composite displays comprised immovable objects and items not considered evacuation worthy. They possessed an amateurish, haphazard quality, characteristic of the institution until the 1960s (Condell 2002: 31), which, even then, fell short of the sort of the exhibition philosophy that museums aspired to (Markham 1938: 84–85; Dean 1993; Lord and Lord 2002; Hughes 2010). The exhibition in the Naval Gallery sought to represent sea and air power. The display included ship and submarine models; *materiel*, such as torpedoes, mines and depth charges; the above-mentioned Short Seaplane; and pictures of German fighter aces from the previous war (Blaikley 1940: 8). The Army Gallery looked to represent military power on the land, alongside espionage and politics. Items here included artillery pieces, camouflage, infantry personal equipment, spy tools and documents such as The Treaty of Versailles (ibid.). The Picture Gallery dealt with propaganda and included lithographs and drawings, both satirical and serious in nature (ibid.: 8–9) (Figure 5.4).

Analysis identifies dual meanings to this exhibition. Superficially, it can be viewed as an exhibition on the Great War. This is because apart from newer acquisitions such as the Anglo-German Agreement, signed by Neville Chamberlain and Adolf Hitler after the 1938 Munich Conference, and a model of HMS *Ajax*, which helped sink the German pocket battleship *Admiral Graf Spee* during the 1939 Battle of the River Plate, the material displayed was of 1914–1918 origin

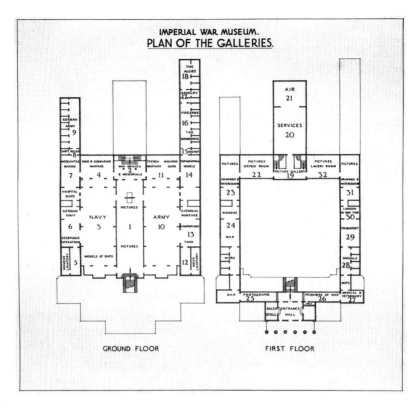

FIGURE 5.4 A floor plan of the Imperial War Museum's galleries before the Second World War. (© IWM Q60569.)

(ibid.: 8). On closer inspection, however, it becomes apparent that the exhibition can also be interpreted as being *about* the new ongoing war.

The exhibition showed visitors objects of direct relevance to the prevailing situation, such as a photograph of Hermann Göring as Oberleutnant of his German fighter wing during the Great War (ibid.). Göring featured regularly in the British media at the time as a high ranking political and military leader in Germany, and most visitors would have recognized him. Another example was an assemblage of gas masks (ibid.: 9). This display could have made distinctly uncomfortable viewing for visitors, given they would have been carrying a more modern – though noticeably less substantial – example with them at the time. The fear that gas-bombs might be used against civilian targets was still very real at this stage of the war (Calder 1992: 55). A third example was the pencil drawing by Henry Rushbury depicting Winston Churchill speaking to an audience in Central Hall, Westminster, on 4 July 1918. Some words from the speech were emblazoned below the picture: 'Germany must be beaten, must know she is beaten, must feel she is beaten!' (Blaikley 1940: 9). An accompanying note informed visitors that 'until recently delicacy has prevented them from showing the drawing, but that they are doing so now because "the sentiments expressed in Mr. Churchill's speech have once more become appropriate and sensible'", to quote writer and novelist Mollie Panter-Downes' (1972: 46) recollection of it.

The significance of putting the drawing on display had a prescient aspect. In February 1940, Churchill was not yet Prime Minister, but had been brought into the Chamberlain War Cabinet as First Lord of the Admiralty. He had been the chief opponent of Chamberlain's policy of appeasement, but now his appointment was seen as a way of harnessing his energies while neutralizing him as a critic (Gilbert 1990). The *Illustrated London News* commented on the exhibition that the Churchill depicted in Rushbury's picture possessed an uncanny likeness to the man who had spoken in Manchester just a week before about the need to fight the war (Anon. 1940a; Anon. 1940b) (Figure 5.5).

That this exhibition was curated almost entirely using material from the Great War belied the clever curatorial work which created a highly relevant experience for visitors (Nielsen 2015). Noting the cogency of individual items selected for display, the *Times* commented about their 'particular bearing on the present-day war conditions' (Anon. 1940c). Indeed, the upshot was an exhibition that directed visitors to *meaning-making* – a process through which exhibits become meaningful (Weil 2002: 70) through an amalgamation of curatorial choices and visitor circumstances (Mason 2005) – which orientated them historically and

FIGURE 5.5 The final exhibit of the Imperial War Museum's wartime exhibition: WinstonChurchill addressing an audience at Central Hall, Westminster, on 4 July 1918. Drawn by Henry Rushbury. (© IWM Art.IWM ART1122.)

contemporaneously against the national picture. In doing so, the exhibition provided psychological nourishment during this dark hour.

From 1938 until 1940, many in the United Kingdom suffered what has been theorized as the 'war of nerves' (Gottlieb 2017). This was an anxiety condition derived from fears about the situation in Europe and the likelihood of another war involving the country. The heightened stress suffered by people who have no control over its source is well documented; so too is the theory that this stress can be mitigated by seeking to become better informed (Barlow 2004: 254–257; Silvia 2012: 157–158). By attending the IWM's wartime exhibition, therefore, visitors gained the opportunity to seek understanding and assurances about the wartime situation and thereby maintain a sense of control.

This exhibition presented a unique curation of the Great War which responded to a unique moment in British history: a period betwixt and between the world wars. Essentially, it fully represented neither one period nor the other. That is because while the coming of the Second World War had shattered the illusion of the 'war to end all war', the effects had yet to be fully felt on the British Isles, giving the new war a sense of distance, but for how long few could predict. This caused acute stress in British society, with people clamouring to know what was awaiting them. Accordingly, and ironically, the curators at the IWM, drawing on experience and artefacts of a conflict that for 26 years had been associated with a 'war to end all war', made projections about the future which, judging from visitor figures, the public readily indulged. But this period was short lived, meaning the exhibition was, perhaps inevitably, time limited. On 7 September 1940, the Blitz began (Overy 2013: 85–86). Two days later, the IWM was forced to close again when a bomb narrowly missed the building and lay unexploded in the surrounding park. Following this, the institution did not reopen until after the Second World War. Over its roughly seven-month opening, the exhibition was attended by 65,496 people, 1,234 on Easter Sunday alone (IWM EN1/1/ REP/032b: 10).

Repositioning the Subject of the Great War

This early wartime exhibition prefigured the way the IWM treated the Great War after 1945. Never before was it presented in a way that enabled connections and comparisons with other conflicts to be made. Hitherto, the Great War had been treated as the 'war to end all war', even when subsequent interwar conflicts disproved this. Moreover, by winking and nodding at the connections and comparisons between the previous world war and the new ongoing one, the exhibition heralded the representation of other conflicts at the institution beyond the Great War. This is a principle which today forms the institution's core subject remit (IWM 2020: 4). The short-lived wartime exhibition represented the emerging reinvention of the IWM, which occurred during the Second World War. Accordingly, the institution's *raison d'être* and rationale – its essential philosophical underpinnings – were transformed: the institution metamorphosed from a museum on the 'war to end all war' to a museum on two world wars and their interconnections. As Anderson (2012: 2) insightfully observed, 'Reinventing the museum is not just adding a program, reinstalling a gallery, or increasing financial reserves – it is a systemic shift in attitude, purpose, alignment and execution'.

Leslie Bradley was the driving force behind the IWM's wartime reinvention, a judgement deriving from analysis of his influence over the institution. Many traditional museum histories coalesce around one significant individual. These individuals are often uncritically regarded as the catalyst for the actions undertaken by an institution (Hooper-Greenhill 1992: 20). Such a focus might be considered justified, however, in Bradley's case. His fundamental influence on the IWM was due to distinct systemic reasons. Indeed, his responsibilities were many and varied, and when he received promotion, he never relinquished the previous role. Accordingly, when Bradley became Director-General in 1936 (ffoulkes 1939: 156), he was also Curator, Secretary to the Board of Trustees and Chief Accounting Officer (IWM EN1/1/REP/032c: ii).

Drawing on John Child's (2005: 6–17) articulation of organizations as being an architectured arrangement of conceptual components, it can be argued that Bradley was a *critical structural component*, given his depth and breadth of responsibility. Interestingly, Bradley's legacy evokes mixed reaction at the museum today. On one hand, he is remembered as an insatiable collector: someone who provided subsequent curators and historians with plentiful material to exhibit and research (Cundy 2012). On the other hand, he is considered a reactionary: conservative in conduct, favouring the Great War only, and regarding the Second World War a nuisance which filled the institution with unnecessary and unwanted objects (Charman 2008: 104; Taylor 2009: 55). To a large extent, this perception echoes that propagated by his successor, Noble Frankland. In one example, Frankland once wrote that:

> when the [IWM's] original object of helping to sustain morale in the war expired with the advent of peace, the new idea which took its place was that this museum would record and remind of a catastrophe which surely could never happen again. When, within a shockingly short time, it did, the original [...] [IWM] seemed to lose its mission. One of its most devoted servants, my immediate predecessor as Director, Mr L. R. Bradley, was quietly planning an institutional demise, which would be slow and dignified and would approximately coincide with his own.
>
> *(Frankland 1995: 127)*

And in another example, he wrote:

> Mr Bradley continued to see the Imperial War Museum through the eyes of its original beholders and those who founded it. [...] The coming of the Second World War shattered this illusion, as it had done for the Royal Institute of International Affairs. In that context, it was not wholly illogical

for Mr Bradley to believe that the best course was to arrange for a gradual and dignified decline towards extinction for the museum which history had turned on its head. It did not occur to him that there was an alternative, or if it did, it was not one which he wished to embrace. He gave the impression of hoping, as he approached the grave, that the museum, which he had served for so long, would do the same.

(Frankland 1998: 164)

But this criticism does not entirely stand up to scrutiny.

As the Second World War approached, Bradley perceived the need for the IWM to assume a wider remit covering both world wars. He otherwise feared for the institution's continuing existence beyond any future hostilities. This concern was later articulated in a letter sent on 24 October 1939 to Trustee Sir James Ross, wherein Bradley warned that he 'could see no future for the Museum if it was to remain merely a Museum [...] [on] the last war but one' (IWM AIR 2/10188a). This worry presumably derived from recognition that institutions such as museums must maintain cultural relevancy in society. Without relevancy, they risk losing public support and resources, and closing. The solution, as identified by Bradley, was to reorientate the IWM's focus. Accordingly, he decided it needed to make a collection of the fresh material from the new world war which would eventually be exhibited alongside existing material from the Great War.

For this solution to be effective, however, the IWM needed to move quickly to conceive and execute a strategy for delivering on this new collection, including ensuring that there was material to collect. Bradley's experience of collecting during and after the Great War showed that full benefit from the process depended chiefly on prompt and comprehensive collecting by the institution (TNA AIR 2/10188b). Established during 1917, the museum missed out on more than two years when acquisitions from limited stocks could have been made, a fact that forever circumscribed its collections. Bradley was determined that such problems would not reoccur (TNA T 162/742/3a). Demonstrating this determination, he wrote to various government ministers during September 1939 urging them to instruct their departments to earmark documents, ephemera and other material for preservation by the museum (TNA AIR 2/10188b; HO 186/2097a; HO 186/2097b). 'How long, for instance', he rhetorically asked the Secretary of State for Air, Sir Kingsley Wood, 'will it be possible to obtain copies of the leaflets which have been dropped in Germany?' (TNA AIR 2/10188b).

Despite this eagerness, no new collection could be made without first the agreement of the institution's Board of Trustees which, guided by the Director-General, were responsible for setting its policy (IWM EN2/1/ACC/004/7b). Interestingly, records suggest that several Trustees had reservations about expanding its scope. This greatly alarmed Bradley for the reason given above. Fortunately, those Trustees who supported an expansion carried the day, and on 22 September 1939, the Board granted its permission pending approval by the Treasury, which was subsequently received on 19 October 1939 (TNA T 162/742/3b).

There is no scope in the present chapter to consider the IWM's collecting of Second World War material, which took place over 1939–1945 and beyond. That comprises a separate discussion. But it is important to consider the effect this whole process had on the institution's curation of the Great War in the post-1945 years. The former changed the latter. Bradley's decision to seek the extension of the IWM fundamentally remoulded the institution. It entered the Second World War as a museum on the 'war to end all war' and exited six years later as a museum on the two world wars. Indeed, during the first permanent exhibition after reopening, the Great War was represented by pictures only (Museums Correspondent 1946). No longer would it be represented through Wellsian framing as the culmination of an old world order that enabled something new and better to flourish. Rather, it started being represented as the first act in a worsening human tragedy. Where once objects and artwork from the Great War occupied dedicated exhibition space (IWM EN1/1/REP/032a), they started being displayed alongside material representing the Second World War (IWM PUB/LON/01/003).

Alys Cundy (2017b: 411–412) has identified an intention by the curatorial team to compare and contrast the two conflicts. This comprised a thematic comparison, where relatable material occupied space near each other (ibid.: 412). The upshot was an era of exhibitions that did not present the two world wars in accessible, chronologically compartmentalized ways, but rather through disconcerting temporal, geographical and thematic disorders, which caused the Great War to appear as having concluded with unfinished business (Malvern 2000: 194–196), in turn causing the post-1918 aspirations for peace to transform, 'hauntologically', into some lost future (Derrida 1994).

Conclusion

This chapter has provided an overview of the work undertaken by the IWM to curate its Great War material during the Second World War. Indeed, this study demonstrates that the institution did not go into hibernation in 1939, but rather continued operating, experiencing institutional mistakes, learning, innovating and reinventing throughout the process.

The coming of the Second World War challenged the IWM in a way which may well have been existential. This chapter tries to make clear that the actions taken to face the various threats were far removed from the pessimistic and purely reactive response which has hitherto been ascribed to the museum and, in particular, its Director-General, Leslie Bradley. The IWM began planning for the wartime evacuation of collection material at a surprisingly early date. It was forced however to face greater problems than other national museums and galleries when carrying out this process, such as the collection's greater immobility. After the war began, the IWM reopened, until the onset of the Blitz reversed that decision. For this reopening, it had created a successful public offer from the limited resource provided by the un-evacuated collections. And finally, the Director-General proved to be alive to the IWM's need to collect material from the new war, if the museum was to remain culturally relevant.

The findings presented above reveal that the curation of the Great War at the IWM during the Second World War era catalysed an active programme of museographical development there, particularly over 1939–1945. On one hand, this programme ensured the institution's long-term continuance, despite the challenges encountered in the process. On the other, it enabled irrevocable changes to the institution's physical and metaphysical structure. In any case, the programme ensured that the IWM could survive the Second World War and, most significantly, become the museum in existence today.

Notes

1 The initials were in common usage as shorthand for Imperial War Museum, prior to being adopted officially in 2011 as an abbreviation for Imperial War *Museums* (a title inclusive of all five IWM sites) (IWM 2011).
2 A quasi-autonomous non-governmental organization responsible for advising the government over matters pertaining to museums and galleries (Carlisle 1988a, b).
3 A non-governmental organization promoting the professional development of museums (Lewis 1989).

References

Published Sources

Ambrose, T. and C. Paine. (2018) *Museum Basics: The International Handbook.* Abington: Routledge.

Anderson, G. (2012) A Framework: Reinventing the Museum. In G. Anderson (ed.), *Reinventing the Museum: The Evolving Conversation on the Paradigm Shift*, pp 1–9. Lanham, MD: AltaMira Press.

Anon. (1940a) The Imperial War Museum Reopens. Illustrated London News, 3 February: 135.

———. (1940b) Mr. Churchill in Manchester. The Manchester Guardian, 29 January: 6.

———. (1940c) The Imperial War Museum. *Times*, 26 January: 11.

Apsel, J. (2016) *Introducing Peace Museums.* Abingdon: Routledge.

Barlow, D.H. (2004) *Anxiety and Its Disorders: The Nature and Treatment of Anxiety and Panic.* New York, NY: The Guilford Press.

Blaikley, E. (1940) Reopening of the Imperial War Museum. *Museums Journal* 40: 7–8.

Boylan, P.J. (2006) The Museum Profession. In S. Macdonald (ed.), *A Companion to Museum Studies*, pp 415–430. Malden, MA: Blackwell Publishing.

Budgen, D. (2018) Literature. In U. Daniel, P. Gatrell, O. Janz, H. Jones, J. Keene, A. Kramer and B. Nasson (eds.), *1914–1918-online. International Encyclopedia of the First World War [online].* Berlin: Freie Universität Berlin. DOI: 10.15463/ie1418.10329/1.1. Available from <https://encyclopedia.1914–1918-online.net/pdf/1914–1918-Online-literature-2018-06-29-V1.1.pdf> [accessed 6 December 2019].

Burcaw, G.E. (1997*) Introduction to Museum Work.* Walnut Creek, CA: AltaMira Press.

Calder, A. (1992) *The People's War: Britain 1939–1945.* London: Pimlico.

Carlisle, E.H., Countess of. (1988) *A History of the Commission: Standing Commission on Museums and Galleries, 1931–1981; Museums and Galleries Commission*, 1981–1986. London: Museums and Galleries Commission.

Charman, T. (2008) 'A Museum to Man's Greatest Lunatic Folly': The Imperial War Museum and its Commemoration of the Great War, 1917–2008. In Anon. (ed.), *A Part of History: Aspects of the British Experience of the First World War*, pp 99–106. London: Continuum.

Child, J. (2005) *Organization: Contemporary Principles and Practice*. Malden, MA: Blackwell Publishing.

Committee of Public Accounts. (1957) *Special Report and First, Second and Third Reports from the Committee of Public Accounts Together with the Proceedings of the Committee, Minutes of Evidence, Appendices and Index*. London: HMSO.

Condell, D. (2002) The History and Role of the Imperial War Museum. In B. Korte and R. Schneider (eds.), *War and the Cultural Construction of Identities in Britain*, pp 25–38. Amsterdam: Rodopi.

Cooke, S. and L. Jenkins. (2001) Discourses of regeneration in early twentieth-century Britain: From Bedlam to the Imperial War Museum. *Area* 33 (4):382–390.

Cornish, P. (2004) 'Sacred Relics': Objects in the Imperial War Museum, 1917–1939. In N.J. Saunders (ed.), *Matters of Conflict: Memory and the First World War*, pp 35–50. Abingdon: Routledge.

Cundy, A. (2012) Illuminating Our History [online]. Available from <http://blogs.iwm.org.uk/research/2012/05/illuminating-our-history/> [accessed 5 March 2020].

———. (2015) Thresholds of memory: Representing function through space and object at the Imperial War Museum, London, 1918–2014. *Museum History Journal* 8 (2):247–268.

———. (2017a) Objects of War: The response of the Imperial War Museum, London, to the First and the Second World Wars. *Post-Medieval Archaeology* 51 (2):261–273.

———. (2017b) The Imperial War Museum and Material Culture. In A. Einhaus and K.I. Baxter (eds.), *The Edinburgh Companion to the First World War and the Arts*, pp 402–418. Edinburgh: Edinburgh University Press.

Dean, D. (1993) *Museum Exhibition: Theory and Practice*. London: Routledge.

Deans, P.W. (2019) *The Imperial War Museum's Work To Safeguard Its Collections during The Second World War* [online]. Available from <http://www.mghg.info/blog/2019/5/3/the-imperial-war-museums-work-to-safeguard-its-collections-during-the-second-world-war> [accessed 17 December 2019].

Derrida, J. (1994) *Specters of Marx: The State of the Debt, the Work of Mourning and the New International*. London: Routledge.

Desvallées, A. and F. Mairesse (eds.) (2010) *Key Concepts of Museology*. Paris: Armand Colin.

Faith, Thomas I. (2016). Gas Warfare. In U. Daniel, P. Gatrell, O. Janz, H. Jones, J. Keene, A. Kramer and B. Nasson (eds.), *1914–1918-online: International Encyclopedia of the First World War [online]*. Berlin: Freie Universität Berlin. DOI: 10.15463/ie1418.10813. Available from <https://encyclopedia.1914–1918-online.net/pdf/1914-1918-Online-gas_warfare-2016-01-25.pdf> [accessed 25 April 2018].

ffoulkes, C. (1939) *Arms and the Tower*. London: John Murray.

Frankland, N. (1995) Review of, Gaynor Kavanagh, museums and the First World War, a social history. *Journal of the History of Collections* 7 (1): 126–127.

———. (1998) *History at War: The Campaigns of an Historian*. London: Giles de la Mare Publishers.

Gibbs, N.H. (1976) *Grand Strategy: Rearmament*. London: HMSO.

Gilbert, M. (1990) *Prophet of Truth: Winston S. Churchill, 1922–1939*. London: Minerva.

Gottlieb, J. (2017) Umbrellas, Hats, and Gas Masks: The Objects of the War of Nerves, Britain 1938–1939. In *Conference on Objects In and After Hostility: The Materiality of Conflict*. Held 30–31 March at Newcastle University and Northumbria University.

Hall, S. (2013) The Work of Representation. In S. Hall, J. Evens and S. Nixon (eds.), *Representation*, pp 1–47. London: SAGE Publications.

Harries, M. and S. Harries. (1983) *The War Artists: British Official War Art of the Twentieth Century*. London: Michael Joseph.

Hooper-Greenhill, E. (1992) *Museums and the Shaping of Knowledge*. London: Routledge.

Hughes, P. (2010) *Exhibition Design*. London: Laurence King Publishing.

Imperial War Museum (IWM) (1939) *Annual Report of the Director-General to the Board of Trustees, 1938–1938*. London: HMSO.

———. (2011) *IWM Launches New Brand* [online]. Available from: <https://www.iwm.org.uk/sites/default/files/press-release/New_Brand_Press_Release.pdf> [accessed 11 January 2020].

———. (2020) *Annual Report and Accounts, 2019–2020*. London: HMSO.

Kavanagh, G. (1994) *Museums and the First World War: A Social History*. London: Leicester University Press.

Lewis, G. (1989) *For Instruction and Recreation: A Centenary History of the Museums Association*. London: Quiller Press.

Lord, B. and G.D. Lord (eds.) (2002) *The Manual of Museum Exhibitions*. Walnut Creek, CA: AltaMira Press.

Malvern, S. (2000) War, memory and museums: Art and artefact in the Imperial War Museum. *History Workshop Journal* 49:177–203.

Markham, S.F. (1938) *Museums and Art Galleries of the British Isles (Other Than the National Museums)*. Edinburgh: Carnegie United Kingdom Trustees.

Mason, R. (2005) Museums, galleries and heritage: Sites of meaning-making and communication. In G. Corsane (ed.), *Heritage, Museums and Galleries: An Introductory Reader*, pp 200–214. Abingdon: Routledge.

McCamley, N.J. (2003). *Saving Britain's Art Treasures*. Barnsley: Leo Cooper.

Mercer, A. (2013) The changing face of exhibiting women's wartime work at the Imperial War Museum. *Women's History Review* 22 (2): 330–344.

Murdoch, J. (1994) Defining Curation. In G. Kavanagh (ed.), *Museum Provision and Professionalism*, pp 137–141. London: Routledge.

Museums Association. (2015) *Code of Ethics for Museums* [online]. Available from <https://www.museumsassociation.org/download?id=1155827> [accessed 11 January 2020].

Museums Correspondent. (1946) Changed War Museum. *Times* 27 November: 7.

Nielsen, J.K. (2015). The relevant museum: Defining relevance in museological practices. *Museum Management and Curatorship* 30 (5Lieut): 364–378.

North, F.J., C.F. Davidson, and Swinton, W.E., Lieut. (1941) *Geology in the Museum*. Oxford: Oxford University Press.

O'Brien, T.H. (1955) *Civil Defence*. London: HMSO.

Overy, R. (2013) *The Bombing War: Europe, 1939–1945*. London: Penguin Books.

Panter-Downes, M. (1972) *London War Notes, 1939–1945*. London: Longman.

Pearson, C. (2017) *Museums in the Second World War: Curators, Cultures and Change*. Abingdon: Routledge.

Plenderleith, H.J. (1934) *The Preservation of Antiquities*. London: The Museums Association.

———. (1937) *The Conservation of Prints, Drawings, and Manuscripts*. Oxford: The Oxford University Press.

Robinson, J.M. (2014) *Requisitioned: The British Country House in the Second World War.* London: Aurum Press.

Romero Salvadó, F.J. (2013) *Historical Dictionary of the Spanish Civil War.* Lanham, MD: The Scarecrow Press.

Silvia, P.J. (2012) Curiosity and Motivation. In R.M. Ryan (ed.), *The Oxford Handbook of Human Motivation,* pp 157–166. Oxford: Oxford University Press.

Standing Commission on Museums and Galleries. (1948) *Third Report: The War Years and After.* London: HMSO.

Taylor, J. (2009) Interpreting the Second World War. In E. Kjeldbæk (ed.), *The Power of the Object: Museums and World War II,* pp 52–81. Edinburgh: MuseumsEtc.

Weil, S. (2002) *Making Museums Matter.* Washington, DC: Smithsonian Institution Press.

Wellington, J. (2017) *Exhibiting War: The Great War, Museums, and Memory in Britain, Canada, and Australia.* Cambridge: Cambridge University Press.

Wells, H.G. (1914) *The War That Will End War.* London: F. and C. Palmer.

Wilkinson, H. (2014) *Negotiating Change: Curatorial Practice in UK Museums, 1960–2001.* Unpublished doctoral thesis. Leicester: University of Leicester.

Archival Sources

IWM

EN1/1/COB/049/4 Draft Minutes of the Meeting of the Board of Trustees Held on Thursday, 7th December 1939.

EN1/1/REP/032a 21st Annual Report of the Director-General to the Board of Trustees, 1938–1938.

EN1/1/REP/032b War History of the Imperial War Museum, 1933–1943.

EN1/1/REP/032c 20th Annual Report of the Director-General to the Board of Trustees, 1937–1938.

EN2/1/ACC/004/7a Letter from L. R. Bradley to B. B. Cubitt, 1 February 1941.

EN2/1/ACC/004/7b Letter from E. J. Forsdyke to L. R. Bradley, 5 February 1941.

EN2/1/CON/004 Safe Custody of National Art Treasures in the Event of War.

EN2/1/GOV/111a Storage of National Art Treasures: Note of a Meeting Held at Lambeth Bridge House on 3rd of May, 1948.

EN2/1/GOV/111b Storage Accommodation Required by the Imperial War Museum in the Event of War.

EN2/1/MUS/002/3a One-page untitled document detailing the name and location of the refuges and contact details of their owners.

EN2/1/MUS/002/3b Six-page untitled document headed with Class I on page 1, Class II on page 4, Class III on page 5, and Class IV on page 6.

EN2/1/MUS/002/3c Photographic Albums.

EN2/1/MUS/002/16 Letter from E. de Normann to Curator and Secretary, 24 September 1937.

EN2/1/MUS/003/1ba Letter from L. R. Bradley to Principle Air Raid Precautions Officer, 13 November 1939.

EN2/1/MUS/003/1bb Letter from D. T. Griffiths to L. R. Bradley, 11 December 1939.

EN2/1/MUS/003/1bc Letter from D. T. Griffiths to L. R. Bradley, 19 March 1940.

PUB/LON/01/003A Short Guide to the Imperial War Museum.

The National Archives of the United Kingdom

AIR 2/10188a Letter from L. R. Bradley to J. Ross, 24 October 1939.

AIR 2/10188b Letter from L. R. Bradley to Secretary of State for Air, 11 September 1939.

HO 186/2097a Letter from L. R. Bradley to The Lord Privy Seal, 12 September 1939.

HO 186/2097b Letter from L. R. Bradley to Secretary of State for the Home Department and Minister of Home Security, 14 September 1939.

MEPO 2/3489 Letter from D. T. Griffiths to Superintendent, 29 November 1939.

T 162/742/3a Letter from L. R. Bradley to Secretary, 22 September 1939.

T 162/742/3b Letter from Wm S. Douglas to The Trustees, 19 October 1939.

PART II

Museums and Materialities

6

EAST OF THE JORDAN

Curating and forgetting the First World War and Arab Revolt along the Hejaz Railway

Nicholas J. Saunders

The idea of excavating modern conflict sites, especially of the First World War, as a worthwhile scientific endeavour and a performative kind of sensorial remembrance was largely unknown – certainly unconceptualized and untheorized – until the late 1990s. Since then, the advent and adoption of an increasingly interdisciplinary modern conflict archaeology (e.g. Saunders 2007; Desfossés et al 2008; Stichelbaut 2018) has enhanced and familiarized the idea that archaeological excavation of that conflict's sites is both a legitimate undertaking and a way of remembering and respecting the war dead, especially when it leads to the identification and/or re-interment of human remains (e.g. PAP 2010; Loe et al 2014; MoD/VUK 2019) and thereby reclaims some of 'the missing'. This of course is an eloquent reaffirmation of the anthropological nature and consequences of these archaeological investigations.

My aim here is to explore a particular aspect of such activities – one based on the notion that surveying and excavating conflict sites that are currently being damaged or destroyed is a particular kind of curation, and one which offers a degree of preservation in the absence of any formal curatorial policy and furthermore has the potential for honouring the dead in a more informed and respectful way. As Faniel et al (2020: 1) have observed, the interdisciplinary team-based settings of an archaeological excavation 'are ripe for collective curation'. This idea of course is underpinned in part by the long-acknowledged practice of 'preservation by record' – where the threat to an archaeological site requires total investigation before it is too late (Foyle 2015; Huggett 2015). While this most often concerns the rescue archaeology of sites in danger of motorway or urban development, it is also urgent (and particularly appropriate) when it involves conflict-related sites of suffering and loss (and sometimes only recently discovered) and which are in imminent danger.

DOI: 10.4324/9781003263531-9

Looting of personal effects and miscellaneous military hardware from First World War human remains has long been a serious issue along the old Western Front of France and Belgium (Saunders 2007: 11) and also occurs in eastern Europe, Russia, and elsewhere (e.g. Zalewska and Czarnecki 2021: 77–78). In southern Jordan, the search for 'Turkish Gold' and more mundanely the desire for 'free' building materials (stone, metal, wood) has been a constant probably since the 1920s. The ever-present threat of removing materials and damaging the integrity of such sites often precludes the possibility that such objects can ever be investigated, interpreted, or curated. They simply disappear from history. When possible, undertaking archaeological and anthropological investigations creates a body of knowledge and understanding that did not exist before and so represents a valuable form of curation.

This is of course but part of the ongoing debate concerning overcoming the challenges of preserving and curating modern conflict heritage – not least via a strategy of deploying technology driven solutions (Stichelbaut et al 2021). And although not dealt with here, this wider debate also concerns modern warfare damage to ancient and acknowledged heritage – most recently and infamously with the depredations of Islamic State in Syria and Iraq (Jones 2018; Westcott 2020). Modern conflict archaeology strata are often hybrid, mixing levels from various periods of the past with the destruction wrought by the modern conflict involved; consequently, these strata have a unique potential to tell complex stories and to raise the difficult issue of what should be done with material culture associated with them.

The Great Arab Revolt Project (2005–2014)

The Great Arab Revolt Project (GARP) began in 2005 with a reconnaissance of southern Jordan followed by nine years of annual fieldwork mainly in the area stretching from Ma'an south to the border with Saudi Arabia – a distance of 113 km. While the original intention had been to investigate the damaged and mainly abandoned Hejaz Railway stations along this route, it soon became evident that there existed several previously unrecognized and undocumented landscapes in-between these stations and farther out in the desert.

The first of these was an unexpected and extraordinarily rich landscape composed of the remains of over 100 Ottoman tented campsites belonging to the railway battalion labourers who constructed the railroad in this area in 1905–1906 (Figure 6.1). To our knowledge, the existence of this wealth of early-twentieth-century archaeology – capturing the confrontation of tradition and modernity in an almost unknown region of the Middle East – is virtually unacknowledged even in the plentiful literature of the Hejaz Railway which itself hardly mentions the workers' everyday life (e.g. Tourret 1989; Nicholson 2005; Hülagü 2010; Özyüksel 2014). This multinational though mainly Syrian railway workforce left a unique archaeological signature as it moved south mainly following the earlier telegraph path which itself mainly followed that part of the

FIGURE 6.1   Bird's Nest Camp, an Ottoman Hejaz Railway construction camp show-ing a line of tent rings. (© Author.)

Ottoman *Darb al-Hajj al-Shami* pilgrimage route which extended from Damascus to Medina, but had never been investigated archaeologically. It was a unique but unknown landscape with no heritage status and thus completely unprotected.

The size and number of these construction-era campsites became a logistical challenge to GARP but survey and targeted excavation yielded insights into the later Arab Revolt as well as a wealth of material culture and understanding of the desert. Not least of these insights (only hinted at in the historical record) was that this construction landscape was also a conflict landscape – and for two reasons: first, it incorporated defensive features against a technologically low-level threat from the Bedouin between 1904 and 1916 and second because parts of it were briefly and sporadically incorporated into the Arab Revolt conflict landscape between 1916 and 1918.

This second (Arab Revolt) landscape was composed of defensive structures built by the Ottomans to protect the railway from Arab/British guerrilla attack during the Revolt. In some places, such as in Saudi Arabia where Bedouin hostility to the railway had always been more aggressive, this second landscape was amalgamated with the first, i.e. more trenches, more barbed wire, and more strong points. However, in our Jordanian study area, this second conflict landscape was more easily discernible as an anti-insurgency defensive network out in the desert. Its distinctive components included Ottoman Army camps, earth-work 'karakoll' strongpoints (Figure 6.2), trenches, machine-gun posts, small stone-built forts, and as mentioned above, occasional reuse of the earlier con-struction-era campsites. There were also British locations facilitating raids on the railway, and these included 'overnight' armoured car raiding camps, and

FIGURE 6.2   Ghadir al Haj Karakoll North 1; note the proximity to the railway above, and two rows of earlier construction camp tent rings to the right. (© APAAME_20151006_RHB-0179. Photographer Robert Bewley, courtesy of APAAME.)

short-lived advanced landing grounds (ALGs) used by the Royal Flying Corps/ Royal Air Force. Virtually none of the Ottoman or British sites belonging to this 1916–1918 conflict landscape were known or recognized before 2006.

In other words, the existence of two almost unknown landscapes and their material culture record were recognized, investigated, and thereby 'preserved/ curated' by GARP which would otherwise have been lost to looters, treasure hunters, and developers. In retrospect, it seems astonishing that there had been no archaeological intervention of this period in this area between 1919 and 2006, despite the events involving Emir Feisal, T.E. Lawrence, David Lean's later Hollywood version of the same, and even archaeological fieldwork in the same area focused on the Islamic heritage of the pre-railway Hajj route, and which on occasion involved some of the same buildings later repurposed between 1916 and 1918 (see below). The archaeology of these momentous events had entirely slipped through the net in the form of two important Jordanian heritage landscapes.

Already by 2005/2006, many station buildings and much associated infrastructure had been damaged or destroyed – the entire Ottoman station building at Batn al-Ghoul had disappeared, robbed for its ashlar stones at some point around 1970; not a single block survived at this easily accessible site. Other station buildings, such as those at Aqabat Hejazia and Wadi Rutm stations, had also

FIGURE 6.3 Wadi Rutm Station building; extensive damage has revealed the subterranean cistern. (© Author.)

been severely damaged, sometimes robbed for building materials and at other times bulldozed in efforts to discover 'Turkish Gold' believed to have been buried there (Figure 6.3).

It was clear that the desert was a museum of guerrilla warfare, and investigating the Arab Revolt would, in a sense, be curating the desert; the main sites were not traditional museums, nor even recognized or bounded open air ones, but rather abandoned and ruinous places (some known, many not). And so it was not possible easily to replicate innovative curatorial practices from elsewhere, where landscape could be brought within the museum via multimedia exhibits and the museum taken out into the landscape with GPS augmented-reality walks and associated activities (Stichelbaut et al 2021). These southern Jordanian desert places were the components of a hitherto undocumented conflict landscape which, over the intervening 100+ years, had become a complex palimpsest, its often-interleaving features identified and investigated by GARP's fieldwork. By 2014, it was possible to identify the following features:

- The pre-railway Hajj routeway and associated above and below ground features.
- The remains of original Hejaz Railway stations, embankment, and line, and over 100 tented construction camps built by and for the labour battalions who created the railroad and its infrastructure here in 1905–1906.
- Evidence of new Ottoman defensive counter-insurgency features at stations and in the landscape to counter the guerrilla threat of Arab/British raids after the 1917 fall of Aqaba.

- Evidence of destruction wrought on the above during the late Arab Revolt of 1917–1918.
- Remains of the short-lived reconstitution of the railway during the 1920s, followed by abandonment, removal and repurposing of some stretches of line from the 1930s to the 1960s.
- Evidence of the extensive but abortive refurbishment of parts of the railway during the mid-late 1960s, followed by a partial revamping of some sections in 1972 to take heavier phosphate trains to Aqaba (on a new stretch of line).
- The continuing destruction of buildings and landscape features from the 1970s to the present.

In a curatorial sense, it has been possible to identify, contextualize and give some interpretive structure to the physical remains of the Hejaz Railway from 1900 to the present between Ma'an and the border with Saudi Arabia. It is a valuable snapshot of the railway's cultural biography – an assessment too of immateriality, of what is now to a large extent desert-blown intangible heritage but previously was not. It stands on the edge of becoming. The small portable artefacts which were recovered between 2006 and 2014 have a more traditional curatorial home in the storerooms of the Department of Antiquities in Amman, though whether they occupy an acknowledged 'curatorial space' is another matter. Only slightly less expected are the ad hoc collections of Arab Revolt artefacts in local dwellings throughout the area; for example, collections of bullets, shrapnel balls and other objects kept in households near Ma'an Station. At the southern end of GARP's study area, at the Bedouin settlement of Mudawwara, it is less these small objects than the dwellings themselves which have preserved the railway infrastructure, as original Hejaz Railway Station buildings are now occupied by Bedouin families.

As GARP developed, it increasingly revealed the archaeological complexity of the Arab Revolt which lay at its heart. It soon became obvious that by reconnaissance and excavation, previous 'unknown' sites were being moved from invisibility to visibility and thus from the preservation offered by forgetfulness to the threatened status of the known/remembered. GARP research was 'creating' new heritage landscapes – or more accurately retrieving and giving shape and meaning to landscapes which had been selectively forgotten, at least in their material correlates. As Forty (1999: 9) observed of commemorative artefacts, 'they permit only certain things to be remembered, and by exclusion cause others to be forgotten'. For Darlington (2020: 197), the act of omission 'is the art of curation'. While the First World War and Arab Revolt are well remembered in Jordan, their landscapes are neither especially remembered nor given any commemorative value or salience. Harrison (2013: 591–592) makes a similar and perhaps more prescient point that 'Such traces might later re-emerge as a significant source of future collective memories'.

GARP was an interdisciplinary endeavour and thus located at the crossroads of different kinds of memory – Arab, Ottoman Turkish, Western technological/

imperial, military, cultural – and existing in oral tradition and literary forms. The single most influential source was, and arguably remains, T.E. Lawrence's 1926 *Seven Pillars of Wisdom*, which Lawrence himself admitted was a memory of a memory – written in 1919 from recall and notes, then lost, then rewritten from memory again and amended between late 1919 and 1922 (Lawrence 2003: 4; and see Saunders 2020: 234). Unsurprisingly, these events were remembered and interpreted differently in published Arab sources (e.g. Mousa 1966), but also in the oral tradition. GARP interviews recorded contrasting attitudes to Lawrence – pride in ancestors who rode with him during the Revolt, and contemptuous dismissal of his self-aggrandizing behaviour. These landscapes, therefore, embody contested memories by the Bedouin whose traditional lands they remain.

During the lifetime of the project, four issues emerged which intersected different aspects of the term 'curating'. First, was the ambiguous Ottoman attitude towards their empire's extraordinary archaeological heritage, alternating between modernizing, recognition and pride, and geographical ambivalence. Second, was the almost total absence of any archaeology of the First World War/ Arab Revolt before 2006, despite the Revolt's pivotal role in contributing to the Allied victory of 1918, the subsequent creation of the Syrian, Iraqi and Jordanian nations, and as the founding act of the latter's ruling Hashemite dynasty. Third, the absence of any proactive heritage activity aimed at protecting or rejuvenating the Hejaz Railway and its infrastructure for most of the route south from Ma'an to Mudawwara at a time of increased looting and destruction of visible remains. Fourth, was the realization that many if not most investigated sites would be in imminent danger of looting and damage as soon as the fieldwork season was over and so required total excavation wherever possible.

Ottoman attitudes

The Ottomans were apparently content to plunder parts of their empire's pre-Ottoman Islamic past by destroying, selling off, or exchanging objects large and small for European technologies (Shaw 2003: 133). Sultan Abdulhamid II's desire to finance the Hejaz Railway led to his sublimating the past to current political/geo-political considerations. This selective curatorial attitude to the empire's rich archaeological heritage is illustrated by the stripping of castles at Tripoli, Jaffa and elsewhere and by turning a blind eye to Hejaz Railway officials acquiring antiquities near Mada'in as-Salih. The most spectacular example of this saw the elaborate façade of the uncompleted Winter Palace of *Qasr Al-Mshatta* commissioned by the Ummayad Caliph Al-Walid II (CE 743-4) gifted to Germany's Kaiser Wilhelm II in 1903 and now displayed in Berlin's Pergamon Museum (Saunders 2020: 36). And all this occurred at a time of increasing general interest in the empire's pre-Islamic and Islamic past and the inauguration of the Imperial Museum in Constantinople in 1891 to house their remains (Çelik 2016: 35). Both these instances show, as Cornish (this volume) says, that museums are political spaces, whether they like it or not.

The key to understanding this apparent contradiction is that while there was a late nineteenth-century Ottoman policy to build a national archaeological heritage (Shaw 2003; Çelik 2016), the Arab provinces of the empire were not included in this process (Maffi 2009: 6–7). Even Islam's holy sites were not immune as shown by the conversion of the Prophet's Mosque in Medina to a munitions store, and demolition of the city's medieval buildings to make space for an extension of the Hejaz Railway to the mosque itself to remove the holy relics (Saunders 2020: 36–37).

An absent archaeology

The absence of any archaeological engagement with the Arab Revolt other than GARP is both easy and difficult to understand. While it might be thought that physical remains of the pivotal event which created the modern state of Jordan and its Hashemite dynasty would be highly valued, it is also the case that the nation's extraordinary archaeological remains (from prehistory to classical antiquity to the Islamic period) dominates archaeological research and funding. This is entangled in the complex relationships of how Jordanian archaeology has developed from late Ottoman to colonial then post-colonial times (Maffi 2009). One consequence of this is that there is no official/professional interest in investigating or curating the archaeological remains (objects and landscapes) of the struggle to create the modern nation, let alone a museum to hold such remains or specifically dedicated to commemorating the Revolt.[1]

Two other factors are at work here. First, is the attitude, dealt with several decades ago in Western Europe, that the First World War is too recent to benefit from archaeological investigation, especially given the wealth of available historical publications on the conflict in this region (e.g. al-Askari 2003; Barr 2006; Aksakal 2008; Rogan 2015). A recent survey of Jordanian archaeology (van der Steen 2019) fails even to mention the First World War or the Arab Revolt some 13 years after GARP began and started publishing its findings (e.g. Faulkner and Saunders 2009; Saunders and Faulkner 2010).

The second and related point is that the Jordanian authorities did not regard anything after 1750 CE as archaeological and therefore not covered by heritage legislation; it was only with the 2003 Interim Law No. (49) For the Protection of Urban and Architectural Heritage that legal protection was provided for post-1750 CE remains (Ha'obsh n.d.). In a country so rich with the archaeology of various millennia-and-centuries-old imperial presences, and whose own archaeological development has been influenced by British colonial and more recent Israeli influences (Maffi 2009: 26–27), there appears to be little space for the material remnants of its own struggle for national identity, despite the 'cultural heritage diversity of non-traditional tourist attractions … and [a] growing interest in the country to attract new categories of tourists to those attractions' (Ababneh et al 2016: 4).

FIGURE 6.4 Damaged wall of eighteenth-century Ottoman Fassu'ah Fort, repurposed during the Arab Revolt. (© Author.)

It is an interesting comment on archaeology itself that previous research has sometimes come extraordinarily close to discovering and investigating the First World War/Arab Revolt archaeological legacy as it interleaves with earlier more traditional kinds of archaeology in Jordan. Whether this was because the connections were simply missed or regarded as less important than the pre-twentieth-century focus of a particular investigation is difficult to say. It is certainly the case for example that important historical archaeology/Islamic archaeology research has been carried out along the already mentioned Darb al-Hajj al-Shami pilgrimage route which passes through GARP's study area (Petersen 2008, 2012). Despite this proximity which includes Arab Revolt-period features and Ottoman Hajj forts repurposed during the Revolt only occasional passing comments are made (Figure 6.4). Here and elsewhere, the search for earlier more traditional archaeological landscapes has led to the sublimation of the Arab Revolt conflict landscape despite its national importance.

No heritage, no protection?

The absence of any protection or rejuvenation of the railway sits awkwardly between the 2003 legal recognition of post-1750 CE remains as archaeological heritage, the popularity of the Hejaz Railway as a topic for heritage studies in academic circles (e.g. Eman 2005; Orbaşli and Woodward 2008; Abu Khafajah and Al Rabady n.d.), sporadic but potentially significant tourist interest, and occasional press statements concerning inter-governmental schemes between Jordan and Turkey (and sometimes Saudi Arabia) to rebuild or reconfigure the railway in whole or in part. In other words, talking about curating/preserving the multidimensional physical and cultural aspects of Jordan's past and pan-Islamism as embodied and symbolized by the Hejaz Railway has not been matched by any substantive physical actions (Saunders 2020: 52–54).

The only visible act of traditional curation and preservation in GARP's study area has been at Ma'an Station, where in 2006 there was a small and about-to-be-closed museum inside the fine Ottoman building built for Heinrich August Meissner, the German engineer tasked with constructing the Hejaz Railway – and hence often called 'Meissner's House'. The building was subsequently occupied by the then Prince Abdullah (later King Abdullah I) in 1920 as the centre of the first Jordanian government and known thereafter as Abdullah's Palace and more recently still as Ma'an Palace (Figure 6.5). In the 1990s, it opened as a

FIGURE 6.5 Ma'an Palace (Abdullah's Palace/Meissner's House) at Ma'an Station in 2006. (© Author.)

museum telling the story of Jordan's history from the Arab Revolt to the present. In 2003, it was announced that a 1.4 million US dollar renovation project had been authorized (CSBE 2003). By 2006, it was essentially a ground floor room with several old glass-topped display cases containing miscellaneous railway paraphernalia, several trench-art bracelets (made of artillery shell drivebands), photographs of Abdullah and his family, and a large 1918 Jordanian flag on the wall. The museum closed in 2007, and the renovation soon became the centre of a dispute over standards of work – it has not reopened since; the whereabouts and condition of its curated and possibly unique artefacts are unknown.

A less traditional curatorial act here was mainly symbolic and took place in 1926 when stones from Ma'an were used to build the exterior of Abdullah I's new Raghadan Palace in Amman (RP n.d.). Almost certainly this referenced the king's reuse of the Ottoman building at Ma'an Station. This symbolic curation is further marked in everyday transactions today as Ma'an Palace is depicted on the reverse of the Jordanian five dinar note, and Raghadan Palace on the reverse of the 50 dinar note. Ma'an town, Ma'an Station, and the Hejaz Railway coalesce historically and culturally to be of great significance to the Hashemite dynasty and the Jordanian state, yet the connecting thread of the railway remains in heritage limbo.

Elsewhere, the only kind of curation-preservation that has occurred was partial and coincidental, a by-product of plans for commerce not heritage. The first and most extensive example was a 1960s scheme to refurbish the railway line and infrastructure from Ma'an to Medina. The plan was ambitious, costed at £10 million over three years from 1966, financed by Syria, Jordan, and Saudi Arabia, with the contract awarded to a consortium of mainly British companies – 'The Hejaz Construction Company'. By 1967, the embankment and many bridges had been completed and 30 km of new track laid (Saunders 2020: 53) – which means that much of what GARP encountered dated to the 1960s not 1916–1918 (or even the 1920s). Less preservation than conservation, this rebuilding was an unusual kind of curation – saving original locations and some features but augmenting others into a hybrid reconstruction (Figure 6.6). GARP's archaeologists had to differentiate between original 1905–1906 construction of station buildings and infrastructure and their 1960s reconstruction faithfully carried out in accurate rebuilding – sometimes recycling original materials all similarly patinated by decades of desert sun.

The rebuilding project was abandoned after the 1967 Arab-Israeli 'Six Day War', with post-1970 damage to the refurbished buildings blending with Arab Revolt era damage to present a convincing but seriously misleading impression of continuity and survival. In some ways, the refurbished buildings and track would have been fake heritage, and certainly the passage of time (some 40+ years) plus added destruction suggests that fake heritage accrues value. The problem is that with no indication that many of these structures are damaged 1960s-rebuilds 'temporal amnesia ... can muddy the boundaries of authenticity' (Darlington 2020: 211, 215).

FIGURE 6.6 The Blockhouse; construction phase (1905–1906) railway defence showing clear signs of major 1960s reconstruction and subsequent damage. (© Author.)

The second example was a commercial development between Ma'an and Batn al-Ghoul; this saw the reconfiguration of this stretch of railway line and embankment from 1972 to take the heavier phosphate trains travelling from El Hasa Station (north of Ma'an) and a purpose-built separate extension to the ruinous original Aqabat Hejazia Station down to Aqaba (the 116-km Batn al-Ghoul to Aqaba stretch did not exist before this time) (Figures 6.7 and 6.8). This continued

FIGURE 6.7 Modern phosphate train on the strengthened/reconfigured rail and embankment section near Batn al-Ghoul in 2008. (© Author.)

FIGURE 6.8 Excavation of ruinous remains of Aqabat Hejazia Station adjacent to revamped railway with new facility for phosphate trains in the background. (© Author.)

use of part of the original Hejaz Railway route has in a sense preserved its progress through this ancient landscape, though has not protected many of the stations and structures flanking that route, such as the 'Round Fort' investigated by GARP in 2011, and which has been severely damaged by bulldozing (Figure 6.9) (Saunders 2020: 124–126). It is worth emphasizing that various Hejaz Railway/ Arab Revolt features associated with this still operating stretch of the railway are as likely to be damaged or destroyed as the more remote ones dealt with below. Ironically, while the Batn al-Ghoul to Aqaba line dates only to 1972 and was never part of the Hejaz Railway, today as it passes by Wadi Rum it hosts the area's only heritage/tourist activity – 'The Great Arab Revolt Show' which recreates a 1916 Bedouin attack on a train (Saunders 2020: 54). Nearby, at the village of Disi, the site of a short-lived Royal Flying Corps Advanced Landing Ground, there is the small privately run 'Laurence Museum', full of a locally curated miscellany of Arab Revolt and other memorabilia.

Another example has seen a degree of curation/preservation by virtue of abandonment and forgetfulness along the original route from Batn al-Ghoul to Mudawwara and beyond to the border with Saudi Arabia. This stretch of line preserves the course of the embankment laid out by Meissner's Ottoman labour battalions in 1905–1906 to a considerable degree, despite having its railway lines and sleepers removed after 1925, partly by locals as building material, and then by Australian troops in 1941 during the Second World War to build a new (and subsequently abandoned) extension line to Naqb Ashtar/Ras en Naqb. And this stretch of the embankment and building infrastructure saw significant rebuilding during the 1960s refurbishment as well.

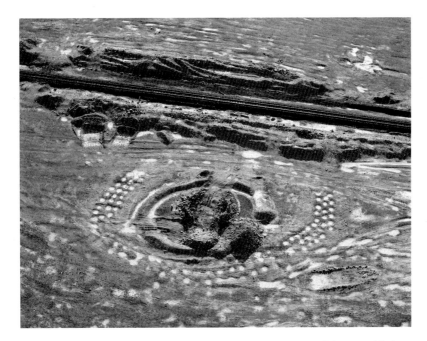

FIGURE 6.9 The Round Fort, showing heavy recent (2012) bulldozer gold-digging damage, and the Arab Revolt-era defensive 'wolf pits'. (© APAAME_20151006_ RIIB-0114. Photographer Robert Bewley, courtesy of APAAME.)

A curious fate awaited the rail track and wooden and metal sleepers removed by locals inasmuch as they formed a new vernacular architecture – reused as beams to reinforce house walls and roofs and as fence posts to demarcate gardens and land (Figure 6.10) (Saunders 2020: 51). In 2006 and 2007 there were still backyards full of such original Hejaz Railway materials for sale across the area – this whole phenomenon being another unusual kind of curation. The removal of such economically useful and recyclable material led to a forgetting (and hence protection) of the embankment itself, and fortuitously also of the 'unknown' Ottoman defensive features beyond the stations – the extensive counter-insurgency landscape discovered and investigated by GARP between 2006 and 2014. In some of these previously unknown military sites, there was an intriguing kind of impromptu curation where Ottoman troops, cast adrift in hostile and remote locations, picked up prehistoric tools and other items, moved them around (presumably as curiosities), then abandoned them inside the defensive site they had manned.

Increasingly, however, these comparatively isolated parts of the railway south of Batn al-Ghoul to the Saudi border are afflicted by opportunistic looting as well as more serious damage. As this remote part of Jordan has attracted more attention, the long abandoned ruinous stations and nearby sites have suffered accordingly, and the protection hitherto offered by remoteness, a lack of useful

FIGURE 6.10   Reuse of Hejaz Railway steel sleepers as gate posts in 2006. (© Author.)

raw materials, and forgetfulness has been replaced by economic opportunities and the ever present though misguided lure of 'Turkish gold'. In 2009, a one-billion US$project was begun in this remote area. The 'Disi Water Conveyance Project' pipes water from the Qa-Disi aquifer north to Amman and runs parallel to the Hejaz Railway line at several points in the GARP study area. Problems concerning local employment issues led to social unrest and several fatalities, with one of the work camps located just a few hundred metres from several key Arab Revolt sites. Ironically, part of the pipeline work was awarded to a Turkish company and so after 100 years, Turks were once again digging trenches in southern Jordan (Saunders 2020: 335 n.86). The main point, however, is that the presence of a workforce in a remote area and in proximity to Hejaz Railway sites, however ruinous, can lead to intentional and unintentional damage to natural and cultural heritage.

Preservation by record

In light of the above, it was evident that preservation by record was the only way in which the First World War/Arab Revolt in this region could be recognized, systematically investigated, interpreted, and curated. While much damage had been done to the known station sites in the preceding decades, it was also the case that the presence of foreign archaeologists over succeeding years signposted new areas for local interest. Preservation by record was also vital because of the realization, mentioned above, that there were several landscapes involved: the well-known Hejaz Railway line embankment (its stations and infrastructure), a hardly acknowledged but extensive railway construction landscape in-between the stations, and nested within these two landscapes, a hitherto largely unrecognized third and later landscape of First World War/Arab Revolt guerrilla warfare, often ephemeral and sometimes distant from the railway itself.

The 'new' sites of the construction landscape were numerous and often sizeable, offering unique insights into the distinctive social archaeology of labour gangs and construction teams in an inhospitable environment at the beginning of the twentieth century. Widespread ignorance of their existence had been a powerful protection. Quite different were the 'new' sites of the Arab Revolt landscape (and their imagined relationship with Turkish gold) that were in imminent danger of being lost almost immediately after their discovery unless investigated in their totality. The desert has eyes, and we knew that our presence and activities in certain locations were observed by those we could not see.

Equally significant, and another, juxtaposing, way of looking at the same data, was to see the area as composed of two distinct twentieth-century conflict landscapes. Their existence was but faintly hinted at in the literature on the Hejaz Railway but was becoming ever more apparent in investigating the physical remains in the desert. The first of these was part of the pre-1914 railway-construction-era landscape where defences were slight and few and far between and aimed only at deterring occasional attacks by Bedouin armed with muskets. In our area, these modest defences dated to around 1905–1906 and included designed-in loopholes for rifles in some station buildings, and a single blockhouse out in the desert between Bir Shedia and Aqabat Hejazia stations (Saunders 2020: 113–116). The second conflict landscape was characterized by more frequent and substantial defences belonging to the Arab Revolt of 1916–1918 and designed to counter Arab-British guerrilla attacks featuring modern rifles, machine guns, artillery, armoured cars, and aircraft. These landscapes, each representing a social-technological-military 'world' of its own, were interleaved with each other in different locations – recognizing and interpreting their interrelationships was a vital step in considering how they might be understood and thereby more accurately curated.

It is worth stating here that further south, in what today is Saudi Arabia, the pre-1914 situation was somewhat different. As noted above, Bedouin hostility towards the railway had been more aggressive in this area, and the Ottomans fortified stations (or reinforced existing pre-railway Hajj forts) to such an extent that Major Arthur J B Wavell, cousin of the later Field Marshal Earl Wavell, who was travelling on the railway in 1908, observed that 'All the stations south of Medain Salih are fortified with trenches and barbed wire' (Wavell 1912: 58). In our study area, however, this seems not to have been the case until after the Arab Revolt was launched in 1916.

For GARP, preservation by record involved three stages: first, recording and targeted excavation of well-known existing features – mainly stations – some long abandoned and ruinous, others revamped as working locations; second, reconnaissance fieldwalking of the 113-km railway route from Ma'an to Mudawwara, following up Bedouin information, and rapid survey and selective excavation of discovered sites (i.e. construction-era campsites and Arab Revolt-era sites); third, speculative/intuitive exploration (often far from the railway) based mainly on accessing archive sources (documents and photographs) combined with Google Earth imagery and applications, and followed by survey and excavation of discovered sites. The most significant result of this stage was the 2012 discovery (and subsequent investigation) of two ephemeral British armoured car raiding campsites known as Tooth Hill Camp 1 and 2 (Saunders 2020: 184–192).

The result of these investigations contributed to two distinct kinds of curation. First, was a comprehensive listing, mapping, and selective excavation of twentieth-century sites in this part of southern Jordan – many of which were previously 'unknown' and an increasing number of which are either no longer extant or are heavily damaged. The material culture from these investigations was deposited with the Department of Antiquities in Amman. In other words, GARP discovered, investigated, and gave transdisciplinary analytical shape and correlative historical detail to several twentieth-century landscapes created by the Hejaz Railway and the Arab Revolt, and embedded within a millennia-old cultural landscape with which it sometimes intersected. These investigations created a body of knowledge concerning the Arab Revolt which had not existed before; they supplemented and enriched a sporadic (mainly British military) archival record; and they revealed connections with the archaeologies of earlier historic and prehistoric periods.

Second, was a more traditional museum-based curation, the 18-month-long exhibition, *Shifting Sands: Lawrence of Arabia and the Great Arab Revolt*, held at the National Civil War Centre, Newark, UK, from October 2016 to March 2018 (Figure 6.11). This exhibition provided an opportunity to bring together objects

FIGURE 6.11   The *Shifting Sands* exhibition at Newark, 2016–2018. (© Author.)

directly from our desert investigations and exhibit them alongside better known and more famous items and thereby breathe new curatorial life and understanding into all.

Conclusion

Curating a palimpsestic conflict landscape little known archaeologically before 2005 was and remains a complex challenge for many reasons discussed above. This landscape is also, in part, embedded within an oral tradition regarded variously as folklore and mythology and is permeated by stories of buried gold and influenced by tales (true and false) of T.E. Lawrence. It is also the quintessential Arab Revolt landscape of the origins of the Hashemite Kingdom of Jordan. This is an extraordinary and volatile mix of issues, yet the landscape has not attracted any sustained contemporary/conflict archaeological interest beyond the investigations of GARP, and despite its potential for various kinds of structured (and mainly eco-friendly) tourism and cultural heritage management.

One consequence of this during GARP investigations was that well-known and newly discovered sites had to be investigated and documented rapidly because of the threat of looting, mining, opportunistic souveniring, and economic development. GARP, designed initially to investigate the ruined station landscapes of the Hejaz Railway from Ma'an to Mudawwara, had to rapidly reconfigure to include and investigate/curate a large and unexpected heritage landscape – composed of several landscapes nested within one another.

However, preservation by record depends on understanding what is being preserved. It is all too easy to regard that which is being investigated is that which is sought. Several GARP examples illustrate the point. Large campsites composed of parallel rows of tent rings initially were seen as Ottoman Army locations sited in the desert to protect against Arab-British guerrilla attacks in 1916–1918. It soon became evident that these were railway construction camps not Arab Revolt-period Ottoman Army camps (neither of which had been investigated before); here was a vast and unexpected 1905–1906 construction-era landscape and one which had its own conflict component in minimal defences against a low-level Bedouin threat.

The Hejaz Railway embankment and its often-ruinous buildings provided more insight as they seemed like century-old survivors of the Arab Revolt. Nothing could have been further from the truth. Along different sections of the railway, the embankment had been straightened and strengthened in order to take heavier phosphate trains since 1972, and many Ottoman railway buildings and bridges had been (sometimes substantially) rebuilt during a (subsequently abandoned) 1960s refurbishment project. Their damaged appearance by 2005 was not a fortuitous survival of the Arab Revolt of 1916–1918 but the result of far more recent gold-digging and robbing for building materials during the 1970s and 1980s. Here, GARP investigations were preserving/curating contemporary landscapes of rebuilding and looting only a few decades old.

This landscape was a true palimpsest – a twentieth-century interleaving of mainly conflict-driven elements incorporating pre-1900 Ottoman historical landscapes themselves embedded within an earlier Islamic Hajj routeway, which itself is traceable back to Byzantine and Roman/Nabatean spice and slave routes, and back even further to prehistoric times. What has been curated, by reconnaissance, discovery, survey, excavation, and analysis, is a rich and hitherto largely unrecognized multi-layered landscape – itself but a small part of a much larger routeway landscape from Damascus to Medina, and indeed beyond.

Note

1 The 100th anniversary of the Arab Revolt was commemorated in Amman in 2016. While there is currently no archaeological presence of the Revolt in any Jordanian museum, the Martyrs' Memorial and Museum in Amman has a display of some Arab Revolt memorabilia, and in the Great Arab Revolt Hall of the Royal Tank Museum, also in Amman, there is a panorama showing a replica Rolls Royce Armoured Car against a painted desert scene of the Revolt (Winterburn 2013).

References

Ababneh, A., F.M. Darabseh and A.S. Aloudat. (2016) The management of natural and cultural heritage: a comparative study from Jordan. *The Historic Environment: Policy & Practice* 7(1):3–24. DOI: 10.1080/17567505.2016.1142686

Abu Khafajah, S. and R. Al Rabady. (n.d.) *The Hijazi Railroad Line: A Cultural Landscape of a World Heritage Quality.* Available on Academia.edu, at http://www.academia.edu/1219541/The_Hijazi_Railline_a_cultural_landscape_with_world_heritage_quality. [Accessed 21 April 2014].

Aksakal, M. (2008) *The Ottoman Road to War in 1914: The Ottoman Empire and the First World War.* Cambridge: Cambridge University Press.

al-Askari, J.P. (2003) *A Soldier's Story: from Ottoman rule to independent Iraq.* London: Arabian Publishing.

Barr, J. (2006) Setting the Desert on Fire: T. E. Lawrence and Britain's secret war in Arabia, 1916–1918. London: Bloomsbury.

Çelik, Z. (2016) *About Antiquities: Politics of Archaeology in the Ottoman Empire.* Austin (TX): University of Texas Press.

CSBE. (2003) New Commissions for September 2003. Renovation of the Founding King's Palace in Ma'an. *Centre for the Study of the Built Environment,* July–December. https:www.csbe.org/2003-2 [Accessed 14 June 2021].

Darlington, J. (2020) *Fake Heritage.* London: Yale University Press.

Desfossés, Y., A. Jacques and G. Prilaux. (2008) *L'archéologie de la Grande Guerre.* Rennes: Éditions Ouest-France.

Eman, A. (2005) The dynamic of linear settings: The Hijaz Railroad. *Monuments and Sites in Their Setting – conserving cultural heritage in changing townscapes and landscapes,* pp 839–843. Proceedings of ICOMOS 15th General Assembly and Scientific Symposium, 17–21 October 2005, Xi'an, China. http://openarchive.icomos.org/id/eprint/411 [Accessed 21 April 2014].

Faniel, I.M., S. Whitcher, E. Kansa, J. Jacobs, and P. France. (2020) Identifying opportunities for collective curation during archaeological excavations. *International Journal of Digital Curation* 15 (1):1–13.

Faulkner, N., and N.J. Saunders. (2009) War without frontiers: The archaeology of the Great Arab Revolt. In B. Peacock (ed.), *The Frontiers of the Ottoman World*, pp 431–451. Proceedings of the British Academy 156. Oxford: Oxford University Press.

Forty, A. (1999) Introduction. In A. Forty and S. Küchler (eds.), *The Art of Forgetting*, pp 1–18. Oxford: Berg.

Foyle, J. (2015) Is it time to rethink our ideas about preserving world heritage? Financial Times website https://www.ft.com/content/545458d4-fae9-11e4-9aed-00144feab7de [Accessed 25 April 4 2018.

Ha'obsh, M. (n.d.) Cultural Heritage in the Hashemite Kingdom of Jordan. http://culturalheritage.ceistorvergata.it/Participant_Contribution/Cultural_Heritage_in_Jordan_CH.pdf [Accessed 19 May 2018].

Harrison, R. (2013) Forgetting to remember, remembering to forget: late modern heritage practices, sustainability and the 'crisis' of accumulation of the past. *International Journal of Heritage Studies* 19 (6):579–595.

Huggett, J. (2015) Preservation by record. *Introspective Digital Archaeology*. Available at introspectivedigitalarchaeology.com/2015/05/25presewervation-by-record/ [Accessed 1 May 2018].

Hülagü, M.M. (2010) *The Hejaz Railway: The Construction of a New Hope*. New York: Blue Dome.

Jones, C.W. (2018) Understanding ISIS's destruction of antiquities as a rejection of nationalism. *Journal of Eastern Mediterranean Archaeology & Heritage Studies* 6 (1–2):31–58.

Lawrence, T.E. (2003) *Seven Pillars of Wisdom, a triumph. The Complete 1922 Text*. (Second edition with amendments. Jeremy and Nicole Wilson). Fordingbridge: Castle Hill Press.

Loe, L., C. Barker, K. Brady, M. Cox, and H. Webb. (2014) *Remember Me to All: The Archaeological Recovery and Identification of Soldiers Who Fought and Died in the Battle of Fromelles, 1916*. Oxford: Oxford Archaeology.

Maffi, I. (2009) The emergence of cultural heritage in Jordan: The itinerary of a colonial invention. *Journal of Social Archaeology* 9 (1):5–35.

MoD/VUK. (Ministry of Defence and Veterans UK). (2019) Burial of 13 WW1 soldiers brings closure to crowdfunded archaeological project. https://www.gov.uk/government/news/burial-of-13-world-war-one-soldiers-brings-closure-to-crowdfunded-archaeological-project.

Mousa, S. (1966) *T.E. Lawrence: An Arab View*. London: Oxford University Press.

Nicholson, J. (2005) *The Hejaz Railway*. London: Stacey International.

Orbaşli, A., and S. Woodward. (2008) A Railway 'Route' as a Linear Heritage Attraction: The Hijaz Railway in the Kingdom of Saudi Arabia. *Journal of Heritage Tourism* 3 (3): 159–175.

Özyüksel, M. (2014) *The Hejaz Railway and the Ottoman Empire: Modernity, Industrialisation and the Ottoman Decline*. London: I.B. Tauris.

PAP (The Plugstreet Archaeological Project). (2010) The Funeral of Pte. A.J. Mather. http://www.plugstreet-archaeology.com/burialajmather.php [Accessed 1 January 2014].

Petersen, A. (2008) The Ottoman hajj route in Jordan: Motivation and Ideology. *Bulletin d'études orientales, Supplement LVII*: 31–50.

———. (2012) *The Medieval and Ottoman Hajj Route in Jordan: An Archaeological and Historical Study*. Oxford: Oxbow.

Rogan, E. (2015) *The Fall of the Ottomans: The Great War in the Middle East*, 1914–1920. London: Allen Lane.

RP (n.d.) *The Royal Palaces*. Raghadan Palace. http:www.kinghussein.gov.jo/royal_palaces.html [Accessed 12 June 2021].

Saunders, N.J. (2007) *Killing Time: Archaeology and the First World War*. Stroud: Sutton Publishing.

———. (2020) *Desert Insurgency: Archaeology, T.E. Lawrence and the Arab Revolt*. Oxford: Oxford University Press.

Saunders, N.J. and N. Faulkner. (2010). Fire on the Desert: Conflict Archaeology and the Great Arab Revolt in Southern Jordan 1916-1918. *Antiquity* 84 (324):514–527.

Shaw, W.M.K. (2003) *Possessors and Possessed: Museums, Archaeology, and the Vizualization of History in the Late Ottoman Empire*. Berkeley: University of California Press.

Stichelbaut, B. (ed.) (2018) *Traces of War: The Archaeology of the First World War*. Veurne: Hannibal Publishing.

Stichelbaut, B., G. Plets, and K. Reeves. (2021) Towards an inclusive curation of WWI heritage: integrating historical aerial photographs, digital museum applications and landscape markers in "Flanders Fields" (Belgium). *Journal of Cultural Heritage Management and Sustainable Development* (online). http://hdl.handle.net/1854/LU-8683291

Tourret, R. (1989) *Hedjaz Railway*. Abingdon: Tourret Publishing.

Van der Steen, E. (2019) The archaeology of Jordan: A condensed history. *Journal of Eastern Mediterranean Archaeology and Heritage Studies* 7 (2):149–164.

Wavell, A.J.B. (1912) *A Modern Pilgrim in Mecca and a Siege in Sanaa*. London: Constable.

Westcott, T. (2020) *Destruction or Theft? Islamic State, Iraqi Antiquities and Organized Crime*. Geneva: Global Initiative Against Transnational Organized Crime.

Winterburn, J.B. (2013) Sarh Al-Shaheed, the Martyrs' memorial and Museum. *Military History Matters* 34 (June): 66–67.

Zalewska, A.I., and J. Czarnecki. (2021) Conflict gas-scape: Chemical weapons on the Eastern Front, January 1915. In N.J. Saunders and P. Cornish (eds.), *Conflict Landscapes: Materiality and Meaning in Contested Places*, pp 66–84. London: Routledge.

7

CONFLICT LANDSCAPE AS MUSEUM AND MEMORIAL

The Walk of Peace from the Alps to the Adriatic

Željko Cimprić

Introduction

On 24 May 1915, when the army of the Kingdom of Italy attacked the Austro-Hungarian army from the Swiss border to the Adriatic, the First World War had been raging for 10 months across the Balkans, Eastern Europe and the Western Front. For the Austro-Hungarian army this meant moving part of its strength to a third, south-western, front, with the limited objective of merely stopping the attackers and preventing them from moving further into the monarchy. In the north, defensive positions ran for 500 km over Alpine peaks, while in the east, they stretched across the Julian Alps for over 90 km and along the state border all the way to the Adriatic Sea. Austrian territory on the right bank of the river Soča (It. Isonzo) was abandoned to the attackers without a fight. The only exceptions were a bridgehead defending the city of Gorizia in the south, along with a smaller bridgehead in the lee of the mountains near the town of Tolmin further north, which defended vital road and rail communications running behind the front and into the Austrian interior.

The nature of this front called for a different way of fighting than that which prevailed on the lowland plains and farmland that characterized most of the Eastern and Western fronts. A century later we still talk about a battlefield 'carved in stone', telling the stories of mountain warfare. The entry of Italy into the war was most welcome to the *Entente* partners, Britain and France, who had offered much to persuade it to join them. Nevertheless, this aspect of the war tended to be overshadowed by events on other battlefields, despite a comparable slaughter occurring there. The Italian army battered itself against the Austro-Hungarian line of the Soča/Isonzo, but after 29 months and 11 bloody offensives, it failed to achieve any strategically important progress. Compared to the others, this was the most static battlefield of all (Schindler 2001; Thompson 2008; Macdonald and Cimprić 2011).

DOI: 10.4324/9781003263531-10

After the war, the territory of the former Soča/Isonzo Front became part of Italy, which celebrated victory in the 'fourth war for the unification of Italy'. This set the scene for the preservation and creation of collective memory and ultimately also Italian national identity. The process was strongly encouraged by the Italian establishment and was taken to new heights after the establishment of Mussolini's Fascist regime. A nationalistic and heroic interpretation of the Great War was central to the Fascist world-view (Cornish 2018: 227–228). By contrast, the defeated protagonist, Austria-Hungary, had collapsed, leading to a redrawing of the map of Europe. For the new nations that arose from the wreck of the Haspburg Empire, the war might have been the catalyst for their independent existence, but it was not *their* war (Gerwarth 2017: 187–198; Cornish and Saunders 2019: xviii). Focused on creating new political and social structures, while dealing with internal disorder and border conflicts, they had no time to reminisce about the world war. This was particularly true of the country that now bordered Italy to the east – the Kingdom of Serbs, Croats and Slovenes (Gerwarth 2017: 195–198). Only two decades later, another war would be followed by even more radical political changes.

Remembering War and the Kobarid Museum

Great differences in the way the First World War was remembered in the decades after the end of the Second World War are manifested by history schoolbooks from the three neighbouring countries on the territory of the former battlefield. In Italy, this subject received considerable attention. In Austria, school books included at least some basic information about war events. By contrast, in some Slovene school books, the Soča/Isonzo Front and the battlefield in the Alps were not even mentioned (in the Federal Republic of Yugoslavia, the school system was in the remit of each republic). To this day, it is impossible to find street signs in Slovenia commemorating these important historical events, which took place on what is now Slovenian national territory and involved (among others) Slovene participants. Despite such disregard for this chapter of history, memory lived on in many local families and every few years a book of war veteran's memoirs appeared (e.g. Matičič 1922; Prešeren 2014). Certain individuals felt indebted to a generation that had effectively been deprived of a voice and launched private initiatives to preserve the memory of the events in which that generation had taken part.

An early and ambitious initiative of this kind was former Austrian army colonel Walther Schaumann's effort to create a 'Walk of Peace' in the Italian Dolomite mountains during the 1970s. Volunteers from Austria and neighbouring countries cleaned some 300 km of military roads over 25 years and eventually moved their activities eastwards to the Carnic Alps. In Slovenia, the first large temporary exhibition on the First World War in the region was organized in 1989 by Drago Sedmak, a custodian of the Museum of Nova Gorica. In the same year, preparations for a museum exhibition in Kobarid (Caporetto) also got underway. The idea, initiative and leadership came from a single person – the amateur historian Zdravko Likar, who was striving to make Kobarid better known to the wider public as a town of historic importance. People welcomed this initiative, feeling a sense of duty to their forefathers – the long-suppressed stories of combatants of the Great War. The museum opened its doors on 20 October 1990 after one year of preparation, which included building work as well as creating the exhibition, in which the author of this paper was involved. It presented the public with the story of mountain warfare and the battle of Kobarid, best known to the international public from Ernest Hemingway's 1929 novel *A Farewell to Arms*.

The independence process that was gathering momentum in Slovenia at the time did not interfere with or influence the museum project. Moreover, the concept of the permanent exhibition put no special emphasis on any Slovene elements, and we wondered at the beginning whether this would provoke any criticism; perhaps surprisingly, it didn't. The entire museum story focuses on the description of mountain warfare on the Soča/Isonzo Front and on the experience of all combatants, without characterizing them as 'good guys' or 'bad guys'. This interpretation of events – the absence of chauvinism and bias – earned the Museum the highest museum prize in Slovenia in 1992, and a year later, the Council of Europe Museum Prize for 1993 (KM n.d.). As a museum on a former battlefield, its activity gradually expanded out into the surrounding environment. Initially, two cannon and the remains of a truck were placed along the roads near the town entrance: the remains of weapons pushed into the river by the Italian soldiers who found their path blocked by a damaged bridge during the retreat from the battle of Kobarid in October 1917. Along with new signposts with the town's name in three languages (Kobarid, Caporetto and Karfreit), this gave the visitors an impression of Kobarid as a place of historic importance.

In its first decade, the museum protected several high-altitude remains in the mountains and cleaned and renovated Italian Army trenches on Kolovrat Mountain, where an open-air museum was established (Košir et al 2019). In the vicinity of Kobarid, the Kobarid Historical Trail was established, following a circular route on either side of the river Soča. To this purpose, a suspension bridge was built on the same site where the Italian army had built one to connect with their bridgehead position in Kobarid. Interest in the former Soča/Isonzo Front was now growing, and similar activities were initiated by individuals and groups elsewhere in the area of the former battle-zone. In many cases, the interventions were not set up and carried out in an appropriate or professional way, and, most seriously, there was a lack of connection and cooperation between the various initiatives.

It became obvious that the museum would not be able to fulfill its ambition of expanding its activity to a wider area with only the income from entrance tickets and its own limited resources. These circumstances led the museum's founder, Zdravko Likar, to envision an institution that would connect and harmonize all these activities, while also acting as a study centre. Despite the already established use of the phrase by the 'Friends of the Dolomites' (Fod n.d.), he named the project the *Walks of Peace in Posočje Foundation* and convinced the Slovenian government to officially validate the creation of the project under this name on 21 September 2000. It was based on a national and international level within the remit of five government ministries. Three months later, the Foundation was set up and headquartered in Kobarid adjacent to the museum. Its main objective was the preservation, renovation, and presentation of the Soča Front heritage.

The Walk of Peace

In the following years, the Foundation cooperated with amateur societies to organize parts of the former battle-zone into so-called 'open-air museums' and to clean and renovate various monuments and sites of memory. In the early summer of 2007, a 110-km Walk of Peace was inaugurated in the upper Soča valley. The walk was split into five sections, allowing visitors to take one-day tours. The entire length of the walk connects six open-air museum along with 25 monuments and sites of memory. Public reaction was very positive. Slovenian municipalities in the central and southern part of the former battlefield and the neighbouring Italian authorities were all interested in preserving and presenting the remains of the Great War in their territories in the same way. In 2011, a three-year international Slovenian-Italian project was initiated to extend the Walk of Peace southwards all the way to the Adriatic Sea. The Foundation was the initiator, coordinator and organizer of the project, and the presidents of Slovenia and Italy visited the area and became its patrons.

The formal inauguration of the 'Walk of Peace from the Alps to the Adriatic' took place in 2015, on Europe Square between the Italian town of Gorizia and its Slovenian counterpart Nova Gorica. A year later, the Walk was added to the UNESCO tentative list of intangible cultural heritage as part of First World War heritage. The entire length of the Walk, from its northernmost point to the southernmost one in the city of Trieste, is divided into 15 sections (Figure 7.1). The first five are in the mountains of the Upper Soča valley, the next three run across the hills to the towns of Gorizia and Nova Gorica, while the last seven sections cross the Karst plateau all the way to the sea. The Upper Soča valley sections have been well visited and appropriately marked for over 10 years. In the central and southern parts, the standards are somewhat different, mainly as a result of the Walk running near roads and not as a trail in open country. Visitors can orientate themselves with the help of brochures, specialized maps and a guide published by the Foundation (Koren 2008). The keenest visitors walk the entire route, section by section, although most prefer to drive between the various 'points of interest'. The level of organization or renovation of the different open-air museums, cemeteries and battlefield sites varies greatly, depending largely on the degree of motivation of the local authorities. Specifically, numerous administrative hurdles have presented themselves on Italian territory.

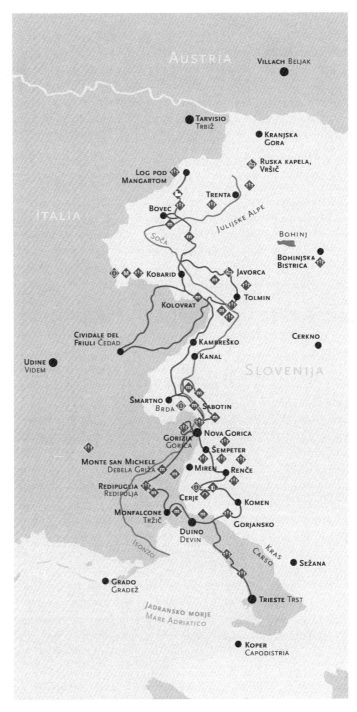

FIGURE 7.1 Map of The Walk of Peace. (© Pot Miru/Walks of Peace in the Soča Region Foundation.)

In the north, the Walk starts in the village of Log Pod Mangartom, next to the tunnel which was used for water drainage from the Cave di Predil lead mine. The Austro-Hungarian army used the mine elevators and the tunnel to provision its units, as the Italians had blocked the road over the Predel pass with artillery fire. In front of the tunnel entrance is a large cemetery, where the men who fought on the mountain of Rombon and in the Bovec area are buried. The Walk follows the creek of Koritnica along its right bank, to the two fortifications at the bottom of the mountain and down towards the Bovec basin. On Ravelnik hill near Bovec, the local historic society cleaned up the positions of Austro-Hungarian units, who maintained a defensive posture here from August 1915 until the final battle at the end of October 1917 (Figure 7.2). Above the village of Kal-Koritnica, visitors can climb the remains of a small Austro-Hungarian artillery fortification, with beautiful views over the Bovec basin and the neighbouring mountains. The trail then continues across the suspension bridge to the left bank of the Soča river, with the second and third sections requiring some experience of mountain hiking on the part of its visitors. It runs mainly along military provision paths to the rear of the nearby front line. Ambitious walkers can, with additional time and effort, use it as a starting point for the ascent to the trenches, artillery positions and other preserved structures.

Between the Bovec basin and the valley near Kobarid lies the next open-air museum, a well-fortified system of Italian Army trenches. The Italians were only able to complete such extensive work after building a military mountain road, which walkers can now use to walk down to the village of Dreznica and further down into the valley to Kobarid. Here they can find extensive information

FIGURE 7.2 Ravelnik open-air museum near Bovec, reconstructed Austro-Hungarian line. (© N.J. Saunders.)

FIGURE 7.3 The 'Bes' Chapel on Mt Planica, built in memory of Italian soldiers who died. (© Author.)

about the entire Walk of Peace and the related historical events at the Foundation headquarters and in the Kobarid museum. Naturally, many people visit both of these institutions before starting their visit to the various sections of the path or to the surrounding mountains. The walk continues along the Kobarid historic path up to the Italian ossuary of fallen soldiers, then on the left bank of the Soča river, turning back up towards Dreznica in the area of the Kobarid bridgehead. From here on, the supply roads of the Italian army lead to the ridges of the second defence line, the so-called 'line of defence at any cost' (*La linea della difesa ad oltranza*). This line ran from the top of the highest surrounding mountain, Mt. Krn (2244 m), to the Soča river valley. Along the road stands the 'Bes' chapel, built by members of the Italian mountain corps during the war (Figure 7.3) and restored in 1996 and 2003.

To the East, under the southern slopes of the Krn mountain range, the path descends over mountain pastures to a *rifugio* where mountaineers can find food and shelter in the summertime. This is the starting point for visits to the high-mountain battlefield, stretching 1,000 m higher over the mountains of Krn and Batognica. In these mountains, men's lives were in constant danger not only from deadly weapons, but also from mighty forces of nature which, over two long winters, brought seven to eight metres of snow. Italian supply roads, built for transport with mules, lead up to the former battlefield, while the Walk of Peace continues lower, across mountain pastures up to Mount Mrzli Vrh, which was the most infamous of all mountain battlefields. Italian units engaged in uphill attacks over the course of 29 months suffered terrible losses. In some places, the opponent's trenches were little more than 10 m away. There is an open-air museum in this area, in the format of a circular path and renovated caverns.

A visit to this mountain completes the highest part of the Walk, which then continues towards the sea over lower ridges and plains, running down the valley only in certain points near Tolmin and the Gorizia area. One such descent is in the former Austro-Hungarian rear area in the valley of Tolminka, where hikers are in for an impressive surprise. On a hill about 100 m above the valley stands the commemorative church of the Holy Spirit, built by members of the Austro-Hungarian mountain brigade over eight months in 1916, based on plans by the Viennese architect Remigius Geyling. The Art Nouveau style church in is built on stone foundations and preserves the names of 2,565 fallen soldiers, burnt into large oak panels opening from the internal walls like pages of an enormous book (Figure 7.4). The external wooden walls display coats of arms of the 20 Austro-Hungarian regions, while the bell tower is decorated with a sun dial and the inscription 'Pax'. The paintings in the interior and colourful stained glass windows present a wonderful subject for hikers with a passion for photography. With a wooden structure to maintain, the church has been renovated several times over the past century. A witness to this is a memorable inscription added by the Italian authorities after the 1934 renovation 'Hatred does not reach beyond the ashes of the dead'. The church was awarded European Heritage Site status by the European Commission in 2018.

FIGURE 7.4 Memorial Church of the Holy Spirit, Javorca Church, built by 3rd Austro-Hungarian Mountain Brigade between 1 March and 1 November 1916. (© Author.)

FIGURE 7.5 The German Ossuary, Tolmin, built between 1936 and 1938; it contains the remains of 1,000 German soldiers. (© N.J. Saunders.)

The walk then follows the flow of Tolminka river on its right bank, reaching the military cemetery of Loce on the northern outskirts of the town of Tolmin 6 km later. The soldiers commemorated in the Javorca church are buried here. On the southern outskirts of Tolmin, on the bank of the Soča river, stands a German ossuary (Figure 7.5). At the end of the 1930s, around the time when Italy built three ossuaries on the annexed territories along the Soča river, Hitler's Germany built this single counterpart. No large German units were present on this front until the final Battle of Kobarid in October 1917, which pushed the combat area all the way to the Piave river near Venice. The ossuary holds the remains of approximately 1,000 German soldiers who fell in this area. On the opposite bank stand two hills of roughly 500 m: Mengore and Cvetje (formerly St. Lucia), known as the Tolmin Bridgehead at the time of the fighting. During the battle of Kobarid, these two hills were the starting point for the attack of German divisions. Mengore now hosts an easily accessible open-air museum with restored trenches and caverns (Figure 7.6). Still visible in the concrete walls are inscriptions in German and Croatian.

From the village of Volce, under Mengore hill, the Walk leads up to the ridge of Kolovrat, to the Slovenian-Italian border. The latter feature has become famed as the scene of a notable action during the Battle of Kobarid that featured a young Erwin Rommel. It was his own account of his leadership there, in his 1937 book *Infantry Attacks*, which brought him to the attention of Adolf Hitler, leading to his rapid rise to the rank of Field Marshal (Rommel 1937; see Potočnik 2021). The visitors can reach the ridge by foot on a trail or by a road suitable for motorized vehicles. They have the same choice if they decide to access the area

FIGURE 7.6 Mengore open-air museum; Austro-Hungarian caverns. (© Author.)

starting from Kobarid, since the Kolovrat mountain stretches between Kobarid and Tolmin and reaches southward in a horseshoe shape. Most visitors decide to drive along these sections and make stops only in places offering panoramic views. Above the point where the ridge changes direction, at Hill 1114, stands a large open-air museum with restored trenches, observation post and underground shelters (Figure 7.7). Part of the trenches is covered with the original metal sheets used during the war, revetted with metallic meshes and equipped

FIGURE 7.7 Hill 1114, Kolovrat Ridge; reconstructed trench. (© Author.)

with concrete-reinforced embrasures. In the summertime, this part of the Walk is the most visited. The best views can be seen from the border stone on the top of the hill. In spring and autumn, this 'open-air classroom' is visited by many school groups from Slovenia and Italy. It is an excellent place to discuss different historical periods in the area between the Alps and the Adriatic, as well as topics related to geography and nature.

During the war, this area had an extremely high concentration of Italian artillery units, which impressed the few British military men present. In his detailed descriptions of the Soča battlefront, Hugh Dalton (later to become Chancellor of the Exchequer, but then a Lieutenant in the Royal Garrison Artillery) stated:

> Observation was beautifully easy on these high hills and in this clear air. What worlds away is this country with its wonderful cloudless sunshine from the dismal flat lands of the Western Front! Said one enthusiast of ours, 'This is a gunner's heaven!' It is a country with a strange beauty of its own; it is, in its own measure, rough and mountainous, and it is within sight of other loftier mountains to the north west.
>
> *(Dalton 1919: 32)*

On the way across the ridge towards the south, it is worth stopping at three other points: the fortified Globocak peak, the panoramic point St. Marijino Celje and the top of Mt. Korada, whose observation point was frequently used by the high command of the Italian army. The visitor can imagine the scene as it was described by a notable wartime visitor, Rudyard Kipling. He was impressed by the Italian artillery, writing 'here were batteries upon batteries of the heaviest pieces' (Kipling 1917).

From here on, the path descends to the Vrhovlje pass between the Soča Valley and Goriska Brda hills, descending softly into the plains of Friuli. This was the safe rear area of the Italian army, which is nowadays more likely to impress a tourist with excellent wines and culinary delights than with stories of the Great War. The Goriska Brda region is becoming widely known as the 'Tuscany of Slovenia'. Near the pass, the hiker faces the choice of either continuing along the ridge on the left bank of the river or descending down the panoramic road below the ridge towards the open-air museum of Mt. Sabotin. This, the highest point overlooking the town, was the pillar of the Austro-Hungarian defence of the Gorizia bridgehead. The Italians conquered the mountain and the town of Gorizia in August 1916 during the Sixth Battle of the Isonzo after 14 months of fighting in five previous offensives. A cavern system created by the defenders was then used for artillery positions, firing upon the Austro-Hungarian positions on the left bank of the river until the final battle. An 8-km stretch of the left bank was gradually conquered by the Italians between 1915 and 1917, starting from the curve in the river and the lowest hill (383 m), across the adjacent hills, up to the highest point at Mt. Sveta Gora (681 m) in the 11th offensive. Continued attacks on the neighbouring Mt. Skabrijel

(San Gabriele) were unsuccessful, turning it into the bloodiest battlefield of the whole Soča Front.

From Mt. Sabotin and Mt. Sveta Gora, the path descends to the twin cities of Gorizia/Nova Gorica; the latter built on the Yugoslavian side of the border after the Second World War. On the right river bank, now on the Italian side of the border, but the site, during the fighting, of an Austro-Hungarian bridgehead position, stands the Oslavia ossuary, completed in 1938, and hosting the remains of almost 58,000 Italian soldiers. In the vicinity we can also find the monument on Mt. Calvario (241 m) commemorating those who fell during in the Italian offensive of August 1916 and several other memorials. The castle overlooking the centre of the town hosts an interesting First World War museum, *Il Museo Della Grande Guerra di Gorizia* (see Martina, this volume).

After its retreat from Gorizia, the Austro-Hungarian army continued the defence of the eastern outskirts of the town and fortified the surrounding hills. Nova Gorica was therefore literally built over the trenches of both armies. Testifying to the consequences of this positional warfare, are numerous cemeteries spread across the entire former battlefront rear, from the Banscice Plateau, over the plain of Gorizia, the Vipava valley and the Karst Plateau, all the way to the coast. As the Austro-Hungarian monarchy collapsed, many of these graveyards remained neglected for long periods of time, while only traces of others remain. Only in the last few decades did Central and Eastern European governments and organizations begin significant efforts for the preservation and restoration of these historical sites. The Walk of Peace Foundation of the Soča valley played an important part in this process.

The Walk passes a few cemeteries east of Nova Gorica and then climbs to the highest southwestern point of the Slovenian side of the Karst plateau, to the panoramic tower and museum on the Cerje hill (343 m). The site offers an exceptional view of the former battlefield of the Gorizia region and the Karst. From here on, the Walk splits in three directions, following the chronology of wartime events. From the beginning of the conflict, the Italian army strove to conquer elevated defensive positions on the edge of the Karst Plateau, with repeated uphill attacks from the Soča river to the west, being made for 14 months. These events are featured in the first and westernmost leg of the Walk. At the end of summer 1916, in their sixth offensive, the Italians conquered this area and the dry valley of Vallone, which today separates the Italian and Slovenian sides of the Karst Plateau. Down this valley and along the banks of the Doberdob lake runs the second, shortest and lowest leg of the Walk running towards the sea. The third and longest leg is the eastern one, crossing the plateau in a long bow, climbing on Mt. Grmada (Hermada) and finally reaching a cliff overlooking the bay of Trieste.

Observation points and open-air museums along the Walk are more important today than previously, due to the fact that since 1918 what used to be a dry rocky plain has become largely overgrown with bushes and patches of wooded areas. On the western leg, after crossing the Vallone valley, the first point of this

FIGURE 7.8 Monte San Michele: underground emplacement for Italian 149-mm artillery, built between 1916 and 1917 by the Italian Third Army. (© Author.)

kind is the Brestovec hill (206 m) open-air museum with its system of Italian artillery tunnels. The path leads to the next hill on the left bank of the Soča river, the notorious Monte San Michele (275 m). Over the course of six offensives, the mountain was pierced with countless trenches, military shelters and a system of large artillery casemates and tunnels (Figure 7.8). After the war, the Italians placed several memorials here to commemorate the engagement's various units. Nowadays they are accompanied by a small museum presenting the historical events with the aid of digital technologies. Two panoramic platforms were built over the northern and southern slopes, with views similar to the ones from the Cerje panoramic tower.

As the Walk descends through the village of San Martino del Carso (Martinscina) towards the foot of the plateau, there is an Austro-Hungarian military cemetery, created after the end of the war. Positioned near the main road, it is easy to spot from afar due to the high cypress trees planted on its grounds. It was created by the reinterment of 14,550 bodies, relocated from smaller graveyards in the battlefield's rear areas. One kilometre further, on the slope of the plateau above the town of Redipuglia, stands the eponymous and largest Italian ossuary, holding the remains of over 100,000 Italian soldiers. This is the location of the main national commemoration of the 4 November, until a few decades ago known as *La Giornata della Vittoria* (Victory Day), and now called *La giornata dell'Unitá d'Italia e delle Forze Armate* (Italian Unity and Armed Forces Day). In the first years after the war, a cemetery was built on Sant'Elia hill at the foot of the plateau and on the opposite side of the main road. After the ossuary was built, the area was repurposed as a memorial park with replicas of the original tombstones and various artillery pieces of both armies placed among the trees. The original cemetery had been unique in that its graves were marked by the debris of the war. Under the hill stands the Museum of the Third Army, run by the Italian army.

Continuing along the edge of the plateau, the Walk first reaches the open-air museum called the *Dolina dei Bersaglieri* and fortified trenches, and then the theme park *Parco Tematico della Grande Guerra* above the town of Monfalcone. The intricate system of trenches and artillery positions here was part of the Austro-Hungarian defence system until the sixth Italian offensive and was additionally fortified by the Italian army after its conquest. Four kilometres further on, the Walk reaches the southernmost point of the Soča Front: the castle of Duino on a high cliff running parallel to the coast towards Trieste. This is also the final point of both the shortest leg of the Walk of Peace, running along the Vallone valley and along the banks of the Lake of Doberdo, as well as its longest, easternmost leg. The peculiarity of the latter, running entirely within the former Austro-Hungarian rear area, is the natural karst cave formations, which represented safe shelters for the soldiers during artillery bombardment. This area has many cemeteries and memorial sites, particularly those commemorating Hungarian units, which were particularly heavily engaged in this sector throughout the war.

Mt. Grmada (323 m) above the castle of Duino presented a natural obstacle – which was additionally fortified – that blocked the advance of the Italian army towards Trieste. The mountain is full of trenches, natural caves and tunnels drilled by the defending army. In recent years, the Italian partners of the Foundation have been striving to extend the Walk towards Trieste and all the way to Venice in the West. Many more initiatives will be required, both in Slovenia and in Italy, to link isolated remains of the war in the former rear areas of the battlefront to a comprehensive network that can recount the historical events of the Great War in the region.

Final Thoughts

Across the world, when people think about the First World War, they mainly imagine the Western Front in France and Belgium. This was also the case in the recent centennial commemorations of war events accompanied by a new wave of literature, films and other media productions. When discovering the 'forgotten' Soča front, visitors are impressed by the extraordinary amount of preserved heritage and traces of historical events: hundreds of kilometres of artillery and communications trenches, military roads, thousands of tunnels, fortified positions and shelters, as well as memorial sites and cemeteries. One of the main reasons for this preservation is that the war on this battlefront took place in the rocky alpine and karst landscape, unsuitable for farming and other activities that would interfere with the remains.

Following the disastrous defeat at the Battle of Caporetto/Kobarid, the Italian Second and Third Armies retreated to Italy in just two to three days, leaving

FIGURE 7.9 Post-1918 reuse of war metal in the Soča Valley. (© N.J. Saunders.)

behind everything they accumulated in long years of positional warfare. After the war, the material and equipment that was moveable was largely repurposed for everyday needs by the impoverished local population (Saunders et al 2013: 51–52; Košir 2019: 181–186). Thus the thatched roofs of and shelters on mountain pastures got replaced by corrugated metal sheets, barbed wire served as fencing for pastures, gardens were surrounded with metal mesh revetting found in trenches, slabs of concrete from embrasures paved cowsheds (Figure 7.9). The cables of former ropeway conveyors were equipped with hooks to send bales of hay into the valley, military roads and water reservoirs came in handy for many remote villages, while farms and homesteads had an abundance of picks, shovels and other tools left behind by engineering units.

Due to poverty, border changes and political circumstances brought about by new political regimes, another world war, and migrations to larger towns and cities, the area has become more sparsely populated. The impact of human interventions in Great War heritage is therefore relatively limited. A greater impact comes from natural changes to the landscape, mainly the overgrowth by scrub of the lower-lying parts of the central and southern sections of the former battlefront. In the high mountains, a visitor can move on and off the beaten track with magnificent views across the entire battlefield, while lush vegetation tends to impede such exploration in lower areas throughout spring and summer. For this reason, the Walk in such sections adheres to the concept of a network of preserved remains, special interest areas and prime panoramic spots, rather than a single line on the map. This principle has provided the basis of the illustrated guide describing the historical heritage found on the Walk, published by the Foundation in several languages (Koren 2008).

Soon after the war's end, the Kingdom of Italy began organizing several areas of battlefield remains on newly conquered land, albeit limited to the southern part of the front. The authorities named these areas *Zone Sacre* (sacred areas), which made political sense given the 600,000 lives sacrificed to 'redeem' these lands for Italy. Organized mass visits with commemorative events were encouraged. Nowadays, organized visits remain part of the activities of various associations, societies and parishes, while many individuals and families are drawn by stories of their ancestors. National memory of, and official engagement with, the Great War in the region was far stronger in Italy than elsewhere. Consequently, it is little surprise that the number of written accounts of the war by Italian combatants found in archives and published sources far exceeds the quantity of accounts of other nationalities. Research into and acquisition of such material in other countries remains challenging.

Personal accounts of those who experienced the front first-hand are a significant contribution to our understanding of the war and can greatly enhance visitors' appreciations of the Walk. Compared to the generally monotonous landscape of other European battlefields, the dynamic terrain of the Soča Front remains virtually unchanged from the time when even certain rocks would be given a name. In some instances, soldiers stared at such features for months and mention them in their accounts; the Italian soldier Caccia Dominioni commented after a bombardment near Ajba, '... the Austrian trenches are destroyed. The Devil's Rock that before was shaped like a mushroom, now looks like a pyramid' (Dominioni 1993: 110).

It is a challenge to carry these stories across borders through translations into other languages. For the foreseeable future, the most privileged of all visitors to the former battlefield remains the Italian hiker, who can explore the area with a selection of Italian-language books to hand. While visitors can avail themselves of museums, information centres, local amateur explorers and collectors of material remains, and more recently digital media, the insight and knowledge of an experienced guide is the best option. The renewed interest in this historical era in Slovenia and other Central and Eastern European countries, combined with free movement across nowadays invisible state borders, has brought visitors of diverse nationalities to the region. The material and immaterial heritage of the First World War tells a story shared by many nations, therefore activities aimed at its preservation and presentation are of the utmost importance. They are part of several EU-funded cross-border programmes and projects creating partnerships between organizations from many different countries (see Brandauer, this volume).

Within these frameworks, the cooperation between Slovene and Italian partners is particularly important, since the population of the area near the border between the two countries lived through bitter and tragic experiences over the past century. Two world wars and the actions of different political regimes have left a permanent scar on the generations who lived through these historic times. The 'Walk of Peace' in the Foundation's name is therefore representative of the institution's mission to focus on the friendly co-existence of neighbouring nations within its wider endeavours for world peace. In striving to achieve this, the Walk, with its interconnection of *lieux de memoire*, museums and a dramatic conflict landscape, might be said to have created the world's largest open-air museum.

References

Cornish, P. (2018) Afterword: The Mobilisation of Memory, 1917–2014. In J. Wallis and D. Harvey (eds.), *Commemorative Spaces of the First World War*, pp 225–235. London: Routledge.

Cornish, P. and N.J. Saunders. (2019) Preface. In U. Košir, M. Črešnar and D. Mlekuž (eds.), *Rediscovering the Great War: Archaeology and Enduring Legacies on the Soča and Eastern Fronts*, pp xvi–xix. London: Routledge.

Dalton, H. (2004) [1919] *With British Guns in Italy*. Uckfield: Naval and Military Press.

Dominioni, P.C. (1993) *1915–1919 Diario di Guerra*. Milan: Ugo Mursia Editore, s.r.l.

Fod. (n.d.) *Friends of the Dolomites website*. www.friends-of-dolomites.com

Gerwarth, R. (2017) *The Vanquished*. London: Penguin.

Kipling, R. (1917) Podgora. *Daily Telegraph*, 9 June. London. Available at http://www.kiplingsociety.co.uk/rg_mountains_podgora.htm

KM. (n.d.) The Kobarid Museum: Awards. https://www.kobariski-muzej.si/en/museum/201802121741285002/awards/

Koren, T. [transl. B. Klemenc] (2008) *The Walk of Peace: A Guide along the Isonzo Front in the Upper Soča Region*. Kobarid: The 'Walks of Peace in the Soča Region Foundation'.

Košir, U. (2019) Legacies of the Soča Front – from Rubbish to Heritage (1915–2017). In U. Košir, M. Črešnar and D. Mlekuž (eds.), *Forgotten Fronts, Enduring Legacies: Archaeology and the Great War on the Soča and Eastern Fronts*, pp 181–18. London: Routledge.

Košir, U., N.J. Saunders, M. Črešnar and G. Rutar. (2019) Between Tourism and Oblivion: Rombon and Kolovrat – Conflict Landscapes on the Soča Front, 1915–2017. In U. Košir, M. Črešnar and D. Mlekuž (eds.), *Forgotten Fronts, Enduring Legacies: Archaeology and the Great War on the Soča and Eastern Fronts*, pp 90–108. London: Routledge.

MacDonald, J. and Ž. Cimprić. (2011) *Caporetto and the Isonzo Campaign: The Italian Front 1915–1918*. Barnsley: Pen and Sword.

Matičič, I. (1922) *Na krvavih poljanah*. Ljubljana: Učiteljska tiskarna.

Potočnik, A. (2021) Controversy in the Julian Alps: Erwin Rommel, Landscape, and 12th Battle of the Soča/Isonzo. In N.J. Saunders and P. Cornish (eds.), *Conflict Landscapes: Materiality and Meaning in Contested Places*, pp 85–106. London: Routledge.

Prešeren, J. (2014) *Vojak 1915–1918*. Celje. Celjska Mohorjeva družba.

Rommel, E. (2009) *[1937] Infantry Attacks*. Minneapolis: Zenith Press.

Saunders, N.J., N. Faulkner, U. Košir, M. Črešnar and S. Thomas. (2013). Conflict landscapes of the Soča/Isonzo Front, 1915–2013: Archaeological-anthropological evaluation of the Soča Valley, Slovenia. *Arheo* 30: 47–66.

Schindler, J. (2001) *Isonzo: The Forgotten Sacrifice of the Great War*. Santa Barbara: Praeger.

Thompson, M. (2008) *The White War*. London: Faber and Faber.

8

DIGGING A TRENCH IN AN UPSTAIRS GALLERY

Commemorating the Great War in rural Dorset

Martin Barry

Early in 2015, a planning meeting of Wimborne's Priest's House Museum and Garden management team decided to meet the challenge of commemorating and interpreting the centenary of the 1916 Battle of the Somme. A full gallery exhibition was agreed, with a centrepiece being a First World War trench display in the museum's Temporary Exhibition Gallery on the first floor of the building. For a battle (and a war) which took place underground and in the air, it seemed fitting that a trench had somehow to be 'dug' in an upstairs gallery.

The Priest's House Museum and Gardens is in a Grade II★ Listed Building on the High Street of the market town of Wimborne in East Dorset, England (Figure 8.1). Until 2019, the museum's displays were in ten rooms spread across a complicated merging of several buildings, dating from the sixteenth century to the early eighteenth. The oldest part of the site is an 'L'-shaped stone-and-flint hall and north wing, a structure probably one and a half storeys high, with a second storey and attic space added in the early seventeenth century. A timber-framed south wing was added around this time. The courtyard between the two wings was filled in by a two-storey building in the mid-eighteenth century, its ground floor becoming today's museum entrance and shop. The front of the original building was fully covered by these later additions, and a brick-built single-storey kitchen was added to the rear and extends well into what is now the garden.

During the nineteenth century, the ground floor became a diverse retail space for merchants including a stationer, a grocer and an ironmonger. The ironmongers were the Coles family who lived and worked in the house from 1872 and were responsible for developing the garden and the central path and planting beds, kept and maintained today mostly in their original form. It was Hilda Coles (1907–1987), the granddaughter of the first ironmonger, who in 1962, with the Wimborne Historical Society, opened a library and small museum in the

DOI: 10.4324/9781003263531-11

FIGURE 8.1 The Priest's House Museum and Gardens, Wimborne, 2004. (© Author.)

building. Hilda ran the museum in three rooms on the ground floor for 25 years with a team of volunteers and support from the local community. She died in 1987 and left the building to the Governors of Wimborne Minster Trust with a request that the house become a museum for the town and surrounding district of East Dorset. The building was restored by East Dorset District Council between 1990 and 1991, the most visible alteration being the return of the bow-fronted windows from the original Victorian period shops. Ten rooms were now adapted to become display space and a programme to develop permanent galleries began between 1991 and 1995.

The galleries were:

Ground Floor – Ironmongers Shop, Stationery Shop, Georgian Parlour, seventeenth Century Parlour, Victorian Kitchen and Service Range

First Floor – Childhood Gallery, Costume Gallery, Archaeology Gallery and Temporary Exhibition Gallery

The Service Range, which incorporated a Victorian Schoolroom, was also used as a study space. In addition to the public galleries, the Museum also had a research library, storage space in the attic, management offices and a garden tearoom

The galleries are representative of the scope of the museum's collection and include a nationally significant collection of Victorian valentines' day cards. Object donations from the public do occur but are random when it comes to collections categories. In addition to the first-floor Temporary Exhibition Gallery, there was a large glass fronted 190 cm wide by 185 cm tall cabinet at the end of the seventeenth-century parlour on the ground floor housing temporary displays. Three permanent members of staff, a Director, Assistant Director and Learning Officer are supported for the day-to-day running of the museum and tearoom by around a hundred volunteers. The museum is operated by 'The Priest's House Museum Trust', a limited company, run by a board of trustees elected by members, known as 'friends', of the trust. A separate trust, 'The Priest's House Museum Collections Trust', owns the collections.

The Heritage Lottery Fund has supported two large capital projects. The first, in 2012, developed the tearoom into a larger enterprise, created a community learning space and a modern reserve object storage facility; the second, starting in 2019, redeveloped the main building. As well as modernizing the gallery spaces and overall access to the site, the original sixteenth-century courtyard was restored. The Trust's vision today remains the same as that of Hilda Coles, who believed the museum should be 'a "live" museum – a centre of education and culture, continually changing its displays and appealing to children as well as to adults' (Priest's House Museum 2019). At the end of 2019, the Trust decided to rebrand the museum as 'The Museum of East Dorset' in order to reflect the wider role within the larger community of East Dorset as a whole and not just Wimborne.

The Author and the Priest's House

The author's relationship with the Priest's House began in 1996 with personal visits which highlighted the challenges facing a community museum. These included how to balance meaningful interpretation, relevant exhibitions programmes, community engagement and day-to-day running, with difficult infrastructure and enthusiastic but mainly unqualified volunteers. Consultancy work in 2004 led the author to produce a 'Disabled Visitors' Access to Collections Audit' for the museum. Other consultancies followed including a role in the 'One Hundred Year Heritage of the First World War for Wimborne and East Dorset' project funded with a £56,100 Heritage Lottery Grant which ran between 2014 and 2019. Most significantly, the author has curated several First World War displays and exhibitions for the museum since 2008. The first, 'Mementos and Memories', was offered to the museum to commemorate the 90th anniversary of the Armistice in 2008. The museum was in the application phase of a £450,000 Heritage Lottery Fund grant and had neither time nor resources to produce anything themselves. The display told the story of three soldiers and how they were linked by common objects from the war. The objects were a Princess Mary Gift Box ('Mary Tin') from 1914 (Figure 8.2), a 'Service Rations Department' rum jug, and a gas attack warning rattle. Two of the soldiers were cousins but the third was unknown to them. They share a common descendant, however, as the author's youngest son is the great-grandson, great nephew, and great-great grandson of the three men.

FIGURE 8.2 Princess Mary Gift Boxes from Christmas Day 1914, along with accompanying 'comforts'. (© Author.)

This use of an emotional 'hook' to draw the visitor further into the story and create a sense of connection beyond the surface subject matter became the main design characteristic of the author's subsequent museum displays and follows Connerton's description of how 'we preserve versions of the past to ourselves by using words and images' (1989: 72). So many of the displayed materials are not physically accessible to visitors, because of their fragile or hazardous nature, and an emotional element was seen as a way of making the exhibition more personal. Later displays usually ran from Remembrance Day, 11 November, until early March in most years. Each had an emotive pull that encouraged the visitor to enter the lives, experiences and feelings being interpreted from a century ago.

'A Christmas Wish', the story of Princess Mary's Christmas Gift to the troops in 1914, was hosted in 2009, using the seventeenth-century parlour case. People from Wimborne and East Dorset were invited to bring in their 'Mary Tins' during an open day held that summer. Each tin was photographed with the intention to use the images together with associated images and stories of the soldier-recipients of the 'Gift', as background and supporting material for a future display. A third display, 'Remembered Faces' which ran from 2010, had no objects, just six photographic postcards of real people from the First World War. All had messages to friends and family written on the back; four were British, two German.

The 'Tommy's Kit' exhibition ran in 2011 and displayed a range of uniform items and equipment carried by the average British infantryman of 1916. It used all the seventeenth-century parlour glass case and also a smaller tank case and was accompanied by a continuous loop of popular First World War music. The personal items, including photographs, letters, souvenirs and sundry items a soldier would have in his pockets, and the music gave a more intimate feel to an exhibition, designed to 'trap and hold information long after the human organism has stopped informing' (Connerton 1989: 73).

The 'Families' exhibition, held in 2012, featured photograph-postcards depicting seven soldiers and their families. There were young soldiers with parents and younger siblings, older soldiers with elderly parents and soldiers with, very often, young families. The enlarged images were accompanied by original and modern poetry and prose. The poetry offered one element of emotional engagement, but the most striking examples were down to the reactions by the public to the visible emotions on the faces in the enlarged images. These emotions had not always been noticeable in the original 14 cm by 6 cm photograph. Another significant design choice was having a total of seven images, because one in seven British soldiers was killed during the war.

None of the exhibited objects came from the museum's collections, but rather belonged to the author. This was not an issue for the museum as these displays were small, self-contained events, presented on their own once a year for around 10 weeks; nevertheless, the situation concerning such small-scale exhibitions was about to change. By the end of 2012, the museum director was looking to the upcoming centenary of the First World War. Four years of commemorating a world-wide event in our history was starting to catch the public's attention and imagination. Even with the author providing exhibitions during this period, the centenary would now hopefully involve the whole community of Wimborne and East Dorset and had to be addressed.

Exhibiting on a Shoestring

The financial challenges facing community-based museums are manifold, with operating costs being the largest burden. Heating, lighting, ground rent and business rates are among the regular expenditures the museum must pay. This does not leave any money to 'buy in' exhibitions. The reserve collection gives a little scope to rotate or refresh existing displays but cannot present entirely new visitor experiences. Such museums' original displays were usually created using the best objects available at the time, and the reserves are mostly duplicates of these.

Public donations can bolster collections, but are usually single items or, at best, small groups of objects. The Priest's House Museum has a strict acquisition policy to prevent the building being filled with random, albeit interesting, 'stuff'.

The objects must add something to the existing collections and permanent displays or be relevant to Wimborne or East Dorset. This does 'top up' the collections, even allowing the permanent objects to be replaced with a better example, but does not bring much new into the museum.

As with most museums, it is the Temporary Exhibition Gallery space that draws visitors, either regulars to see what is new, or tourists to have a day out. Temporary exhibitions drive both interest and footfall. They give a museum scope to go off at a tangent and present something very different from the permanent displays. Local historical societies, special interest groups and private collectors often furnish content for this constant refreshing of the temporary exhibitions. These have included:

> 'What's in a Map', history of the local Ordnance Survey Map (2017).
> 'Hats for all occasions', a collection of 44 different hats and other forms of headwear (2018).
> 'Rena Gardiner – A Dorset Artist', exhibition of prints and books (2018).

Another source of temporary exhibitions is other museums. The goal of the Priest's House, through the redevelopment project, is to meet national guidelines for exhibition security and insurance. This allows for significant objects, even from national collections, to be loaned to the museum to enhance the temporary displays. All transportation, curating and ongoing conservation costs are the responsibility of the Priest's House, but the loans are free. St. Barbe Museum and Art Gallery in Lymington, Hampshire, already with this level of display security in place, held an exhibition in 2017, 'Neo-Romantic Art: the McDowall Collection', which included works by leading artists including John Piper, Graham Sutherland, Paul Nash and Henry Moore (St Barbes Museum 2020). This upgrading creates more scope for the museum to remain vibrant and relevant in the face of the increasing difficulty of persuading people to devote their leisure time to visiting it. But the costs mentioned above will be significant. There will always be a need for private, 'home-grown' exhibitions.

The Priest's House Museum and the Great War

In common with communities across the United Kingdom, Wimborne and East Dorset have many War Memorials. Men joined up and went to fight for 'King and Country', many destined not to return. The memorials in the area record around 1,225 names. Those who remained at home were also affected either by the changes from a peacetime to a wartime economy or by the impact of a loved one lost or wounded. Many local buildings and businesses changed roles during the war and the legacies of this momentous social transformation are still evident in the community.

A determination to investigate, record and interpret this legacy for the benefit of the local community inspired the 'The One Hundred Year Heritage of the First World War for Wimborne and East Dorset' project. Partly funded by another Heritage Lottery Fund grant, of £56,100, the project was overseen by a working party of trustees and volunteers. A project manager was appointed along with several consultants, including the author, each paid for specific tasks during the four and a half years from the summer of 2014 until the presentation of the final report in late 2019. These dates corresponded with the centenary of the start of the war up until the date of the first Remembrance Day on 11 November 1919. The central element of the project was to provide biographies for the 1,225 names on the various war memorials in the area. This was tasked to a small group of dedicated volunteers who each took responsibility for either a parish or village in the study area. The project manager and the Deputy Director had overall responsibility, with advice and research support from the author.

The project held two conferences, August 2016, and November 2018, and there was a final project report (HLF n.d.). There was also 'Tommy's Sisters', a film written, directed and produced by a community theatre group and starring amateur actors from the local area (SoP n.d.). Although the dialogue was dramatized, the characters and their stories were drawn from actual histories of families in the Wimborne area.

The museum hosted a number of open days, starting in 2013, to engage and inform the local community about the structure and aims of the project and to attract stories and perhaps objects of family connections with the war, the latter possibly for display. Incidentally, but importantly in this context, the Priest's House's own First World War collection contains very few objects, comprising only some service medals, several documents and a wooden tea caddy made by a German prisoner of war who worked on a local farm.

Two displays were curated – the first from June 2014 until July 2015 was part of an exhibition that filled the first floor Temporary Exhibition Gallery. Part of the gallery had a sectioned-off area with a small window looking into a reconstructed nurse's accommodation at Hazebrouck railway station in Flanders which had been used to accommodate British nurses who served on hospital trains between the Western Front and English Channel ports. The display included a mannequin dressed in British army uniform depicting a member of the Royal Army Medical Corps. Three glass tank cases were positioned around the walls of the gallery, each containing objects lent to the museum by local people who attended the open days. Another tall case was positioned in the centre of the gallery and held a display called 'Pack Up Your Troubles' (Figure 8.3) which showed a range of items carried by a British soldier.

The title implies that the central theme is the contents of 'Your Old Kit Bag', as per the song of the period; but in fact British infantrymen did not carry kitbags, all their belongings, issued and personal, were carried in the Large and Small Packs of their 1908 Pattern Webbing Sets. The objects on display were a mix of original and reproduction items, and this was the first large-scale use at the Priest's House of material sourced from re-enactment suppliers, rather than just original artefacts. The case backboard had an enlarged panel depicting

FIGURE 8.3 'Pack Up Your Troubles' display, June 2014. (© Author.)

an infantry company in full kit route marching through the countryside. The rear of the panel, the back of the freestanding glass case, had enlarged images of nurses and Royal Army Medical Corps members that linked to the adjacent Hazebrouck display.

The second display, which ran from November 2014 until March 2015, was an expanded version of 'A Christmas Wish', again telling the story of Princess Mary's Christmas Gift of an embossed brass box to soldiers and sailors serving at Christmas 1914 (Figure 8.4). The display also included printed images of 'Mary Tins' brought into the museum by local people. Each panel had the name and regiment, and if possible, a photograph of the original recipient. Other displays and exhibitions during the centenary include 'The Story of Pip, Squeak and Wilfred – British Service Medals of the First World War' (2015), 'Somme' (2016), and 'After the War' (2018), an exhibition showing how commemoration and remembrance developed after the Armistice into the 1920s and how those processes are reflected upon a century on. Many of the above displays and exhibitions, especially 'Pack Up Your Troubles' and 'Somme', made use of

FIGURE 8.4   'A Christmas Wish' display, November 2014. (© Author.)

reproduction objects. Why did this happen? Are reproductions or copies a valid resource to use in a museum?

Reproductions

Perhaps the two most limiting factors when displaying First World War objects are their rarity and fragility. Relatively cheap to make and easy to replace, uniforms especially were never expected to last very long, certainly not for over a century (see Price-Rowe 2018). Consequently, those examples that have survived now command very high prices in the world of militaria collecting. A British uniform, 1908 Pattern webbing set and Brodie steel shrapnel helmet, for example, cost upwards of £8,000. Even when such genuine items are used, as with the exhibition 'Tommy's Kit', the security and conservation of these valuable items makes it only possible to display them inside a locked glass case.

Another difficult category of objects to display is the ephemera and paraphernalia of everyday soldier life. Even if objects such as food tins and packets, ration packs, maps and documents still exist, they are very likely to be showing their age. The likelihood of finding a 'bully beef' tin not rusted through and with the paper label clean and intact is slim indeed. The only recent example of such objects surviving intact is that of the supplies stored in Captain Robert Falcon Scott's Antarctica Expedition base on Ross Island (The Independent 2009). The sub-zero temperatures preserved foodstuffs and packaging in a near perfect condition. Even if these rare and unique items were made available for museums to borrow, however, the ambient temperature of a museum gallery without climate control would cause them to deteriorate very quickly. So, what to do?

Re-enacting provides an answer. The Khaki Chums – a living history and research group which disbanded in 2018 after strong condemnation from former military personnel (Jim30 2011) – had a trading company called 'Khaki Devil' (Khaki Devil 2015).[1] This company still provides accurate reproductions of First World War uniforms and equipment serving re-enactors, television and film, historians, living history groups and the museum industry. 'Tommy Pack Fillers' a business run by former 'Chum' Geoff Carefoot, produces accurate replicas of everything from resin hand grenades to 1916 'Fray Bentos' corned beef labels (Carefoot 2016). All these items are faithful reproductions, copied in all cases from the originals. Theatrical 'props', although superficially convincing, do not always have this level of detail. In most cases, their exposure to the audience is fleeting and only needs to convey an impression. But what if a director or film maker wishes to have 'authentic' props regardless of this? Could a film or plays' budget afford such in-depth research? Where do they obtain such accurate material? The answer is simple, they use the re-enacting supply industry because 'unlike emulations or duplicates, copies mainly follow and reflect the past' (Lowenthal 1985: 301).

The 'Somme'

Perhaps not surprisingly, given the prominence of the battle in British public memory of the Great War (Reynolds 2013: 360–367), an exhibition was held between July and November 2016 to commemorate the centenary of the Battle of the Somme (1 July to 18 November 1916). This involved creating a replica of a section of British reserve trench during the build up to the offensive. The following is a detailed account of how this exhibition came about and was realized.

Original Concept

The original location was a 2.4-m wide glass full height case in the Costume Gallery which offered space and access for such a project. One end of the case was to have a figure, dressed as an officer, under cover in a dugout, whilst the other end had an infantryman exposed to the elements in an open section of trench. This was to show that although the officer had a modicum of shelter from the elements, he was as vulnerable to injury or death by shellfire as the exposed infantryman. The display was to be based on a support trench and dugout some 100 m behind the front line. A support trench would have a greater range of objects on view. Forward trenches in comparison would not offer the same breadth of sundry, more domestic 'comforts' and items of everyday life as a support trench. In the event, the Costume Gallery case was being used for another exhibition, so the Museum Director suggested using the entire Temporary Exhibition Gallery for an important and emotive display which would commemorate the bloodiest battle in British military history.

Budget

Apart from providing advertising, there was no money from the museum to produce this exhibition. All uniforms, equipment, sundries and personal items came from the author's collection. Four specific items were sourced to play key roles in the display:

An officer's folding 'Cabinetta' campaign bed from the period made by W & S Wales Limited.

An original 1910 telephone converted for use as a trench telephone.

A steel trench telephone cable support excavated from the Somme battlefield.

Several steel 'corkscrew' barbed wire supports, also excavated from the Somme battlefield.

Timber and fixings were purchased by the author.

Design

The structure was to use two adjacent sides of the room (Figure 8.5), one side, going into a corner, would have a reconstruction of an officers' covered dugout, the other side, running out from the same corner, would have a section of trench

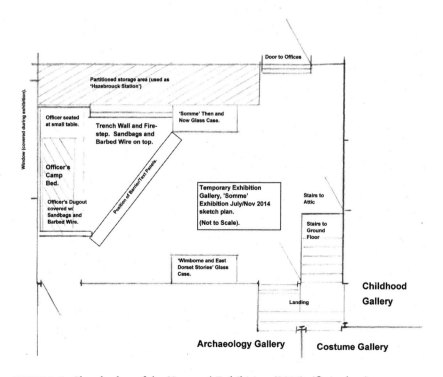

FIGURE 8.5   Sketch plan of the 'Somme' Exhibition (2016). (© Author.)

complete with fire-step, sandbag parapet and barbed wire. At the end of the trench section there was to be a tall glass tank case with objects depicting the Somme in 1916 and 2016. Another case opposite was to display objects and stories about the Somme gathered from the residents of Wimborne and East Dorset. A diagonal 80-cm-high barrier ran from the start of the dugout to the end of the trench. This prevented anyone touching or removing the objects on display and provided a useful stand for text-based interpretation panels. The dugout and trench section were constructed off-site, numbered, disassembled, transported to site and reassembled in the gallery.

Officers' Dugout

This was constructed using a rectangular wooden frame, 2.85 m long by 1.0 m deep and 1.9 m high. The end walls and back wall were panelled in rough timber and the floor made from narrow wooden slats. The roof was made from a sheet of corrugated plastic painted to resemble corrugated iron. The front side was open as this allowed the display to be viewed in cross section. A section of 'duckboard' was placed along the front of the dugout to form a plinth for displaying larger, standing objects. Edges and gaps were covered with hessian, and the roof was edged with sandbags and barbed wire (Figure 8.6).

The largest single object was the officers' folding campaign bed from the period. A mannequin, dressed as an infantry officer, was seated at a small folding table with a reproduction trench map, original notebook and indelible pencil, trench whistle, Webley pistol and other sundry items representing the officers'

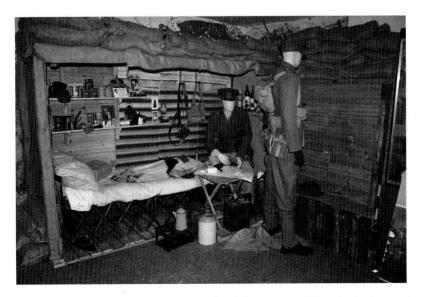

FIGURE 8.6 The 'Somme' Exhibition: Officer's Dugout and Trench display during assembly in 2016. (© Author.)

daily responsibilities and activities. Shelves around the dugout held an array of objects likely to be in such a structure in 1916, including issue food ration tins, sundry personal 'comforts' and items only allowed to officers, such as wine and spirits.

Trench Section

This 1.8-m wide by 1.9-m high section was constructed from timber with vertical planking. The fire-step, a step for soldiers to mount in order to see over the parapet of the trench during night-time sentry duty or to repulse attacks, was made from horizontal planking supported by vertical log sections around 30 cm tall. The section was also topped with sandbags and barbed wire. A mannequin dressed and equipped as a British infantryman of 1916 stood by the fire-step looking towards the enemy. He had a few sundries around him depicting his modest resources as compared with the more 'lavish' provisions of the officer, including a small trench stove for brewing a mug of hot tea or heating tins of 'bully' beef.

Sandbags

Using sandbags filled with real earth was impractical, being too heavy for the wooden framework to support and possibly introducing contaminants and insect pests to the museum environment. The solution was quite 'theatrical'. Around 40 Black plastic bin liners were inserted into hessian sandbags and filled with paper shredding and tied at the neck. This gave bulk to the sandbag and allowed them to be moulded into position without being too heavy. Additionally, 20 sandbags were filled with old clothing and used as heavy anchor points at the corners of the display with the lighter paper filled ones placed on top.

Barbed Wire

Real barbed wire would have been too hazardous to use in a public display, not only for the visitors but also for the display builder. Around 30 m was needed but fake, 'theatrical prop', barbed wire made from leather was too expensive at around £5.00 per metre. The solution was to make it 'in-house'; 2-mm silver aluminium florists wire was chosen as the construction medium. A 10-m length was passed through a mounted hook and folded into a double strand. It was then loosely twisted together. Every 15 cm along the length 10-cm pieces of wire were twisted around the long lengths and clipped to resemble 'barbs'. Several lengths were constructed using this process. They were easy to bend into the familiar coil shape or kept as straight runs where appropriate. All the wire was mounted on the original steel posts from the Somme, creating a hybrid of genuine and reproduction.

FIGURE 8.7 The 'Somme' Exhibition: Display case containing reproduction and original relics from the Somme battlefield. (© Author.)

Glass Cases

The case next to the trench section (Figure 8.7) held a mix of original items excavated from the Somme battlefield as well as some modern reproductions. The aim of the display was to convey a sense of time passing from 1916 until 2016 through what had happened to several mundane, everyday objects, in this instance, food ration tins.

A stack of these tins, below a photograph of army cooks on the Somme, was presented in one corner. Several food tins in varying stages of decay swept down to the middle of the case and ended in a pile of rusty fragments. These decaying tins and rust, all excavated from the Somme battlefield, represented the slow passage of time from real to rubbish, yet all had to be purchased for this display from militaria dealers on the internet. This presents a new 'value' of, what is really, 'rubbish'. Thompson (2017: 27) describes the seemingly impossible transfer of an object from transience to durability when it reaches zero value and zero expected life span at the same time, becoming rubbish. He goes on to say that unless 'it turns to dust, it may be discovered and successfully transferred to durability' (ibid.). Here, some of the display has actually 'turned to dust', the fragments of metal food containers discarded into rubbish pits on the Somme are used to illustrate the final stage of decomposition. Perhaps this extends Thompson's theory and makes even 'dust' durable?

The centre section of the case had a barbed wire support stake with sections of original battlefield wire linked through it. The case opposite contained a small number of objects and text panels that represented the Wimborne stories gathered by the museum in the run-up to the exhibition, including two poems written by a woman whose father, having joined the army under-age, had suffered mental trauma after the Somme battle that manifested in later life as brutality towards his young children. Poetry was her way of dealing with and reconciling her fathers' behaviour.

Conclusion

The aim of this chapter has been to show what can be achieved at a local level with usually limited finances, a counterbalance perhaps to the experiences and approaches of larger better funded museums. The perspective has been rural rather than metropolitan and has focused too on the important if often under-acknowledged role of individual collectors, avocational experts, volunteers and donators in local museums and their relationships with objects. In an ideal world, with ample funding and an enlightened approach by local and central government to the benefits of preserving and interpreting our history and heritage, it may be possible to continually refresh how and what a museum presents to the visitor without damaging the integrity of the object 'memories'. If we avoid the 'tyranny of tradition' (Janes 2004: 388) and create 'dream spaces' (Kavanagh 2000), then exhibitions would flow as do other forms of contemporary public interaction.

Against this view, there is of course the need to attract and engage visitors, and to keep the museum open, without being disrespectful to the soldiers' service and sacrifice, and thus 'doing no harm to history' (Winter 2018). Keeping museums interesting and relevant might sometimes come dangerously close to the accusations of 'Disneyfication' – of parodying the original – made to re-enactors, though perhaps might be closer to what Jay Winter (2018) has called 'infotainment', which at least implies the intention to educate the visitor or provide insight into the situation behind the re-enactment.

Using methods of 'infotainment' that engage without straying over the line of respect can be achieved, and it is hoped that some of these practices, deployed in the 'Somme' Exhibition displays described above, go part way to demonstrating this. Ultimately, it must also be acknowledged that *all* museum visitors deserve to be engaged at their own particular level of interest (Cornish 2017).

Note

1 It is worth noting that military re-enacting has become more controversial and less accepted as a legitimate form of interpretation over the past 20 years. The hobby of dressing and acting the part of British soldiers from the First World War has attracted controversy and hostility. The disbanding of the Khaki Chums was in response to ex-servicemen questioning the appropriateness of the Chums attending Remembrance Sunday 2011 at London's Cenotaph.

References

Carefoot, G. (2016) Great War Period Ration and Food Labels. [Online]. [17 November 2019]. Available from: http://www.tommyspackfillers.com/ration.asp

Connerton, P. (1989) *How Societies Remember*. Cambridge: Cambridge University Press.

Cornish, P. (2017) Concept and Space in the Imperial War Museum's First World War Galleries. In N.J. Saunders and P. Cornish. (eds.), *Modern Conflict and the Senses*, pp 14–28. London: Routledge.

HLF. (n.d.) *The One Hundred Year Heritage of the First World War for Wimborne and East Dorset, Priest's House Museum and Garden, Wimborne, Dorset. Funded by the Heritage Lottery Fund 4/12/2013*. Final Report. https://www.heritagefund.org.uk/our-work/one-hundred-year-heritage-first-world-war-wimborne-and-east-dorset

Janes, R. (2004) Persistent Paradoxes. In G. Anderson (ed.), *Reinventing the Museum*, pp 375–394. Walnut Creek: Altamira Press.

Jim30. (2011) Army Rumour Service. [Online]. [29 October 2019]. Available from: https://www.arrse.co.uk/community/threads/who-are-the-khaki-chums-and-why-do-they-parade-at-the-cenotaph-on-nov-11.172383/

Kavanagh, G. (2000) *Dream Spaces – Memory and the Museum*. Leicester: Leicester University Press.

Khaki Devil. (2015) About Us. [Online]. [10 December 2019]. Available from: http://www.khakidevil.co.uk

Lowenthal, D. (1985) *The Past is a Foreign Country*. Cambridge: Cambridge University Press.

Price-Rowe, C. (2018) First World War Uniforms: Lives. *Logistics, and Legacy in British Army Uniform Production 1914–1918*. Barnsley: Pens & Sword.

Priest's House Museum. (2019) About Us. [Online]. [14 November 2019]. Available from: http://www.priest-house.co.uk/about-us/the-museum.html

Reynolds, D. (2013) *The Long Shadow*. London: Simon & Schuster

SoP (n.d.) 'Tommy's Sisters'. *State of Play* website https://stateofplayarts.co.uk/tommys-sisters-2/

St Barbes Museum. (2020) Past Exhibitions. [Online]. [8 January 2020]. Available from: https://www.stbarbe-museum.org.uk/whats-on/exhibitions/past-exhibitions/neo-romantic-art-the-mcdowall-collection/

The Independent. (2009) Frozen in Time: Captain Scott's Huts. [Online]. [4 December 2019]. Available from: https://www.independent.co.uk/news/science/frozen-in-time-captain-scotts-huts-1844262.html

Thompson, M. (2017) *Rubbish Theory – The Creation and Destruction of Value*, 2nd ed. London: Pluto Press.

Winter, J. (2018) 'Keynote talk'. *Curating the Great War Conference*. Imperial War Museum. London. 13–14 September 2018.

9

CURATING THE GREAT WAR IN POLAND

The prisoner-of-war camp at Czersk

Dawid Kobiałka

In 2014, the first remains of a former prisoner-of-war (PoW) camp in Czersk, Poland, were discovered. These were largely relics of barracks, dug-outs and trash pits. They were recorded thanks to Open Access Light Detection and Ranging (LiDAR) derivatives in the form of hillshade models. Since that time, this unique heritage has become the object of closer, non-invasive archaeological research. This chapter discusses and summarizes various archaeological and social initiatives regarding the Czersk camp that have been taking place since the discovery.

History and context

An important part of the Great War's so-called 'Eastern Front' was located in modern-day Poland. The physical vestiges of this warscape – trenches, craters made by explosive munitions, dugouts and machine gun nests can still be discerned. Furthermore, numerous war cemeteries, where soldiers of both sides – largely Russians and Germans – are interred, are still extant (Zalewska and Kiarszys 2017). Countless smaller artefacts lie buried among these larger physical remains. A further Great War legacy exists in the form of traces of German PoW camps. These are in fact the rarest iteration of Great War heritage in the region. While it is estimated that 38 such camps existed, most were dismantled after the war and historical records relating to them are sparse, selective and one-sided.

The urgent need to build special sites for soldiers' detention was a direct consequence of the first victories of the Kaiser's army in East Prussia in August and September of 1914. Hundreds of thousands of Russian soldiers were taken into captivity in only a few weeks of fighting. It is estimated that just at the Battles of Tannenberg and the Great Masurian Lakes 92,000–95,000 Russian soldiers were taken into captivity by the German army (Dąbrowski 2015: 150). They were

DOI: 10.4324/9781003263531-12

imprisoned mostly in two camps in West Prussia: Tuchola (Tuchel) and Czersk (Kobiałka et al 2017). During the following months of the war, the number of prisoners steadily grew. In the war as a whole, according to Jastrzębski (2008: 19), one and a half million soldiers of the Triple Entente were taken into captivity by the Germans just before the end of 1915.

Thus, Germans started to build PoW camps, in German *Kriegsgefangenenlager* (Pope-Hennessy 1920; Doegen 1921) in which Russians and later on French, English, Serbians, Italians and Romanians would be imprisoned. It was decided that the camps had to be located at a safe distance from the Fronts. West Prussia was chosen as one of the provinces where the camps would be built. One of them was in Czersk (*Kriegsgefangenenlager Czersk*) (Figure 9.1). Such sites shared a similar pattern of infrastructure. The one in Czersk consisted of administration

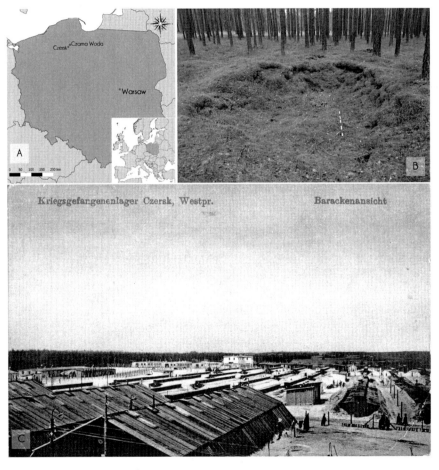

FIGURE 9.1 (A) Location of sites discussed in the article. (© Author.) (B) A camp structures documented during field research. (© Author.) (C) A rare Great War German propaganda postcard showing Czersk camp. (© Author.)

buildings, wooden barracks partially excavated into the ground (in German *Erdbaracke*), dug-outs, canteens, quarantines zones, lazarettes, bakeries, bathhouses, warehouses, workshops, fences of barbed wire and a PoW cemetery. Rare German propaganda postcards as well as several photographs taken in the camp offer a peek into a camp landscape (Figure 9.1).

Franciszek Smagliński – a parish priest of one of the churches in Czersk – only 20 years after the Great War asked:

> What is this place? This is a place of eternal rest of thousands of the (First) World War victims. This is a Russian cemetery, the only heritage of the huge prisoner-of-war camp in Czersk that survived until the present.
>
> *(Smagliński 1993: 1; transl. author)*

Indeed, from a certain point of view, the priest's observation is reasonable. The camp was closed and dismantled after the war, and only a relatively small number of historical documents concerning it have been preserved. Additionally, their nature is peculiar and one-sided. During research, the collections of the National Archives in Bydgoszcz, the archives of the town hall of Czersk, as well as documents found in the archive of the Historical and Ethnographic Museum of Julian Rydzkowski in Chojnice, were studied (see also Marcinkiewicz 2016). These records consisted of a few German propaganda postcards and photographs of the camp, some sketches of the prisoners, a simplified plan of the camp and documents relating to the exhumation of deceased French and British soldiers from the camp cemetery, carried out in the 1920s. From a historical point of view, the most valuable material is a list of almost 5,000 soldiers who died in the camp, which mentions the christian names and surnames of soldiers, their regiments and the dates and causes of death. Nonetheless, the prisoners are presented merely as items on a list. This tantalizing document does not enable us to delve deeper into the experience of these men. We can only guess at their emotions, feelings and worries, their strategies for surviving incarceration or their ability to adapt to camp life. And we can ascertain nothing about their engagement with the materiality of the camp.

The site itself was considered a forgotten landscape, a space spread between myth and reality (Smagliński 1993). It was generally accepted that nothing of the camp had survived into modern times. But this understanding changed in 2014, just two years later, when hillshade models of high resolution DEM (Digital Elevation Model) (Airborne laser scanning/LiDAR-derivative) were made available as Open Access on a Polish platform geoportal[1] (see Kobiałka 2019a). The first remains of dug-outs were noticed by the author and Mikołaj Kostyrko during their surveying of the visualizations. This was the beginning of an archaeological interest in the value of the camp heritage that we have been researching ever since (e.g. Kobiałka 2018, Kobiałka et al 2017).

Here, various archaeological and social initiatives regarding the Czersk camp that have been taking place since the discovery are discussed. The last part of this paper analyses one of the most important results of the research carried out as part of the project entitled *Między Pamięcią a Zapomnieniem: Archeologia a XX-wieczne Dziedzictwo Militarne na Terenach Zalesionych* (*Between Memory and Oblivion: Archaeology and 20th Century Military Heritage in the Woodlands*): a collection of objects from the camp which are examples of trench art (see also Kobiałka 2018, 2019b). It gives a glimpse into the diversity, complexity and creativity of human beings under detention during the first global apocalypse.

Between past and present at Czersk camp – curating Great War heritage

The recent development of Great War archaeology in Poland resembles the situation in Belgium where it was local, non-professional historians, regionalists, enthusiasts and metal detectorists who were the first to appreciate the historical and cultural value of the broken, rusted, decayed, buried objects and structures from the Great War found in the Belgian soil (Saunders 2007: 12–17). In other words, they were first to value Great War 'trash' as heritage. Archaeology did not initially recognize this heritage as possessing any archaeological value. That changed at the beginning of the twenty-first century. Now, the archaeology of the Great War is one of the most dynamically developing fields of archaeological interests in Belgium (e.g. Stichelbaut et al 2017; Gheyle et al 2018).

Without doubt, the archaeological value of Great War heritage is attracting increasing interest in many countries (Cresswell 2005; Saunders 2007; see also Stichelbaut and Cowley 2016). Poland is no exception. The project entitled *Archaeological Revival of Memory of World War I*, headed by Anna Zalewska (Zalewska 2016, Zalewska and Kiarszys 2017), is an excellent example of an archaeological engagement with the material remains of the Great War in Poland (see also Karczewski and Karczewska 2014; Czarnowicz, Ochał-Czarnowicz, and Kołodziejczak 2016). Equally worth mentioning are recent examples of invasive (Rola et al 2015) and non-invasive archaeological research (Kobiałka et al 2017) on Great War Polish PoW camps. However, the objects and structures buried in the ground had been in most cases discovered by enthusiasts, regionalists and metal detectorists for at least two decades. Sadly, archaeologists often arrive at a site too late, to discover that many artefacts have already been illegally robbed and destroyed.

The contemporary Czersk camp landscape is covered with pine forest, fields of crops and meadows. Surviving historical documentation is limited, so it has been archaeological research, rather than archival scrutiny that has facilitated the reclamation of some of the camp's material memories. As mentioned, part of the research methodology was the use of LiDAR derivatives which initially enabled the recording and documentation of approximately 150 camp structures (Kobiałka et al 2017). Two clusters of dug-outs, barracks, trash pits and other categories of camp structures were registered. Now in 2020, after six years of research, the location of more than 600 structures is known (Kostyrko 2018).

Remains of barracks, dug-outs, administration buildings and others required field verification by fieldwalking. Moreover, a diverse assemblage of material culture was documented during the field research that reflects on a day-to-day life of prisoners and administration staff in the camp. Among the artefacts there were uniform buttons and buckles, iron bowls and mugs, tin cans, glass bottles for wine, beer and medicine, spoons, forks, mess tins, fragments of barbed wire fence, axes and shovels, to mention but a few. Aerial and geophysical surveys also played an important role in the integrated non-invasive research in Czersk, allowing the documentation of the camp's structures. All in all, one thing is sure, to paraphrase Smagliński: *the cemetery is not the only heritage of the huge prisoner-of-war camp in Czersk that survived until the present* (Figure 9.2).

The research methodology was not limited to the previously mentioned methods. One of the first steps was searching for material culture related to the camp that might be stored in museums, or local memorial rooms or be in the possession of those whose grandfathers were prisoners or guards in Czersk. Only one of the memorial rooms owned some artefacts related to the camp. It was an *Exhibition of Nature of the Tuchola Forest and the River Wda (Wystawa Przyrody Borów Tucholskich i Doliny Rzeki Wdy)* in Czarna Woda. Part of the exhibition includes

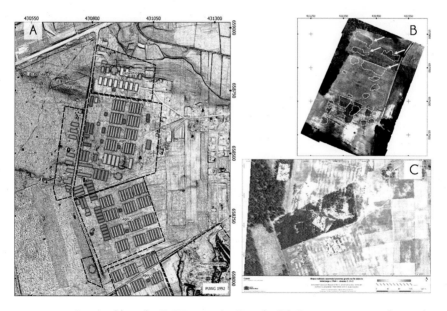

FIGURE 9.2 Researching the PoW camp in Czersk. (A) Reconstruction of a northern part of the camp based on LiDAR-derivatives and historical records. (© M. Kostyrko.) (B) Aerial photo of part of the camp unforested today (dark arrows indicate possible features related to the camp, white arrows indicate cropmarks unrelated to the camp). (© M. Kostyrko.) (C) Result of geophysical survey – background is an aerial photo taken in 1964 showing marks left by PoW structures. (© R. Ryndziewicz and courtesy Głowny Urząd Geodezji i Kartografii.)

objects given by the descendants of those who were imprisoned in the camp or whose fathers, grandfathers were German guards (*Wachmann*) there. The remaining part of the collection contains artefacts that were legally found by the Ilfing Association while surveying the camp terrain.

Great War heritage does not just belong to the past. It is, in many ways, part of the present as well. The past of the camp can be considered as a space that potentially could link and bind various social and cultural groups – indeed, it is multi-vocal (e.g. Hodder 2008; Hamilakis 2011). Whatever terms one uses – archaeologies of the contemporary past (Buchli and Lucas 2001), an archaeology of the recent past (Olsen and Pétursdóttir 2014) or an archaeology in and of the present (Harrison 2011) – archaeological research concerning material heritage of recent decades has a strong social and cultural value/impact. Furthermore, it is archaeology that should be understood as a verb, as *practising*, building certain social and cultural attitudes towards the value and meaning of the material heritage of the recent past as such. It was this understanding of the goals of archaeology that provided the framework for the following initiatives that took place at Czersk camp.

The first initiative was the organization of an exhibition entitled *Between Memory and Oblivion: An Archaeology of a Prisoner-of-War Camp in Czersk from the First World War* (*Między Pamięcią a Zapomnieniem: Archeologia Pierwszowojennego Obozu Jenieckiego w Czersku*). It was one of the results of the NEARCH project[2] and was led by the author. The aim of the exhibition was to show the local communities of Czersk that there are still many remains of the camp and to highlight the important role of such material heritage. Various posters that discussed the archaeology of the recent past, social and cultural aspects of archaeological research, non-invasive archaeological methods and the results of our research on the Czersk camp were used as a case study (Figure 9.3A).

The second initiative was a 'lesson of living archaeology' for a group of disabled people from Czersk and neighbouring villages. In the course of this 2017 initiative, archaeologists and invited guests together explored the history of the forests around Czersk. For the disabled the opportunity to learn about archaeology and the material past of the Czersk camp was a true adventure, as Renata Breszta – a tutor of the group – noted (pers. comm., 22 May 2018) (Figure 9.3B). Once again, the possibility of personally discovering and touching a rusted mug or bowl used by prisoners was a valuable experience for those who took part in the event. In 2018, the lesson was repeated – this time a team of archaeologists engaged disabled people in a geophysical survey at the camp.

Last but not least, an aggregation of spatial data obtained through the interpretation of the LiDAR data and the analysis of spatial distribution of metal artefacts at the camp terrain supported the preparation of a Monument Record Sheet (*Karta Ewidencyjna Zabytku Archeologicznego*). Now, six years after the beginning of the first archaeological survey in the Czersk camp, this rare Great War heritage is under legal protection of the heritage authorities (Figure 9.3C).

FIGURE 9.3 (A) Image from the exhibition *Between Memory and Oblivion: An Archaeology of a Prisoner-of-War Camp in Czersk from the First World War*. It represents prisoners returning to the Czersk camp from forced labour, overlayed by the pine forest that now covers the site. (© (A) Kobiałka.) (B) A group of disabled people attend a 'living archaeology' session at the camp site. (© Author.) (C) The distribution of metal artefacts was key to assessing the extent of the site. (© Author.)

Heritage of the Czersk camp: Trash as (trench) art

One of the key advantages of archaeological research on PoWs and their camps is the opportunity to focus on the ways in which material culture was creatively used and reused during the time of imprisonment. An additional advantage of such studies is the fact that PoW material culture has been underestimated for a long time and is mostly unknown. Trench art can be regarded as a special category of PoW camp material culture (Carr 2011; Rydén 2018).

In 2000, Saunders (2000: 45) defined trench art as 'any item made by soldiers, prisoners of war, and civilians, from war *matériel* directly, or any other material, as long as it and they are associated temporally and/or spatially with armed conflict or its consequences'. I adopt this definition in this paper. Indeed, trench art of the Western Front of the Great War is relatively well recognized and researched. It is mostly the result of studies of Saunders (2000, 2003, 2004, 2007). According to Saunders, trench art embodies the totality and fragmentary of war experience. It gives insight into entanglements between people and objects during military conflicts. It often expresses what was unvoiceable (non-discursive). And as Saunders (2004: 22) goes on to say:

> Until recently, anthropology largely avoided twentieth-century industrialised war, as did archaeology; art history ignored the phenomenon of trench art; museums (even those dedicated to war) often appeared to marginalise everything except weaponry and uniforms, and military history concerned itself almost exclusively with grand strategies and tactical battles. In the interstices between this array of compartmentalized approaches exists a virtually unexplored and infinite number of overlapping worlds, where human experience is embodied in the relationships between people and objects.

However, one can say that the strongest aspects of Saunders research are also the weakest. To be more precise, although the British archaeologist analyses the great spectrum and variety of manifestations of trench art, his studies focus mostly on the Western Front. The material culture of the Eastern Front is almost absent in his research. My point is simple: one cannot understand the nature and diversity of the Great War and trench art without taking into account the Eastern Front which was such an integral part of the First World War.

The unique value of trench art from the Czersk camp comes from the fact that it is an example of a material culture of the Eastern Front. Additionally, and also very relevantly, the assemblage is related to just one specific site and period of time (1914–1919). It holds material (thing) memories that one cannot find in the written records.

The most typical category of trench art made and remade at PoW camps consists of objects related to eating and drinking. As already pointed out by some studies (e.g. Karpus and Rezmer 1997), living conditions in the German Great War's camps were very tough. Prisoners were allowed to possess only a limited number of personal belongings. Practical items like mugs or bowls, spoons etc. were of the greatest value. In fact they might be considered priceless: if a prisoner lacked a bowl in which he could receive a ladleful of soup or a mug into which tea could be poured, then he would go without. Such objects could literally mean the difference between life and death. Consequently, they were made and remade from every suitable material that could be accessed by the prisoners. Unsurprisingly, this category of object was among those recovered at the site of the Czersk camp (Figure 9.4).

Figure 9.4A presents one such an example, a small tin can. It may have entered the camp in a parcel sent to Czersk by the Danish Red Cross or by a prisoner's family. The can is empty; the contents most probably eaten by a prisoner. However, it was not simply thrown away as a useless metal trash. Two fragments of wire were coiled around the can and then intertwined to make a handle. In this way,

FIGURE 9.4   (A) A prisoner mug made from a tin can and fragments of metal wire. (© Author and courtesy Wystawa Przyrody Borów Tucholskich i Doliny Rzeki Wdy.) (B) A glass made from a cut-down bottle. (© Author and courtesy Wystawa Przyrody Borów Tucholskich i Doliny Rzeki Wdy.) (C) Trench art aluminium prisoner numbers. (© Author and courtesy Wystawa Przyrody Borów Tucholskich i Doliny Rzeki Wdy.) (D) Death certificate of prisoner number 9948 – Wassili Stoiku, a Romanian PoW who died in the camp on 22 January 1917. (© Author and courtesy Archiwum Państwowe w Bydgoszczy.)

a drinking mug was created. One can discern that the wire had to be cut off by the use of a sharp tool (pincers?). This object was so robustly made that it could still serve as a drinking vessel today. Other finds indicated prisoners also used drinking glasses, which they manufactured from beer bottles (Figure 9.4B).

One very typical and iconic aspect of PoW camps across both world wars was the allocation of camp numbers to imprisoned soldiers, and this held true for Czersk too. However, the camp numbers from Czersk are intriguing items (Figure 9.4C). Perhaps surprisingly, these prisoner identity tags were not always issued by the Germans, but were – at least sometimes – made by the prisoners themselves. Interestingly, the individuality and identity of each soldier is manifested in the way in which camp numbers were carved and decorated. The differing techniques and varying sizes attest to the fact they were made by the PoWs. The holes drilled through them indicate that they were intended to be attached to uniforms and coats.[3] This practice of forcing PoWs to participate in their own registration and identification as prisoners is not unique to Czersk or indeed to the First World War – see, for example, the varied identity tags made by British prisoners of the Japanese during the Second World War (for example, Imperial War Museum EPH 30, EPH 72, EPH 101).

It has to be highlighted that these small, aluminium plaques with inscribed camp numbers each relate to particular human beings – PoWs from the Czersk camp who had names and surnames; they were fathers, husbands, uncles, etc. Without any doubt, each numbered tag encapsulates different memories and experiences. To put it metaphorically, the camp numbers have human faces, as Burström (2009) would have put it. For example, it became clear from archival research that the number 9948 was Wassili Stoiku, a Romanian PoW who died at the camp on 22 January 1917. He was 36 years old and was a Greek Catholic. He died soon after arriving at the Czerk camp from the Romanian Front. The cause of death – as the record states – was inanition of the body (i.e. exhaustion and starvation) (Figure 9.4D). And as well as serving as emblems of personal suffering, these artefacts are testaments to human creativity and ingenuity. They took time, effort and precise workmanship to create. They are also possessed of an artistic or ornamental quality that transcends their ostensible purpose. When we look at this sort of trench art, we cannot but feel that we are standing very close to its makers.

The prisoners' creativity is manifested and embodied in an astonishing variety of ways. Without any doubt, time spent in Czersk camp was a difficult and painful experience (Figure 9.5). The number of almost 5,000 soldiers who are buried

FIGURE 9.5 (A) A view of the camp cemetery; (B–D) metal plaques with prisoners' names and numbers. (© Author.)

at the camp cemetery is an unquestionable proof (Marcinkiewicz 2016). Rare written testimonies of the prisoners confirm the horror and tragedy – as one of them recollected after the war:

> The next day after unloading us from the cattle boxcars we were made to clear large areas of the forest. Emaciated by starving from the very first day of captivity, we had to work beyond human capability. – If you want to have a roof over your head for the winter – shouted the guards – you have to work hard. After clearing this part of the forest you will build dug-outs here. Nobody will do it for you.
>
> *(Milewski 1993: 9; transl. author)*

The camp cemetery yields a further category of prisoner of war trench art – their own grave markers. The prisoners were buried in multiple graves, initially marked by wooden crosses, later of reinforced concrete. They bore metal plaques with prisoners' names and numbers carved into them. These plaques should be perceived as a unique and very characteristic kind of trench art from the Czersk camp. The carvings are in the Cyrillic alphabet, for which reason it can be safely assumed that they were made by prisoners. Interesting to note that all the plaques on one cross are made in a single style, most likely by one prisoner – physical evidence of an unknown social situation. Trench art literally memorializes the prisoners in this instance (Figure 9.5).

Remaking and reusing were characteristic ways in which trench art could be produced. The plaques confirm this insight and also remind us that the remaking is not confined to any specific era of an artefact's 'social life'. Many crosses at the cemetery lack such plaques. That is why it is now impossible to determine who is buried at each grave. In 2018, ethnographic research was carried out among local communities in order to collect additional memories concerning the past and present of the cemetery – the most obvious and important heritage of the camp. One of the informants told a story of how local children used to play at the cemetery in the 1960s. Boys liked to go fishing too. At the time, Polish stores were literally empty – it was a time of deep communism and the permanent lack of even most elementary goods was part of day-to-day life. However, the young boys from Czersk and other local villages were very creative. They used the plaques from the Czersk cemetery as fishing weights to stabilize their floats. Trench art does indeed provide examples of human creativity in a many unexpected ways.

Prisoners were also forced labourers – essentially slaves – who were hired by the local people of Czersk to work for them. A wooden casket is an example of this process (Figure 9.6). In 1914, four sons of Augustyn Budziński were ordered to fight for the Kaiser. Budziński then decided to hire two prisoners from the Czersk camp who would help him run a pottery workshop. Eventually, in 1918, the prisoners ran away. Before that, they made the wooden box as a material sign of gratitude for good treatment and a roof over their head during the war. In an interview with a grandson of Budziński, it was revealed that the casket is a

FIGURE 9.6 (A–B) A wooden box made by two prisoners from the Czersk camp. (© M. Piechocki.) (C) The Budziński family. (© M. Piechocki.) (D) Pottery workshop where the prisoners worked during the war. (© M. Piechocki.)

'family treasure and true relic' (Marek Piechocki, pers. comm., 17 May 2017). It is this combination of materiality and sensoriality that truly characterizes trench art (Figure 9.6).

Conclusion

Materiality, memory, decay, death, fragmentation, emotions, human craft, ambivalence and meaning: archaeology at its purest is about all these things (Shanks 2012). And all of these things are remembered and manifested in and though material culture from the Czersk camp. Accordingly, this Great War heritage does not simply belong to the past. It is, in many ways, part of the present as well. The past of the camp can be considered as a space that links and binds various social and cultural groups. Describing some of the scientific and social initiatives that have recently been taking place in the Czersk camp was one of the main goals of this chapter. It is archaeology that a century after the closing of the Great War's PoW camps can shed new light on materialities of these landscapes and on PoW experiences of life behind barbed wire. These insights of archaeology cannot be underestimated.

Material culture was used and reused creatively by the prisoners. In short, for them, trash was priceless. Material culture was part of a strategy to survive and remain human in inhuman times. Prisoners made and used different material stuff. However, it has to be mentioned also that the opposite process took place: paradoxically, objects make people as much as people make objects (Saunders 2004: 6).This is the strength of a theoretical and practical contribution of archaeology within a multidisciplinary discourse of PoWs and PoW camps. These objects are no less valuable than memoirs or letters as embodiments of the PoW experience. As the discussion around the trench art from the Czersk camp indicates, trench art has the power to reveal very intimate memories, thoughts, worries, fears, hopes and beliefs related to day-to-day life in the camp.

The Great War is often understood and conceived as the first industrialized conflict (see Saunders 2013: 18). It can be said that entire countries were changed into war supplies factories that built millions of weapons of thousands of types to kill the enemy. However, archaeological analyses of material culture found at such sites as the Czersk camp can offer a more individual perspective on the matter. The creativity of prisoners, faced with challenging circumstances, imbued mass-produced material with new forms, functions and meanings. Trench art is a material culture with a human face, so to speak (e.g. Burström 2009). Above all, trench art is the art of human creativity. It allows us to experience the producers, owners and users of these unique artefacts almost literally. That is why trench art can play an important social and cultural role in presenting and curating the experience of the Great War heritage to a wider public.

And the camp, as Saunders (2007) might put it, is a space that binds together the dead and the living, the past and the present, ideas and materialities, the human and the non-human and, ultimately in this case, the archaeologists and the local communities interested in preserving the heritage of those who were detained a century ago in the Czersk camp.

Acknowledgements

I would like to thank Kornelia Kajda and Mikołaj Kostyrko for joint research on the archaeology of the camp in Czersk. A big thank you to my wife Anna Kobiałka who graphically refined figures for this article. Finally, Marek Piechocki told me the story behind the wooden casket and allowed me to reproduce photographs from his private archive (Figure 9.6). This work was supported by the National Science Centre, Poland under Grant no. DEC-2016/20/S/HS3/00001.

Notes

1 http://mapy.geoportal.gov.pl/imap/?locale=pl&gui=new&sessionID=3698782).
2 See more at http://www.nearch.eu/.
3 For an example of an official issue German PoW identity tag of the period, see EPH 52 in the Imperial War Museum's collections – a tag issued at Doberitz prisoner of war camp.

References

Buchli, V. and G. Lucas (eds.). (2001) *Archaeologies of the Contemporary Past.* London: Routledge.

Burström, M. (2009) Looking into the recent past: extending and exploring the field of Archaeology. *Current Swedish Archaeology* 15–16:21–36.

Carr, G. (2011) Engraving and Embroidering Emotions upon the Material Culture of Internment. In A. Myers and G. Moshenska (eds.), *Archaeologies of Internment*, pp 129–145. New York: Springer.

Carr, G. and H. Mytum. (2012a) The Importance of Creativity behind Barbed Wire. Setting a Research Agenda. In G. Carr and H. Mytum (eds.), *Cultural Heritage and Prisoners of War: Creativity Behind Barbed Wire*, pp 1–15. New York: Routledge.

———. (eds.) (2012b) *Cultural Heritage and Prisoners of War: Creativity Behind Barbed Wire.* New York: Routledge.

Cresswell, Y. (2005) Behind the Wire: The Material Culture of Civilian Internment on the Isle of Man in the First World War. In R. Dove (ed.), *'Totally Un-English'? Britain's Internment of 'Enemy Aliens' in Two World Wars*, pp 45–61. Amsterdam-New York: Rodopi.

Czarnownicz, M., A. Ochał-Czarnowicz and P. Kołodziejczak. (2016) Karpackie epizody Wielkiej Wojny – badania, ochrona i rewitalizacja zespołu pobojowsk z okresu pierwszej wojny światowej w rejonie Kamienia nad Jaślikami i Jasiela. *Topiarius. Studia Krajobrazowe* 2(1):43–61.

Dąbrowski, J. (2015) *Wielka Wojna 1914–1918.* Oświęcim: Napoleon V.

Doegen, W. (1921) *Kriegsgefangene Volker, Band I: Der KriegsgefangenenHaltung Und Schicksal in Deutschland.* Berlin: Verlag für Politik und Wirtschaft.

Gheyle, W., B. Stichelbaut, T. Saey, N. Note, H. Van den Berghe, V. Van Eetvelde, M. Van Meirvenneand and J. Bourgeois. (2018) Scratching the surface of war. Airborne laser scans of the Great War conflict landscape in Flanders (Belgium). *Applied Geography* 90:55–68.

Hamilakis, Y. (2011) Archaeological ethnography: A multitemporal meeting ground for archaeology and anthropology. *Annual Review of Anthropology* 40:399–414.

Harrison, R. (2011) Surface assemblages. Towards an archaeology *in* and *of* the present. *Archaeological Dialogues* 18(2):141–161.

Hodder, I. (2008) Multivocality and Social Archaeology. In H. Junko, C. Fawcett and J.M. Matsunaga (eds.), *Evaluating Multiple Narratives. Beyond Nationalist, Colonialist, Imperialist Archaeologies*, pp 196–200. New York: Springer.

Jastrzębski, W. (2008) Miejsce obozu jeńców w Tucholi w strukturze niemieckich obozów dla jeńców wojennych w latach 1914-1918. In Z. Karpus (ed.), *Tuchola: Obóz Jeńców I Internowanych 1914–1923, Volume 3: Warunki Życia Jeńców i Internowanych*, pp 19–28. Toruń: Wydawnictwo UMK.

Karczewski, M. and M. Karczewska. (2014) Archeologia I wojny światowej na giżyckim odcinku frontu wschodniego. In R. Kempa (ed.), *Wielka Wojna na Mazurach 1914–1915. Studia z Dziejów Frontu Wschodniego I Wojny Światowej*, pp 393–403. Giżycko: Towarzystwo Miłośników Twierdzy Boyen.

Karpus, Z. and W. Rezmer. (1997) *Tuchola. Obóz Jeńców i Internowanych 1914–1923, Volume 1.* Toruń: Wydawnictwo UMK.

Kobiałka, D. (2018) 100 years later: The dark heritage of the Great War at a prisoner-of-war camp in Czersk, Poland. *Antiquity* 92 (363): 772–787.

———. (2019a) Living monuments of the Second World War: Terrestrial laser scanning and trees with carvings. *International Journal of Historical Archaeology* 23 (1): 129–152.

———. (2019b) Trench art between memory and oblivion: A report from Poland (and Syria). *Journal of Conflict Archaeology* 14 (1):4–24.

Kobiałka, D., M. Kostyrko and K. Kajda. (2017) The Great War and its landscapes between memory and oblivion: the case of prisoners of war camps in Tuchola and Czersk, Poland. *International Journal of Historical Archaeology* 21 (1):134–151.

Kostyrko, M. (2018) *Biografia Przeszłych Krajobrazów w Perspektywie Danych Teledetekcyjnych.* *Unpublished PhD* thesis. Poznań: Institute of Archaeology.

Marcinkiewicz, A. (2016) Cmentarz obozu jeńców wojennych w Czersku w świetle materiałów archiwalnych ze zbiorów Muzeum Historyczno-Etnograficznego w Chojnicach. *Zeszyty Chojnickie* 32:250–259.

Milewski, J. (1993) Szlakiem zapomnianej zbrodni pruskiej I wojny światowej w Czersku w Borach Tucholskich. *October 8. Gazeta Kociewska* 40:8–9.

Olsen, B. and Þ. Pétursdóttir (eds.) (2014) *Ruin Memories: Materialities, Aesthetics and the Archaeology of the Recent Past.* Abingdon-New York: Routledge.

Pope-Hennessy, U.B. (1920) *Map of the Main Prison Camps in Germany and Austria.* London: Nisbet.

Rola, J., M. Stasiak and M. Kwiatkowska. (2015) Badania sondażowe na terenie obozu jenieckiego z I wojny światowej w Pile. *Wielkopolskie Sprawozdania Archeologiczne* 16:253–258.

Rydén, J.B. (2018) When bereaved of everything: objects from the concentration camp of Ravensbrück as expressions of resistance, memory, and identity. *International Journal of Historical Archaeology* 22:511–530.

Saunders, N.J. (2000) Bodies of metal, shells of memory: 'trench art', and the Great War re -cycled'. *Journal of Material Culture* 5:43–67.

———. (2003) *Trench Art: Materialities and Memories of War.* Oxford: Berg.

———. (2004) Material Culture and Conflict: The Great War, 1914-2003. In N.J. Saunders (ed.), *Matters of Conflict. Material Culture, Memory and the First World War,* pp 1–25. London, New York: Routledge.

———. (2007) *Killing Time: Archaeology and the First World War.* Stroud: Sutton.

———.(2013) Anthropology and archaeology of the First World War. *Cadernos do CEOM, Patrimônio, Memória e Identidade* 26 (38):17–31

Shanks, M. (2012) *The Archaeological Imagination.* Walnut Creek: Left Coast Press.

Smagliński, F. (1993) Utuliła ich pomorska ziemia. *Echo Czerska. Miesięcznik Komitetu Obywatelskiego* 11(43):1.

Stichelbaut, B., W. Gheyle, V. Van Eetvelde, M. Van Meirvenne, T. Saey, N. Note, H. Van den Berghe and J. Bourgeois. (2017) The Ypres salient 1914–1918: Historical aerial photography and the landscape of war. *Antiquity* 91(355): 235–249.

Stichelbaut, B. and D. Cowley (eds.) (2016) *Conflict Landscapes and Archaeology from Above.* Farnham/London. Ashgate/Routledge.

Tarlow, S. (2012) The archaeology of emotion and affect. *Annual Review of Anthropology* 41(1): 169–185.

Zalewska, A. (2016) The 'gas-scape' on the Eastern Front, Poland (1914-2014): Exploring the Material and Digital Landscapes and Remembering Those 'twice-killed'. In B. Stichelbaut and D. Cowley (eds.), *Conflict Landscapes and Archaeology from Above,* pp 147–165. Farnham-London: Ashgate-Routledge.

Zalewska, A. and G. Kiarszys. (2017) Absent Presence of Great War Cemeteries in the Municipality of Bolimow, Central Poland. In A. Zalewska, J.M. Scott and G. Kiarszys (eds.), *The Materiality of Troubled Pasts. Archaeologies of Conflicts and Wars,* pp 55–82. Warsaw-Szczecin: Roadside Lesson History Foundation, Institute of Archaeology, Szczecin University.

10

CURATING THE MACEDONIAN CAMPAIGN

Andrew Shapland

In 2012, the Archaeological Museum of Thessaloniki in northern Greece put on a temporary exhibition called 'Archaeology Behind Battle Lines' (Adam-Veleni and Koukouvou 2012). It marked an important anniversary: the centenary of the foundation of the Archaeological Service in Macedonia, which was formed as a result of the military conquest of Thessaloniki by Greek forces in 1912 during the First Balkan War. It shows the importance of archaeology to the Hellenic State that the archaeology of Macedonia was given protection even before the 1913 Treaty of London had been signed, marking the formal absorption of Thessaloniki and its surrounding area into Greece. The exhibition covered the first ten years of the Archaeological Service, finishing with objects brought by refugees from Asia Minor in 1922 as a result of the disastrous Greek campaign to expand the borders of the state further east (Koukouvou 2017). In this part of the world, the Great War was part of a much longer period of conflict which helped to determine the borders and populations of the modern Greek state.

Among the exhibits were objects excavated at the site of Chauchitza by Stanley Casson in 1921–1922. He later recalled that:

> As I found the graves of these well-armed warriors I could not but reflect on the progress of civilisation, for above those graves I had first, before excavation, to clear away countless shell-fragments, cartridges and all the oddments of modern war, before I could arrive, a few feet lower down, at the armaments of our ancestors.
>
> *(Casson 1935: 275)*

The countless shell-fragments Casson describes were the product of the British front line around Lake Doiran, where three major battles against Bulgarian and German forces were fought between 1916 and 1918. The Iron Age cemetery of

DOI: 10.4324/9781003263531-13

Chauchitza was discovered accidentally in a camp behind the lines by a YMCA volunteer named Robert Gaddie in 1917 (Casson 1935: 274; Maitland 2017). Captain Casson, who was serving both as an intelligence officer in the British Army and acting as assistant curator in the British Salonika Force Museum in Thessaloniki, investigated the site and found more burials. In 1921, he returned to excavate the site properly and the finds became some of the first additions to the collection of the Archaeological Museum of Thessaloniki (Casson 1921). The original finds from the site had ended up in the National Museum of Scotland in Edinburgh and the British Museum in London. Other warrior graves from Macedonia became part of the Louvre collections. Casson himself resumed his academic career, writing an important book on the history and archaeology of Macedonia before signing up again at the outbreak of the Second World War and dying while on military service in 1944 (Casson 1926; Myres 1945).

This chapter will explore the intertwined nature of archaeology and warfare during the Macedonian Campaign which began with the arrival of Allied troops in Thessaloniki, also known as Salonika, in October 1915 and ended with their withdrawal in 1919. Although the Campaign was not on the scale of the Western Front and has largely been forgotten by comparison, at its peak the Allied Army numbered 600,000 soldiers (Wakefield 2017: 8). A combination of political necessity, military activity and archaeological opportunism resulted in the discovery and reporting of large numbers of sites and finds in the area of Macedonia under Allied control. The presence of archaeologists such as Stanley Casson serving in the British and French forces fostered the development of archaeology in the region, only a few years after it had become part of Greece. These foreign archaeologists cooperated with Greek archaeological officials, resulting in two museums being formed in Thessaloniki, one for British finds and the other for French finds. The museums were dispersed in 1919 with many of the finds being donated to the UK and France by the Greek government. Such objects, as the 2012 exhibition showed, have a dual significance as a result of their archaeological and First World War context.

Foundation of the Museums

Allied troops arrived in Salonika in October 1915 in order to go to the aid of Serbia, which was threatened by the imminent entry of Bulgaria into the First World War on the side of the Central Powers.[1] By the time French and British forces arrived in Serbia, it was too late to stop the Bulgarian advance, and by the end of 1915, they had retreated back into Greece. A change in the Greek government since the dispatch of the expedition had seen the country affirm its neutrality. For the time being, therefore, the Bulgarian Army respected Greece's borders. But Greece was unable to disarm the Allied force or make it leave its territory. The French and British occupied the area surrounding the strategically important port of Salonika (Thessaloniki) and dug themselves in. Their fortifications became known as the 'Birdcage' because so much barbed wire was used, but it was the associated trenches which became significant from an archaeological point of view because as they were dug, antiquities started coming to light. This was an inevitable consequence of trench digging on other fronts too (Saunders 2010: 4–7), but in Macedonia it was particularly productive for the archaeology of the region because of the nature of the Campaign, the rich archaeological landscape, and the way these discoveries were reported and collected.

The British and the French took control of different areas of Macedonia, partly as a result of differences of opinion between the British and French commands about the aims of the Campaign. This was reflected in their approach to antiquities: the French Army included a formal scientific expedition which began to explore the French zone and undertake excavations. The British Army instead relied on archaeologists who had joined up, a number of whom had ended up in intelligence roles because of their knowledge of Greece and the Greek language. Among these was Ernest Gardner, who signed up as a Lieutenant in the Royal Naval Volunteer Reserve while Professor of Archaeology at the University of London, and who had previously served as Director of the British School at Athens.

In December 1915, Gardner persuaded his superior, Col. Cunliffe-Owen to issue orders that any antiquities found were to be reported. As a result, early in 1916, when the Greek Government in Athens expressed concern about the protection of antiquities in Macedonia, particularly those of the Byzantine period, Gardner was tasked with finding a mutually agreeable solution. In February 1916, a meeting was called between British and French representatives and the Greek official (Ephor) in charge of Byzantine antiquities, Adamantios Adamantiou. It was agreed that finds were to be reported and brought to Thessaloniki, where they could be inspected by the Ephor (Gardner and Casson 1919: 10–12). In this way, the antiquities laws could be upheld despite neutral Greece effectively being occupied by the Allied army, and orders to this effect were signed by its commander, General Maurice Sarrail.

As a result of the agreement, two museums were established in Thessaloniki. French finds were kept in the ancient church of Saint George, also known as the Rotunda (Farnoux 2012). The French took the opportunity to expand earlier Greek excavations in the area of the Rotunda and nearby Arch of Galerius, both important examples of Roman architecture (Hébrard 1920). From the start, the French were more willing to initiate archaeological excavations in and around Thessaloniki. Archaeologists and historians served in the formally constituted *Service Archéologique de l'Armée d'Orient*, whose activities were justified as being part of the Army's scientific mission, in the spirit of Napoleon (Mendel 1918). Many of its members had previously worked in Greece as members of the French School at Athens.

Meanwhile the British based their museum at another Thessaloniki landmark, the White Tower, a remnant of the city's mediaeval walls on the harbourside. Gardner sought permission to use this building at the suggestion of Harry Pirie-Gordon, another archaeologist, who was at that time in charge of

FIGURE 10.1 Lt Cdr Ernest Gardner in the British Salonika Force Museum at the White Tower, Thessaloniki. (© IWM Q31874.)

the Eastern Mediterranean Special Intelligence Branch in Salonika (Gill 2006). It was the ideal place for Gardner to combine his formal role as intelligence officer, since it was also used as a signals station and offered a view over the harbour, with his informal position as museum curator (Figure 10.1). Gardner's assistant in both activities was 2nd Lieutenant Marcus Tod, University Lecturer in Greek Epigraphy at Oxford (Gill 2011: 393–395). As an Italian Liaison officer in Salonika approvingly noted of the British Army: 'Archaeologists were found particularly useful in "I" work, because their training rendered them thoroughly capable of weighing, sifting, and co-ordinating evidence, and deducing accurate or at least reasonable conclusions' (Villari 1922: 71).

At first, Gardner's intelligence role consisted largely of reading the newspapers from Athens in order to write reports on the political situation in Greece but over time his knowledge of modern Greek meant that he took a more active role in intelligence gathering, and he left the White Tower Museum in 1917. He was succeeded briefly by Thomas Eric Peet, an Egyptologist serving with the Army Service Corps, before another officer took over, Major Alexander Wade, who served as curator until the end of the War. Unlike Gardner and Peet, or Stanley Casson, who was Wade's deputy as museum curator, Wade was an amateur archaeologist with no experience of Greece. Wade was Landing Officer for the harbour but also worked in counter-espionage, boasting of his spy-catching exploits in a book written after the War (Wade 1938). It was under Wade that the museum was moved in 1918 from the White Tower to nearby British Headquarters at the Papapheion Orphanage.

These various museums appear to have served their purpose of allowing Greek officials to inspect finds. Both Adamantiou and Georgios Oikonomos, Ephor of Antiquities visited the White Tower (Gardner and Casson 1919: 12). Oikonomos was succeeded by Eustratios Pelekidis in 1917, when royalist officials were removed from post following the abdication of the King, coinciding with the entry of Greece into the First World War on the side of the Allies. Pelekidis appears to have taken a more active interest in the collection, compiling a catalogue of the pottery of the British finds (Kanatselou and Shapland 2014). The British Salonika Force Museum, as it became known, was open by appointment and became part of the lively entertainment scene along the harbourside for off-duty troops (Gardner and Casson 1919: 12). The atmosphere was dampened by the Great Fire of Thessaloniki in summer 1917 which destroyed much of the city, but the museums continued to function. Over the course of the War, fighting became more intense along the borders of Greece but the British and French continued to accumulate archaeological material in Thessaloniki from discoveries made by soldiers.

Significant Finds

Before the First World War, there had been little systematic archaeological excavation in Macedonia. In the nineteenth century, when the region was part of the Ottoman Empire, a number of antiquarians had come in search of inscriptions, and a collection of antiquities had been formed in Thessaloniki (Adam-Veleni 2017). Although the Greek Archaeological Service had initiated excavations in the city after 1912, there were few resources available against a background of continuing military conflict (Akrivopoulou 2012). The wider Macedonian landscape was known for its distinctive 'toumbes', artificial mounds, some of which had attracted the attention of treasure hunters and which had become of increasing interest to archaeologists. In 1909, Alan Wace and Maurice Thompson proposed a classification dividing them into funerary tumuli, prehistoric settlements and Greek town sites, but they did not conduct any excavations in Macedonia (Wace and Thompson 1909). The First World War explorations of these sites are therefore regarded as the foundation of the prehistoric archaeology of the region (Kotsakis 2017). With the arrival of the Allies in 1915, as Gardner noted, 'the numerous mounds which are familiar to Macedonian archaeologists lent themselves readily to military purposes' (Gardner and Casson 1919: 10). The use of the mounds for military installations and the digging of trenches across the landscape resulted in the accidental discovery of a large number of antiquities. Although some were no doubt kept by soldiers, the existence of orders to report them did result in some of them making their way to the British and French museums. Whereas the curators of the British Salonika Force Museum did little more than visit findspots and conduct the odd limited excavation, members of the *Service Archéologique de l'Armée d'Orient* initiated a number of large-scale excavations in the French zone.

Nevertheless, a number of significant discoveries were made by British soldiers while digging the Birdcage lines in early 1916. These included an inscription from the time of Hadrian dedicated to Manius Salarius Sabinus found by the Royal Scottish Fusiliers and a sixth-century tomb reported by Major Thomas Gayer Anderson (Gardner and Casson 1919: 15–24). Both were reported in the British press, with the grave group featuring in the *Illustrated War News* (Figure 10.2). Gayer Anderson was a career soldier with a strong interest in Egyptology and reported the find to Gardner in a beautifully illustrated letter (Morgan 2017: 132–148). Another officer who had followed orders and reported an archaeological find to Gardner was Lieutenant Archibald Don, a recent graduate from Cambridge with an interest in geology (Gardner and Casson 1919: 12–15). He and his brother had excavated two deposits of Neolithic pottery in a trench dug by their battalion of the Black Watch. It has only recently become apparent that this was at the time the earliest evidence for human occupation in Macedonia, with the oldest sherds dating to the Early Neolithic, around the 7th millennium BC (Dimoula 2017).

Over the course of the War, a number of soldiers, often officers with archaeological interests, contributed sherds found while trench digging or sometimes their own informal explorations of mounds while off-duty. Archaeology for some became a pastime, one of a number of leisure activities for which the Macedonian Campaign unfairly gained the reputation of being a holiday posting (Wakefield and Moody 2011: 146–164). There was a perception that little fighting was going on in Macedonia but after the initial withdrawal in 1915, trench warfare was established along the borders of Greece and there was also a high number of casualties from malaria and dysentery as a result of the climate. As the British front line expanded to the borders of Greece, the number of sites represented in the British Salonika Force Museum increased, growing to 36 by the end of the War. Among the later finds, of particular importance were the Iron Age jewellery from the Chauchitza cemetery mentioned above and a warrior burial of the Classical period discovered by Major Wade and Ephor

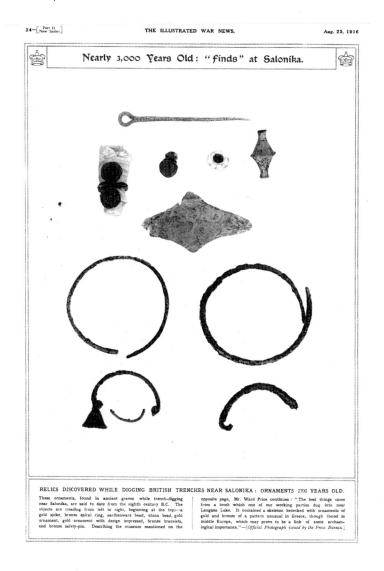

Nearly 3,000 Years Old: "finds" at Salonika.

RELICS DISCOVERED WHILE DIGGING BRITISH TRENCHES NEAR SALONIKA : ORNAMENTS 2700 YEARS OLD.

These ornaments, found in ancient graves while trench-digging near Salonika, are said to date from the eighth century B.C. The objects are (reading from left to right, beginning at the top)—a gold spike, bronze spiral ring, earthenware bead, china bead, gold ornament, gold ornament with design impressed, bronze bracelets, and bronze safety-pin. Describing the museum mentioned on the opposite page, Mr. Ward Price continues : "The best things came from a tomb which one of our working parties dug into near Langaza Lake. It contained a skeleton bedecked with ornaments of gold and bronze of a pattern unusual in Greece, though found in middle Europe, which may prove to be a link of some archaeological importance."—[Official Photograph issued by the Press Bureau.]

FIGURE 10.2   Grave goods from Aivasil pictured in the *Illustrated War News*, 23 August 1916. (Courtesy of D. Wardle; out of copyright.)

Pelekidis while investigating reports of looting near Thessaloniki (Figure 10.3) (Morgan 2017: 148–152). These finds were rapidly published in the *Annual of the British School at Athens* after the War, resulting in a wide-ranging survey of the Neolithic-Byzantine archaeology of Macedonia (Gardner and Casson 1919).

Among the significant finds made by French archaeologists were the warrior burials at the Archaic-Classical cemeteries of Zeitenlik and Mikro Karaburun

FIGURE 10.3   Finds from the Mikro Karaburun warrior grave found by Alexander Wade and Eustratios Pelekidis. (© Trustees of the British Museum.)

(Descamps-Lequime 2017; Picard 1919). These were the location of military camps but were extensively excavated by the archaeologist Léon Rey. The *Service Archéologique de l'Armée d'Orient* also conducted major excavations at three prehistoric mounds and explored many others. Soon after the War, Rey published a volume on prehistoric Macedonia which set these excavations in a wider regional context. Including detailed plans and sections of the mounds, as well as photographs and drawings of pottery, it was a seminal work for the prehistory of Macedonia (Rey 1917). It was dedicated to General Sarrail, who was frequently photographed visiting excavations in order to show that he was a patron of scientific research. One of these photographs gained wide circulation as a postcard (Figure 10.4).

The arrival of British and French archaeologists as part of what later became 'The Army of the Orient' had a long-lasting legacy for Macedonian archaeology. The finds made in the course of military activities, alongside the more directed archaeological exploration, resulted in what would now be described as an archaeological field survey of the landscape. Important sites such as Chauchitza and Dikili Tash were discovered during the War and then continued to be excavated afterwards. In the case of Chauchitza, two soldiers who served in the British Salonika Force, Stanley Casson and Walter Heurtley, returned to Macedonia after the War was over. Heurtley went on to excavate a number of other sites in the 1920s and wrote an important synthesis, *Prehistoric Macedonia*

FIGURE 10.4 General Maurice Sarrail visiting a French excavation. Undated post-card. (Out of copyright.)

(Heurtley 1939). Many of the wartime finds, however, did not stay in Greece as a result of agreements made at the end of the War.

Transfer

The British and French made separate agreements for the dispersal of their wartime museums when Allied troops withdrew in 1919. Ephor Eustratios Pelekidis was keen to establish a new museum in Thessaloniki, bringing together the various collections of finds in the city (Koukouvou 2017: 268–270). Although the Greek antiquities law ensured that the British and French finds belonged to the Greek state, there were provisions allowing the export of certain objects (Galanakis 2017). The French finds were subject to a partage agreement between the Greek Archaeological Service and the Louvre, with finds arbitrarily divided so that the contents of individual tombs were often split between the two (Descamps-Lequime 2017: 74). The British Salonika Force Museum was instead exported almost wholesale to London as a result of Alexander Wade's efforts. Although Ernest Gardner had intended that British finds stay in Greece, Wade offered the museum's contents to the newly formed Imperial War Museum, which refused them, before submitting his proposal to the War Office Trophies Committee. The Committee, although its remit was to collect military memorabilia for the Imperial War Museum, duly sent an order requesting the archaeological material. This resulted in a diplomatic flurry as General Milne, commander of the British Army in Salonika, sought permission from the government in Athens to export the contents of the Museum. The collection was listed and permission was granted, with the exception of two inscriptions which were clearly felt to be of historical significance to the region of Macedonia (Kanatselou and Shapland 2014).

As a result of these agreements, 30 crates of objects were despatched to the Louvre and 29 crates to the War Museum in London. Knowing that the War Museum did not want the archaeological objects, Wade contact the British Museum, which agreed to take them instead. The Louvre and the British Museum dealt with the objects in similar ways: selected objects were immediately put on display, with the warrior burials proving popular. The bulk of the objects, however, remained uncatalogued in the museum basements. In 1919, Stanley Casson assisted with the registration of some of the British Museum's Macedonian objects, but only about 10% were registered at that time. The remainder, almost entirely pot-sherds, were finally registered in 2011 and 2013 (Shapland 2017: 97–100). Some potsherds still bear labels written by soldiers giving the findspot, and Pelekidis' catalogue number, making them archaeological objects bearing the trace of their First World War history.

A number of other finds from Macedonia were brought back by individual soldiers. As a result, there are also objects from Chauchitza in the National Museum of Scotland (Maitland 2017). Wade also donated potsherds to the Ashmolean (Galanakis 2017). The British Museum also accepted a small number of objects from a tomb in Amphipolis, apparently revealed by shellfire, donated by Eric Gardner (Shapland 2017: 97). These, and other objects still in private hands, can be categorized as souvenirs, often brought home by soldiers. By contrast, the objects which went to the Louvre and British Museum functioned more as diplomatic gifts at a time when Greece needed the support of Britain and France as it sought to expand its borders (Clogg 2017: 48).

Curating the Great War

A small number of objects from Macedonia became part of permanent exhibitions at the Louvre and British Museum, but they were, and still are, primarily displayed for their aesthetic or archaeological interest. It was only in 2011 with the Louvre's temporary exhibition, *Au royaume d'Alexandre le Grand. La Macédoine antique*, that attention was drawn to the wartime context of some of these objects (Descamps-Lequime 2011). The exhibition also provided the impetus for the Louvre to work with the Archaeological Museum of Thessaloniki in order to understand the tomb assemblages from Zeitenlik and Mikro Karaburun split up in 1919. As a result, some of the finds made by French soldiers which had remained in Thessaloniki were temporarily put on display in France along archival material and other finds made by the Army of the Orient.

In 2012, the 'Archaeology Behind Battlelines' exhibition in Thessaloniki included, alongside a number of finds from Chauchitza, the Salarius inscription mentioned above, which the Greek government had retained in 1919 (Koukouvou 2017). It was shown alongside the photograph of its discovery by

FIGURE 10.5 The inscription to Manius Salarius Sabinus on display in the 2012 'Archaeology Behind Battle Lines' exhibition at the Archaeological Museum of Thessaloniki. (© Archaeological Museum of Thessaloniki – Ministry of Culture and Sports.)

British troops, emphasizing its wartime context (Figure 10.5). Unfortunately, it did not prove possible to include British Salonika Force finds from the British Museum as had been intended. Nevertheless, the catalogue and related symposium at the British Museum provided the opportunity to explore the archaeological activities of Allied soldiers in Macedonia. Continuing interest in this topic in Greece is shown by a 2018 exhibition, *Archaeology in Times of War at Kilkis,* at the

Archaeological Museum of Kilkis in Central Macedonia[2] and a recent book on the subject (Andreou and Efkleidou 2018). The centenary of the First World War in Greece has been marked with a number of other exhibitions and conferences (Katsaridou and Motsianos 2017; Mourelos et al 2018).

The various centenaries of the First World War in 2014–2018 provided the opportunity for heritage organizations in Britain to join the commemoration activities (coordinated as *14-18 Now*). These largely focused on the Western Front, and to a lesser extent on the British Navy and the Home Front in line with the First World War events the Government chose to focus on commemorating (DCMS 2013). The Gallipoli Campaign was a significant exception, which in some ways stood for the wider reach of the conflict. The Macedonian Campaign remained somewhat neglected, echoing the experience of veterans in the aftermath of the First World War (Palmer 1965: 239–242; Wakefield and Moody 2011: 235–236). There was a small display of Macedonian finds at the British Museum, including coins and other objects from Chauchitza. The Sedgwick Museum of Earth Sciences in Cambridge featured Archibald Don in a display on Cambridge geologists in the First World War (Freshney 2015). Soon after finding the Neolithic sherds mentioned above, Don had discovered a mammoth tusk at the bottom of the trench and sent it off to Cambridge. The display also acted as a form of commemoration since Don died of malaria a few months after the mammoth tusk arrived in Cambridge. A label on the tusk, recording Lieut. A.W.R. Don as the donor and the findspot as 'Nr. Aivali Salonika, 1916', gave an immediacy to the history of the tusk given in the display.

Although the Macedonian Campaign remains largely unknown outside Greece, despite the efforts of organizations like the Salonika Campaign Society, the focus on First World War centenaries has resulted in an increasing number of academic publications on this subject. As well as the various exhibition catalogues and other publications, the British Salonika Force collection at the British Museum is now available in its entirety on its website, and the online collections databases of the National Museum of Scotland and Louvre also include objects excavated by soldiers.[3] The British Museum online database received unexpected media attention in Greece in 2014 when objects from Amphipolis were erroneously linked to an excavation of an important burial mound at the same site; a widely reported conspiracy theory suggested that British troops had looted the mound despite it being of a later date than the British Museum finds and the other side of the front line (Holloway 2014). This demonstrates that collections databases can be used to tell a variety of stories: while they are an important means of making objects in museum collections available, museums also need to provide overviews of their collections, and the circumstances of acquisition. There is the potential for online exhibitions to fulfil this role, in the same way that temporary exhibitions have in recent years. Vodcasts and blog posts are another way to tell these stories (Shapland 2015).

Conclusions

Over time, the archaeological significance of the finds made by British and French soldiers in the First World War Macedonian Campaign has decreased. Some of the sites they explored, such as Mikro Karaburun (Karabournaki) or Aivatli (Lete), have been excavated subsequently, using modern techniques producing more detailed data. The syntheses by Casson and Heurtley have been superseded by the continuing discoveries of the Greek Archaeological Service and other academic projects. The centenaries of the various battles and conflicts which affected Thessaloniki in the early twentieth century have instead stimulated a growing interest in the historical significance of the same objects that were once used to establish the archaeology of the region. Labels which once simply recorded a findspot now have a poignancy as First World War documents. Exhibitions at the Louvre and Archaeological Museum of Thessaloniki have placed these objects in a military context rather than a purely archaeological context. In some ways these exhibitions have come full circle: these finds were first curated in temporary wartime museums in Thessaloniki staffed by British and French soldiers. The postwar deposition of these objects in archaeological museums helped fix their identity as archaeological finds but their significance continues to change as a result of different contexts of display and the stories that are told about them.

Acknowledgements

This paper is dedicated to the memory of Liana Stefani, Director of the Archaeological Museum of Thessaloniki until her untimely death, who was a wonderful collaborator in researching the archaeology of the Macedonian Campaign. The *Archaeology behind the Battle Lines* symposium which we organized brought together a number of scholars, all of whom I would like to thank for their various insights. I would also like to thank Nick Saunders for inviting me to give a seminar on this topic at the University of Bristol and for soliciting this contribution.

Notes

1 For detailed accounts of the Macedonian Campaign see Falls (1933–1935), Palmer (1965), and Wakefield and Moody (2011).
2 With an accompanying website: https://www.warandarchaeology.gr/en.
3 British Museum (https://research.britishmuseum.org/research/collection_online/search.aspx): 3,076 results for 'British Salonika Force'; National Museums Scotland (https://www.nms.ac.uk/explore-our-collections/search-our-collections/): 106 results for 'Chauchitsa'; Louvre (http://cartelen.louvre.fr/): 9 results for 'Armée d'Orient'.

References

Adam-Veleni, P. (2017) Archaeology in Macedonia: Then and Now. In A.J. Shapland and E. Stefani (eds.), *Archaeology Behind the Battle Lines: The Macedonian Campaign (1915–1919) and Its Legacy*, pp 327–355 (BSA Modern Greek and Byzantine Studies Volume 4). Abingdon: Routledge.

Adam-Veleni, P. and A. Koukouvou (eds.) (2012) *Αρχαιολογία στα μετόπισθεν. Στη Θεσσαλονίκη των ταραγμένων χρόνων 1912–1922/Archaeology Behind Battle Lines. In Thessaloniki of the Turbulent Years 1912–1922, Catalogue of the exhibition, Thessaloniki Archaeological Museum, 24 November 2012 - 31 December 2013.* Thessaloniki: Archaeological Museum of Thessaloniki.

Akrivopoulou, E. (2012) Amidst the Blasts of Cannon, Commences the Work of Peace: The Greek State's Concern on Macedonian Antiquities and the Actions of Georgios P. Oikonomos (1912-1917). In P. Adam-Veleni and A. Koukouvou (eds.), *Αρχαιολογία στα μετόπισθεν. Στη Θεσσαλονίκη των ταραγμένων χρόνων 1912-1922/Archaeology Behind Battle Lines. In Thessaloniki of the Turbulent Years 1912–1922, Catalogue of the exhibition, Thessaloniki Archaeological Museum, 24 November 2012–31 December 2013*, pp 61–63. Thessaloniki: Archaeological Museum of Thessaloniki.

Andreou, S. and K. Efkleidou. (2018) *Η αρχαιολογία στη γραμμή του πυρός: αρχαιότητες και αρχαιολογική έρευνα στη Μακεδονία του Α' Παγκοσμίου Πολέμου.* Thessaloniki: University Studio Press.

Casson, S. (1921) Excavations in Macedonia. *Annual of the British School at Athens* 24:1–33.

———. (1926) *Macedonia, Thrace and Illyria: Their Relations to Greece from the Earliest Times Down to the Time of Philip Son of Amyntas.* Oxford: Oxford University Press.

———. (1935) *Steady Drummer.* London: G Bell and Sons.

Clogg, R. (2017) Foreign Archaeologists in Greece in Time of War. In A.J. Shapland and E. Stefani (eds.), *Archaeology Behind the Battle Lines: The Macedonian Campaign (1915–1919) and Its Legacy*, pp 40–57 (BSA Modern Greek and Byzantine Studies Volume 4). Abingdon: Routledge.

DCMS. (2013) 2010 to 2015 government policy: national events and ceremonies. Online: https://www.gov.uk/government/publications/2010-to-2015-government-policy-national-events-and-ceremonies. Accessed 30 January 2020.

Descamps-Lequime, S. (2011) La presence francais en Macédoine de le fin du XVIIIe siècle au début du XXe siècle. In S. Descamps-Lequime (ed.), *Au royaume d'Alexandre le Grand*, pp 56–58. Paris: Somogy Editions

———. (2017) The Excavations Conducted by the *Service Archéologique De L'Armée D'Orient* in northern Greece: New Information from the Archives Kept in France. In A.J. Shapland and E. Stefani (eds.), *Archaeology Behind the Battle Lines: The Macedonian Campaign (1915–1919) and Its Legacy*, pp 69–84 (BSA Modern Greek and Byzantine Studies Volume 4). Abingdon: Routledge.

Dimoula, A. (2017) 'In the trenches': Old Sites, New Finds and the Early Neolithic Period in Macedonia, Greece. In A.J. Shapland and E. Stefani (eds.), *Archaeology Behind the Battle Lines: The Macedonian Campaign (1915-1919) and Its Legacy*, pp 281–298 (BSA Modern Greek and Byzantine Studies Volume 4). Abingdon: Routledge.

Falls, C. (1933–1935) *Military Operations Macedonia, 2 vols.* London: HMSO.

Farnoux, A. (2012) *Η Στρατιά της Ανατολής και η Αρχαιολογία*/Archaeology and the *Armée d'Orient*. In P. Adam-Veleni and A. Koukouvou (eds.), *Αρχαιολογία στα μετόπισθεν. Στη Θεσσαλονίκη των ταραγμένων χρόνων 1912–1922/Archaeology Behind Battle Lines. In Thessaloniki of the Turbulent Years 1912–1922, Catalogue of the exhibition, Thessaloniki Archaeological Museum, 24 November 2012–31 December 2013*, pp 83–89. Thessaloniki: Archaeological Museum of Thessaloniki.

Freshney, S. (2015) For club and country: The Sedgwick Club and WW1. *GeoCam* 12:14.

Galanakis, Y. (2017) 'Spy-Hunter' as antiquary: Major A.G. Wade, cultural politics and the British Salonika Force Collection at the Ashmolean Museum in Oxford. In A.J. Shapland and E. Stefani (eds.), *Archaeology Behind the Battle Lines: The Macedonian Campaign (1915–1919) and Its Legacy*, pp 181–202 (BSA Modern Greek and Byzantine Studies Volume 4). Abingdon: Routledge.

Gardner, E. and S. Casson. (1919) Macedonia II. – Antiquities found in the British zone 1915–1919. *Annual of the British School at Athens* 23:10–43.

Gill, D. (2006) Harry Pirie-Gordon: Historical research, journalism and intelligence gathering in the Eastern Mediterranean (1908–18). *Intelligence and National Security* 21: 1045–1059.

⸻. (2011) *Sifting the Soil of Greece: The Early Years of the British School at Athens (1886-1919)*. Bulletin of the Institute of Classics Studies supp. vol. 111. London: Institute of Classical Studies.

Hébrard, E. (1920) Les travaux du Service archéologique de l'armée d'Orient à l'arc de triomphe « de Galère » et à l'église Saint-Georges de Salonique, *Bulletin de Correspondance Hellénique* 44:5–40.

Heurtley, W.A. (1939) *Prehistoric Macedonia*. Cambridge: Cambridge University Press.

Holloway, A. (2014) *Did British soldiers plunder Amphipolis Tomb in 1916?* Online: https://www.ancient-origins.net/news-history-archaeology/did-british-soldiers-plunder-amphipolis-tomb-1916-002097. Accessed 26 January 2020.

Kanatselou, A. and A.J. Shapland. (2014) Eustratios Pelekidis and the British Salonika Force Museum. In E. Stefani, N. Merousi and A. Dimoula. (eds.), *A Century of Research in Prehistoric Macedonia, Proceedings of the International Conference, Archaeological Museum of Thessaloniki, 22–24 November 2012*, pp 91–100. Thessaloniki: Archaeological Museum of Thessaloniki.

Katsaridou, I. and I. Motsianos. (2017) *Into the Vortex of the Great War: Thessaloniki of the Armée d'Orient (1915–1918)*. Thessaloniki: Museum of Byzantine Culture.

Kotsakis, K. (2017) Trenches, borders and boundaries: prehistoric research in Greek Macedonia. In A.J. Shapland and E. Stefani (eds.), *Archaeology Behind the Battle Lines: The Macedonian Campaign (1915–1919) and Its Legacy*, pp 58–68 (BSA Modern Greek and Byzantine Studies Volume 4). Abingdon: Routledge.

Koukouvou, A. (2017) The formation of the collection of the Archaeological Museum of Thessaloniki and the exhibition "Archaeology Behind Battle Lines": A dialogue. In A.J. Shapland and E. Stefani (eds.), *Archaeology Behind the Battle Lines: The Macedonian Campaign (1915–1919) and Its Legacy*, pp 261–280 (BSA Modern Greek and Byzantine Studies Volume 4). Abingdon: Routledge.

Maitland, M. (2017) Chauchitza at National Museums Scotland. In A.J. Shapland and E. Stefani (eds.), *Archaeology Behind the Battle Lines: The Macedonian Campaign (1915–1919) and Its Legacy*, pp 204–225 (BSA Modern Greek and Byzantine Studies Volume 4). Abingdon: Routledge.

Mendel, G. (1918) Les travaux du service archéologique de l'armée française d'Orient. *Comptes rendus des séances de l'Académie des Inscriptions et Belles-Lettres.* 62: 9–17.

Morgan, C. (2017) The British Salonika Force, the British School at Athens, and the Archaic-Hellenistic archaeology of Macedonia. In A.J. Shapland and E. Stefani (eds.), *Archaeology Behind the Battle Lines: The Macedonian Campaign (1915–1919) and Its Legacy*, pp 121–180 (BSA Modern Greek and Byzantine Studies Volume 4). Abingdon: Routledge.

Mourelos, I., S. Sfetas, I. Michailidis, V. Vlasidis and S. Dordanas (eds.) (2018) *Το θέατρο επιχειρήσεων της Θεσσαλονικίκης στο πλαίσιο του Α' Παγκοσμίου Πολέμο/The Salonica Front in World War I*. Thessaloniki: University Studio Press.

Myres, J.L. (1945) Stanley Casson: 1889–1944. *Annual of the British School at Athens* 41:1–4.

Palmer, A. (1965) *The Gardeners of Salonica: The Macedonia Campaign 1915–1918.* London: Faber and Faber.

Picard, C. (1919) Macedonia I. Les Recherches archéologiques de l'Armée Française en Macédoine, 1915-1919. *Annual of the British School at Athens* 23:1–9.

Rey, L. (1917) Observations sur les premieres habitats de la Macédoine. *Bulletin de Correspondance Hellénique* 41–43:1–310.

Saunders, N.J. (2010) *Killing Time: Archaeology and the First World War.* Stroud: The History Press.

Shapland, A.J. (2015) The Salonika Campaign: archaeology in the trenches. Online: https://www.youtube.com/watch?v=TQR6Flbf_-0. Accessed 30 January 2020.

———. (2017) The British Salonika Force Collection at the British Museum. In A.J. Shapland and E. Stefani (eds.), *Archaeology Behind the Battle Lines: The Macedonian Campaign (1915–1919) and its Legacy*, pp 85–120 (BSA Modern Greek and Byzantine Studies Volume 4). Abingdon: Routledge.

Villari, L. (1922) *The Macedonian Campaign.* London: T. Fisher Unwin.

Wace, A.J.B. and M.S. Thompson. (1909) Prehistoric Mounds in Macedonia. *Liverpool Annals of Archaeology and Anthropology* 2:159–164.

Wade, A.G. (1938) *Counterspy.* London.

Wakefield, A. (2017) A Most Cosmopolitan Front – Defining Features of the Salonika Campaign 1915–1918. In A.J. Shapland and E. Stefani (eds.), *Archaeology Behind the Battle Lines: The Macedonian Campaign (1915–1919) and Its Legacy*, pp 1–18 (BSA Modern Greek and Byzantine Studies Volume 4). Abingdon: Routledge.

Wakefield, A. and S. Moody. (2011) *Under the Devil's Eye: The British Military Experience in Macedonia 1915–1918.* Barnsley: Pen and Sword Military.

11

'OH! WHAT A LOVELY EXHIBITION!'

Exploring the Imperial War Museum's First World War 50th Anniversary Displays, 1964–1968[1]

James Wallis

The 2014–2018 centenary of the First World War witnessed a four-year com-memorative effort across the UK (and beyond) that emphasized a predominantly local and individual duty to remember, achieved via creative remembrance prac-tices that sought to engage and inspire new generations. Viewed from this per-spective, the comparatively scant public and academic interest paid to what went on during the conflict's 50th anniversary seems surprising, given how influential the commemorative legacies that emerged from the 1960s became in shaping Britain's cultural memory of the First World War. In choosing to focus on one particular example from this period, this chapter considers the presentation of wartime photographs in a comparative 'Then and Now' format, which con-stituted an exhibition series held at London's Imperial War Museum (IWM). Individual exhibitions in historical institutions are shaped by 'competing dis-courses such as commemoration, education, patriotism and victory' (Lisle 2006: 842). Analysing what are essentially spatial representations of the past requires paying specific attention to the architecture, layout, design, objects and text of exhibitions, prior to situating these within their larger contemporary cultural context, then scrutinizing the power relations and dynamics between involved stakeholders (Till 2001: 276). This chapter considers First World War visual cul-tures during the 1960s, in terms of reworking official wartime photographs for display within a museum exhibition space (Stylianou and Stylianou-Lambert 2016).

For the IWM, this 50th anniversary represented an important occasion. Britain's national war museum had been born out of a 1917 propaganda ini-tiative, thus owing its very existence to the conflict (Kavanagh 1994; Cornish 2004; Cundy 2015). In recording the involvement of those who had witnessed the conflict, this fledgling institution aspired to keep the events of the 'The Great War', as it was known then, fresh in public memory. Not all were confident, with

DOI: 10.4324/9781003263531-14

the War Cabinet predicting that the institution would struggle to retain public interest for more than 'a few years' (Kavanagh 1994: 135). Documenting a second global conflict two decades later brought about an unforeseen extension to its remit (see Deans, this volume), squeezing rich collections into an impractical building ill-equipped to act as a fully functioning museum (Cooke and Jenkins 2001). By 1960, the institution lacked resonance amidst a time of social change, radicalism and the declining British Empire.

Seeds of change were sown via its newly appointed Director, Dr Noble Frankland, a Bomber Command veteran turned military historian who had derided the IWM's former galleries as 'dingy and neglected' (Frankland 1998: 160). He instigated a large-scale extension and improvement programme that saw the creation of new facilities, the recruitment of professionally qualified departmental staff and an end to sub-standard cataloguing practices and leaking galleries. For him, this process of reinvigoration essentially meant converting a 'warehouse full of curiosities' into historical displays, without neglecting the Museum's role as 'a centre for research and education' (ibid.: 170, 172).

However, the requirement to acknowledge the First World War's 50th anniversary so early on in Frankland's tenure dictated any potential exhibition being on a limited scale and budget. By chance, in May 1963, Mr (later Sir) Peter Masefield wrote to Frankland suggesting a commemorative display idea. It proposed using comparative 'Then and Now' photographic pairs to match up the official First World War photographs with a contrasting image of how exactly the same spot appeared 50 years later:

> For some time, it has seemed to me that there would be historic merit, and some interest in a new briefly commentated, chronological story of those four and a half years as a medium for linking together a carefully prepared review of 'Then and Now – Fifty Years After' photographs which – in years to come – would link the great events of the past with the latter day scene. Although something of this sort was done in 1936 as 'Twenty Years After' – it was <u>not</u> done well (the value lies not only in the carefully selected photographs but also in the achievement of precisely the same angle of precisely the same spot), and a 50 years gap is, I think, more significant'.
>
> *(Masefield 1963)[2]*

Both Frankland and the Museum's Deputy Director were keen to utilize the untapped 'visual evidence' of the material held within its Photographic Archive, so approval quickly followed. By and large, photographs would depict events of 1914–1918 chronologically, to coincide with their respective anniversaries between 1964 and 1968 (for example, see Figure 11.1). Arrangements were made between Masefield and the IWM, allowing the former to obtain present pictures of the battlefields and First World War sites as a 'labour of love' (IWM DP2/008).

FIGURE 11.1 (A) 'Then and Now' Photographic Pair at Anzac Cove (Gallipoli); (B) taken by Christopher Roads. (© IWM Q13431 and IWM CHR10.)

Masefield, Motivations and the 'Then and Now' Concept

The man behind these *Fifty Years After* displays, Peter Masefield, was a well-connected and enthusiastic individual who worked chiefly in the aviation industry.[3] His autobiography reveals a meticulous man, noting that 'From an early age, I had revelled in keeping detailed records and personal accounts…I continued to fill large books and ledgers with notes, statistics and financial records' (Masefield and Gunston 2002: 224). IWM-held archival material includes his personal notebooks that offer extensive detail and breakdown of the 17 battlefield 'sorties' he conducted between August 1964 and June 1969 (IWM DP2).[4]

Masefield's long-standing enthusiasm in the First World War appears to have stemmed from exposure to the wartime experiences of his relatives. His father had served in the 20th Kings Royal Rifle Corps, whilst his second cousin, John Masefield, was the Poet Laureate between 1930 and 1967:

> All wars end; even this War will some day end ... when the trenches are filled in, and the plough has gone over them, the ground will not long keep the look of War. When this War is a romance in memory, the soldier looking for his battlefield will find his marks gone ... Summer flowers will cover most of the ruin that man can make...these places will be hard indeed to trace ... Centre Way, Peel Trench, Muster Alley and those other paths to glory will be deep under the corn.
>
> *(Masefield 1917: 75)*

This eloquent reflection by his relative offers insight into Peter's motives for the photographic comparisons, with the latter drafting a response to the testimony that, by the 1960s, had come to pass:

> What John Masefield foresaw as he wrote from that old front line, while the guns still fired, has come to pass. Only the cemeteries stand in mute testimony to the scenes of battle. But there are other traces; grass mounds which once were trenches, woods still thick with debris, craters of mines will never disappear. So long as one knows where to look, and what to look for, the signs still stand. The old photographs hold the clues.
>
> *(IWM DP2/009)*

Even though the scars of the conflict were not healed in British national consciousness, a 50-year interval had allowed sites to almost fully return to their peacetime form. For that reason, new comparative photographic pairs would act as visual witnesses to both the conflict and subsequent changes to the landscape.[5] Archival records indicate Masefield's occasional reliance upon local inhabitants' knowledge, to assist in establishing where events had happened. In noting 'before long, such sources will have gone', there was a sense of urgency to capture that knowledge whilst still in existence, beyond any palpable belief he held that contemporary photographs would resonate with a 1960s museum audience (IWM DP2/009).[6]

The premise for utilizing a comparative 'Then and Now' concept was taken from an inter-war weekly magazine series called *Twenty Years After: The Battlefields of 1914–18 Then and Now*, edited by Sir Ernest Swinton (Swinton 1936–1937). Its principal feature compared official wartime photographs with images of the same area in peacetime two decades later. Coincidentally, the 'Now' photographs of the morphing Western Front landscape were captured by two IWM curatorial staff, Jack Insall and G.T. Watson. Insall was an observer in the Royal Flying Corps during the war, subsequently taking charge of the IWM's Air Force Section, before becoming Keeper of its Photographic Archive (Insall 1970).

A rich source combining photographs and articles, the magazine ran for 42 editions with a further 22 supplementary parts. Its success was twofold; namely the relatively recent nature of the 'Then' experience permitted the concept of confronting a haunting and traumatic past to function effectively, as a chance to relive remembered experiences. The same spirit animated the contemporaneous battlefield tour undertaken and recorded by veteran and author Ralph Mottram, who wrote 'There is one more peculiarity about the journey which I have taken. It is an attempt to recapture the past in the present' (Mottram 1936: 5).

In this sense, such publications provided a literary space for veterans and ex-servicemen to reminisce and share personal memories, stemming from a spirit of wartime camaraderie intensified by wider war disillusionment of the 1930s. In reaffirming to this group that they had not fought in vain, David Lloyd (1998: 148) has suggested the importance of nostalgia as primary inspiration; they enabled former soldiers unable to visit the battlefields to compare their mental recollections with the pictured landscape. Insall and Watson latterly turned the best of their photographic comparisons into a book, which Masefield referenced as a major source of inspiration (Anon. 1938). Another potential influence was the 1959 BBC televised series 'After the Battle' that featured correspondents returning to the battlefields they had reported from during the Second World War.

The Special Photographic Exhibitions and Visitor Response

Visitors found the Special Photographic Displays located in various recesses and annexes. The physical look of the displays – large 30-inch by 40-inch black and white prints on dark gallery walls – presented a stark picture. Enlarging the photographs from prints to theatrical wall-staging undoubtedly improved their clarity, allowing visitors to contemplate, muse and study them in detail. Whilst their recognizability may have resonated with some, interpretation was guided by text captions that sat alongside a purchasable guide accompanying individual exhibitions (Anon. 1964; 1968).[7] This handbook functioned as an explanatory narrative, chronologically setting out the events of the War via a prescribed order of viewing. A comparatively lengthy guide to the subject matter was intended to grant visitors a sense that they had purchased something greater than a mere catalogue of exhibits, which should retain value beyond the exhibition. Its contents contained a dearth of information about the 'Then' photographs, in terms of who made them, how they were produced and what purpose they had served, sitting in notable contrast to the emphasized presence of Masefield's endeavours.

Despite attempts to guide or perhaps control viewer vision – and hence reception of the images – through accompanying text, it remains difficult to establish with much conviction how visitors actually interpreted the exhibitions; museologist George Hein has described the 1960s as 'one of amazing growth in museums… [but] a low point in systematic empirical visitor studies' (Hein 2002 52). Writing to Masefield in October 1965, Frankland termed the current display '…a great success. People are particularly impressed by the panoramas and these too have helped to get the exhibition favourable publicity in the press. It remains to be seen how, and to what extent, captions on the walls affect the sale of the guidebooks!' (Frankland 1965). The museum archives further disclose that Frankland, Masefield and the final exhibition in the series all featured within an hour-long afternoon ITV television programme in April 1968, titled 'Relics of War: A Visit to the Imperial War Museum' (IWM DP2/019, DP2/020).[8] A number of visitors wrote to Frankland expressing their enjoyment at having seen the special exhibition in the broadcast, additionally stating interest in purchasing any planned 'Then and Now' photographic publication[9] (IWM Central Files EN3/3/31/002 1968).

Beyond favourable popular reception in these quarters, what these encounters evidence is the importance for the IWM of seeking to generate guidebook publication revenue, as well as capitalize upon television as a method for drawing public attention to the ongoing work and activities of the museum (thereby increasing visitor numbers). Though specific data corresponding with the exhibitions does not exist, Annual Attendance Figures to the IWM rose significantly over this period, from 323,681 in 1960 to 650,348 in 1968 (IWM EN4/41/CF/1/1/4/8). And though there is scarce information for total sales figures, Board Meeting minutes reveal that a healthy 5,000 copies of the first exhibition guide had sold by mid-September 1964, with a second print run of 2,000 additional copies duly ordered (IWM Central Files EN3/2/1/1/5-7). Yet by the summer of 1966, one response to Masefield from the Daily Telegraph indicated that the newspaper had featured more about First World War battles than their readers could probably digest, so chose not to feature submitted material about that year's exhibition (IWM DP2/011).

Whilst it can be ascertained that there must have been a public appetite for the levels of detail featured in the Exhibition Guide, another way of deciphering this is as context for veteran visitors (Figure 11.2). Many of the descriptive captions were geographical orientations in relation to roads or features, suggesting the need for a prior knowledge of the battlefield vicinity. Some examples, such as 'the famous Hill 60', advocate an assumed level of visitor knowledge when it came to certain locations and historical events (Anon. 1964: 37). Acting as a form of 'official memory' (see Moser 2010), the in-house archives contain precious few photographic documentation of the displays themselves, other than at their respective openings. Most show people in conversation or meeting and greeting, and the record duly proves useful in revealing the prominence of veterans at the opening of individual displays, thereby corroborating this idea of validation. The 1964 exhibition opening was completed by the President of the Old Contemptibles Society, accompanied by 30 'rank and file' members of the 1914 British Expeditionary Force (including three Victoria Cross winners).

Photographs are expected to authorize and authenticate when 'mobilized within the didactic space of the museum', presented as unbiased visual evidence of the past (Edwards and Mead 2013: 21). Such an expectation may have jarred amongst some visitors, given that as Jane Carmichael has noted, the broader

FIGURE 11.2 Veterans Studying the Special Photographic Displays. (© IWM MH7715.)

purpose of war photographer was shifting significantly, from that of patriot producing propaganda, to at least neutral observer or witness against war – as the anti-war campaigner use of Don McCullin's photographs of the ongoing conflict in Vietnam exemplified (Carmichael 1989: 146; see also Brothers 1997).

Justin Court has posited two pertinent arguments here. First, that beyond discussion of wartime censorship and the interrelated issue of sanitization when depicting death, the conflict's visual record is 'mostly devoid of the ethical problems of representation that dominate other conflicts' (2017: 75; see also Beurier 2004). Certainly, the representational strategies of deploying these photographs in exhibition format did little to engage with the moral dilemmas of the violence and destruction they conveyed. Second, that the bulk of unofficial photographic content depicted within soldiers' private albums (predominantly during the early part of the conflict) tended to be not of trenches, brutal destruction or scenes of battle (other than when identifying memorials of those killed), but simply the day-to-day realities and the personal lived experience of soldiers. As a result, the absence or obscured nature of individual stories contained within the official photographs – that made up this visual exhibition – gave limited opportunities for evocative or empathetic engagement on the part of viewing visitors.

In terms of display content, Masefield was clearly governed by certain limitations of the official wartime photographs. One example was the presence of the Navy, which had a small pictorial record since actions took place over significant distances at sea. Other theatres of war, such as Egypt and Mesopotamia, were incorporated into the official photographic remit from 1917, but were largely inconspicuous within the displays. Gallipoli featured more prominently. The contemporary political situation must explain the marginalization of Russia's role in the conflict, as was the case with the work of Horace Nicholls and G.P. Lewis, the two official photographers who produced 3,000 images of the British Home Front, including women working as shipbuilders and munitionettes (Carmichael 1989: 120–139). The reasoning can be speculated upon; tracing precise locations within built environments would have been challenging, Masefield perhaps wary of the images' more blatant propaganda tone or even made decisions based on factors of cost and convenience.[10] Whatever it was, a conscious prioritizing of pairs from the Western Front took place.

Researching precise locations of images that had been taken in the midst of battlefields proved tricky and time-consuming, so often sites with contours or recognizable features such as streets or roads were chosen (Figure 11.3). The result

A

B

FIGURES 11.3A, B 'Then and Now' Photographic Pair of the Zillebeke Road near Ypres, Belgium. (© IWM Q50706 and IWM PGM352.)

was spectral absence, where the 'soldiers with helmets, rifle and pack trudging in single file in front of a turbulent skyline' shown in the 'Then' photographs did not appear within the 'Now' ones (Holmes 2010: 42). This gave the photographs a potency as remembrance canvases, passive frames onto which individual visitor understanding could be projected. The neutral presentation of the images accentuated this idea further, seemingly more like artworks to be studied and admired, than as carriers of historical information. Jennifer Wellington identifies a similar tension of memory at the Australian War Memorial, in her analysis of its model dioramas. She perceives these prompted '*emotional* connection rather than *understanding* the causal flow of events, the "what happened"...[The diorama] stimulates the viewer to emote, but not to understand... [it] commands its viewer to *remember*' (Wellington 2012: 111–113 emphasis original). Encouraging memory and connection 'with the *idea* of an event' invites response based on empathy and remembrance over historical understanding (Wellington 2012: 117). Much as his second cousin had done 50 years before, the collective result of Masefield's and IWM efforts provided a seemingly romanticized interpretation of the conflict (see Smith 1965). For many visitors then, the monotone photographs must have seemed, as Elizabeth Edwards puts it, 'of other times and other places' (Edwards 2001: 17).

Cultural Representations beyond the Museum

The build-up to the 50th anniversary commemorations of the conflict bore contrasting public attitudes across the UK. On the one hand, there were changing views towards the purpose of Remembrance Day, amidst calls for it to be dropped from the national calendar (Parker 2009: 165). On the other was a surge of public interest to discover more about those who had experienced the conflict, amidst a clamouring to know what it had been like. Numerous memoirs of officers Robert Graves and Siegfried Sassoon, as well as biographies, anthologies and volumes of poetry were all released or republished during this period. Most published works 'did not so much attack the War as lament its consequences', though a number were openly critical of those in High Command (Parker 2009: 172). Such convictions were led by Alan Clark's *The Donkeys* and A.J.P. Taylor's *The First World War – An Illustrated History* (Clark 1961; Taylor 1963). Clark's work was heavily slanted and, despite its vivid style, has since been criticized for poor scholarship and prioritizing sales over historical accuracy (Danchev 1991; Todman 2005: 102). Nevertheless, as easily consumed history, both were popular at a grassroots level, with Taylor's work drawing heavily upon the official wartime photographs. The accompanying tongue-in-cheek captions gave them a sardonic interpretation, starkly different from the formality of their presentation at the IWM. This was echoed in the satirically depicted, commercially successful 1963 theatre production *Oh! What A Lovely War!*, directed by Joan Littlewood (1963). The similar reception amongst military historians did little to dampen the play's broad appeal and popularity (Paget 1996; Reynolds 2013: 331–333).[11]

The IWM Research and Publications Officer at the time, (Professor) Peter Simkins, offered personal reflections on the Special Photographic Exhibitions during an interview in 2012.[12] Having produced the majority of the text for the Exhibition Guides, Peter looked back on the displays as 'pretty low key' at a 'dynamic and adventurous time' for the IWM. Nevertheless, for him, the extent to which public understanding of the conflict was radically shifting was an important factor in explaining how they were received by audiences. Themselves all too aware of the impact of warfare, the Cold War generation was evermore hostile towards traditional authority, targeting the 1914–1918 conflict in light of the morally more clear-cut Second World War. Brian Bond has conjectured that several factors – such as the pervasive fear of nuclear war and the rise of an independent youth culture – shaped contemporary understanding of Britain's role during the First World War (Bond 2002: 51–54). Peter likewise recalled this time of anti-establishment feeling that portrayed the conflict as the 'epitome of cynical, incompetent leadership, needless sacrifice and futility' (Bond 2002: 54).

But the overall conviction is that it was the impact of the 1964 BBC television series *The Great War* that proved the biggest factor in changing the ways in which the British public interacted with, and therefore understood, the First World War (BBC 1964; and see Ramsden 2002; Hanna 2007, 2009: 32–62; Reynolds 2013: 337–342). Its 26 episodes quickly achieved epic status, through visually and emotionally powerful depictions, capitalizing upon the novel medium of television to showcase archival film footage. The IWM was greatly involved in production and provision of historical guidance, on the back of Frankland's desire to showcase collections and contribute towards the War's historiography.[13] The resulting involvement inevitably diverted resource away from in-house exhibitions. The official photographic collection featured heavily within the television series, although their presentation was interpreted by many viewers as the melancholic, haunting images of battlescapes. The opening credits sequence relied upon a montage of rostrum-shots of three official photographs that were to become an iconic cultural memory in themselves (see Todman 2005: 65–66.) Not only more engaging than the mono-sensual, static exhibition boards, the gulf between these portrayals was amplified further by the television series' unprecedented idea of speaking to veterans directly. Recording their experiences thereby presented them as a tangible connection between past and present. For Peter Parker, the spoken rather than written word added 'a new layer of authenticity to the way we reconstructed the past' (Parker 2009: 203). Emma Hanna also interprets this approach – that of increasing interest in the lives and history of ordinary people – as fostering an understanding of the War 'marked by the faces' of individual participants (Hanna 2007: 95). These faces may have been present at exhibition opening events but were mostly absent in its largely impersonal content.[14]

The Special Photographic Exhibitions thus appealed to two key groups. Their conservative, effectively nostalgic presentation sought to reinvigorate the remaining veterans' wartime memories. It was somewhat paradoxical that wartime photographs designed for non-military audiences during the conflict were now being presented to former soldiers here. Second, through their mobilization of a very specific knowledge about the First World War, the Special Photographic Exhibitions held an appeal for what Peter Simkins described as 'the gentleman historian'.[15] With whiffs of traditional museums for the connoisseur, these displays could not convey sufficient impact or appeal amongst those who saw them. Moreover, the significance of this failing meant that any prior understanding or preconceptions visitors held about the conflict – derived from other engaging cultural works – duly went unchallenged.

Concluding Remarks

Exploring postcards and post-war reconstruction in the French Argonne region, social anthropologist Paola Filippucci posited that wartime photographic photographs 'hold and embody the past, both as what has been and as what is no longer: they are perched between absence and presence' (Filippucci 2009: 232). These postcards became a key medium in 'keeping a particular social memory of the war', because of the ways in which they reinvested the conflict with affectivity and sentiment, so as to bridge the domains of memory and history (ibid.: 227). Photography remains a usable, functional and uncompromising tool to recall locations where space and time do not fuse, thereby constructing a sense of place. Such a notion of pictorial means, and its material ability to simultaneously convey enduring presence, absence and indeed resilience to change, represents a vital fact for how we visualize, and resultantly understand, the recent past. As Justin Court (2017) articulates, photography remains a privileged method through which contemporary viewers can still access the First World War as the past, via mass-market illustrated histories that operate somewhere between sensational historical spectacle and objective documentary evidence. The re-photographing concept of 'Then and Now' featured prominently within various centenary-based commemorative outlets – albeit perceived as an unproblematic (digital) medium that has to forge a more synthetic connection, in its requirement to collapse significant temporal distance (see Wallis and Harvey, forthcoming). While discussion around the merits of such works falls beyond the remit of this chapter, it undoubtedly speaks to the timely legacy of these Special Photographic Exhibitions, as an iterative form of commemorative practice that continues to hold sway with audiences 100 years on from the First World War. Indeed Masefield himself was already looking forward to the centenary in 1964, when he wrote 'I hope that today's photographs will help to mark for all time the places where these great events took place, so that – in fifty years' time, when the centenary arrives, there will no difficulty in remembering' (Peter Masefield 1964)

Britain's national War Museum acknowledged the war's 50th anniversary through multiple outputs. The broader national impact of *The Great War* series certainly made this a justifiable decision, in giving less dedication and resource to the Special Photographic Exhibitions. Indeed, this exhibition series offered cost-effective value, drew upon a vast but under-used collections resource and ultimately made the best of limited practicalities at a time when the IWM was changing both its external structure and internal ideology. Frankland looked back on the displays fondly, describing them as 'an interesting comment on the impact of war upon the landscape and the power of subsequent healing and reconstruction' (Frankland 1998: 173). Masefield's intentions, and ultimately his diligence and dedication to breathing fresh life into an innovative conceptual framework, were sound. That this rich photographic record of First World War sites and spaces still exists, as an act of commemoration with its strong onus on responsibility, is certainly testament to Masefield's good sense and passion towards the overall pursuit.

But the main ramification from this episode lies in the official photographs. As a body of work created for a specific purpose, this wartime collection took on new meaning when transferred into IWM ownership and care, as a record of national effort. Whilst this sat with the Museum's remit, this was not a collection designed for the archive, but one that functioned as a public record reliant on distribution and mass consumption. Consequent absorption into other narratives and popular culture meant needing to compete with engaging rival interpretations of the very same material. Along the way, a critical point was reached whereby the knowledge imparted and resonance of these official photographs within the public sphere changed, after which point information was projected onto, rather than extracted from, them.

Even though conservative displays may have reinvigorated veteran memories, the IWM could ill afford to risk solely satisfying a group rapidly dwindling in number. It was moreover an approach that ran counter to the bulk of the other mass-produced works of this period, which were telling the story of the conflict by prioritizing clarity over accuracy. Thus, these photographic displays were accordingly limited in their ability to shape, let alone challenge any existing visitor knowledge, despite their being situated in an environment that was dedicated to authoritative learning. Their legacy would instead come to fruition through later exhibitions and reinventions of the IWM – when the time came to address the fundamental issues of whom its exhibitions were for, and adopting a proactive institutional stance in shaping audience understanding of past conflicts.

Notes

1 This chapter draws on the author's doctoral research conducted between 2011 and 2015, which was a partnership project between the University of Exeter and Imperial War Museums, funded by the Arts and Humanities Research Council. The author wishes to thank Professor Peter Simkins for sharing his recollections into these displays.
2 This correspondence also reveals that Masefield had trialled the concept in France a few years beforehand.
3 He became an IWM Trustee during the Special Photographic Exhibitions and was briefly Chairman of Trustees the following decade.
4 It is not clear why Masefield made a battlefield trip in June 1969, given the final photographic exhibition closed on 30 April 1969.

5 Several Exhibition Guide descriptions reference a transition from war to peace, or pre-War conditions, such as the 1964 Guide citing the 'erasure' of the 'scars of war' (Anon. 1964: 45). This suggests one exhibition driver as being to remind visitors what had occurred in these locations and that they must not forget this, despite nature (and mankind) having reclaimed these once obliterated landscapes. This is supported by an additional discourse about the role of truthfulness and a reliance upon a continuing act of witnessing, which has heavy remembrance overtones.

6 The fact that Masefield often took more than one image at each site and, in the case of comparative aerial photographs, completed 'several flights across the battlefields' (Anon.1964: 49) indicates that, not only was he highly motivated, but that he viewed the camera as an instrument of scientific precision that ensured absolute accuracy (vindicated by his original vision to improve on the 1930s photographic pairs). Within one Exhibition Guide, Frankland's preface speaks of Masefield's 'scholarly and detective work of a high order' (Anon.1964: iii). Masefield additionally brought back numerous battlefield relics from one Somme expedition, some of which were displayed within the 1966 exhibition.

7 Written correspondence between Frankland and one visitor indicates that no exhibition catalogue was produced for the 1966 exhibition, due to the limited resources required to undertake the necessary research (IWM EN3/3/31/002 1966). It seems that by 1968, copies of some individual photographs could be purchased, ranging from postcard size through to 24 by 20-inch prints (IWM DP2/021). 1967 also saw a one-off Special Photographic Exhibition depicting the work of the Commonwealth War Graves Commission, to commemorate its founding 50 years earlier.

8 Efforts to locate a copy of the broadcast were unsuccessful.

9 There were plans for a two-volume publication, but Masefield's external commitments – namely when he was made chairman of the newly created British Airports Authority in 1965 – seemed to prevent this ever getting beyond initial drafts (correspondence between Masefield and Frankland, November 1967, IWM EN3/3/29/004).

10 In his original proposal letter to Frankland (IWM EN3/1/27/3), Masefield expressed a desire to photograph naval bases such as Scapa Flow, industry in Whitehall and aerodromes both in the UK and abroad. His connections to aviation enabled him to contrast aerial landscapes by taking several comparative photographs from the air (including on the Western Front). The fact that he had anticipated his contribution as occupying only two to three years of his spare time at the outset may explain why it proved harder to balance extensive trips and photographic research with his day-to-day workload, as the exhibition series went on.

11 Daniel Todman suggests that the play was 'lent an added authority' through its use of sentimental period songs that prompted an 'essentially nostalgic emotional impact' (Todman 2005: 109).

12 Recorded Interview between James Wallis, Alys Cundy and Peter Simkins, conducted on 21 March 2012.

13 Production tensions between the IWM and BBC manifested over the issue of acknowledging the use of reconstructed footage (see IWM Central Files EN3/2/1/1/3-7).

14 Frankly spoken veteran testimonies formed the basis of an oral history movement, led by Lyn Macdonald and the IWM Sound Archive, during the early 1970s.

15 Recorded Interview, 21 March 2012.

References

Imperial War Museum files
IWM DP2– Papers of Sir Peter Masefield
IWM DP2/008
IWM DP2/009
IWM DP2/011

IWM DP2/019

IWM DP2/020

IWM DP2/021

IWM Central Files EN3/1/27/3. P. Masefield original proposal letter to N. Frankland

IWM Central Files EN3/2/1/1/3-7: Minutes of the Board Meeting of IWM Trustees (9 March 1964–8 March 1965)

IWM Central Files EN3/2/1/1/5-7: Board Meeting Data (24 September 1964–8 March 1965)

IWM Central Files EN3/3/31/002: 'Appreciation', correspondence between N. Frankland and Mr Scott, November 1966

IWM Central Files EN3/3/31/002: Appreciation', correspondence between various members of the public and N. Frankland, April 1968

IWM Central Files EN3/3/29/004. Correspondence between P. Masefield and N. Frankland, November 1967

IWM Central Files 1980. EN4/41/CF/1/1/4/8. Initial Brief for the Redevelopment of the Main Building of the Imperial War Museum. Also, Annex 4 – Analysis of Attendance Figures from 1960

Anon. (1938) *The Western Front – Then and Now*. London: C. Arthur Pearson Ltd.

Anon. (1964) *An Illustrated Guide to the Photographs in the Special Exhibition at the Imperial War Museum, 1964*. London: Her Majesty's Stationery Office.

Anon. (1968) *An Illustrated Guide to the Photographs in the Special Exhibition at the Imperial War Museum*, 1968. London: Imperial War Museum.

BBC. (1964) *The Great War*. British Broadcasting Corporation in collaboration with Australian Broadcasting Corporation, Canadian Broadcasting Corporation and the Imperial War Museum. Produced by T. Essex & G. Watkins. London.

Beurier, J. (2004) Death and Material Culture – The Case of Pictures During the First World War. In N.J. Saunders (ed.), *Matters of Conflict: Material Culture, Memory and the First World War*, pp 109–122. London: Routledge.

Bond, B. (2002) *The Unquiet Western Front – Britain's Role in Literature and History*. Cambridge: Cambridge University Press.

Brothers, C. (1997) *War and Photography – A Cultural History*. London: Routledge.

Carmichael, J. (1989) *First World War Photographers*. London: Routledge.

Clark, A. (1961) *The Donkeys: A Study of the Western Front in 1916*. London: Hutchinson.

Cooke, S. and L. Jenkins. (2001) Discourses of regeneration in early twentieth century Britain: From Bedlam to the Imperial War Museum. *Area* 33:382–390.

Cornish, P. (2004) Sacred Relics – Objects in the Imperial War Museum, 1917–1939. In N.J. Saunders (ed.), *Matters of Conflict: Material Culture, Memory and the First World War*, pp 35–50. London: Routledge.

Court, J. (2017) Picturing history, remembering soldiers: World War I photography between the public and the private. *History and Memory* 29 (1):72–103.

Cundy, A. (2015) Thresholds of memory: Representing function through space and object at the Imperial War Museum, London, 1918–2014. *Museum History Journal* 8:247–268.

Danchev, A. (1991) 'Bunking' and Debunking: The Controversies of the 1960s. In B. Bond (ed.), *The First World War and British Military History*, pp 263–288. Oxford: Clarendon Press.

Edwards, E. (2001) *Raw Histories – Photographs, Anthropology and Museums*. Oxford: Berg.

Edwards, E. and M. Mead. (2013) Absent histories and absent images: Photographs, museums and the colonial past. *Museum and Society* 11:19–38.

Filippucci, P. (2009) Postcards from the Past – War, Landscape and Place in Argonne, France. In N.J. Saunders and P. Cornish (eds.), *Contested Objects: Material Memories of the Great War*, pp 220–236. London: Routledge.

Frankland, N. (1965) Letter from N. Frankland to P. Masefield. 5 October 1965, IWM EN3/2/1/12.

Frankland, N. (1998) *History at War: The Campaigns of an Historian*. London: Giles de la Mare.

Hanna, E. (2007) A small screen alternative to stone and bronze: The Great War Series and British Television. *European Journal of Cultural Studies* 10 (1):89–111.

———. (2009) *The Grea War on the Small Screen: Representing the First World War in Contemporary Britain*. Edinburgh: Edinburgh University Press.

Hein, G. (2002) Learning in Museums. London: Routledge

Holmes, R. (2010) *Shots From the Front – The British Soldier 1914–18*. London: HarperCollins.

Insall, A. (1970) *Observer – Memoirs of the R.F.C. 1915–18*. London: William Kimber & Co Ltd.

Kavanagh, G. (1994) *Museums and the First World War – A Social History*. Leicester: Leicester University Press.

Lisle, D. (2006) Sublime lessons: Education and ambivalence in war exhibitions. *Millennium – Journal of International Studies* 34:841–864.

Littlewood, J. (1963) *Oh! What A Lovely War*. Stratford Theatre Workshop, Theatre Royal, Stratford East. Produced by J. Littlewood, G. Raffles & C. Chilton.

Lloyd, D. (1998) *Battlefield Tourism – Pilgrimage and the Commemoration of the Great War in Britain, Australia and Canada, 1919–1939*. Oxford: Berg.

Masefield, J. (2006) [1917] *The Old Front Line*. Barnsley: Pen & Sword Military.

Masefield, P. (1963) Letter from P. Masefield to N. Frankland. 24 May 1963. IWM EN3/1/27/3.

———. (1964) Speech by Peter Masefield at the opening of the 1964 Special Photographic Exhibition. IWM DP2/008.

Masefield, P. and P. Gunston. (2002) *Flight Path – The Autobiography of Sir Peter Masefield*. Marlborough: The Crowood Press Ltd.

Moser, S. (2010) The devil is in the detail: Museum displays and the creation of knowledge. *Museum Anthropology* 33 (1):22–32.

Mottram, R. (1936) *Journey to the Western Front: Twenty Years After*. London: G. Bell & Sons.

Paget, D. (1996) Remembrance Play: Oh What A Lovely War and History. In T. Howard and J. Stokes (eds.), *Acts of War: The Representation of Military Conflict on the British Stage and Television since 1945*, pp 82–97. Aldershot: Scolar Press.

Parker, P. (2009) *The Last Veteran – Harry Patch and the Legacy of War*. London: Fourth Estate, HarperCollins.

Ramsden, J. (2002) The Great War: The making of the series. *Historical Journal of Film, Radio and Television* 22:7–19.

Reynolds, D. (2013) *The Long Shadow – The Great War and the Twentieth Century*. New York: Simon & Schuster.

Smith, G. (1965) *Still Quiet on the Western Front – 50 Years Later*. New York: William Morrow & Co.

Stylianou, E. and T. Stylianou-Lambert. (2016) *Museums and Photography: Displaying Death*. London: Routledge.

Swinton, E. (ed.) (1936–37) *Twenty Years After: The Battlefields of 1914–18 – Then and Now*. London: George Newnes Publications.

Taylor, A. (1963) *The First World War – An Illustrated History*. London: Hamish Hamilton.

Till, K. (2001) Reimaging National Identity – Chapters of Life at the German Historical Museum in Berlin. In P. Adams, S. Hoelscher and K. Till (eds.), *Textures of Place – Exploring Humanist Geographies*, pp 273–299. London: University of Minnesota Press.

Todman, D. (2005) *The Great War – Myth and Memory*. Hambledon: Continuum.

Wallis, J. and D. Harvey (Forthcoming). Refocussing Perspectives: Photographic Responses to the First World War Centenary through the Lens of *Then and Now*. In K. Lilley (ed.), *Sense of Place: Framing Legacies of the Great War and its Centenary*. Bloomington: Indiana University Press.

Wellington, J. (2012) Narrative as History, Image as Memory: Exhibiting the Great War in Australia, 1917–41. In S. Longair and J. McAleer (eds.), *Curating Empire: Museums and the British Imperial Experience*, pp 104–121. Manchester University Press.

12

TE PAPA'S *GALLIPOLI: THE SCALE OF OUR WAR*

Curating innovation

Kirstie Ross

At 5.30 am, on 18 April 2015, hundreds of guests gathered expectantly in the foyer of the Museum of New Zealand Te Papa Tongarewa (Te Papa), waiting for the official opening of *Gallipoli: The scale of our war*. This is the museum's major contribution to New Zealand's centennial commemorations of the First World War and a presentation of the nation's involvement in that eight-month-long Middle Eastern campaign. Appropriately, the opening coincided almost to the day with the 100th anniversary of the campaign's start when the Australian and New Zealand Army Corps (Anzacs) landed at dawn on a narrow beach on the Gallipoli Peninsula known since as Anzac Cove.

After a powhiri (Maori welcome) and blessing, small groups were invited into *Gallipoli* where they were stunned by its interpretative piece de resistance: eight hyper-real sculptures of individuals involved in the campaign, each realized at almost two-and-a-half-times larger-than-life (Figure 12.1). These spectacular models – a fiercely guarded secret during the exhibition's development – are presented in six moodily lit circular rooms, 'frozen' at a pivotal moment during the fighting at Gallipoli. The rest of the exhibition unfolds chronologically in five alternating thematic galleries, presented almost exclusively from a New Zealand perspective.

Gallipoli's so-called 'giants' were an instant hit. In the first months after it opened, members of the public queued for more than 90 minutes to see the monumental figures created by Weta Workshop, Te Papa's project partner, famous for its work in Hollywood (most notably the *Lord of the Rings* trilogy directed by Sir Peter Jackson). If the size of this audience is taken as the measure, then *Gallipoli* continues to be a phenomenal success: by February 2020, visitor numbers had surpassed three million. Personal feedback and social media commentary add qualitative substance to this statistic. These responses provide convincing evidence of high levels of visitor satisfaction and the multiple ways in which the

DOI: 10.4324/9781003263531-15

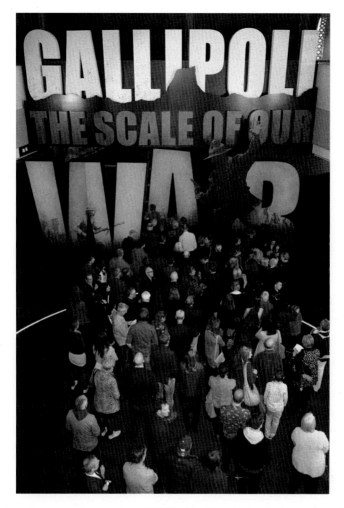

FIGURE 12.1   Guests to the opening of *Gallipoli* wait to be invited into the exhibition. (© Kate Whitely, Te Papa.)

exhibition is appreciated. An Australian journalist summed this up: 'not only is [*Gallipoli*] spectacular, it's intelligent and very moving' (*Sydney Morning Herald,* 1 May 2015). Some academic commentators, too, have highlighted the exhibitions' sensitive treatment of the campaign. For example, celebrated New Zealand historian and former Te Papa employee Jock Phillips was thankful that the partnership had not turned the 'human tragedy of Gallipoli' into 'heroic melodrama' (Phillips 2016b).

Individuals' reactions to *Gallipoli* are subjective yet also socially and historically contingent, the outcome of personal circumstances and collective memory (Schorch 2014; King 2017). Anzac Day has been a key cultural referent for visitor engagement, a corollary to its shaping of New Zealanders' knowledge of the

First World War generally. As historian Margaret Harris notes, this annual civic ritual is 'the primary method of New Zealand engagement with the Great War' (Harris 2014). First observed on 25 April 1916 to mark the anniversary of the Gallipoli landings, Anzac Day is a national holiday for war remembrance in both New Zealand and Australia. Local war memorials, engraved with the names of the war dead are its monumental counterpart, forming national geographies of mourning where military sacrifice and loss are reiterated every April (Phillips 2016a). And in both Anzac nations, the two have also played a significant role in validating an origin story of national identity (Light 2020).

Accordingly, staff at Te Papa assigned to the commemorative project were alert to how this pervasive mnemonic culture might shape the exhibition in a particular way. But equally important – although never discussed in these terms – was Te Papa and Weta Workshop's track records for innovation and its impor-tance for each partner's 'brand'.[1] The following discussion, based on my work as a Te Papa employee and *Gallipoli's* curatorial lead, considers how the pursuit of technical and museological innovation, within the context of an entrenched culture of war remembrance, affected decisions related to the content and form of *Gallipoli*.

The new museology and Te Papa

In the last decade of the twentieth century, New Zealand's national museum, established in 1865, underwent an unparalleled transformation (McCarthy 2018). The result, the Museum of New Zealand Te Papa Tongarewa, was a hybrid museum-art gallery underpinned by the principles of the country's founding document, the Treaty of Waitangi, and a bicultural version of the new museol-ogy. The quickening of national identity and the burgeoning of Maori political and cultural self-determination during the previous two decades had kick-started this radical redevelopment. The revamped museum was correspondingly distinguished by its bicultural governance structure and overt demonstration and promotion of Maori cultural sovereignty.

Te Papa's freshly inked thumb print logo and snappy moniker 'Our Place' boldly asserted its preoccupation with identity, community, and belonging. Like other museums putting the new museology into practice, Te Papa shifted from 'being about something to being for somebody' (Weil 1999: 229). It set out to be an inviting place for all New Zealanders, especially groups who typically ignored museums and art galleries because they did not see themselves or their concerns reflected there. The creation of active and affective experiences that would expand and diversify audiences was another hallmark of Te Papa's public-facing activity. To achieve this objective, it downplayed elite or esoteric forms of knowledge, producing bold cross-disciplinary narrative exhibitions that incorporated popular culture and celebrated the nation. However, this crusade meant that the museums' collections and research by its specialists were at times downplayed.

War at Te Papa?

The reimagined museum delighted the general public, although it was not completely immune from negative commentary, especially from those disappointed by the demise of a separate National Art Gallery. Yet none of the suite of exhibits that New Zealanders flocked to see when the museum reopened in 1998 covered the country's involvement in war, despite it being embedded in popular culture and national identity – key planks of Te Papa's museology. Instead, the interpretation of New Zealand at war continued to be the responsibility of the Auckland War Memorial Museum and the Navy, Army, and Air Force Museums. However, as Te Papa embarked on an exhibition to mark the First World War centennial, its staff revisited this division of labour especially in light of its subject expertise, patchy war-related collections, and government expectations that Te Papa would play a leading role in the anniversary.

Initially, staff at Te Papa and Auckland Museum floated an idea to co-curate a travelling exhibition that showcased the latter's extensive war-related collections. However, this proposal was abandoned in favour of a more audacious strategy that was, in hindsight, a better fit with Te Papa's museological brand. Philosophically, the museum was pre-disposed towards teaming up with partners operating in mass popular culture.[2] One year out from the centennial, Michael Houlihan, Te Papa's then CE, began lobbying the major players in Wellington's famous film industry – known locally as 'Wellywood' – to gauge their interest in co-creating the museum's commemorative exhibition.

In the middle of 2014, with significant government funding secured to underwrite the project, Te Papa embarked on a partnership with Weta Workshop, one of Wellywood's principal players. On its website at this time, Weta was self-described as a 'multi-award-winning design studio and physical manufacturing facility servicing the world's entertainment and creative industries'. By drawing on Weta Workshop's experience of producing and delivering technically ambitious spectacles for popular audiences, Te Papa was poised to break new ground in the presentation of New Zealand's First World War. Sir Richard Taylor, Weta's co-founder, co-owner and creative director, and five times' Oscar winner, became the exhibition's creative director. Te Papa assumed responsibility for spatial design, historical and object-related content, audience advocacy, community consultation, and marketing, while Taylor held the creative purview and final-sign-off on all creative aspects.

By now, Te Papa's board had agreed with Houlihan's recommendation that the exhibition focus on a single story – the 1915 Gallipoli campaign. Gallipoli was the New Zealand Expeditionary Force's (NZEF's) first major experience of combat in the war, which was hailed subsequently as a defining moment for the nation: 'Before the war we were an untried and insular people' wrote Fred Waite, a Gallipoli veteran and the campaign's first historian; 'after Anzac we were tried and trusted' (Waite 1921: 299–300).

The NZEF's deployment to the Middle East had taken New Zealanders by surprise; when the Main Body left New Zealand in October 1914 the assumption was that it was headed for the Western Front. The infamous landings by the Anzacs on 25 April 1915 marked the start of a gruelling, eight-month-long stalemate in Turkey between British and Ottoman forces. Altogether, 16–18,000 New Zealanders served on the peninsula, including 500–600 Maori soldiers. From the outset, the Ottoman Army dominated the British Empire forces. Eventually, after the failure of a second attempt to move inland to the take the Dardanelles, the British War Office acknowledged the futility of the situation. In the wake of severe winter storms, and with careful planning, Anzac and British troops were evacuated from the peninsula, arriving in Egypt by early January 1916 (Fenton et al 2013: 12–25).

In the New Year, the reports of the campaign's demise printed in the New Zealand press considered the meaning of Gallipoli within the context of the war and New Zealand's contributions to it. National and imperial sentiment flowed freely. According to one Christchurch paper: 'Though Gallipoli remains a Turkish stronghold, it also stands as a shrine of British heroism, and the testing ground of Britain's overseas manhood' (*Evening Star*, 11 January 1916). The first anniversary of the Anzac landings, three and half months later, was another public outlet for similar claims as well as a focus for private mourning (Worthy 2002). Over the next century, this mutually reinforcing rhetoric and ritual evolved to become the means through which the campaign's human and tactical costs were redeemed, to morph into a national myth of identity formation and belonging.

For Weta, *Gallipoli's* discursive and performative fusion with nation-building was not an impediment to innovation nor an ideological hurdle to interrogate; it was more akin to a gift. Workshop staff were palpably excited and inspired by the exhibition's subject matter. Public statements made by Taylor and conversations with his team during exhibition development sessions indicated that they considered it an honour to be telling an iconic story *of* the nation *for* the nation. The Te Papa project team, however, had reservations about focussing on a campaign that had long received uncritical popular, political, and scholarly attention. They anticipated existing understandings of the campaign would be reinforced by the exhibition rather than questioned because of Te Papa's reputation as a touchstone for New Zealanders' shared sense of themselves. Yet Te Papa's project team also conceded that a tight focus on the 1915 campaign had its advantages: the New Zealand contribution to Gallipoli was distinctive, dramatic, and self-contained; the proposed chronological and geographical focus made it manageable from a curatorial and narrative perspective, as well as coherent and intelligible for visitors.

The movies, model-making, and the museum

A partnership in which an external firm had creative control of a social history exhibition was ground-breaking for Te Papa. This novel collaboration has been promoted by Te Papa on its website as a combination of the worlds of movies, model-making, and museums, creating an exhibition 'like no other'. The project also represented uncharted territory for the museum's collaborator Weta Workshop. For the exhibition, the firm would be putting aside the manufacture of mythical creatures and fantasy worlds for which it is celebrated in favour of factual content and historical accuracy. But it was clear that Taylor and Weta staff were committed to putting history at the heart of the project: one of the partner's first major agreements was that they would select a handful of key individuals from the historical record, who would act as the exhibition's narrators.

Taylor then came up with a daring concept that would give physical form to this idea. Transfixed by the hyper-real human figures sculpted by Australian sculptor Ron Mueck, he proposed the use of similarly larger-than-life models based on real people whose personal experiences would drive the exhibition's narrative. This was an untested technical proposition, but theoretically, with a staff of artisans, technicians, illustrators and designers, plus a 65,000 m² facility, anything could be made in-house by Weta Workshop – even 'people'. Taylor had confidence that his team's technical ingenuity applied to model-making would provide the 'x' factor that would capture the attention of audiences, especially those with restless minds and limited attention-spans, and apparently little interest in history.

The proposed super-sized, highly expressive human figures were clearly a reversal of the functional anonymity of museum mannequins. But the giant sculptures were also storytelling props and because of this, the scheme flipped the conventional view that a museum is a keeper and interpreter of authentic things. However, again from a practical point of view, making authentic personal stories literally into the exhibition's 'objects' compensated for Te Papa's desultory First World War collections. Another factor behind the model-making scheme was its potential to enhance the partners' reputations. If the giants were executed sympathetically and with the right attention to detail, they would enhance Te Papa's status as a cultural and museological innovator while Weta's spectacular technical wizardry would be given a platform at a popular and internationally feted museum.

Yet the giants were not merely an innovation for the sake of boosting brand awareness; along with the rest of the exhibition's content, they were subject to Te Papa's visitor-centric practises. Curators and audience advocates applied a framework of interpretive principals to the huge hyper-real human models just as they did to other elements in the exhibition's visitor experience. These principles, outlined in internal concept development documents, were:

- A sense of connection: visitors will be able to connect their personal story with that of the exhibition and experience.
- An emotional journey: we will evoke empathy with the many human emotional experiences inherent in these stories.
- Authentic accounts: we set the scene of what actually happened by using first-hand accounts where possible.

- Multi-sensory experience: we will explore these stories and emotions via a variety of sense and modes in order to cater to a broad range of learning styles.
- Space for reflection: we will provide opportunities for quiet contemplation, to allow visitors to reflect on the subject matter and exhibition.[3]

While the Te Papa team was concerned with these and other museological issues, Taylor contracted military historian and preeminent Gallipoli expert Dr Chris Pugsley as Weta's historical director to ensure the accuracy of the giants. By August 2014, and with the approval of Te Papa's board, Pugsley's responsibilities had been extended to cover all historical content in the exhibition. Pugsley by then had already joined forces with Te Papa's curatorial team of four to select Gallipoli's main characters. At this time, Pugsley also reoriented the exhibition's overall narrative so that it was presented chronologically rather than thematically, Te Papa's original intent. Because of this, the biographical selections had to make sense according to a timeline that ran from April to December 1915. Furthermore, at least one of the chosen individuals had to have survived Gallipoli so that a postscript set on the Somme in September 1916 worked.

From a large pool of candidates, eight individuals whose documented experiences would provide the exhibition's affective and narrative scaffolding were chosen. The first three interpretive principals outlined above came to the fore during this process.[4] In making their final choice, Pugsley and the curatorial team employed diversifying criteria – age, occupation, rank and unit, geographical origin or domicile, gender and ethnicity – to ensure that the exhibition presented as broad a cross section of experiences as possible albeit in a military setting.

While most of the disagreements generated by this process were resolved, the approach to representing Maori was intractable. This clash was due to Te Papa's museological principles and Pugsley's empiricism and scholarly conservatism. Members of the Te Papa team, all committed to the museum's bicultural role and the principles of the Treaty of Waitangi, insisted that at least one giant be Maori, whereas Pugsley took a literal position. Comparatively, the number of Maori who served on the peninsula with the NZEF was small – around 500–600 out of around 16,000–18,000 troops. However, this was the Maori Contingent's sole experience of frontline combat during the First World War and the project's Maori curator Puawai Cairns, supported by the exhibition's other three curators, argued that this unique but little-known New Zealand story warranted special attention. Pugsley, on the other hand, maintained that visitors would gain the wrong impression if the representation of Maori in the exhibition was 'disproportionate' to actual numbers. Although there was an impasse on this point, Cairns' firm rebuttal meant that two Maori alongside one Australian, and five Pakeha (New Zealanders of European ancestry), one of whom was British-born, made it into the exhibition.

FIGURE 12.2 Sir Richard Taylor, *Gallipoli's* Creative Director, poses with the sculptures depicting machine-gunners Rikihana Carkeek, Friday Hawkins, and Colin Warden (L-R). (© Michael Hall, Te Papa.)

Although a staid take on storytelling, the chronology implemented by Pugsley had the advantage of creating a seamless, immersive experience. Visitors are thrown into this immediately without context then come face to face with excited 29-year-old farmer Spencer Westmacott, aiming a pistol at the 'Turks' on 25 April. Next is 45-year-old surgeon Percival Fenwick on 4 May, hunched over with resignation, a dead soldier before him. Following Fenwick is 26-year-old journalist Jack Dunn on 4 July, who at the height of summer is perspiring and listlessly trying to keep 'flies' from landing in his corned beef.

A tableau showing three soldiers in the midst of battle on 6 August continues the chronology (Figure 12.2). Here, 25-year-old engineer Colin Warden is sprawled on the ground, fatally shot. The other two, 23-year-old carpenter Friday Hawkins and 25-year-old clerk Rikihana Carkeek from the Maori Contingent, are manning their machine gun, their faces projecting focussed aggression. Grief overwhelms 33-year-old hospital ship nurse Lottie Le Gallais, depicted in mid-November 1915, at the moment news of her soldier brother's death on Gallipoli in July finally reaches her. The final scene shows Cecil Malthus, a 26-year-old school teacher and Gallipoli survivor, standing in a shell crater on the Somme on 15 September 1916, staring blankly into the distance.

A red timeline runs along the floor between the giants and through the five thematic galleries that fill in and elaborate the chronology. This spatial arrangement is akin to plot development and action interrupted by cinematic close-ups, when the thoughts, feelings, and reflections of a main character fill the 'screen'. Featuring a range of interpretation, the thematic galleries cover the months of April–May ('The Great Adventure'); May–June ('Order from Chaos'); July ('Stalemate'); August ('Chunuk Bair'); and November–December ('Saying Goodbye'). The specific moment within the campaign at which each giant is 'frozen' is given context in these galleries with a single panel illustration like a page from a graphic novel. Their pre-war (and post-war) lives are also presented here as digital biographies on touchscreens.

The giants are powerful interpretative media. Their supersizing, ironically, helps visitors to personalize and make sense of Gallipoli at a scale they can comprehend – the war is an individual and subjective experience as much as it is a collective martial one (Stewart 1984). Clearly, though, they work as archetypes; they are a form of emotional shorthand and the embodiment of affect. As one visitor '@steven.ski' noted on Instragram: the 'life-like figures … tower above, oversized – bringing you closer to their emotional state'. Empathy is intensified by individual soundtracks, especially composed for the exhibition, which play in each of the enclosed spaces occupied by the giants. To heighten visitors' immersion within these emotive moments, the only other interpretation consists of words recorded by the individuals at the time, which are narrated by voice actors and animated on the galleries' walls.

Visitors to *Gallipoli* are generally aware that they are encountering a representation of reality: its artifice – and artistry – is openly acknowledged through a series of online, behind-the-scenes, 'making of' videos.[5] Yet while the giants are 'props', and their poses imagined for dramatic impact, their lives were not. Because *Gallipoli's* giants are real people based on historical and verifiable accounts of their war-time experiences, visitors also comprehend them as authentic and truthful entities. Curatorial research, which was based on archival enabled Weta to render them with uncanny realism.

However, without descendants' support and knowledge of family history, Te Papa would not have considered presenting the story of Gallipoli in such a bold way. Te Papa curators located living descendants of the seven men and one woman featured in the exhibition. These included (in 2015) two living children, both in their 90s. Each giant's life story was intangible heritage and a family treasure, so curators liaised with the respective families about how their ancestors should be represented in the exhibition. More pointedly, this was the broader application of Te Papa's bicultural practice of mana taonga, which acknowledges Maori cultural values and knowledge systems and the ongoing connections between source communities and Te Papa's collections and their interpretation.

Family members were profoundly moved that Taylor and Weta Workshop were involved in depicting the experiences of their relatives in order that take centre-stage stage in Te Papa's commemorative exhibition. This approach also echoed the ever-increasing public engagement with the First World War through genealogy and Maori whakapapa (family connections). And not only was family support fundamental for ethical reasons; it also gave curators access to details not always captured in the archive – including confirmation by one daughter that her father, Spencer Westmacott, had all his own teeth.

Innovative words – 'that's where the action was'

There is also a wide range of standard museum interpretation in *Gallipoli*, which is sometimes overlooked because of the attention-grabbing giant sculptures. However, this interpretation ensures that the exhibition provides visitors with multi-sensory experiences appealing to a broad range of learning styles – one of its five interpretive principles. Museum and privately owned objects, historical quotes, miniatures, dioramas, archival photography, oral history, as well as physical and digital interactives, illustrations and graphics and, of course, text, all combine to create a varied visitor experience.

In terms of exhibition text, Te Papa staff relished the opportunity presented by the project to rethink the museum's already innovative and visitor-centric approach to labels. Te Papa employs writers who collaborate with curators to craft accessible text for exhibitions. This entails the application and layering of hierarchies of information and the imposition of strict word limits, as well as translations into the Maori language (te reo Maori). In *Gallipoli*, writers and curators decided to experiment with perspective, replacing the common curatorial eye-of-god with labels that presented soldiers' first-person points of view.[6] They also agreed that labels did not have to be comprehensive – authoritative details about Gallipoli are readily available – and that they would focus instead on immersing visitors in the historical moment rather than over-explaining it to them.

In deploying the collective voice of the literate subaltern, curators and writers were aiming to produce texts that were intimate and enlightening. To keep the action in the present context and 'flashbacks' were kept to a minimum; the origins of the war, for example, are explained in 83 words. Verbatim, contemporaneous quotes presented graphically like magazine headlines helped to achieve this objective. Vocabulary and tone were also carefully considered. Familiarity with primary sources, along with digitized newspapers and dictionaries, meant that language did not stray into parodic 'Boys' Own' territory.

The introductory label, which sets the scene for the first thematic gallery 'The Big Adventure', illustrates the technique adopted for the exhibition:

> We were in Egypt when they told us we'd be invading Gallipoli. The Turks had sided with the Germans in the war, and we were itching to take them on. Apparently they wouldn't be too much trouble. Gallipoli was our first campaign of the war. We landed at Anzac Cover on April 25th, ready to back the Aussies. We clambered up the rugged hills – that's where the action was. Our great adventure had begun.

The next label, which accompanies a display of winter clothing near the end of the exhibition, shows how this writing style was applied to objects:

> In November, it suddenly got bloody cold. No more wandering about half naked with a grin on your face. We were given a greatcoat, extra socks and

shirts – and rum each night. We got woollens from home too. Fred Crum was chuffed with his balaclava: 'I can't believe Nan made it. It's A1 and fits like a glove. There's very little face showing … I've got Mrs Ashton's socks on and they're lovely.'

These words interpret items of unprovenanced and generic military uniform. Described in this way, the objects become connected imaginatively to a specific time and place in the past, while evoking a familiar scenario for the reader. The text alludes to the shock of being on Gallipoli during unexpected winter storms, which hastened the evacuation of the peninsula in December. It also gestures towards home, hinting at the emotional and material networks of one soldier within his family and community at home.

Limitations to innovation – a soldier's tale?

The content of the second label, which is also an allusion to how 'New Zealand society as a whole was enmeshed in the Great War', can be traced to recent First World War historiography concerned with a broader conception of military history and war studies (Hunter and Ross 2014: vii). This work pays attention to relationships between combatants and civilians during times of conflict, including their emotions and subjectivities, as well as race and gender and the long-lasting physical and psychic impacts of war. New sources too are considered for new insights and new lines of enquiry they offer. The spirit of this research can be discerned in some museums displaying war, including the Historial de la Grande Guerre in Péronne (Winter 2012: 160–161), In Flanders Fields Museum (Chielens et al 2014), and the Historical Military Museum of the *Bundeswehr* in Dresden (Pieken 2013), and in exhibitions such as Melbourne Museum's *Love and Sorrow* (Damousi et al 2021).

However, from a curatorial perspective, the incorporation of this scholarship and other fresh ways of thinking about commemorating war became difficult in *Gallipoli* because of the size of the giants and the challenges of sustaining an immersive chronological experience within a fairly modest 750 square metres. Structuring the exhibition's emotional arc and narrative according to combat experience also limited opportunities to explore a range of subjectivities. Even in *Gallipoli*'s most overt evocation of connections between a soldier in the field and his home, the soldier's inner thoughts and feelings drive the storyline. This moment occurs halfway through the exhibition within a replica of the dugout of NZEF commanding officer William Malone. Weta created this structure from Malone's photos and sketches; even the props displayed on a bedside table, including the photo of his wife Ida, are based on primary sources. Visitors, alone or in pairs, can enter these cramped quarters; digital images of Malone's family in New Zealand are projected onto the back of the bivouac (Figure 12.3).

FIGURE 12.3 A visitor reads a copy of William Malone's final letter to his wife Ida, within a replica of Malone's Quinn's Post dugout. (© Norm Heke, Te Papa.)

Once inside the dugout, visitors can also eavesdrop on extracts read from a tender letter that Malone wrote to Ida on the night of 5 August, as he contemplated the possible outcome of the imminent attack on Chunuk Bair:

> I expect to go through all right but, dear wife, if anything untoward happens to me, you must not grieve too much. There are our dear children to be brought up. You know how I love and have loved you, and we have had many years of great happiness together. I am prepared for death, and hope God will have forgiven me all my sins.

Malone was a practicing Catholic, and these words no doubt served as a moral and spiritual stock-take for him in the face of the unknown. While Malone's heightened emotions are focussed on home, his loved ones at home have no voice, and their absence is keenly felt in this intimate setting. If visitors fail to guess from the tone of content that these were Malone's last words to Ida, they learn about his death on Chunuk Bair, three days later after he wrote them, in the next gallery.

This example is notable for its singularity. However, it was not meant to be exceptional. During the planning and concept development phase of the exhibition, curators and audience advocates had hoped to demonstrate such connections in a more sustained way. The hospital ship nurse Lottie Le Gallais, for example, was selected as mediator between Gallipoli and New Zealand. But the opportunity to fully realize this objective vanished as the realities of presenting the giants and telling the campaign story took over. In this case, it was the spatial demands of the giant machine gunners' triptych and displaying two machine guns, one from a private collection with impeccable Gallipoli provenance, in the 'Chunuk Bair' theme.

Because of the spatial needs of what is the martial narrative's dramatic high-point, little space was left to cover the final months of the campaign and the evacuation of troops from the peninsula. The modest nature of home front objects in Te Papa's collections also conspired against ambitions to extend the geographical and emotional reach of the exhibition. Curators compromised by making a feature of the New Zealand hospital ship *Maheno* in the 'Saying Goodbye' theme. Lottie Le Gallais served on the *Maheno* which picked up the sick and wounded from Gallipoli between August and November 1915. The ship, its outfitting for military service funded entirely by New Zealanders, was described as 'the latest practical token of that intense patriotism of New Zealand and its unalterable attachment to the grand Imperial connection' (cited in Hunter and Ross 2014: 186). This back story allowed the *Maheno* to function in two ways. Presented as an engaging cutaway miniature model the *Maheno* demonstrates tangible connections to home as well as the medium for telling the story of the medical evacuation of troops from the peninsula. However, this narrative sleight of hand means 'Lottie' tends to be interpreted by visitors as a cipher of grief and a victim of the horror of war (Figure 12.4).

Active engagement

The sheer spectacle of the giants and their show-stopping hyper-realism had the potential to overturn Te Papa's commitment to active audience engagement. In an attempt to offset this risk of passive viewing, Te Papa staff lobbied for adequate space to be set aside in the galleries for physical interactives. Of the interactives that made it into *Gallipoli*, two were designed to encourage visitors to share their own thoughts and feelings. The first of these, in the 'Stalemate' theme, asks them to empathize with the troops on Gallipoli who, in 1915, relied on an erratic postal service to keep in touch with loved ones. Here visitors are invited to write a postcard to friends and family, stimulated by two questions: 'If you knew you might never make it home what would you miss most? What would you say to your loved ones?'.

The second appears near the exit of *Gallipoli*. Folded-paper red poppies are used here as vehicles for visitor comments. The following words prompt reflection:

> Gather a poppy and share your thoughts – someone's name, a war story, your response to the exhibition, or your feelings on conflict. Feel free to lay your poppy at the feet of the solider ahead of you, or take it home.

The development of this interactive activity revealed diverging attitudes amongst members of the Te Papa project team towards this universal symbol

FIGURE 12.4   The sculpture of the nurse Lottie Le Gallais tells the story of women at war but also acts as a cipher for grief and horror. (© Michael Hall, Te Papa.)

of war remembrance. New Zealanders wear red poppies on Anzac Day, a tradition that began in 1922 (Saunders 2014: 111), and curators and audience advocates debated whether this long association with this mnemonic practice would circumscribe contemporary reflections. The counter argument, which ultimately prevailed, was that alternatives would have no meaning visitors.[7]

Within days of *Gallipoli* opening, it was clear that the decision to use red poppies was justified. By April 2016, an estimated 280,000 poppies had been left as tributes in the gallery – representing approximately 40 per cent of the total number of visitors to *Gallipoli* in that period. Nicola Caldwell and Lee Davidson's study of one per cent of the poppies (3,001) left in *Gallipoli* over its first

12 months revealed a range of messages, most of them falling under the rubric of commemoration and reflection. However, Caldwell and Davidson reported certain subtle variations in these responses. Not entirely unexpected, 20 per cent contained clichés commonly associated with war remembrance yet 11 per cent expressed anti-war sentiments. Many – 13 per cent – directly addressed soldiers, some thanking them for their service. On the other hand, national identity is barely mentioned, with just 13 messages (one per cent) in the sample using it to frame their message, while ten per cent shared family connections (Caldwell and Davidson 2016: 3). It seems that visitors are making sense of *Gallipoli* at personal than rather collective scale.

War memorial museum?

The evidence presented by Caldwell and Davidson supports Australian historian Christina Twomey's observation that, since the 1980s, '[p]ersonalised stories of trauma, suffering, loss and pain [have come] to occupy a legitimate space in the public discussion of Anzac' (Twomey 2013: 88). But the privatization of sentiment does not mean that other components of mnemonic culture have lost their purchase in structuring the meanings of war in the two Anzac nations. The strong hold of war memorials on New Zealand's commemorative imagination was clear during the planning stages of *Gallipoli* when Taylor proposed that the exhibition concludes with a replica tomb for an unknown soldier.[8] After rigorous debate, the idea was abandoned on the grounds that its inclusion would have transformed Te Papa, a secular forum, into a de facto war memorial which would have consequences for Maori cultural protocols around death.[9] It also seemed heavy-handed, given that the national as well as provincial and local war memorials were already part of Wellington's cityscape. Eventually, a giant figure presented within the context of the Western Front was approved as a more fitting end to the exhibition. However, the invitation made to visitors to leave poppies at this giant's feet resembles a popular practice at the Australian War Memorial's Roll of Honour; it signals that this space at Te Papa is, like the war memorial, dedicated to remembrance (Figure 12.5).

Weta Workshop's desire to list the names of the NZEF's 2,779 Gallipoli fatalities was another manifestation of the firm's unproblematic deference towards existing commemorative modes. In this case, Weta wanted to replicate in the exhibition the nominal acknowledgment of the war dead, a defining feature of New Zealand's war memorials. The Te Papa project team deflected this proposal on the grounds that it was, at best, too literal. Designers found an alternative: a graphic and symbolic representation of the loss of a life denoted by a red cross against the date of death along the exhibition's timeline. In this way, visitors make their journey through *Gallipoli* along a path of service, sacrifice, and loss (Figure 12.6).

FIGURE 12.5   At the end of the exhibition, visitors leave folded poppies with messages in the Western Front shell crater occupied by the sculpture depicting Cecil Malthus. (© Norm Heke, Te Papa.)

FIGURE 12.6   *Gallipoli's* timeline, seen here at the gallery dedicated to the Battle for Chunuk Bair. (© Norm Heke, Te Papa.)

Conclusion

Gallipoli now holds the record for the most visited exhibition, ever, in New Zealand. Its millions of visitors, muted criticism, and industry awards suggest that an immersive 'blockbuster' exhibition has been an appropriate vehicle for war remembrance. Ultimately, institutional concerns about whether a commemorative exhibition at Te Papa about the First World War could attract visitors were unfounded. Visitor-centric 'new museology' and rigorous historical research combined with Weta's cutting-edge technical expertise and canny knowledge of audiences continues to find favour with visitors primed for a version of the campaign popularized by mass media.

But *Gallipoli* was also part of a broader four-year commemorative and cultural phenomenon – a critical context for its development and reception. Events marking the occasion had enormous support from New Zealanders, if figures from a government survey are any indication. According to the Ministry for Culture and Heritage, which oversaw the centennial of the First World War, 93 per cent of those surveyed engaged with commemorative activities during the anniversary period (Ministry for Culture and Heritage 2019: 30). Therefore *Gallipoli* is also a snapshot of New Zealand's evolving culture of remembrance; it illuminates how dominant forms of New Zealand's culture of remembrance, such as the war memorials, retain their relevance (Heathorn 2005: 1104).

Conversely, collective identity, a defining feature of Anzac remembrance, is no longer the powerful marshalling force it once was for those engaging in the story of the First World War. *Gallipoli's* striking innovation, the giants, folds neatly into an alternative iteration of Anzac remembrance which has been ascendant since the 1980s. The key referents for this version of Anzac are 'the traumatising effects of war, and sympathy for its victims' (Twomey 2013: 88). That this trope has gained widespread purchase across the two Anzac nations is illustrated by messages written on poppies left in *Gallipoli:* 'Gut wrenching to think so many people lost their lives for a pointless war' as one visitor put it (Caldwell and Davidson 2016: 21).

Also central to Anzac's revival are 'emotion and affect, through the medium of the individual story' (Twomey 2013: 95). Both were at the heart of *Gallipoli,* its eight main characters selected from the historical record for their potential to elicit empathy from visitors and their ability to tell the story of the campaign at a human scale. Those working at the radical edges of cultural production and scholarship might consider *Gallipoli* a missed opportunity: while innovation was a driving force behind this approach, ultimately it could be seen as a handmaiden of the status quo, enabling the Gallipoli to become more firmly fixed in the bedrock of a popular and conservative culture of war remembrance.

Acknowledgements

I would like to thank the editors for their invitation to contribute to this collection and for their patience. All opinions expressed in this chapter are my own.

Notes

1 For example, Te Papa nominates itself as 'New Zealand's innovative national museum' on its twitter account.
2 In 2002, the museum had been the venue for New Line Cinema's very successful touring exhibition *The Lord of the Rings Motion Picture Trilogy: The Exhibition.*
3 Six complementary behavioural outcomes were also identified; after seeing the exhibition, visitors would be emotionally moved and experience empathy; understand the impact of war on individuals and the nation; know and understand more about Gallipoli and the First World War; grasp the unique characteristics of the Gallipoli campaign; and make personal connections between past and present and to be motivated to act on these insights.
4 Taylor was not involved in these discussions; his overriding concern was how Weta could make the history selected by the experts 'come alive', as he put in an early project pitch.
5 See https://www.tepapa.govt.nz/discover-collections/read-watch-play/behind-scenes/behind-scenes-gallipoli.
6 For this reason, the curatorial team used extracts from veterans' oral histories very sparingly. Although authentic first-person accounts, they were recorded with historical hindsight, many decades after the campaign.
7 Te Papa was not unique in its adoption of the red poppy. It was ubiquitous during the centennial, with many projects utilizing and exploring its symbolism, notably *Blood Swept Lands and Seas of Red*, the 2014 installation of almost 900,000 ceramic poppies in the moat of the Tower of London.
8 While Anzac Day and war memorials had become sites of anti-war and feminist protest in New Zealand during the 1960s and 1970s, their popular uptake was revived in the following decades. This crested in 2004 when New Zealand's unknown warrior was repatriated and reburied at the National War Memorial in Wellington.
9 After one has been associated with the sacred or tapu state of death, certain rituals (tikanga) are conducted, which includes cleansing oneself with water, in order to return to an everyday (noa) state. For this reason, a bowl of water is available at the end of *Gallipoli.*

References

Baird, K. and J. Phillips. (2020) Centenary (New Zealand). In U. Daniel, P. Gatrell, O. Janz, H. Jones, J. Keene, A. Kramer and B. Nasson (eds.), *1914–1918-online. International Encyclopedia of the First World War*, Berlin: Freie Universität Berlin. https://encyclopedia.1914–1918-online.net/article/centenary_new_zealand (accessed 21 January 2021).

Caldwell, N. and L. Davidson. (2016) *Visitors messages on Gallipoli Poppies: An archive of affective engagement. (unpublished research report).* Wellington: Victoria University of Wellington.

Chielens, P., D. Dendooven and A. Vandenbilcke. (2014) *In Flanders Fields Museum Guide.* Ieper: In Flanders Fields Museum.

Damousi, J., D. Tout-Smith and B. Zino (eds.) (2021) *Museums, History and the Intimate Experience of the Great War.* Abingdon: Routledge.

Fenton, D., C. Lord, G. McLean and T. Shoebridge. (2013) *New Zealand and the First World War.* Auckland: Penguin Books.

Harris, M. (2014) Commemoration, Cult of the Fallen (New Zealand). In U. Daniel, P. Gatrell, O. Janz, H. Jones, J. Keene, A. Kramer and B. Nasson (eds.), *1914–1918-online. International Encyclopedia of the First World War*, Berlin: Freie Universität Berlin. https://encyclopedia.1914–1918-online.net/article/centenary_new_zealand (accessed 21 January 2021).

Heathorn, S. (2005) The mnemonic turn in the cultural historiography of Britain's Great War. *The Historical Journal* 48 (4):1103–1124.

Hunter, K. and K. Ross. (2014) *Holding on to Home: New Zealand Stories and Objects of the First World*. Wellington: Te Papa Press.

King, S. (2017) *Centennial Stances, Museums, Morals, and the First World War*. MA thesis (Museum and Heritage Studies). Wellington: Victoria University of Wellington.

Light, R. (2020) *Anzac commemoration in Australia and New Zealand, 1965–2015*. PhD thesis (History) University of Auckland.

McCarthy, C. (2018) Te Papa Wellington: Te Papa Press.

Ministry for Culture and Heritage. (2019) *WW100 First World War Centenary Programme Final Report*. Wellington.

Phillips, J. (2016a) *To the Memory: New Zealand's War Memorials*. Nelson: Potton & Burton Nelson.

———. (2016b) *Gallipoli: The scale of our war. Gallipoli: The New Zealand story in colour, reCollections*, 11, 1 https://recollections.nma.gov.au/issues/volume_11_number_1/exhibition_reviews/gallipoli (accessed 26 January 20211).

Pieken, G. (2013) Contents and space: New concept and new building of the Militärhistorisches Museum. In W. Muchitsch (ed.), *Does War Belong in Museums?*, pp 63–82. Bielefeld: Transcript Publishing.

Saunders, N.J. (2014) *The Poppy: A History of Conflict, Loss, Remembrance and Redemption*. London: Oneworld.

Schorch, P. (2014) Cultural feeling and the making of meaning. *International Journal of Heritage Studies* 20 (1):22–35.

Stewart, S. (1984) *On Longing: Narratives of the Miniature, the Gigantic, the Souvenir, the Collection*. London and Baltimore: Johns Hopkins University Press.

Twomey, C. (2013) Trauma and the reinvigoration of Anzac. An argument. *History Australia* 10 (3):85–108.

Waite, F. (1921) *The New Zealanders at Gallipoli*. Auckland: Whitcombe and Tombs.

Weil, S. (1999) From being about something to being for somebody: The ongoing transformation of the American Museum. *Daedalus* 128 (3):229–258.

Winter, J. (2012) Museums and the representation of war. *Museum and Society* 10 (3): 150–163.

Worthy, S. (2002) 'A Debt of Honour': New Zealanders' First Anzac Days. *New Zealand Journal of History* 36 (2):85–200.

PART III

Audiences and Engagement

13

CURATING *THE SENSORY WAR, 1914–2014*

Emotions, sensations and the violence of modern war

Ana Carden-Coyne

The centenary commemorations of the First World War (2014–2019) invigorated new historical research that supported heritage projects, community collaborations, museum exhibitions and commissioned art projects, digitization projects and podcasts for the public to curate 'do-it-yourself' exhibitions (Evans 2008; Jones 2013; Cornish 2016: 513). However, the rising temperature of 'centenary fever' in the UK led to political jostling about the causes, meaning and legacies of the conflict and partisan debates were conducted in the media. A questionable celebratory tone was preferred by some English politicians, following £50 million of government investment into heritage projects, overseen by the Prime Minister David Cameron's special representative Dr Andrew Murrison MP.[1] Museums questioned if there was a 'danger of glorifying' the First World War despite solemn curatorial efforts, while historians warned against reproducing the triumphalism of the interwar period, despite the more restrained approach taken in the Irish Republic (Crotty and Melrose 2007; Madigan 2014; Tuathaigh 2014).[2] These anxieties were also seen in other countries shaped by the war, or those with contested memory cultures, shedding further light on unresolved national, transnational, political and historical questions in France (Hanna and Horne 2016); Germany (Mombauer 2017); Australia (Beaumont 2015) and in relation to the Armenia genocide (Laycock 2015) or language politics in Belgium's commemorations (Wouters 2012). Despite discourses that reflected on loss and peace, the reinterpretation of this global First World War was revitalizing nationalist agendas (Van Der Auwera and Schramme 2014). One commentator concluded that in a few short months, the centenary was fast becoming an 'unhappy anniversary' (Bowman 2014). Through this period, historians and curators were attuned to political claims upon both the national mood and the war's alleged meaning, challenging 'cherished visions' shaped by post-war myths

DOI: 10.4324/9781003263531-17

and 'partial truth', thus bringing to the fore the complexities of doing public history (Jones 2014; Moore 2014; Mycock 2014; Cornish 2016: 514).

Nevertheless, heritage and community projects did generate positive responses, such as to the historical accounts and testimonies, national and local museum exhibits, the transformation of heritage spaces into First World War spaces, television documentaries, films, radio programmes, musical theatre and plays, historical art exhibitions and contemporary art commissions and public installations. Attempts were made 'to push beyond familiar historical narratives' to provide 'a richer and more nuanced national conversation about the meaning of the war in twenty-first century Britain' (McCarthy 2016: 505). For instance, a diverse body of publicly funded cultural and art projects, under the *14–18 Now* programme, were commissioned, attracting mass support from audiences.[3] This creative work, often directly working with families and communities, attracted approximately 35 million people, including descendants of the war generation motivated by threading together collective and personal memories (Roper and Duffett 2018). The stakes were high for curators, commissioners and artists, with a great responsibility to speak for communities, to complicate dominant narratives, while navigating the fraught political climate (Baxter 2020). The burden of politicization, however, did not deleteriously affect the delivery of public history and museum engagement, as we will see.

Creativity in curation can act as an antidote to divisive debates, and museum spaces as a sanctuary from the toxic tone of political and media contestation. Paul Cornish notes of the Imperial War Museum's transformation of its First World War galleries, taking a contemporaneous approach to voices of the past, and a sensory approach to objects and visitor experiences, 'eschews lacing any post-war interpretation on wartime events and decisions' (Cornish 2017: 19). Despite the heavy politicization of the war's meaning, by the end of 2018 'centenary fever' cooled down with the mood of reflection.[4] It is in this context that this chapter raises several questions, which aims to be useful for public historians and curators, and those who will engage cultural institutions and collections in creative acts of commemoration in the future. It explores a set of questions that emerged while preparing and staging a commemorative exhibition based on both historical and contemporary art that I co-curated in 2014–2015, entitled *The Sensory War, 1914–2014*. The exhibition opened on 10 October, 2014, following a three-year intensive process of research resulting in the selection of 178 works, via the partnership between myself (Centre for the Cultural History of War, University of Manchester), David Morris (Senior Curator, Whitworth Art Gallery, WAG) and Tim Wilcox (Head of Exhibitions, Manchester Art Gallery, MAG). It ran for five months from October 2014 to February 2015, attracting an estimated 203,000 visitors, and had an accompanying educational and outreach programme.

The chapter aims to demonstrate that the vanguards of academic research can, in partnerships with key public institutions, make important interventions into public discourse despite the fact that publicly funded institutions may be pressured to shy away from taking such risks. It considers the audience feedback in order to consider what audiences found useful and rewarding when they engage the past and the present through visual art. This is particularly important when the meaning and legacies of wars harbour such uncertainty and constellation through politics, and therefore I will use this example to explore the question about how cultural work might commemorate contested wars in the future, given that wars are often not resolved, they are contested, raked over or silenced, and also carry with them national myths that are difficult to disentangle while remaining respectful. I argue that the role of artists is useful as conduits for communities to shape meaning, heal trauma and foster deep contemplation through creativity and imagination.

Feeling the Exhibition: Emotions in Visitor Data and Public Responses

This exhibition began first and foremost as a response to the resident collections at MAG and the WAG, which meant the curators did not foresee in the planning stages that the centenary would be controversial. Would that have toned down our curatorial decisions, wall panels and labels? MAG's twitter feed data is helpful in considering how visitors responded emotionally to the exhibition, which often contained graphic and confronting subject matter.[5] One visitor comment stated: 'Absolutely stunned by the Sensory War@mcaartgallery absolute perfect balance in commemorating the centenary without glorifying or judging'. Arguably some of the more challenging elements of the exhibition (including works on sexual violence), far from being off-putting, offensive or insensitive were seen as an important realistic corrective at a time when commemoration was becoming celebration. Artists in the show were continually seen by audiences as sustaining a powerful voice that countered the sanitization of war: 'You want to look away but are somehow continually drawn back in'. Another tweet declared, 'THE UNBELIEVABLE TRUTH' of a 'landmark show'.

The visual conversation around the sheer violence of war was also felt as urgent: 'we still can't get *The Sensory War* exhib out of our minds after seeing it yesterday. Incredible. Urge everyone to go'. *The Sensory War* was an exhibition about the impact of modern war on human sensory experience, and what the visitor feedback demonstrated was that art also elicits sensations, feelings and strong emotions that were not found to be inappropriate even if, as one tweeter found it, 'gut wrenching' or another 'was shaken in what feels like an important way'. Another tweeter referred it the exhibits as 'harrowing' but this was not felt as an exploitation of emotion, nor a trauma trigger, but rather something more 'remarkable' in its uniqueness during the centenary. The tone we strove for was still commemorative, and, as one visitor described 'sobering'. Indeed, another concluded that 'Few exhibitions, if any, leave me speechless & mentally drained but it's important that people should see A Sensory War'. The nature of twitter is interesting in this respect, as it enabled visitors to reach out to each other to see the exhibition as part of their own critical and perhaps even moral education.

To be sure, we considered what audiences might want from the remembrance activity of the First World War; both locally, in Manchester – albeit with visitors from diverse backgrounds – and in terms of the international resonance and interest in the centenary. Curating an art show about this world-wide conflict, and its colonial underpinnings, enabled us to think about what was specific to our northern communities and how it linked with the wider global story, a perspective that we found was much welcomed. Education teams are expert at engaging communities often excluded from national (and nationalist) commemorations, such as the South Asian and Afro-Caribbean communities, and communities from the African, Middle Eastern and European diasporas, and their experience could also inform the curation of an exhibition, particularly one about world war that has been so foundational to national memory and embedded in citizenship in the UK. With such a collaborative approach to historical research, curation and education (or learning as it is called at MAG), we thought it was crucial to bring together the historical collections with contemporary art works to create a deeper resonance of the past in the present.

The Sensory War collaborated with the Manchester Literature Festival, which sponsored the author Kamila Shamsie to conduct workshops in the space and to write a response to some key works, resulting in *War Stories. Mostly Not Mine.*[6] Students from Manchester College also created dramatic performances in front of the works. Multi-arts collaborations help broaden the reach of discussion, enabling different voices and perspectives. *The Western Front Association* (WFA) also conducted tours of the exhibition, bringing in further visitors. Visitor data includes letters to the gallery expressing thanks for the opportunity to see the 'wonderful collection'. Another in this group appreciated the direct response of artists to the experience of war: 'a very impressive exhibition, full of realistic impressions and detail … As someone whose parents never talked about war, though they wanted the children to know, I grew up at the time hearing about my Uncle who was killed in 1918, yet I was sheltered from the reality'. From the deeply personal response to hidden family stories of the First World War, we also saw visitors identify a revelation in more contemporary artworks, which far from alienating in their style were found to be 'very moving and thought provoking'. As one visitor from WFA said: 'The exhibition of artwork from war and other conflicts was superb. It vividly showed the effects of war on both participants and the landscape'. This was indeed our curatorial premise: to consider the First World War as a turning point but then to explore the impact of modern technological war across the subsequent hundred years through the eyes of modern and contemporary artists.[7]

The exhibition attracted younger audiences, who remarked on the exhibition's thematic rather than chronological structure, spread across two floors, While this was also quite demanding, even relentless, one PhD student concluded that the exhibition 'managed to negotiate an extremely complex array of styles, themes, methods and subject' and cited another student who said, 'the overwhelming feeling I was left with was of a need to recognise that narratives and commemorations of war need to be complex, if they are to reflect more thoroughly the realities of war'.[8] As one visitor tweeted, the exhibition structure was 'thoughtfully put together' despite its 'Chilling' images that 'are haunting me this morning'. The exhibition did risk upsetting people, and indeed one visitor said it was 'traumatising ... some very powerful works etched on my brain. I could weep'. There was something powerful about the collation of works in this way, through the interconnected themes of embodied emotions and sensations in response to technological war as it became increasingly damaging and toxic over the century, that as one tweeter concluded: 'Astonishing. I don't think I'll ever forget it'.

Art's role as a memory trigger was not necessarily traumatic for some of the visitors who came from a local dementia day care centre and a nursing home, whose activity coordinator informed one of the learning managers that while short-term memory loss is a common symptom, long-term memories remain 'fairly intact'. The on-site workshop *stimulated all their senses* and brought back memories of the war years, which initiated conversations, some of which continued after the sessions had finished'. And the family feedback was that their relatives 'were more alert and talkative when they returned home'.[9]

With the potential to traumatize our audiences, there were certainly major decisions that had to be made about key works. One group of visitors that had important professional reflections to make were art therapists who used the exhibition for a training and development workshop, and to consider challenges they face in their profession when working with traumatized victims. One therapist described having intense visceral reactions: 'challenging, very raw. ...felt infuriated, vulnerable and yet also grateful'.[10] It also enabled a degree of reflection on the profession of art therapy, and the experience of being a witness as well as a practitioner. Art therapists play such crucial roles in working with victims of war and conflict, torture, and displacement, as well as in assisting refugees and asylum-seekers, what we curators learned from this group was not just the power and poignancy of artists' unique insights, but its educational value in enabling health workers to support victims suffering emotional and mental trauma as a result of war and forced displacement. The artworks had a professional benefit in providing valuable, visceral and empathetic insights into war experiences, and a potential to benefit vulnerable people living in the community in Manchester.

The sensory response to the First World War that artists visualized continued to shape artistic developments through to the twenty-first century. This revelation became the key curatorial framework to explore the impact of war on the body, the mind, the senses and the environment – and to understand those fields *synaesthetically* – as mutually informing the human sensory response. The exhibition concept drew upon the 'sensory turn' in academia which enabled us to draw out the acoustic, haptic, textural, material, psychological and affective aspects emerging from the visual content of paintings, etchings, sculptures, films and video works. This was developed into a wider story of war art in the twentieth and twenty-first centuries, and sensory themes emerged from the research beyond the historical to the contemporary conduct and impact of war.

The Sensory War, 1914–2014

Curatorial Background

The starting point for the exhibitions was both the collections of the two institutions and my research into First World War art and culture, with support from the Arts and Humanities Research Council (AHRC), resulting in my monograph, *The Politics of Wounds: Military Patients and Medical Power* (2014), where two major curated themes of 'pain and succour' and 'rupture and rehabilitation' were explored through experiences, documents produced by, and representations of, medical personnel (doctors, surgeons, nurses, physiotherapists) and their patients – medical, surgical and post-operative recovery and living with (often significant) disabilities, all of which has been the subject of artists for centuries but especially in response to the First World War. This material informed the exhibition and we were able to borrow some of the key works in my research monograph to put on display in Manchester. The exhibition mined the collections of the MAG and the WAG and also secured many important historical and contemporary works from public and private collections in Britain, Europe, the US and Iran.

Manchester was also crucial for its position as a major regional centre of First World War recruitment and training, war medicine, rehabilitation and artistic endeavour. Significantly, in 1914, Lawrence Haward was appointed director of the city's gallery and he began collecting directly from the studios of artists who would become part of the British Official War Artists' scheme established by the War Office and Ministry of Information. Hence MAG possessed an important collection, including a few rare Paul Nash pastel drawings and a major work by Henry Lamb. Haward wrote about modern war not as romantic adventure and heroic make-believe, but bitterness and courage, folly and waste. The artist, he wrote, was dependent on 'the stimulus of external reality for their conceptions' and is 'affected by the changes in the *condition of the world which war produces*', grappling with traumatic experiences 'to give expression to aesthetic emotion'. Modern war, Haward said, was not as a romantic adventure (as the Victorians would have it) nor was it a performance of heroic make-believe, but rather 'it is bitterness and courage, folly and waste' and artists 'will reflect that world and the human emotions it arouses' (Haward 1916). Haward's words were powerful testimony for the artists of the period who strove to communicate the sensation and impact of modern war.

The exhibition sought to shine a light on the way that artists across the century had seen modern war as a rupture in human and technological history, in its targeting and radical altering of sensory experience. In the two world wars, many artists had been combatants, had worked as doctors and stretcher bearers, or had been wounded themselves, and many had been witnesses who documented what they encountered. Artistic practices could communicate – even ameliorate – the sensory and deeply intimate experience of war. We felt obligated to examine the war through to the twenty-first century, comparing and contrasting the past and present, and how artists have shifted from visual and tactile media, such as painting, drawing, etching and lithography, which evokes bodily pain or the fragility of flesh, to a more immersive, sensory experiences in sound, film and video. The medium is also a means of expressing sensory war. While military and press photography of this period brought a new capacity to coldly document such lethal displays, artists found a different way of seeing and *feeling*.

Trauma and loss – of body, mind, senses and environments – were central themes in artistic responses to war and conflict over the century, we might also consider aspects of beauty, reconstruction and hope for humanity. The art of war and conflict generates psychological and neurological reactions to chemical war and bombing; sounds of silent mourning stir deep emotions and visual imaginations, and video works immerse us in the sensorial world of postmodern aerial warfare, from the helicopter to the predator drone. From the horrors of the First World War to today's conflicts, artists reveal the trauma of war but also inspire with a recuperative message. In the spirit of peaceful intervention and political challenge, artists have communicated the worst and best of humanity: abject suffering and the hope of resilience.

Ten Sensory Themes and 178 Works

Ten themes for the show emerged quickly in the process: Militarising Bodies, Manufacturing War; Female Factories; Aerial Warfare and the Sensation of Flight; Pain and Succour; Rupture and Rehabilitation; Embodied Ruins; Shocking the Senses; Bombing, Burning and Distant War; Chemical War and the Toxic Imaginary; Ghostlands: Loss, Memory and Resilience. These themes enabled us to range across a century of change in modern war and geographical locations and across artistic practices. We wanted to explore the critical perspective of artists, their role as storytellers, as well as their agency in challenging the politics of militarism and the violation of human rights in wartime with the values of justice, humanity and peace.

To tell this story of artists responding to modern war, we began with the significance of technology's sensorial and affective impact, evident in C.R.W. Nevinson's iconic painting *Explosion* (1916). It reverberates with the sonic assault of high-powered artillery explosions and bombs that annihilated landscapes and shattered bodies into oblivion. The sheer force of the sensory is captured in the jagged lines and Vorticist colour; light, ash and dirt rise up as the boom of the explosion fragments time, the atmosphere, smell, taste and ear-shattering. As a driver for the Friends' Ambulance Unit in 1914, he had found himself helping the overwhelmed French Army medical services at a facility in Dunkirk, tellingly named 'The Shambles'. Nevinson almost broke down from the strain caused by immense firepower, the ensuing chaos and its gruesome results: 'I felt I had been born in the nightmare. I had seen sights so revolting…shrieks, pus, gangrene and the disembowelled', but also felt determined not to 'shrink' from it. He recalled, 'I was pursued by the urge to do something, to be "in" the War, and although I succeeded in the end and was "in" it, I was never "of" it' (Nevinson 1938: 99, 95). He suggests here a sensation of tension between the proximity and distance to the violence of modern war, and it was this paradox that the exhibition curators also sought to explore.

This section of the exhibition, *Militarising Bodies, Manufacturing War*, owed something of its spirit to Trudi Tate's discussion of the professed modernity of new military hardware, and how the authorities helped to manufacture consent for the war through home-front displays and 'tank banks' (Tate 1998). Artists evoked the material texture of this technology, and, as was common at the time, depicted soldiers' bodies as machine-like, David Bomberg's *Sappers at work: a Canadian tunnelling company* (1918), and in Nevinson's *Returning to the Trenches* (1916), the sounds of bayonets clashing like machine parts in an almost audible clanging rhythm. Feminist historians have discussed the phenomenon of the 'munitionette' and wartime female factory labour as militarizing their bodies, which collapsed the distinction between the home front and front-line, though less has been said about the artistic representation (Woollacott 1994; Grayze 2016). Artists' depictions of female labour went beyond national stereotypes, despite arising from propagandistic commissions. The gendered 'tospsy-turveydom' of women in heavy industries, engineering and railways was observed but so too were the skills gained by women in working with explosives and the risks they endured, such as in Archibald Standish Hartrick's *Women's Work, On Munitions: Heavy Work, Skilled Work*, and *Dangerous Work: Packing TNT* (1917) or Nevinson's *Building Aircraft: Acetylyne Welding* (1917), among others. Hence, a dedicated sub-section was called *Female Factories*, a title I appropriated from the infamous female prison of colonial Tasmania, to suggest that the work was dangerous and exploitative.

The technology and spectacle of air power, as aeroplanes were adapted from reconnaissance tools to manned weapons, was also documented by artists. In the section called 'Aerial War and the Sensation of Flight', we exhibited Nevinson's own hand clinging to the side of the open aircraft but also the iridescent beauty of *Archies* (1916), painted on glass. In both the first two sections, we showed vibrantly coloured paintings from the Second World War too, including Wyndham Lewis' *A Canadian War Factory* (1943) and Laura Knight's *Ruby Loftus Screwing a Breech Ring* (1942), as well as the more sombre drawings of Eric Ravilious' *View from the Cockpit of a Moth* (1942) and Paul Nash's *Arrival of the Stirlings* (1942), among others.

Moving from the technology of the two world wars to their destructive impact on human flesh was key to the exhibition. The next section called 'Pain and Succour' focused on the physical and psychological wounds and the medical response, stemming from my research into triage, medical evacuation, surgery, disability and rehabilitation for *The Politics of Wounds* (2014). The standout painting from MAG's collection was by Henry Lamb. Though born in South Australia, he was educated at Manchester Grammar School when his father, Horace, took up the Professorship of Mathematics at the University where I work. He then studied medicine at the University Medical School, before abandoning his studies for art and Europe. When war broke out, he felt compelled to return to England and finish his studies, which he did at St Guy's hospital, before joining the RAMC Northumbrian Field Ambulance Unit in Salonika between 1916 and 1917, and later receiving a Military Cross. But it was not until 1920, when Lawrence Haward commissioned Lamb to turn the drawing of *Succouring the Wounded in a Wood on the Doiran Front* (where the British fought the Bulgarian forces) into a major work for Manchester's commemorative collection.

The resulting *Advanced Dressing Station on the Struma, 1916* (1921) (Figure 13.1) painted from the memory of his service in Macedonia, perhaps reflected on his own invalidity from gas poisoning and influenza in 1919. The scene of a dressing station set deep in the forest is classically modernist in design but bears strong religious overtones that lend emotional weight to the image of helping

FIGURE 13.1 Henry Lamb. *Advanced Dressing Station on the Struma (1916)*. Painted in 1920–1921, from a wartime drawing made by the artist on the Salonika Front. (© Manchester Art Gallery.)

the wounded. The central group focuses on the relationship between a wounded man and a stretcher-bearer, who attends him with a cup of water, a great relief that many soldiers wrote about as the comfort given between men. Thirst and cold were understood much later in the war as signs of haemorrhage and shock. The stretcher-bearer's hand gently touches the wounded man's head, providing comfort symbolic of the Christian *pietà* (the iconography of Mary cradling Christ's body), also an artistic and humanitarian trope. However, Lamb's rendition is an effigy of masculine care and the intimate brotherhood of shared suffering. Placed on the ledge of a shallow trench, the stretcher resembles an altar. In the right-hand corner is a Thomas splint used for compound fractures, which could result in death. Pathos is created by the soldier whose head is buried in his hand, referencing malaria or psychological strain. The central figure stares pensively into the distance. The composition of this painting symbolizes the pain and succour of the entire conflict. Lamb does not paint with the clinical distance of the doctor; he paints with the empathy of the humanitarian. We hung this epic work on a single wall, alongside the large-scale unfinished oil, Henry Tonks' *An Advanced Dressing Station in France* (1918, IWM).

Smaller scale, pencil and watercolour drawings also convey the sensory experience of wounding, such as Harold Sandys Williamson's hospital scene, *Human Sacrifice: In an Operating Theatre* (1918). It provides a cold, even sinister, interpretation of the wounded patient as an experimental subject of medical science, a theme explored extensively in my book. Incongruously this delicate watercolour is crafted with sharp precision. Fragile flesh is concealed under the clinical aesthetic, as scalpel-like lines render the operating theatre hygienic and surgical. Williamson worked as a theatre orderly at the No. 6 General Hospital where he observed operations closely while recovering from an infected ankle. He wrote to his parents of the lightning speed of operations conducted under pressure: '*They are very quick. I think they could take you to pieces completely in half an hour*'. Here, white-gowned doctors loom over the patient, peering inside his body. He is an anonymous object of modern surgery more than a wounded man in pain. We also discovered the work of 59-year-old Alsatian artist Rosine Cahen, who sketched wounded French soldiers she visited in hospitals of Paris and Monte Carlo, with whom she clearly developed a rapport while capturing personal moments of recovery. Cahen's light-touch handling of pastel, chalk and charcoal exude calmness. The men are imbued with dignity rather than voyeurism, reflecting the gentle relationship developed with them.

For the related section called 'Rupture and Rehabilitation: Disability and the Wounds of War', art historian Dorothy Price assisted us in securing works of a major German artist of the interwar period. Never before exhibited in the UK, Heinrich Hoerle's 12 lithographs *Die Krüppelmappe* (*The Cripples Portfolio* 1920) were featured on one large wall. Six plates explore the difficulties of veterans' daily lives, such as unemployment, chronic pain, inadequate prostheses and domestic adjustment. *The Married Couple*, for instance, portrays an intimate scene between disabled veteran and wife. Their faces express shared suffering, as she gently touches his prosthetic arm, lovingly cradled like a baby, perhaps even gripped by anguish. Affective sensations are conveyed in the touch of this prosthetic object. The other six plates depict the dreams and hallucinations of the war disabled, where, as Dorothy Price states, 'missing hands take on terrifying qualities of possession, torment and persecution' (Price 2014: 47). In addition, Price helped us secure the loan of a renowned work, *Drei Invaliden* ('Three Invalids' 1930). Artists such as Hoerle confronted the political rhetoric and scientific fantasy of cyborg aesthetics and the superhuman capacity of prosthetics with the reality of living with war disabilities. Prosthetics, designed with light metals and the rhetoric of machine perfection, cinematization, mechanization and associated discourses of virility supported the desire that body parts and human sensory capacity could be replaced.

Contemporary artists explore similar themes also through the lens of colonialism and racial inequality. In Kader Attia's slide-projection installation, *The Debt* (2013), archival photos of African and Algerian soldiers in the First World War are used to critique French colonialism, erased from the cultural memory of the conflict. This linked with the New Zealand medical illustrator Herbert Cole, whose sketch of Private Harper's facial mutilation is a stark reminder that the Pioneer Battalion (NZ Expeditionary Force) which raised 2,227 Maoris for a European conflict, suffered catastrophic casualties. The exhibition had to acknowledge that the colonial origins of the war have cast a long shadow and that minorities and Indigenous peoples were exploited and forgotten. Richard Moss's surrealist photograph *Untitled* (2011) is a portrait of a Congolese teen-soldier, whose mutilated face conveys how modern plastic surgery is only available to the few. As Suzannah Biernoff writes, 'portraits have the potential to humanize suffering, but they also bring us face to face with the inhumanity of war', starkly visualizing the long shadow that colonialism has cast into the twenty-first century (Biernoff 2014: 40).

From the damaged and rehabilitated body, a conceptual twist was made by considering the way that artists saw the destroyed landscape and the wrecking of military hardware as 'Embodied Ruins'. This section included MAG's rare Paul Nash drawings using crayon, gouache and pastel. They depict the annihilation and beauty of the frontline, such as in little red poppies growing over barbed wire (*The Field of Passchendaele* 1917; *Desolate Landscape, Ypres Salient* 1917 (Figure 13.2); *Landscape: Hill 60* 1918). While enlisted with The Hampshires, Nash began his drawings around Hill 60. Battle debris, churned mud and rancid water-filled craters in the undrained Flanders clay are depicted as physical metaphors of the ruined human body. Muirhead Bone was commissioned as an Official War Artist in both world wars. His *Torpedoed Oil Tanker* (1940) makes the vessel appear human or bestial, its hull broken open like a flesh wound with a chasm of twisted metal intestines. Using different media, artists have conveyed this intimate connection of the corporeal and environmental in sites of conflict. Larissa Sansour's film *Nation Estate (2012)* brings dark humour to her 'clinical dystopia' of Palestinians 'living the high life' in their skyscraper state. But the

FIGURE 13.2 Paul Nash. *Desolate Landscape, Ypres Salient* (1917). (Crown Copyright – Expired.)

futuristic fantasy is pierced by a menacing helicopter, a shattered glass window, an olive tree rupturing the floor. The challenges to statehood appear both environmental and man-made.

Artists have also revealed war as a sensory assault on the mind, and hence 'Shocking the Senses' was a section that included works exploring breakdown and psychological injury, such as Eric Kennington's evocatively titled pastel work, *Bewitched, Bemused and Bewildered* (1917), which depicts a dishevelled soldier trying to navigate a trench in a state of disorientation (Figure 13.3). Using lithograph, the German artist Otto Dix imagined the frightened, electrified face of a soldier ('Wounded Man Fleeing', *Der Krieg* 1924). Contemporary art brought the trauma of the First World War into the present day in Douglas Gordon's film *10ms-1* (1994), for which we built a special room to house its large, tilted screen. Gordon re-edited the famous medical film of a shell-shocked patient (diagnosed with hysteria) so that the barely clothed man repetitively falls down after trying to get up. The original film re-enacted 'before cure' scenes staged by Dr Arthur Hurst. Deception was used as a therapeutic measure, while contriving evidence of his successful treatments (Jones 2012). Gordon's looped version amplifies the trauma through the lens of medical spectacle. In addition, curator David Morris secured the loan of Italian artist Pietro Morando's sketches made while a prisoner-of-war in Hungary. The harrowing depictions of torture, starvation and death are such that one cannot help but think of them as a precursor to the death camps of the Shoah. Richard Serra's Iraq War protest poster, 'STOP BUSH', a

FIGURE 13.3 Eric Kennington. *Bewitched, Bemused and Bewildered.* A 1917 pastel drawing conveying the sensory dislocation inherent in trench warfare. (Crown Copyright – Expired.)

crayon drawing of the infamous hooded victim of Abu Ghraib made to stand on a box with electrical wires attached to his body. It is a sobering reminder of the way that war and occupation rationalize the perpetration of torture.

In 'Chemical War and the Toxic Imaginary', the exhibition explored works stretching from the First World War to the late twentieth-century wars in the Middle East and even linking them. Paul Nash's painting of stretcher-bearers carrying a patient enveloped by a toxic, green haze set the tone for this section of the exhibition (*Wounded, Passchendaele* 1918, Figure 13.4). It was also a rare figurative work that fascinated visitors. Continuing the tradition of official war artists, John Keane, during the First Gulf War when Iraq invaded neighbouring

FIGURE 13.4 Paul Nash. *Wounded, Passchendaele* (1918). A rare instance of this artist depicting human figures on an equal standing with their ruined and toxic environment. (Crown Copyright – Expired.)

Kuwait, created works that nodded to the First World War. Keane used a famous line from Wilfred Owen's poem *Dulce et decorum est* to evoke the panic that gas attacks cause, as soldiers fumble to get their masks and protective clothing on quickly. Next to Otto Dix' lithograph *The Sleepers of Fort Vaux (Gas Victims)* was the young Iranian artist Sam Samiee's heart-breaking painting *Sleeping Children*, drawn from news photographs of the 5,000 Kurdish civilians murdered and maimed by mustard gas and nerve agents dropped on Halabja on 'Bloody Friday', 16 March 1988. The work of another Iranian artist, Backtash Sarang, was also important in addressing the taboo subject of the chemical weapons used in the Iran-Iraq War. *Untitled (box)* (2006) refers to an object carried by Iranian soldiers which, Sarang states, is 'heavy with the memories of war, of the hospital environment and the burial shroud'. The war continues for the families who care for chemically affected soldiers: 'The legacy of war is with the ones who remain, injured in one way or another, who still suffer long after the wars end; they die the slow death and are often neglected and forgotten'.[11] Contemporary artists are able to show that chemical war is not a thing of the past. French Canadian artist

Sophie Jodoin's searing charcoal drawings of people trapped or screaming from inside gas masks (2008 series) became the signature for the show.

In 'Bombing, Burning and Distant War', the exhibition returned to the technology of the power of aerial bombing, air power, noise and distant war – war on the ground and war delivered from far away. Leon Underwood's *Concrete Observation Post, Mount Kemmel (1919)* depicts soldiers observing long range shell fire with binoculars and telescopes, from the safety of their bunker. In Georges Leroux's painting Hell *L'Enfer* (1918), the French frontline, where he served, is enveloped in fire and smoke emanating from the phosgene and liquid fire used in the Battle of Verdun. It is an imagining of hell on earth, incinerating heat and the vaporizing of bodies. Eyewitnesses to these horrors are vital sources of history and memory. Thus, we secured a set of original drawings, never seen in the UK before, made by the *Hibakusha* (bomb-exposed people), victims of the atomic catastrophes of Nagasaki and Hiroshima. These are not professional artists but ordinary people, whose traumatic visions of atomic deserts, charred bodies, black rain and melting flesh continued to haunt victims decades later. Nancy Spero's ink works of women fleeing bombs and helicopters (*Bombs and Victims* 1966) and the harrowing scene of a Bosnian woman gang raped in her home (Peter Howson's *Croatian and Muslim* 1994) demanded consideration of the predominant treatment of women as territory to be violated and conquered.

Across the twentieth century, warfare has been conducted both up-close and dispassionately. Increasing geographic distances, however, have not produced emotional distance, the consequences of which are explored in the dramatic reconstruction video by Omer Fast. In *5,000 Feet is the Best* (2011), which refers to the best distance to drop a predator drone missile, we hear the testimony of a veteran Marine describing the operations. Beauty and destruction are contrasted in the macabre spectacle of laser-beams, 'The Light of God', markers that enable the strike of a Hellfire missile from a remote operation room: 'it looks like it's coming from heaven…pwuh…right on the spot…coming out of nowhere from the sky—it's quite beautiful'. Camera feeds from a drone strike are projected onto screens in the Pentagon. This distant war – from above, from long-range, from a computer screen – returns to haunt the pilot's dreams. War eventually comes home, into the minds of men.

The final section was 'Ghostlands: Loss, Memory and Resilience' which began with MAG's haunting landscape of *Mount Kemmel*, by Ian Strang (1919), a rediscovered work that required conservation. While devastating technologies assaulted the body and the mind as never before – sight, hearing, touch, taste, smell – something extra-sensory was also felt, a sixth unspeakable sense, like perceiving the ghosts of the war dead. For Din Q Le's large three-screen video, we built a dark, immersive room. The Vietnam War or 'the American War', as the Vietnamese prefer, is the subject of local and diasporic memory explored through the haunting image and sound of helicopters in the past and present day. Documentary and news footage is intercut with scenes from *Apocalypse Now*, and interviews with village farmers, who remain traumatized. Yet, the image and sound of dragonflies – sacred symbols in Southeast Asian cultures – hovering over the rice paddies brings peace and calm to this torrid history. Terrifying helicopters are transformed into agricultural tools; trauma shifts to hopeful emotions of resilience. Visitors could also take a break, listening with headphones to the minute silences of Armistice Day ceremonies recorded since the 1920s (*Kennotaphion* 2011).

The Sensory War explored the body's memory and the imagination of the physical and emotional suffering of others, such as in Katie Davies observational film of multiple funerary cavalcades repatriating deceased British soldiers through the town of (Royal) Wootton Basset. *The Separation Line* (2012) evokes the sensations of borders as artefacts of division to explore the possibility of empathy and communication, in a quiet reflection on mourning and memory. Exiting the exhibition, the last artwork shown was by British photojournalist turned artist, Simon Norfolk. *Balloon Seller outside a former Tea House* (2001) offers a glimmer of hope. The wreckage-filled landscape, scarred from years of conflict, is momentarily brightened by the fragile, colourful objects once banned under Taliban rule.

Conclusion

In conclusion, the sensory theme explored across a century of historical works from the world war period, in conversation with contemporary art, enabled new conversations to emerge. Despite the political wrangling and denigration of historians' critical work in public discourse, it did not deter the purposefulness of the collaborative spirit nor disengage our audience in the North. Director Maria Balshaw described it as a 'challenging and thought-provoking meditation on the century long impact' of the war, that would 'strike a chord with the people of Manchester'.[12] The visitor data bears this out, as *The Sensory War* brought into public dialogue the sensory, physical and psychological damage of modern war on both combatants and forgotten civilians, sensitively explored through the eyes of artists, without losing the necessary solemn and reflective tone of the centenary. The exhibition demonstrated that rather than simply using the historians' research as background context, when institutions foster collaboration in co-curating, the dynamism of expertise working together and with diverse communities, exhibitions of meaning and depth can be forged.

Notes

1 PM Speech at Imperial War Museum on First World War centenary plans, 11 October 2012. https://www.gov.uk/government/speeches/speech-at-imperial-war-museum-on-first-world-war-centenary-plans.
2 Vox Pops: Is there a danger of glorifying WW1 during the **centenary** events?', *Museums Journal;* November 2012. 112 (11):23-23, ½. http://www.museumsassociation.org/museums-journal/comment/01112012-vox-pop-ww1?utm_source=ma.

3 See 14–18 Now: Contemporary arts commissions for the First World War Centenary, included Jeremy Deller's Somme tribute We're here because we're here, Peter Jackson's They Shall Not Grow Old, Danny Boyle's Armistice beach memorial, Pages of the Sea, William Kentridge's The Head and the Load, Rachel Whitread's Nissen Hut, Dalby Forest, and dancer-choreographer Akram Khan's Chotto Xenos.

4 Extrapolating from Ann Rigney's work and following a workshop of the same name co-hosted with Laura Doan at the University of Manchester in 2014.

5 All content from the Manchester Art Gallery Twitter feed has been given with permission, with all the data anonymized.

6 https://www.manchesterliteraturefestival.co.uk/pages/art-gallery-commissions-337.

7 Letters to one of the Learning Managers at Manchester Art Gallery, 2015.

8 Imperial War Museum's blog for PhD students. K. Butler, 'Finding New Ways to Understand the Impact of War: 'The Sensory War, 1914–2014' exhibition', 18 March 2015. http://blogs.iwm.org.uk/research/2015/03/finding-new-ways-to-understand-the-impact-of-war-the-sensory-war-1914-2014-exhibition/.

9 These citations come from correspondence to one of the Learning Managers at Manchester Art Gallery are provided with permission on condition of anonymity.

10 Ibid.

11 Cited in *The Sensory War, 1914–2014*, catalogue, p. x.

12 Maria Balshaw, Director's Foreword, *The Sensory War, 1914–2014*, catalogue, p. 5.

References

Baxter, K. (2020) Practices of Remembrance: The experiences of artists and curators in the centenary commemoration of WW1. *Arts* 9 (2):59.

Beaumont, J. (2015) The politics of memory: Commemorating the Centenary of the First World War, *Australian Journal of Political Science* 50 (3):529–535.

Biernoff, Suzannah. (2014) The Ruptured Portrait. In A. Carden-Coyne, D. Morris and T. Wilcox (eds.), *The Sensory War, 1914–2014*. Manchester: Manchester Art Gallery catalogue.

Bowman, J. (2014) Unhappy anniversary. *New Criterion* 32 (6):52–55.

Carden-Coyne, A. (2014) *The Politics of Wounds: military patients and medical power in the First World War*. Oxford: Oxford University Press

Cornish P. (2016) Imperial War Museums and the Centenary of the First World War. *Twentieth Century British History* 27:513–517.

Cornish, P. (2017) 'Sensing War: Concept and Space in the Imperial War Museum's First World War Galleries'. In P. Cornish and N.J. Saunders (eds.), *Modern Conflict and the Senses*, pp 13–28. London: Routledge.

Crotty, M. and C. Melrose. (2007) Anzac day, Brisbane, Australia: Triumphalism, mourning and politics in interwar commemoration. *The Round Table* 96 (393) December: 679–692.

Evans, M. (2008) Opening up the battlefield: War studies and the cultural turn. *Journal of War and Culture Studies* 1 (1): 47–51.

Grayzel, S. (2016) *Women and the First World War*. London: Routledge.

Hanna, M. and J. Horne. (2016) France and the Great war on its centenary. *French Historical Studies* 39 (2): 233–259

Haward, L. (1916) *The Effect of War Upon Art and Literature*. Manchester: Manchester University Press.

Jones, E. (2012) "War Neuroses" and Arthur Hurst: A Pioneering Medical Film about the Treatment of Psychiatric Battle Casualties. *Journal of the History of Medicine and Allied Science* 67:345–373.

Jones, H. (2013) As the centenary approaches: The regeneration of First World War Historiography. *The Historical Journal* 56 (3): 857–878.

———. (2014) Goodbye to all that?: Memory and meaning in the commemoration of the first world war. *Juncture* 20 (4): 287–291.

Laycock, J. (2015) Beyond National Narratives? Centenary histories, the First World War and the Armenian Genocide. *Revolutionary Russia* 28 (2):93–17.

Madigan, E. (2014) A seamless Robe of Irish experience: the First World War, the Irish and centenary commemoration. *History Ireland* 22 (4):14–17.

McCarthy, H. (2016) Public history and the centenary of the First world War in Britain. *Twentieth Century British History* 27 (4):505.

Mombauer, A. (2017) The German centenary of the First World War. *War and Society* 36 (4):276–288.

Moore, C. (2014) 1914 in 2014: What we commemorate when we commemorate the First World War. *Canadian Historical Review* 95 (3) September:427–432.

Mycock, A. (2014) The First World War Centenary in the UK: 'A Truly National Commemoration'? *The Round Table* 103 (2) March:153–163.

Nevinson, C.R.W. (1938) *Paint and Prejudice*. New York: Harcourt, Brace and co.

Price, D.C. (2014) Horrors, Hallucinations, Pity and Prostheses: German Artists and the First World War. In A. Carden-Coyne, D. Morris and T. Wilcox (eds.), *The Sensory War, 1914–2014*, pp 44–50. Manchester: Manchester Art Gallery catalogue.

Roper, M. and R. Duffett. (2018) Family legacies in the centenary: Motives for First World War commemoration among British and German descendants. *History and Memory* 30 (1):76–115.

Tate, T. (1998) *History, Modernism and the First World War*. Manchester: Manchester University Press.

Tuathaigh, G.O. (2014) Commemoration, public history and the professional historian: An Irish perspective. *Estudios Irlandeses — Journal of Irish Studies* 9:137.

Van Der Auwera, S. and A. Schramme. (2014) Commemoration of the Great War: A global phenomenon or a national agenda? *Journal of Conflict Archaeology* 9 (1): 3–15.

Woollacott, A. (1994) *On Her Their Lives Depend*. Berkeley: University of California Press.

Wouters, N. (2012) 'Poor little Belgium?' Flemish-and French-language politics of memory (2014–2018). *Journal of Belgian History* 42 (4):192–199.

14

FORGOTTEN WAR? COPING WITH FIRST WORLD WAR TRAUMA, AND STRATEGIES FOR CENTENARY COMMEMORATION IN THE FEDERAL STATE OF TYROL, AUSTRIA

Isabelle Brandauer

Historical background

The end of the First World War clearly marks a break in the history of the former Austro-Hungarian Crown Land of Tyrol.[1] Almost 24,000 Tyrolean men lost their lives in the war (Böhm 1962: 7).[2] In 1919, the region was divided by a new border at the Brenner Pass, and the southern part was given to the Kingdom of Italy, according to the peace treaty of Saint-Germain-en-Laye (Schober 1982: 237). It was to take more than 80 years until an objective historiography set its focus on the traumatic events of the war years and their immediate results (Überegger 2004: 63–122).

The war against Italy did not come entirely unexpectedly for the Habsburg monarchy. The Italian kingdom had been allied to Germany and Austria-Hungary in a defensive alliance, as part of the so-called 'Dreibund', since 1882. But, following the outbreak of war in 1914, Italy had declared its neutrality. The desire of many Italians to 'redeem' Austrian territory inhabited by Italian speakers, and indeed to establish a border on the Alpine watershed, was an open secret. Germany tried in vain to persuade Austria-Hungary to make territorial concessions to Italy to keep it neutral. But, in March 1915, Italy entered into secret negotiations with the Entente powers, Britain, France and Russia, ultimately signing the Treaty of London on 26 April of the same year. According to this treaty, Italy was obliged to enter the war on the side of the Entente within a month. If the war was won, Italy was promised all that it wanted from Austria as well as gains in the Balkans and even in Turkey. The southern part of Tyrol was the object of particular attention during the negotiations.[3] On 23 May, 1915, the Italian ambassador in Vienna handed over Italy's declaration of war.[4] Thus, the war for Austria-Hungary developed from a war on two fronts (against Serbia and Russia) to a war on three fronts (Schaumann et al 1992).

DOI: 10.4324/9781003263531-18

This caused major problems for the Habsburg monarchy, especially in the early stages of the war against Italy, because the main part of the regular armed forces was engaged on the Eastern Front. It was not until October 1915 that the first regular regiments could be transferred to the new southwestern front. Therefore, to protect the front line between Italy and Austria-Hungary, which was more than 600 km long, reservists, police auxiliaries and the *Standschützen* militia had to be called to arms.

The *Standschützen* was a militia of riflemen specific to, and the traditional defenders of, the Tyrol and Vorarlberg. Their deployment and organization for the protection of the border with Italy had already begun in 1914, in view of the alliance partner's unpredictable behaviour. As a supplement to the standard Austrian militia force – the Imperial-Royal *Landsturm* – members of rifle clubs and veterans associations were enlisted as *Standschützen*. The first calls went out in the autumn of 1914 (Brandauer 2015: 8–17). After inspections, almost 35,000 men were called up in May 1915, of whom approximately 18,000 were considered capable of serving at the front. Since the *Standschützen* lacked sufficient military training, it was understood that they urgently required experienced leadership and instruction. The German Empire was asked for help (Jordan 2008). Despite the fact that it was not formally at war with Italy, this ally sent its *Alpenkorps* to support the *Standschützen* until the arrival of regular Imperial and Royal Army troops from Serbia and the Eastern Front. However, help was not only needed in the form of military reinforcement but also in terms of construction of barracks and trenches. Through this joint effort, the allies succeeded in stabilizing the front line by mid of October 1915 and established a basic infrastructure (Voigt 2017).

Despite the arrival of Austro-Hungarian regular troops on the Southwestern-Front, and repeated offensives by the Italians, the front line there saw little significant change until late 1917. The stasis was dramatically shattered in October of that year, when the Central Powers won a crushing victory at the Battle of Karfreit/Caporetto. The victorious Hapsburg Army and its German ally pursued its beaten foe into Italy, as far as the Piave River just 20 km from Venice. However, due to increasing problems in keeping the troops supplied when Austria itself was stalked by famine, and because of the ever more unstable domestic political situation in the Empire, this victory ultimately proved useless for the Central Powers. The dissolution of the Austro-Hungarian Empire was already underway before the signing of the Armistice of Villa Giusti, on 3 November 1918, formally confirmed its defeat on the Italian front.

After the end of the First World War, the southern part of Tyrol was under Italian military administration and completely shut off from Austria and other countries, which meant that personal traffic and cross-border trade with the northern part of Tyrol came to a standstill. Newspapers were strictly censored; correspondence was limited or did not take place at all (Steininger 1997: 19–20). In May 1919, the peace negotiations between the victorious Allies and the Central Powers or their successor states were about to start in Paris. For Austria and Tyrol especially the question of what was going to happen with South Tyrol was of greatest importance. However, after the end of the war, Italy vehemently claimed the territories that had been promised in the Treaty of London, although Italy's grasp for South Tyrol seemed to be endangered because of point IX of the Fourteen Points[5] declared by the American president Woodrow Wilson. The position of the United States of America concerning South Tyrol therefore was of great significance (Schober 1989: 34–35; Dotter and Wedrac 2018). In the end, all efforts of the Tyrolean government to prevent the division of the country at the Brenner Pass were in vain. The decision concerning the assignment of South Tyrol to Italy had already been made in April 1919 with Wilson's personal statement that he himself favoured that solution. With the final peace agreements of 2 September 1919 the loss of South Tyrol without any further details regarding its autonomy or the protection of the German speaking minorities was eventually confirmed (Schober 1991: 81–127). The official annexation of South Tyrol by the Italian kingdom took place on 10 October 1920.

Historiography of the First World War and university research after 1918

It seems that the traumatic experience of the defeat, the collapse of the Habsburg Empire and, especially in Tyrol, the loss of South Tyrol prevented a scientific approach to First World War research for a long time. Indeed, the history of the war was the history of a political entity that no longer existed – creating a historiographical issue that was not just limited to Austria, but also afflicted other former provinces of the Hapsburg Empire (Košir et al 2019: xvii–xviii; 2–3). The historiography of the First World War in the Austrian interwar period was initially in the hands of former officers and was all about justification or selective perception of history. Furthermore, military history did not seem to be a relevant field of research for university or academic studies. These developments and restricted access to the archives and their records meant that a critical approach to the First World War could not take place during the First Austrian Republic (1919–1934). Access to the archives and an academic approach towards war research, however, did not improve after the Second World War. 1945 rather marked 'an end than a new beginning for Austrian military historiography and the historiography of the First World War in particular' (Überegger 2004: 94; Überegger 2011).

Dealing with war and military history did not appear to be worthwhile until the end of the 1950s. Only with the opening of the archives and access to the records in 1956 did a hesitant scientific approach begin. Eventually, from the mid-1960s onwards, universities discovered the field of war history and began to question the semi-official officer-historiography as well as the outcomes of its research for the first time. Despite this paradigm shift, Austrian historiography of the First World War was not able to keep up with international research developments for quite a while. The turn towards new scientific fields in terms of cultural history or the history of mentalities and everyday life took place slowly.

The First World War remained a side issue within historical research. It was not until the 1990s that modern approaches eventually found their way into the Austrian universities of Vienna and Innsbruck. At the latter a special research and education focus: *Erster Weltkrieg*, has now existed since 1995 (Überegger 2011: 63–114).These developments featured a strong focus on topics of regional history.

However, after a significant and, of course, expected increase of academic papers (which mainly dealt with regional history), as well as intensive lecture activity[6] during the commemorative years of 2014–2018, scientific interest seemed to have lapsed somewhat by the end of 2018, a quite different trajectory to that of other European countries. Currently, there is no dissertation or research project associated with the history of the First World War at the Department of History and European Ethnology at the University of Innsbruck.[7] However, an ongoing project at the Department of Architectural Theory and Building History has been working on the concept for a documentation centre located at the village of Kartitsch in Eastern Tyrol[8] since 2018, developing communicative strategies to bring the cultural heritage of the war to a wider audience. The special quality of this project lies in its interdisciplinary and cross-border approach, which involves the Tyrolean and South Tyrolean State Offices for Historical Monuments and the Department of Archaeologies at the University of Innsbruck, as well as companies and experts in the fields of preservation, conservation and documentation.[9]

Another outcome of the research focus *Erster Weltkrieg* is the publication, since 2007 of several comprehensive studies by University of Innsbruck Department of Archaeology in the series 'Nearchos – Archäologisch-militärhistorische Forschungen'.[10] Furthermore, an archaeological survey took place on the Carnic Main Crest (*Karnischer Kamm*)[11] in 2007, which resulted in a detailed plan for the reclamation of the former front line and the presentation of the history of the First World War. However, at that time, the project failed because of a lack of funding. The results of the survey were later incorporated into a project to preserve selected sites of historic interest at the Carnic Main Crest headed by the Tyrolean State Office for Historical Monuments. The reason that the Carnic Main Crest is at the centre of scientific attention is that it is the only section of the former front line between Austria-Hungary and Italy that is nowadays left on Austrian territory.[12]

In fact, the initiatives on the Carnic Main Crest reach back into the 1970s, when the front line was made accessible during the course of a project called 'Freedom paths' (*Friedenswege*), carried out by the association of the *Dolomitenfreunde* in cooperation with the Austrian Alpine Club. In the course of the current project, an inspection of the terrain on an 11.4-km-length of the line took place in four prospection campaigns between 2014 and 2018. The survey report provided the basis for the notification that finally put three sections of the terrain under heritage protection on the 14 November 2018. The next project phase, in combination with the already-mentioned documentation centre in Kartitsch, is currently in the planning stage. There are also lectures about the material culture of the First World War taking place at the Institute of Archaeology in a biannual sequence, as well as field trips to the sites of both World Wars.

Austria and the federal state of Tyrol 2014–2018

In 2014, as the centenary of the beginning of the war started, in Austria as in many other European countries, a succession of exhibition openings, book launches and other commemorative events began. Furthermore, autumn 2014 marked the zenith of the exhibition activities in Austria.[13] More than 40 exhibitions opened throughout Austria in the commemorative year 2014; and this figure does not include various small exhibitions that were not widely publicized. The number of new publications and specialist articles published between 2014 and 2018 defies enumeration and is in the hundreds, if not thousands. Below, the most important exhibitions in Austria will be briefly discussed before we look at the commemorative activities in the federal state of Tyrol.

Exactly on the 100th anniversary of the murder of the Austrian heir to the throne, Franz Ferdinand, the opening of the newly designed exhibition hall 'First World War', took place at the Heeresgeschichtliches Museum in Vienna. In this gallery, a comprehensive chronological structure leads visitors through the years 1914–1918. This narrative is supplemented by cross-sectional areas that deal with thematic matter, such as war-enthusiasm, wounding and death, women in war, war propaganda and war memoirs. According to the curators, the redesign was particularly important to show visitors the broadest possible picture of events in the war years. In terms of what is displayed, the reinterpretation, which remains in place following the end of the centenary period, presented new acquisitions and previously unseen objects to the public. Naturally, it also built upon the extraordinary and unique collection of artefacts directly related to the Sarajevo attack that the museum possesses. The museum had to turn down loan requests from across the world for some of these iconic objects, which include the blood-stained uniform jacket worn by the assassinated Archduke and the car in which he and his wife were murdered.

It should be noted, however, that the Heeresgeschichtliches Museum's exhibition is a conventionally designed presentation, firmly based on objects that are emblematic of wartime events. It is therefore not surprising that, coinciding as it did with the centenary, this reworking of the museum's First World War displays rekindled a decade-long debate regarding the feelings of many that the Heeresgeschichtliches Museum is in need of a complete revision of the way in which it interprets its collections. The main criticism is that the majority of the historically significant objects in the museum are presented without comment. A critical and contextual embedding of the exhibits is mostly lacking (Weiss 2020). A conference at the end of January 2020 debated the perceived institutional weaknesses of this national institution. It opened a discussion about the need for a contemporary museum environment, in which historical military objects are critically examined and embedded in a democratic culture of remembrance.[14]

An ambitious project in the digital field was the online exhibition of the Austrian Media Library (Österreichischen Mediathek). From 2014, starting with events preceding the outbreak of war, it documented the course of the First World War using archival sources. This exhibition went online in a total of six editions, taking the story up to the foundation of the First Austrian Republic in the Autumn of 1919. The media library provided historical audio and film material on the First World War in an online chronicle. The project was completed at the end of 2018 and is still available online.[15]

The most comprehensive presentation of the war was in the exhibition 'Exultation and Misery: Living with the Great War 1914–1918' (*Jubel & Elend. Leben mit dem Großen Krieg 1914–1918*) at Schallaburg Castle in Lower Austria. This exhibition, which some called the 'most ambitious project of the year of commemoration' spanned 25 rooms, with a footprint of 1,300 square metres. This, to put it in context, was actually larger than the permanent First World War Galleries opened in the same year at London's Imperial War Museum (see Cornish 2017: 15). The Schallaburg exhibition was particularly notable because it was structured thematically rather than chronologically. The themes explored included: The World of 1914, Nations in Arms, Euphoria and Disillusionment, The Propaganda War, Front and Home Front, The Russian Revolution and 1918 as the End and Beginning. Throughout, the exhibition focused on the individual lives and fates of people and ended with memories of the war and questioned why another World War erupted just a few years later.[16] A connection to the present was established in a 'conflict laboratory', in which visitors could engage with a nine-stage escalation model of conflict, classified by conflict researcher Friedrich Glasl, in an interactive workshop.[17] Another novel concept was that every visitor was given the opportunity to create an anthology of their visit from printed sheets that could be collected from each room. These could be bound into a volume in the final room.

The exhibition at the Schallaburg in Lower Austria was one of several large-scale exhibitions in the Austrian federal states. However, in other regions, these exhibitions tended to deal primarily with the history and impact of the First World War on the respective federal state.[18] In the state of Tyrol, a dual approach was followed in the commemorative years 2014–2018, with several exhibitions in federal state museums running alongside a programme of official representative commemorative events, held jointly with the European region of Tyrol-South Tyrol-Trentino. The series of official events began on 16 October, 2014 with a commemorative train (Figure 14.1). This carried 400 Austrian and Italian schoolchildren from all three parts of the former crown land Tyrol, accompanied by historians and teachers, to the Galicia region of Poland. There they visited the memorial sites and locations of the former Eastern Front of the First World War. The high point of this flagship project of the European region, which served to remember the numerous young men who lost their lives on the Eastern Front in autumn 1914 was a commemorative act by the governors of Tyrol, South Tyrol and the Trentino at the Kraków main market. Under the banner 'Bridges for Peace',

FIGURE 14.1 Euregio train to Galicia at the Brenner station on 16 October 2014. (© Federal State of Tyrol/Die Fotografen.)

a symposium was held in Innsbruck-Igls in May 2015 and, on the anniversary of the Italian declaration of war, on May 23, 2015 the official national commemoration in Innsbruck took place.

As part of this national commemoration, the victims of the First World War were once again commemorated in the presence of all three governors and with the blessing of a memorial cross. Reference was also made to the project 'At the Front 1915–2015' (*An der Front 1915–2015*). As part of this project, which had been implemented jointly by the Federation of Tyrolean Rifle Companies, the South Tyrolean and Welsch Tyrolean[19] Rifle Associations, 75 commemorative crosses (Figure 14.2) were erected on the former front line between Austria-Hungary and Italy. The end of the official commemoration was the 'Thinking Days (*Denktage*) 1918/2018', which took place from 2 to 4 November in Innsbruck and in the municipalities of the European region. With a diverse programme, the Thinking Days were dedicated to remembering and commemorating the end of the First World War and the proclamation of the Republic of Austria. Discussion panels made it possible to deal with local challenges in the European region and thus to build bridges with the present.

Within the federal state of Tyrol during this period, the First World War was the main topic in several exhibitions. With the opening date of their large exhibition at the Ferdinandeum on 8 May 2015, the Tyrolean state museums consciously distanced themselves from the 'overdose'[20] of cultural initiatives in 2014, in order to be able to draw the fullest attention. This understandable step, which met with criticism from the media, ultimately paid off in view of the number of visitors to the exhibition 'Front – Homeland. Tyrol in the First World War'

FIGURE 14.2 Consecration of the 75 commemorative crosses on the Waltherplatz in Bolzano on 18 April 2015. (© South Tyrolean Rifle Association.)

(*Front – Heimat. Tirol im Ersten Weltkrieg*).[21] The exhibition did not adopt a military-historical perspective, but focused on the lives of soldiers and the civilian population in order to shed light on the war's social-historical, economic and cultural impact and reveal its legacy in Tyrol. Smaller special exhibitions in the 'TIROL PANORAMA with Kaiserjäger Museum' in Innsbruck were devoted to topics such as the war on the Tyrolean border (2015), the 200th anniversary of the Tyrolean Kaiserjäger[22] (2016), the cavalry (2017) and wartime medical provisions (2018).

Another ambitious project was the exhibition *Pro Patria!? Kartitsch 1914–1918*, which was shown from May to the end of October 2015 in the community hall in Kartitsch (Figure 14.3). The aim of the exhibition was to portray the complete militarization of Kartitsch, which lay just below the front line on the Carnic Main Crest, in the course of the war and its impact on the population. The changes in the infrastructure of the village, in view of its comprehensive military utilization, were shown. Other topics were personal disasters, great and small, experienced by individuals from the village and the surrounding communities, demographic change and the influence of war events on daily life and the daily routine of local residents of all ages. The aftermath and legacies of the war up to the present day were also dealt with. A particular focus was on different war experiences – the years of the First World War were related from the perspective of both male and female inhabitants of Kartitsch, insofar as the current state of research permitted. The modern population of Kartitsch was closely involved in seeking out exhibits and personal testimonies of the war, thereby contributing to the realization of the exhibition and engendering a community identification with it.

FIGURE 14.3 Exhibition poster for *Pro Patria!? Kartitsch 1915–1918*. (© Municipality of Kartitsch/dazdesign.)

Conclusion

In summary, it can be seen that a unifying theme of the diverse projects and initiatives that marked the commemorative years in Austria, especially in the exhibitions and publications, was a turn to new narratives. In most exhibitions, with a few exceptions, there was a clear shift away from event history and political narratives towards thematically arranged structures that focused on people and their individual destinies. Through a critical selection of topics and a focus on sociocultural, everyday history issues, some novel iterations of memory politics were stimulated. The commemorative years of the First World War saw almost all the Austrian federal states furnish visitors to their exhibitions with a measure of orientation in the history and experience of the war. However, the focus – apart from that offered by the more comprehensive perspective adopted at the Schallaburg – was clearly on local or regional historical narratives. Meanwhile the principal national First World War exhibition was criticized for failing to contextualize or fully interpret its displays. Taken together, these facts seem to confirm that the Republic of Austria is still unable to write a universal Austrian history of the First World War and underscores the different effects of the war years on the Austrian provinces and their collective World War memory.

Notes

1 In terms of area, Tyrol was the third largest country in Cisleithania after Galicia and Bohemia. See K. k. Statistische Zentralkommission (1916: 1).

2 See Böhm(1962:7). The last census was held in Austria-Hungary in 1910. Thereby, 928,787 people, including 457,703 men, were counted in Tyrol. For the following years, the numbers were calculated using various coefficients. This resulted in an increase of approximately 10,000 people in the male population until about 1913. See K. k. Statistische Zentralkommission (1916: 4).

3 The problem of using the term 'South Tyrol' is discussed in Heiss (2000). Until the separation of Tyrol after the First World War, the term South Tyrol was used broadly in terms of territory and used in a differentiated manner. With the separation of the parts of the country, the term South Tyrol was quickly reduced to the future area of the province of Bolzano, i.e. the German-speaking Tyrol, as a demarcation from the Italian-speaking Trentino.

4 On the historical and cultural-political developments in South Tyrol from 1915, see Grote and Obermair (2017).

5 Point IX of the 14-point programme, in which Wilson already described the main features of a reorganization of Europe in early 1918, said: 'A re-adjustment of the frontiers of Italy should be effected along clearly recognizable lines of nationality'. See https://www.britannica.com/event/Fourteen-Points (accessed on 9 January 2020).

6 In the summer semester of 2014, the lecture series 'The First World War in an International Perspective. Austria-Hungary in the field of tension between the Entente and the Central Powers' began. Videos of the 13 lectures were published on YouTube: https://www.youtube.com/playlist?list=PL5eolwFmTdvgg4koMJHTY7c5jQA-GDEAZv (accessed on 16 January 2020). See also the publication list of completed dissertations and theses on the website of the Institute of History and European Ethnology at the University of Innsbruck at https://www.uibk.ac.at/geschichte-ethnologie/institut/oesterreich/forschung.html (accessed on 16 January 2020).

7 See https://www.uibk.ac.at/geschichte-ethnologie/institut/oesterreich/forschung.html (accessed on 16 January 2020).

8 The First World War shaped the life of the Kartitsch community decisively and, as it were, catastrophically in all areas of life. Before the war, there were 104 houses and 774 inhabitants in the municipality. At the beginning of the war in 1914, around 100 men from Kartitsch and Hollbruck, and from some families even three or more boys and men, were called up for military service. Already in the first year of the war, almost a tenth of those who were inducted into Russia would fall or be reported missing. By the end of the war in November 1918, Kartitsch alone had 40 soldiers to mourn.

9 See http://www.baugeschichte.eu/lehre/info/?no_cache=1&elementID=516 (accessed on 16 January 2020).

10 There are currently four publications: Brandauer (2007); Wiedemayr (2007); Stadler et al (2008); Stadler (2015).

11 In autumn 2006, the Institute of Archaeology headed by Univ. Prof. Dr. Harald Stadler conducted a survey on a section of the Carnic Main Ridge. Initially based on archaeological settlement research, the focus shifted due to the situation on site to the findings of the First World War. The field research included explorations from an archaeological point of view as the basis of a feasibility study for subsequent extensive archaeological fieldwork. Various preparatory work in different alpine areas made it possible to document the findings in a specially developed recording system. In the course of inspection in the area of the Obstanser Lake, 26 findings were classified and recorded using a specifically defined description key (see Stadler 2006). The findings were recorded using Holdermann's description key (see Holdermann and Manner 2003).

12 The positions and fortifications on the Plöcken Pass in Carinthia had already been converted into an open-air museum in the early 1980s.

13 For a detailed analysis of the commemorative years in Austria and other European states, see Bachinger and Lein (2017).

14 See https://www.textfeldsuedost.com/hgm-neudenken (accessed on 29 January 2020).

15 See https://www.mediathek.at/der-erste-weltkrieg/ (accessed on 27 January 2020).

16 See http://www.rapp-wimberger.com/jubel-elend (accessed on 13 January 2020).

17 See https://www.oejc.at/index.php?id=269&L=0%2522%252FRK%253D0%2525 (accessed on 13 January 2020).

18 For example, in the Burgenland: 'Land at war. The "Burgenland" 1914-1918', in Upper Austria: Exhibition series 'Upper Austria in the First World War', in Styria: 'Styria and the Great War', in Salzburg:'War, trauma, art. Salzburg and the First World War', in Carinthia: '1914 – the beginning of the end'.

19 That is, another term for 'Trentino'.

20 See https://apps.derstandard.at/privacywall/story/2000008382146/wo-der-erste-weltkrieg-erst-1915-begann (accessed on 7 January 2020).

21 From 8 May to 1 November 2015, the exhibition counted 16,942 visitors.

22 This elite light infantry unit was recruited exclusively in Tyrol and Vorarlberg and was part of the Imperial and Royal Army of Austria-Hungary.

References

Bachinger, B. and R. Lein (eds.) (2017) Gedenken und (k)ein Ende? Das Weltkriegs-Gedenken 1914/2014. Debatten, Zugänge, Ausblicke. *Studien zur Geschichte der österreichisch-ungarischen Monarchie 23*. Wien.

Böhm, K. (1962) *Die Gefallenen Tirols 1914–1918 und 1939–1945. Zur 150-Jahr-Feier 1809–1959*. Innsbruck: Wagner.

Brandauer, I. (2007), Menschenmaterial Soldat. Alltagsleben an der Dolomitenfront im Ersten Weltkrieg 1915–1917. *Nearchos – Archäologisch-militärhistorische Forschungen 1*. Innsbruck: Golf Verlag.

———. (2015) Der Alarmfall "I"und die Aufstellung der Innsbrucker Standschützenbataillone. In W. Meighörner (ed.), *Wissenschaftliches Jahrbuch der Tiroler Landesmuseen 2015*, pp 8–17. Innsbruck: Studienverlag.

Cornish, P. (2017) Sensing War: Concept and Space in the Imperial War Museum's First World War Galleries. In N.J. Saunders and P. Cornish (eds.), *Modern Conflict and the Senses*, pp 13–28. London: Routledge.

Dotter, M. and S. Wedrac. (2018) Der hohe Preis des Friedens. *Die Geschichte der Teilung Tirols 1918–1922*. Innsbruck: Tyrolia.

Golowitsch, H. (1985) *'Und kommt der Feind ins Land herein …'. Schützen verteidigen Tirol und Kärnten*. Nürnberg: Buchdienst Südtirol.

Grote, G. and H. Obermair (eds.) (2017) *A Land on the Threshold: South Tyrolean Transformations 1915–2015*. Oxford: Lang.

Heiss, H. (2000) 'Man pflegt Südtirol zu sagen und meint, damit wäre alles gesagt.' Beiträge zu einer Geschichte des Begriffs 'Südtirol'. *Geschichte und Region/Storia e regione* 9:85–109.

Holdermann, C. and H. Manner. (2003) Ein Aufnahmesystem zur siedlungsarchäologischen Erfassung am Beispiel des alpinen Bereichs. Ein Beitrag zur Analyse historischer und prähistorischer Raumnutzungskonzepte. *Archäologische Informationen 26.* Bonn: Habelt.

Jordan, A. (2008) Krieg um die Alpen. Der Erste Weltkrieg im Alpenraum und der bayerische Grenzschutz in Tirol. *Zeitgeschichtliche Forschungen 35*, Berlin: Duncker und Humblot GmbH.

K. k. Statistische Zentralkommission (ed.) (1916) *Österreichisches statistisches Handbuch*, Wien: Gerolds.

Košir, U., M. Črešnar and D. Mlekuž (eds.) (2019) *Rediscovering the Great War: Archaeology and Enduring Legacies on the Soča and Eastern Fronts.* London: Routledge.

Schaumann, W. and P. Schubert. (1992) *Süd-West-Front. Österreich-Ungarn und Italien 1914–1918.* Klosterneuburg: Mayer.

Schober, R. (1982) *Die Tiroler Frage auf der Friedenskonferenz von Saint Germain.* Innsbruck: Wagner.

———. (1989) Die Friedenskonferenz von St. Germain und die Teilung Tirols. In K. Eisterer and R. Steininger, Die Option. *Südtirol zwischen Faschismus und Nationalsozialismus. Innsbrucker Forschungen zur Zeitgeschichte 5*:34–50. Innsbruck: Haymon.

———. (1991) Südtirol von der Friedenskonferenz bis zur österreichisch-italienischen Krise 1928. *Tiroler Heimat* 55:81–127.

Stadler, H. (2006) *Projekt: Karnischer Kamm/Osttirol, Archäologischer Survey des Instituts für Archäologien. Arbeitsbericht zu den Geländebegehungen 27.09. –29.09.2006.* Innsbruck.

———. (2015) Russland und Tirol im Ersten Weltkrieg: Archäologisch und historische Annäherungen zum Thema Kriegsgefangenschaft. *Nearchos - Archäologisch-militärhistorische Forschungen 4.* Innsbruck: Golf Verlag.

Stadler, H., R. Steininger and K. Berger (eds.) (2008) Die Kosaken im Ersten und Zweiten Weltkrieg. *Nearchos - Archäologisch-militärhistorische Forschungen 3.* Innsbruck: Studienverlag

Steininger, R. (1997) *Südtirol im 20. Jahrhundert. Vom Leben und Überleben einer Minderheit.* Innsbruck: Studienverlag.

Überegger, O. (2004) Vom militärischen Paradigma zur ,Kulturgeschichte des Krieges'? Entwicklungslinien der österreichischen Weltkriegsgeschichtsschreibung im Spannungsfeld militärisch-politischer Instrumentalisierung und universitärer Verwissenschaftlichung. In O. Überegger (ed.), *Zwischen Nation und Region. Weltkriegsforschung im internationalen Vergleich. Ergebnisse und Perspektiven. Tirol im Ersten Weltkrieg. Politik, Wirtschaft und Gesellschaft 4*, pp 63–122. Innsbruck: Wagner.

———. (2011) Erinnerungskriege. Der Erste Weltkrieg, Österreich und die Tiroler Kriegserinnerung in der Zwischenkriegszeit. *Tirol im Ersten Weltkrieg. Politik, Wirtschaft und Gesellschaft 9.* Innsbruck: Wagner.

Voigt, I. (2017) *Zeugnisse von der Dolomitenfront. Das Alpenkorps in Bildern, Berichten und Fotografien.* Bozen: Athesia.

Weiss, S. (2020) Kritik an Heeresgeschichtlichem Museum: Initiative will Neuaufstellung. In *Der Standard*, 27 January 2020.

Wiedemayr, L. (2007) Weltkriegsschauplatz Osttirol. Die Gemeinden an der Karnischen Front im östlichen Pustertal. *Nearchos - Archäologisch-militärhistorische Forschungen 2.* Innsbruck: Golf Verlag

15

CURATING THE MASONIC PEACE MEMORIAL

Mark J.R. Dennis

Freemasonry as practised by the United Grand Lodge of England (UGLE) is a fraternal organization, and UGLE is its governing body in England and Wales. The masculine nature of the organization led to many direct links to the First World War through membership by servicemen, veterans, and leaders in society. This chapter focuses on the English/British perspective of the First World War as reflected in the museum displays and architecture of Freemasons' Hall in London. The present building was originally conceived as the Masonic Peace Memorial, a title which was changed at the start of the Second World War. There were Freemasons in most of the war's combatant nations on both the Allied and Central Powers sides. Their story waits to be told but is outside the scope of this paper.

The Museum of Freemasonry has existed in various forms since 1837. By 1914, it had a dedicated space in Freemasons' Hall London and displayed decorative arts and curios among its library cases. It formed a natural focus for the presentation of items relating to the war. The Armistice was commemorated directly by items donated for display in the museum and use in specific lodges. Sir David Watson, commanding the Canadian Division, presented gavel blocks made from the ruins of Ypres Cathedral to Grand Lodge and to Canada Lodge on Armistice Day in 1918.

In 1919, the Grand Master, HRH The Duke of Connaught, announced an appeal to rebuild the headquarters of English freemasonry as a memorial to the masonic war dead (Library and Museum of Freemasonry 2014: 39–40). The reconstruction of Freemasons' Hall as a Masonic Peace Memorial embedded remembrance of the war in the structure of English freemasonry. The building functions both as the headquarters and the main London meeting place for members of UGLE. It also houses the most recent iteration of the Museum of Freemasonry (until 2019 this was termed The Library and Museum of Freemasonry). This was a specific requirement in the architectural competition

DOI: 10.4324/9781003263531-19

as freemasons are asked to 'advance in their masonic knowledge daily', and the facility was seen as a key support to this.

The First World War's architectural symbolism of Freemasons' Hall (Dennis 2009) is here focused on the impact of these elements on the interpreting and embedding of the war in the structure rather than purely the symbolic meaning and historical importance. These features seem to have an ongoing effect on the organization by keeping remembrance at the forefront in a way that is not found in most non-military organizations.

Elements of the architecture directly reference the conflict, the building was entirely funded by masonic donations and the fundraising campaign allowed freemasons to earn and be awarded badges, termed 'jewels', that materialized their level of contribution to the appeal and were worn in much the same way as military medals. The image chosen to represent the appeal is now commonly termed the 'Hallstone Angel'; this is technically incorrect as it represents 'winged peace', but it does follow the conventional incarnation of Peace as an angel. This figure, carrying a stylized temple, appeared on the jewels which marked varying levels of contribution. Key amongst these are those for lodges which made an overall contribution of ten guineas for every member of a lodge (silver gilt and worn on a collarette by the master of the lodge in perpetuity) and an average of ten guineas across a masonic Province or District (Silver gilt and enamels) (Dennis 2009: 83–85). The continuous wearing and passing on of these jewels perpetuate the remembrance of the appeal and the conflict. The jewel was issued with an explanation of the symbolism, and this is generally used when the lodge jewel is passed on to a new master of the lodge. This explanation was written by Cyril Saunders Spackman, the designer of the jewel, and is quoted in full as part of the jewel's entry in the 1938 museum catalogue.

> The jewel is in the form of a cross, symbolising Sacrifice, with a perfect square at the four ends, on the left and right squares being the dates 1914–1918, the years in which the supreme sacrifice was made. Between these is a winged figure of Peace presenting the representation of a Temple with special Masonic allusion in the Pillars, Porch and Steps. The medal is suspended by the Square and Compasses, attached to a ribband, the whole thus symbolising the Craft's gift of a Temple in memory of those brethren who gave all for King and Country, Peace and Victory, Liberty and Brotherhood.
>
> *(Tudor-Craig 1938: 108)*

The museum collections contain many examples of these 'Hallstone Jewels' awarded to famous and lesser-known freemasons. From the late 1990s until 2016, the full range of variants including additional jewels for the commemorative meal at Olympia and the jewel for 'special collectors' were displayed in an exhibition case on the fundraising appeal. During this period also, active collecting located a photograph of an individual wearing all the possible jewels.

The image of the Hallstone Angel also appears on ephemera for the meal held at Olympia in 1925, including on the card cover of a set of matches (Library and Museum of Freemasonry 2006: 60–61).

This image of the angel is repeated in the building through the three vestibules that lead from the main staircase eastwards on the first floor to the Grand Temple. The Memorial Shrine at the start of these vestibules was designed by Walter Gilbert (1871–1946). It takes the form of a bronze casket resting on an ark amongst reeds; the boat is indicative of a journey which has come to an end. Across the front are four gilded figures portraying Moses, Joshua, Solomon, and St George (not an image from freemasonry and here representing patriotism in the context of this being the Grand Lodge of England and not the other nations of the Union). In the four corners stand pairs of winged Seraphim (angels) carrying golden trumpets. The background to the figures is foliage appropriate to the Western Front and the trenches. On the top of the casket the Royal Navy, Royal Marines, army and flying services are represented by kneeling figures. Above the shrine is a stained-glass window (Figure 15.1) which shows on each

FIGURE 15.1 Memorial window in Freemasons' Hall London. (© Museum of Freemasonry.)

side columns of pilgrims rising to their reward. On the left side are soldiers from the war. The central device is the Hallstone Angel, but uniquely here the figure holds a representation of the actual tower of the building. The same image but with the generic temple is also present in the stained glass of the administrative staircase of the building, ensuring that members would pass it every time they attended a meeting.

The museum too is located on the first floor of the building, in line with the processional way to the main ceremonial rooms. This made it part of the life of the building and not merely an attraction to be visited. Contemporary photographs of the museum at its 1933 opening show its displays as a mixture of ceramics, glassware, furniture, and curios. The 1938 catalogue by Sir Algernon Tudor-Craig (Tudor-Craig 1938) lists the content of the museum structured by the then display cabinets. There are relatively few items listed that relate to the war, apart from the previously mentioned gavel block. The remaining items referenced include a maul found in the ruins of Arras, which clearly speaks to the perceived links between actual stonemasons and the symbolic stonemasonry encountered in the ceremonies of freemasonry; while a halfpenny, mounted with a plaque explaining that it was auctioned for £6-6-0 (£6.30) in aid of interned freemasons, links to aspects of brotherhood and charity.

This apparent lack of resources for war-themed displays disguises the large reservoir of material held in the minute books of individual lodges and the prevalence of self-published lodge histories. Many lodges also have 'treasures' which have been presented by members and even, on occasion, have formed lodge museums. These are the main source of social history material outside the museum's permanent collections. The histories in particular are available to all researchers visiting the Museum of Freemasonry and remain a relatively untapped source. The near universality of military and military related service in the early twentieth century means that most lodge histories reference the war, albeit often only to commemorate service. These resources seem to have been little used by the museum in this period between the wars.

More common in the pre-Second World War collection are jewels (badges) donated to the museum on the founding of lodges. These are a unique link to the concerns of the men forming those lodges. The imagery of many dating from the period 1918–20 is emblematic of peace, hope for the future and commemoration of service. Perhaps the most poignant to this author is Memory Lodge No. 4264, formed to commemorate a member of St Mark's Lodge No. 2423 who had been killed in the war. Lodges named after individuals were not encouraged, and so the lodge name, combined with the image of a war memorial bearing his initials and the phrase 'he did his duty', served to link the lodge to the individual.

Significantly, although the focus here is the First World War, it appears that the Second World War was a catalyst for donation of many earlier items. Many of the prisoner of war items dating from the Great War arrived during the period, perhaps to ensure safekeeping or as a gesture of patriotism and defiance. The museum itself was in storage (for parallels, see Deans, this volume), which proved fortunate as the museum windows were blasted-in when a V1 flying-bomb struck the street nearby.

The museum first opened to the general public on a permanent basis with the in-house creation of the 'Permanent Exhibition' in the early 1980s. This was again predominantly a decorative arts display but did have a section showing the charitable actions of freemasons incarcerated at Ruhleben Prisoner of War camp at Spandau, Germany, in making a donation to the Freemasons' War Hospital. During this period, the galleries of the museum only attempted limited interpretation of the collections, concentrating instead on explaining freemasonry to visitors, hence the emphasis on exhibiting the principles of freemasonry including charity and the use of membership to improve morale under conditions of duress.

The museum developed larger scale temporary exhibitions from the creation of an independent charitable trust in 1998. These sought to face outwards to attract a wider audience and were often undertaken in partnership with subject specialists or academics. Perhaps unconsciously the First World War featured in a significant number of these, either as core subject or in support of the main theme (although this author would assert that the building itself has significant affect in the constant rehearsing of the remembrance of that period by tour guides and researchers). This may also have reflected the content of the museum's collection, as during this period decorative items were gradually replaced with narrative and subject-led displays during a period of learning and collections research.

From 2001 to 2013, major summer exhibitions were created in another part of Freemasons' Hall that gave greater access and flexibility. 'Art of the Apocalypse' in 2002, with the subtitle 'Trench Art from the Spanish Armada to Bosnia', featured a significant number of First World War related items, drawn from the museum's own collections but also loaned from individual lodges. A notable feature of many of these was the use of war matériel as construction elements for lodge fittings. The exhibition, co-curated by Professor Nicholas Saunders, took a material culture-anthropological approach to the subject. It catalysed not only a different approach to the collections by the museum but also informed two publications (Dennis and Saunders 2003; Dennis 2009).

The exhibition was structured around the groups making items and their motivations for doing so. Items were loaned from individual lodges. Navy Lodge loaned a collecting box made from HMS *Iris*, one of the converted Mersey ferries used in the raid on Zeebrugge in 1918; Royal Naval Anti-Aircraft Lodge provided a range of items, including a shell case decorated with brass labels indicating the places of the unit's deployment, and officers' jewels made from the duralumin of a crashed Zeppelin (believed to be LZ 129 commanded by Heinrich Mathy and a key source of souvenir duralumin). The exhibition also featured stereo cards of the wreckage from which the jewels were made (Dennis 2009: 80). An artwork of conflict through the ages was created as a backdrop to the exhibition incorporating artefacts over a symbolic battlefield and centred on the First World War (Figure 15.2). Elements of this exhibition remained on display until 2016 in a single case reflecting freemasonry in adversity and

"You shall hear of wars
and rumours of wars"

FIGURE 15.2   Artwork designed by the author for the exhibition *Art of the Apocalypse*.
(© Museum of Freemasonry.)

including the regalia and image of the internee lodge previously shown in the
'Permanent Exhibition'.

On the basis that 'what you really collect is always yourself '(Baudrillard 1996:
97), the collecting within these lodges had the potential to tap into a deeper
level of meaning than just the retention of historical memory. The need to connect physically with the events that had been important to the earlier members seemed evident. Some items in this exhibition, notably a gavel made
from elements of a German Mauser rifle that had been used in meetings within
the war zone and later presented to an English lodge in gratitude (Library and
Museum of Freemasonry 2014: 81–82), and the already-mentioned gavel block
would become repeated exhibits over the next decade (Figure 15.3). They were
in some respects becoming palimpsests as they crossed from their original meanings and ownership and became layered with the differing roles they played in
each succeeding display.

The next First World War related exhibition was held in 2006 and came from
an unexpected source. The concept for 'Most Glorious of Them All: Masonic
Holders of the Victoria Cross' was generated not by the in-house staff of the
museum but following lobbying by an individual freemason, Granville Angell.
His passion for researching the masonic winners of the Victoria Cross and collecting artefacts with a link to them led to one of the most internally popular
exhibitions created in the decade. The opening night was marked by the display
of two actual VC groups from the Firepower Museum of the Royal Regiment of

FIGURE 15.3 Gavel made from elements of a German Mauser rifle and presented initially to St Catherine's Park Lodge. (© Museum of Freemasonry.)

Artillery and was attended by senior freemasons. The impact of this exhibition within UGLE proved to be greater than the museum had anticipated, as the discovery of the strong link between the VC and freemasonry would generate two further commemorations by UGLE independent of the museum itself. The exhibition aimed to be comprehensive in featuring all the VC winners identified; this resulted in a tension between proven artefacts connected to the individuals, items where the link was only circumstantial, items linked to their lodges, and more generic military badges or models that were purely illustrative. Almost all the items in the exhibition apart from lodge jewels came from private collections rather than from the museum itself. Although the subject matter spanned the entire history of the VC, the two World Wars were the major focus.

The war was not only featured in exhibitions directly about conflict. In 2011, 'Building Solomon's Temple' arose from a partnership with a University College London academic Dr Beverley Butler and showed the link between the legend of the Biblical temple and freemasonry. It may seem to be an unlikely source of war-related narrative and material; but despite this, the presence of freemasons in Palestine during the war and the following Palestine Protectorate proved an evocative story and items collected during that period featured in the exhibition. These were subsequently loaned to the School of Oriental and African Studies (SOAS) for a major exhibition on 'The British in Palestine'. Key amongst these were elements of stone from the 'King Solomon' quarries under the Temple Mount in Jerusalem. Some of these were not even worked, being very simply inscribed by the men concerned. This sensorial link to the actual temple would have been significant for freemasons but not for others. This collection of quarry stone by the military freemasons is a very clear example of expressing their identity as freemasons in time of conflict. Souvenir items purchased commercially included gavel sets with quarry stone heads, providing a twist on the selling of trench art souvenirs. Here the vendors clearly understood what could be provided for a rather niche market. The ashlars (cubic stones) for every lodge room in the Peace Memorial were made from the same material. Saunders (2003: 226–227) makes the point that 'trench art constitutes the world of the living during war, and, while retaining its original form, transforms after war to create another world' for those who follow. This transformation of meaning is attached to many of the objects in the collections of the museum.

The museum commemorated the centenary of the outbreak of war in 2014 with 'English Freemasonry and the First World War'. This considered a wide range of issues beyond the purely military and material aspects of the conflict. In contrast to previous exhibitions which had been artefact-led, archival material was used extensively, and this allowed the narratives to expand into previously un-exhibited subject areas. Archival items have, of course, their own materiality and create sensory and emotional affect through this (Lester 2018); the presence of manuscripts created in Prisoner of War camps, and official documents that influenced the path of English freemasonry, allowed visitors to connect directly with the period. The Museum of Freemasonry is a tri-domain organization with the archive and library. The combination of the written record and the printed word with the three-dimensional objects gave far greater emotional and intellectual impact to this exhibition.

The expanded range of subjects included the contested history regarding freemasons who were citizens of enemy powers. The anti-German fever of 1914 led to UGLE members who were citizens of those powers being excluded from their lodges. This had unforeseen consequences with, for example, members of the Polish National Lodge being excluded despite their hopes for a Poland independent of the Habsburg Empire. Lodges also changed their names where there was a German link. Prince William Frederick Lodge became the Ethical Lodge and substituted a female figure for the Prussian eagle on its jewels. Examples of these jewels were on show alongside original correspondence relating to the decision to exclude members and the opposition to this from some freemasons.

Freemasons in Prisoner of War camps were again illustrated, using well-known incidents that featured members. A ceramic plaque from the Royal Masonic Hospital commemorating the freemason dead of the previously mentioned Ruhleben Prisoner of War camp included the name of Captain Charles Fryatt (Figure 15.4). He had attempted to ram a surfaced U-Boat and when later captured had been executed by the Germans. During the preparation phase of the exhibition the museum collaborated with historian Mark Baker, who was campaigning for Fryatt to be better remembered and who was in contact with his descendants (Harwich and Manningtree Standard 2016). War leaders were also featured in the exhibition including Admiral of the Fleet John Jellicoe and Field Marshal Horatio Kitchener, but the relative lack of original items led to a

THE EQUIPMENT OF THIS WARD WAS PRESENTED BY THE BRITISH FREEMASONS WHO WERE INTERNED IN RUHLEBEN, GERMANY, DURING THE GREAT WAR, 1914 TO 1918, AS A TOKEN OF THEIR DEEP GRATITUDE TO THE CRAFT FOR THE FRATERNAL HELP AND RELIEF EXTENDED TO THEM DURING THAT PERIOD OF CAPTIVITY AND DISTRESS: AND IN MEMORY OF THEIR FELLOW PRISONERS, BRO. CAPTAIN C. FRYATT, S.S. BRUSSELS, BRO. CAPTAIN E. RUSSELL, S.S. "BURY", BRO. CAPTAIN A. CORDINER, S.S. "HEWORTH", TO WHOM DEATH BROUGHT RELEASE

PERCY C. HULL, P.D.G.O. ENG

FIGURE 15.4 Ceramic plaque from Royal Masonic Hospital commemorating the generosity of interned freemasons and memorializing their casualties. (© Museum of Freemasonry.)

decision that this 'celebrity' aspect should be downplayed apart from one of the classic, Kitchener recruiting posters.

The use of original manuscripts could take the exhibition in unexpected directions. In a minute book compiled by members of Cappadocia Lodge of Instruction, which met in the prisoner of war camp at Yozgad, Turkey, was an intriguing quote about a member who 'was undergoing confinement for being in telepathic communication with some person or persons unknown' (Library and Museum of Freemasonry 2014: 56).[1] This led to the discovery of a link with a popular book published in 1919 outlining an escape attempt based on a supernatural hoax. The book *The Road to En-Dor* (Jones 2014 [1919]) explained that prisoners who were also members of the lodge attempted to convince their captors that they had secret knowledge of a treasure hoard and that if released they would share it. Items were loaned by the Lodge of Antiquity No. 2, one of whose members had retained them after the conflict. The minute book of the lodge was displayed for the first time in public alongside improvised regalia. This was the first time that a freemason connection to the incident had been displayed but the story had proved inspirational to the well-known author Neil Gaiman (2014) and the book republished. It is a good example of how the apparently niche subject of freemasonry is, in fact, often linked to wider events of more general interest.

In 2015, the exhibition 'Healing with Kindness: Centenary of the Royal Masonic Hospital' featured the origins of the hospital in the Freemasons' War

Hospital in south London. On the outbreak of the First World War in 1914, UGLE proposed running and meeting the expenses of a hospital for the War Office. The Freemasons' War Hospital opened in September 1916 and treated over 4,000 service personnel. Photographs and documents tracked the mutation of a pre-war idea of a nursing home into the hospital on two sites in London and subsequently as the Royal Masonic Hospital continued in its post-war form. The museum archive has substantial records of the hospital and also photographs of the nurses and buildings. Freemasons amongst the patients were able to request hospital visits by fellow masons, and a wide programme of entertainment was provided (Library and Museum of Freemasonry 2014: 69–76).

The Museum of Freemasonry subsequently attempted to move away from war related exhibitions considering that they had become repetitious. In 2016, 'Brethren Beyond the Seas' avoided an obvious marketing link to the war by concentrating on the bicentenary celebrations of UGLE in 1917 and the freemasons from across the Empire that had contributed to them, although with the strap-line 'This exhibition explores the development of the Grand Lodges within the British Empire and marks the contribution of their forces to the First World War'. There was a major war component within this as the presence of overseas freemasons and the curtailing of the celebration was due to the ongoing hostilities in 1917. Building on the exhibition of two years previously, this exhibition sought to celebrate the creation of Grand Lodges that had evolved and become independent from UGLE across the Empire and its predecessor bodies (in the case of the USA). There was again an emphasis on archival material rather than the object-led approach of the previous exhibitions although the now familiar gavel and gavel block re-emerged on display. They had transformed, becoming emblematic of military freemasons of New Zealand and Canada rather than items of trench art.

A new long-term exhibition 'Three Centuries of English Freemasonry' also opened in late 2016. The war was not featured as a separate topic but was referenced by a display entitled 'suitcase story' with the personal effects of individual masons being displayed as they were found in the cases used to contain their regalia. One mason chosen was Alfred Allo who had come to England as a child refugee during the conflict, and amongst a display of the traditional named fitted-leather pouches used to carry masonic aprons to meetings was one bearing the name of a war casualty. A display covering the inclusive nature of freemasonry explained that the blind could join and that a lodge, Lux in Tenebris, had formed specifically to cater for those who had lost their sight in the war. On opening this exhibition, many displays elsewhere in the museum were removed, including a long-standing display case featuring the internee and Prisoner of War lodges of the conflict.

As the museum scaled back its war related displays, the momentum was maintained by UGLE itself taking an increasing interest in commemorating the links between the freemasons and the war. During the early 2000s, the Armistice was not marked by a two-minute silence in the building, nor were poppy wreaths

FIGURE 15.5 Symbolic VC figures commemorating the inauguration of the paving stones outside Freemasons' Hall, London. (© Louise Pichel.)

laid at the memorial casket. This changed in the next decade as research on the VC winners restored the war to memory in the run-up to the centenary. In 2017, UGLE installed, as part of its own tercentenary celebrations, a set of commemorative stones listing all recipients of the Victoria Cross during the First World War who had been members of UGLE (no distinction was made between those who had been freemasons at the time of the award and those who joined subsequently). Life-size plywood cut-out figures printed with the details of each award winner were created and, after display, offered to the Provinces of UGLE (regions) where the winner had been a member. There was debate regarding the most appropriate silhouette to use for the figures, particularly as the winners were tri-service and included colonial troops. In the end the classic 'British Tommy' was used (Figure 15.5). The unveiling of the stones was a public event attended by HRH The Duke of Kent, Grand Master of UGLE, with veterans and a Guards band (Cunningham 2017). The names on the stones used Granville Angell's research and during installation an additional name was located requiring an immediate replacement of one of the stones. Appropriately enough the man's surname was Mason. The stones now form a permanent part of the streetscape and are situated by the main doors to the building beneath the tower.

The centenary of the armistice in 2018 was commemorated by members of UGLE in a special meeting of Victoria Rifles Lodge in the Grand Temple at Freemasons' Hall. The lodge officers were dressed in replica soldiers' uniforms and a Lewis machine gun was placed in the centre of the room. The experience was sensorial, with a soundtrack of gun barrage leading to silence and a fall of paper poppies. More than 500 masters of Hallstone Lodges attended, wearing their jewels. Non freemason Simon Callow was employed to read poetry from the war (Shepherd 2019). This performative and sensory event was very much in line with the ways in which freemasons use their ceremonies. This throws into relief a problem with the traditional museum in that by prioritizing vision and meaning it fossilizes rather than captures activity. The sensorial aspects of this ceremony are now lost, as is the sound of the Mauser gavel mentioned earlier. Dudley suggests of the material displays in museums that 'Too often we interpret that world … not as we should, from *within* it, but as if we were outside it, dis-embodied, looking on' (Dudley 2010: 10).

There remains great potential to evoke the manufacture and use of the items we are discussing, perhaps through sound fields, and tactile elements that allow the imagination to jump from the visual to the sensorial. Curating the museum of a living organization is a strong and emotive prompt to action in order to com-municate effectively the experience of its members. At time of writing one of the Ypres gavel blocks is being returned to its owner, Canada Lodge, and will in future be used in their ceremonies. The Mauser gavel may now be mute but the sound of a wooden gavel hitting a beam from Ypres Cathedral may be captured and heard again. It is a fate that would have startled the builders and users of the cathedral but in some respects may provide an echo of the mallets used to place the beam during the medieval construction of the cathedral. It thus has multiple meanings and could be used to evoke the loss of the cathedral more effectively as part of a soundscape that might also include the Catholic chants of worshippers in the cathedral and the crackle of the fire that consumed it.

In the same year, UGLE partnered with researcher Brian Deutsch to curate a photographic display of freemasons from the war, focussing on more socially important or decorated individuals. This was augmented by a large panel dis-play of war-related images in the circulation corridor of the second floor of Freemasons' Hall. This was an area of the building that had never been pre-viously used for display. A smaller version of the exhibition appeared in the corridor by the museum and featured famous freemasons of the war, including the future King George VI and King Edward VIII. Deutsch, as curator of this exhibition, explained the rationale thus:

> A lot of them have connections to Freemasonry, but the theme of the exhibition is humanity and caring, which is a banner of Freemasonry,' … 'I wanted to show how the spirit of life will ultimately triumph. A lot of that is because the comradeship during the war carried on afterwards. A lot of soldiers actually became Freemasons following the war after seeing what it meant for their officers.
>
> *(Deutsch 2019)*

The following year this photographic display was further augmented by illustra-tions of the masonic VC winners using images taken from cigarette cards. This coincided with the unveiling in the building of a stone carved in the form of a VC. Although the focus was again on the First World War, the point was made that this extended the commemoration to all masonic winners of the decoration.

Sergeant Johnson Beharry VC, recently joined as a freemason, was in attendance, as was the Duke of Kent. Granville Angell was involved again, and the previous Grand Secretary (Chief Executive) commented in his speech to the Duke that Angell's tenacity had led to the placing of the stone there instead of at the National Memorial Arboretum as first intended.

> I can think of no more fitting place for it to be than here in Freemasons' Hall, the Masonic Peace Memorial Building, where I suspect far more Masons will see it and which is the spiritual home of Freemasonry.
> *(Freemasonry Today 2019)*

This most recent commemoration combined the tenacity of an individual, the official wishes of UGLE, and a traditional form of masonic ceremony. The presentation of a worked stone VC also linked operative and speculative masonry with the architecture of the former Peace Memorial. A prototype of the VC stones from outside the building had been deposited in the museum, and at the date of writing this is on long-term loan to the masonic museum in Canterbury, Kent. All the bodies that had contributed to the commemoration of the war in the building were thus drawn together at the close of the centenary events.

At the time of writing, a small display themed around the war remains in the South Gallery of the Museum. The previously mentioned Ypres gavel block is flanked by artefacts relating to the French and English constitution lodges 'Builders of the Silent Cities'. These were lodges created for members of the Commonwealth War Graves Commission, and the name is an oblique reference to the cemeteries themselves. The jewels of the lodges show a generic War Graves Commission cemetery. An epergne commemorating the victory, and an 'Armistice Glass' engraved with the date and time of the cessation of hostilities, complete a modest display that is very much focussed on armistice, remembrance, and the aftermath of the war. Here the gavel block takes its latest meaning as the most authentic artefact in the collection to catalyse a display about the Armistice.

The curating of the Masonic Peace Memorial has over the last century been a partnership between architects, museum professionals, passionate private scholars, and UGLE itself. The items used to create exhibitions now have a biography of their own and point to more targeted research on the multiple meanings that they contain. The future direct role of the First World War in displays at the Museum of Freemasonry is uncertain; but the building, and the collection it holds, continues to be a significant embodiment of the war in display, architecture, and streetscape.

Note

1 Lodges of Instruction are informal lodges that are permitted to perform masonic ceremonies, but not to initiate new members.

References

Baudrillard, J. (1996) *The System of Objects*. (transl. J. Benedict). London: Verso.

Cunningham, A. (2017) Bravest of the Brave: Freemasons Awarded the Victoria Cross Are Honoured. *Arena Magazine* 29 (Summer): 22–23. London: Metropolitan Grand Lodge/ Metropolitan Grand Chapter.

Dennis, M.J.R. (2009) Brothers in Arms: Masonic Artefacts of the First World War and Its Aftermath. In N.J. Saunders and P. Cornish (eds.), *Contested Objects, Material Memories of the Great War*, pp 73–87. London: Routledge.

Dennis, M.J.R. and N.J. Saunders. (2003) *Craft and Conflict*. London: Savannah-Publications.

Deutsch, B. (2019) Bond of Brothers. *FMT the Official Journal of the United Grand Lodge of England* 45 (Spring):20–21.

Dudley, S.H. (2010) Museum Materialities: Objects, Sense and Feeling. In S.H. Dudley (ed.), *Museum Materialities: Engagements, Interpretations*, pp 1–18. London: Routledge.

Freemasonry Today. (2019) Victoria Cross Remembrance Stone conclusion. Freemasonry Today. https://www.freemasonrytoday.com/ugle-sgc/ugle/speeches/victoria-cross-remembrance-stone-conclusion-willie-shackell. Accessed 6 December 2019.

Gaiman, N. (2014) How Neil Gaiman took the road to En-Dor. The Guardian. https://www.theguardian.com/books/2014/feb/28/neil-gaiman-road-endor-eh-jones. Accessed 9 December 2019.

Harwich and Manningtree Standard. (2016) Special exhibition in Harwich to mark 100 years since the death of Captain Fryatt. Harwich and Manningtree Standard. https://www.harwichandmanningtreestandard.co.uk/news/14567497.special-exhibition-in-harwich-to-mark-100-years-since-the-death-of-captain-fryatt/. Accessed 9 December 2019.

Jones, E.H. (2014) [1919] *The Road to En-Dor*. London: Hesperus Press.

Lester, P. (2018). Of mind and matter: The archive as object. *Archives and Records* 39 (1): 73–87.

Library and Museum of Freemasonry. (2006) *The Hall in the Garden: Freemasons' Hall and its place in London*. Hersham: Lewis Masonic.

———. (2014) *English Freemasonry and the First World War*. Hersham: Lewis Masonic.

Saunders, N.J. (2003) *Trench Art: Materialities and Memories of War*. Oxford: Berg.

Shepherd, T. (2019) Victoria Rifles Lodge No.822 hosts Armistice Centenary Meeting. *Arena Magazine* 35 (January):20–22. London: Metropolitan Grand Lodge/ Metropolitan Grand Chapter.

Tudor-Craig, Sir A. (1938) *Catalogue of Contents of the Museum at Freemasons' Hall in the Possession of the United Grand Lodge of England*. London: United Grand Lodge of England.

16

WHAT NEED OF TEARS?

Collaborative memorial-making in the centenary of the Great War

Stephen Dixon

Introduction

During the centenary of the Great War, the United Kingdom witnessed an upsurge of memorialization, from focused local initiatives to art installations on an epic scale, with contemporary artists questioning conventional attitudes to commemoration and rethinking traditional forms of public memorial. Exemplary and high-profile acts of memorialization embraced public spectacle (Danny Boyle's *Pages of the Sea*, 2018), performance and public engagement (Jeremy Deller's *We're Here Because We're Here*, 2016), the evocative language of materials (Cornelia Parker's *War Rooms*, 2015) and the emotive resonance of archive material (Peter Jackson's film *They Shall Not Grow Old*, 2018).

At the same time, many more centenary projects have directly engaged the public, working at a local, grass-roots level, to engage individuals and communities in collaborative acts of memorialization. Within this context, ceramicist Stephen Dixon and film-maker Johnny Magee, both of Manchester School of Art, collaborated on a number of commemorative curatorial projects with museums in Staffordshire. These projects set out to examine our relationship to conflict and its commemoration, engaging with collections and exploiting the mnemonic resonance of historic artefacts. The projects were linked by their connection to the specific locality of Staffordshire and to the Staffordshire Potteries' historic material connection to ceramics.

Dixon and Magee operated as artists and curators for the exhibitions *Resonance* (2015), *Resonate* (2015–2016), *The Lost Boys* (2016), *Passchendaele: Mud and Memory* (2017) and *Refugee Tales* (2017–2019). Collectively, these five projects aimed to employ the emotive agency of collections, archives and excavated objects, to engage cultural memory and to examine and commemorate specific issues of conflict. These issues were encountered in the First World War but are also

DOI: 10.4324/9781003263531-20

relevant to our own times, from the plight of refugees to the exploitation of under-age soldiers. Each of the exhibitions resulted in some kind of memorial, sometimes in the form of an artefact, sometimes as a film, and often collaborative and temporary. In addition, each of these projects featured a significant element of direct public participation in the resulting artworks and exhibitions, and this is an aspect which gained in importance as the projects developed. This chapter outlines each of these exhibitions and explains how an iterative methodology of co-creation was instigated and tested over the course of the five curatorial projects.

Resonance: Reflections on the Great War through Artwork Inspired by Staffordshire Collections

The first of these projects, *Resonance*, was a touring exhibition, commissioned in 2014 by a consortium of seven Staffordshire museums, including the Wedgwood Museum and the Potteries Museum and Art Gallery in Stoke-on-Trent.[1] The brief given to Dixon and Magee was to develop an exhibition of new artworks made in response to the collections of First World War memorabilia held in the archives of the seven museums. Additionally, each of the museums was keen to involve the public and to develop a hands-on, participatory element to the touring exhibition.

The project created a number of dilemmas. First, how could the artists take a critical position – as artists are wont to do – in relation to the broader issues relating to war, conflict and commemoration, whilst at the same time maintain respect for the personal sacrifice and individual suffering of participants? And second, how would they avoid evoking nostalgia and sentimentality when making artworks dealing with such resonant and emotional historic events? The solution was to focus on materiality and to work in dialogue with the evocative qualities of the historic objects in the collections, letting the objects speak for themselves wherever possible. They were also keen to be mindful of contemporary events that might resonate with the historical events of the First World War.

Another, more practical issue was the proximity of the museums to one another; it was clear that the artists could not simply create a body of work and tour an identical exhibition from one museum to the next. This was resolved through working closely with the curators at each museum (actively co-curating each of the exhibitions) responding directly to the objects in each of the museums' First World War collections and adding at least one new artwork to the exhibition each time the tour moved on. This resulted in a significant number of new artworks, some of which appeared at all of the venues, while some appeared only once, and others were reworked or reconfigured. A small selection of these artworks is outlined below.

Collections of Real Photo Postcards were a common element in all of the museums' archives. Kodak introduced the No. 3A Folding Pocket Camera in 1903, which enabled photographers to develop photographs directly onto

FIGURE 16.1 Johnny Magee, *The King's Own Yorkshire Light Infantry* (2015). (© Johnny Magee. Photographer Johnny Magee. Medium: Scanned Real Photo Postcard, coloured and digitally printed. Dimensions: 49 cm high × 69 cm wide. Location: Private collection.)

standard-size postcard backs which could then be sent through the post. This form of documentary photography had become popular by the beginning of the First World War, particularly in the military training camps on the home front. One such was situated at Cannock Chase in Staffordshire, the venue for the first exhibition. Magee scanned and digitized a number of these Real Photo Postcards, which were then enlarged and colourized for the exhibition (Figure 16.1). The effect of colourizing the images was to collapse the temporal distancing effect of the sepia originals, bringing the humanity of the sitter closer to the viewer.[2] New photographic images were added to the exhibition by Magee as the tour progressed.

Dixon also worked with Real Photo Postcards (sourced from ebay to supplement those found in the museum archives) to produce a series of 'Buttoncards' for the third venue of the tour, the Ancient High House, Stafford (Figure 16.2). This was a provocative and iconoclastic work, made in 2015, at a time of very real iconoclasm in the Middle East. The artist's collection of Real Photo Postcards, featuring both British and German soldiers, were dehumanized and literally defaced, by stitching excavated First World War military buttons onto the postcards.

In addition to postcards, the artists came across crested china artefacts in several of the Staffordshire collections. crested china was a form of popular commemorative ware, collected by British tourists on their summer holidays, from the 1880s to the 1930s (Southall 1982). The genre was in its heyday during the Great War, documenting and commemorating significant events, political

FIGURE 16.2 Stephen Dixon, *Buttoncard* (2015). (© Stephen Dixon. Photographer Stephen Dixon. Medium: Real Photo Postcard, military buttons, thread. Dimensions: 14 cm high × 9 cm wide. Location: Private collection.)

figures and particularly the military hardware of war. It adopted a patriotic and sometimes even propagandist line.[3] Dixon saw an opportunity to expand the genre by extending the typology of First World War crested china, while at the same time taking a more critical perspective.

The timing of the first exhibition was perfect to examine the contentious events of the Christmas Truce of 1914 (fraternization, exchanges of gifts and impromptu football games), an event described by Sir Arthur Conan Doyle as 'One Human Episode amid all the atrocities that have stained the memory of the war' (Brown and Seaton 2001). Dixon modelled and cast a British footballer/soldier, replicating

FIGURE 16.3   Stephen Dixon, *The Beautiful Game* (2014). Detail. (© Stephen Dixon. Photographer Tony Richards. Medium: transfer printed earthenware. Dimensions of figures: 15 cm high × 7 cm wide × 6 cm deep. Location: Private collection.)

the scale and generic modelling style of crested china. This was followed by a German soldier, and then some goalkeepers, and eventually two complete football teams, which were exhibited as *The Beautiful Game* (Figure 16.3). Significantly, each figure was named after a soldier who had witnessed and written about the events of the Christmas Truce, and each carried the badge of his regiment as a crest. In this way, the work acted as both literal and physical testimony to the veracity of the event. In the first exhibition, at Cannock Chase Museum, *The Beautiful Game* was displayed alongside the Congreve letter[4] in which General Sir Walter Congreve VC described the 'extraordinary state of affairs' of the truce in a Christmas day letter from the front line and also talks about a football game 'I hear it was further north, 1st R.B. playing football with the Germans opposite them'.

As mentioned above, each of the host venues was interested in developing a public engagement element within the touring exhibition. This was initiated through participatory workshops at each of the museums, where the public were invited to bring in photographs and documents relating to a family member who had served in the First World War. During these workshops, the participants were assisted in developing their documentary material into portrait drawings, following a template derived from commemorative First World War mugs. These drawings became the artwork for digital ceramic transfers, which were subsequently printed onto bone china mugs (Figure 16.4). The commemorative mugs were then displayed in the artwork *Column* in the touring exhibition, with batches of newly decorated mugs added as the tour progressed and more workshops were completed. Initially the 'column' of mugs was plain white, but the

FIGURE 16.4 Stephen Dixon and project volunteers, *Column* (2015). Detail. (© Stephen Dixon. Photographer Tony Richards. Medium: transfer printed bone china. Dimensions of each tankard: 8 cm high × 10 cm wide × 7 cm deep. Various locations (the tankards were returned to their makers after the touring exhibition).)

un-decorated mugs were gradually replaced by decorated ones, thereby adding more rows and columns of combatants to the installation and emphasizing the underlying message of the artwork – the gradual involvement of more and more of the population as the Great War progressed. Repeated visits to the touring exhibition would reveal this developing narrative.[5]

Resonate

The local success of the touring *Resonance* exhibition led to an invitation from the British Ceramics Biennial to produce an installation on the Spode factory site in Stoke-on-Trent, to commemorate the 5,608 soldiers of the North Staffordshire Regiment who lost their lives in the First World War (Cook 1970). This gave the artists the opportunity to explore some of the commemorative and collaborative themes developed in *Resonance* on a much larger scale and in a more open-ended and experimental context.

The resultant work, *Resonate*, was a multi-media installation featuring sculpture, ceramics, sound and public participation. Dixon's monumental sculpture provided the centrepiece of the installation (Figure 16.5). It was made from two tons of Staffordshire Etruria marl clay, the clay on which Stoke-on-Trent stands, and was based on the head of the Nike figure from the Inter-Allied Victory Medal, which was designed by William McMillan R.A. and issued to all who served in the armed forces. However, the classical form and celebratory sentiment

FIGURE 16.5   Stephen Dixon, Johnny Magee and project volunteers, *Resonate* (2015). (© Stephen Dixon and Johnny Magee. Photographer Joel Chester Fildes. Medium: unfired Etruria marl clay, bone china flowers and scaffolding. Dimensions: 300 cm high × 200 cm wide × 240 cm deep. Location: Temporary installation, now dismantled.)

of McMillan's victory medal were challenged by the industrial aesthetic of the sculpture's supporting structure, which in contrast adopted the functionalism and brutal materiality of trench architecture. At three metres high, the clay sculpture required a unique method of construction: blocks of clay were laid from the ground up in hollow concentric circles, following the profile of the head, in a process somewhere between coil-building and igloo-making. The massive combined weight of the clay was carried on a scaffolding armature, with each block of clay tied to the core by nylon cord and ceramic 'buttons'.

The installation was animated by Magee's complementary soundscape, which evoked and orchestrated the familiar and incidental sounds and poignant popular music of the Great War, and was based on a digitally manipulated version of the Jerome Kern classic *They Didn't Believe Me*, with additional piano music performed by Rachel Taverner.[6] The combination of this eerie and evocative sound-track with the open, echoing space of the Spode factory created an emotional, reverential atmosphere for the installation.

Building on the co-creation methodology instigated in *Resonance*, public and voluntary participation was built into this new project from the start. Volunteers working with the British Ceramics Biennial assisted Dixon in the construction of the monumental clay head, and an 'army' of flower-makers led by Rita Floyd produced hundreds of hand-made bone china forget-me-nots for use in the installation. When the exhibition opened in September 2015, visitors to the Biennial were invited to reflect on the nature of loss, sacrifice and commemoration and to attach the white ceramic flowers to the scaffolding structure. They were also invited to attach their own personal tributes, in the manner of impromptu roadside shrines and personal memorials, and to document their unique family stories of the First World War as part of the installation. Unexpectedly, although many of the visitors did commemorate fallen relatives in their tributes, others attached more general reflections on the nature of war:

We fear wolves and snakes, when mankind is the biggest historical killer.[7]

Over the six weeks of the exhibition, the sculpture was gradually encased in a blanket of flowers, tags and tributes, while the clay head slowly dried out, shrinking and fracturing around its scaffolding armature.

The sculpture was a temporary installation and was dismantled at the end of the Biennial in November 2015, but it retains a legacy in Magee's artist film *Things Just Happen Anyway*. The film celebrates the materiality of the installation, documenting the sculpture in its final, fractured form, and elements of the original sound-sculpture were recycled into the sound-track. It was featured at the Crafts Council's *Real to Reel* film festival during London Craft Week in May 2016.

The Lost Boys: Remembering the Boy Soldiers of the First World War

The artists' developing partnership with the British Ceramics Biennial was extended through another project, *The Lost Boys*. This was a community engagement project examining the issue of underage soldiers in the First World War, funded by the Arts and Humanities Research Council and the Heritage Lottery Fund, in conjunction with the *Voices of War and Peace* public engagement centre in Birmingham.

At the outbreak of the First World War, the legal age limit for armed service overseas in the British Army was 19 years, but volunteers were not required to produce evidence of their age at recruitment stations, and underage recruitment was commonplace, particularly following the call for volunteers for Lord Kitchener's New Army in 1914. By the end of the war, an estimated 250,000 underage soldiers between the ages of 14 and 18 had seen active service (Van Emden 2012). *The Lost Boys* project engaged young volunteers of the same age range, as active co-researchers to undertake archival research with the support of the Staffordshire Museums Consortium, the Staffordshire Regiment Museum and Staffordshire County Council archives. Working in collaboration with the British Ceramics Biennial's Education Project Manager Katie Leonard, a team of volunteers from local schools and colleges in the Stoke-on-Trent area was recruited. The young volunteers initially researched the British Army records online and searched for wartime articles and reports on the Sentinel (the local newspaper) database at Staffordshire County Records Office. The British Army records did not yield the information required, as dates of birth were recorded as stated by the soldier at the point of his recruitment. However, the death notices in the Sentinel database revealed more useful information, where the true ages of the young soldiers were revealed, as something of a badge of honour, by their grieving but proud parents and relatives.

These local soldiers' stories and the associated documents became the raw material for a series of ceramic pieces made by the volunteers. In the first phase, a collaborative work, *At Heart a Man*, was made by Dixon and the young volunteers from Staffordshire. They worked with a mixture of open source and archive materials on-site at Manchester School of Art, to produce a printed ceramic installation of 32 ceramic plates, made using laser-printed decals and digital transfer prints, which brought to light some of the tragic personal stories of underage soldiers in the Great War (Figure 16.6). The installation was shown

FIGURE 16.6 Stephen Dixon and project volunteers, *At Heart a Man* (2016). Detail. (© Stephen Dixon. Photographer Tony Richards. Medium: transfer printed earthenware. Dimensions: 26-cm diameter. Location: Manchester Metropolitan University.)

at the Wedgwood Museum in March 2015, and this initiated further research in the Wedgwood archives.

The second phase of the project focused more directly on individual case studies of underage soldiers from the North Staffordshire regiment, drawing on the information sourced by the students in the Staffordshire County Archives. Exploiting the context of Staffordshire's historical connections to the ceramics industry, the young volunteers continued to explore the commemorative potential of ceramic objects, in the form of translucent porcelain lithophane tiles, which revealed the portraits of individual soldiers when illuminated on a light-box.[8]

In parallel to *the Lost Boys* research, the students were given access to the war journal and letters written by Major Cecil Wedgwood, DSO, during his service on the Western Front. Paradoxically, Wedgwood was an over-age soldier, serving in the line at the age of 53,[9] after his repeated requests to re-enlist were finally accepted. He was killed at La Boiselle on 3 July 1916, leading the 7th Battalion, North Staffordshire Regiment at the Battle of the Somme. Some poignant and poetic extracts from Wedgwood's journal were selected by the volunteers and imprinted into a further series of porcelain tiles:

> 'last night was beautifully clear as I lay and looked at the stars'
> 'think of me in a comfy bed instead of a damp dug-out'
> 'the roads and paths are seas of mud'
> 'well done the potters'
> 'when I get home I will do nothing and grow roses'

The project's results were exhibited in *The Lost Boys: Remembering the boy soldiers of the First World War*, at Manchester Metropolitan University Special Collections Gallery in June 2016.

Passchendaele: Mud and Memory

Another commemorative exhibition project followed in 2017, this time at the National Memorial Arboretum, the national centre for remembrance, to mark the centenary of the Battle of Passchendaele. One of the most brutal of First World War campaigns, this battle is associated in the public imagination with the horrific battlefield conditions, particularly the clinging mud of Belgian Flanders. Allied casualties are estimated at 250,000 soldiers, with a similar number of German casualties, and many of their bodies were never recovered or identified (MacDonald 1993).

Dixon saw this as an opportunity to engage even further with the materiality of the war and to make a sculpture from the actual material that the soldiers fought and died in. A trip was made to Flanders, to the Weinerberger Brick factory which quarries 'blue' clay from beneath the battlefield site at Zonnebeke nearby Ypres. The earthenware clay is mixed in the factory with sand, powdered slate and paper pulp, and extruded to make airbricks for the

FIGURE 16.7 Stephen Dixon, *Passchendaele: Mud and Memory* (2017). (© Stephen Dixon. Photographer Tony Richards. Medium: earthenware (brick clay from Zonnebeke and Stoke-on-Trent). Dimensions: 126 cm high × 97 cm wide × 78 cm deep. Location: Tyne Cot Visitors Centre, Passchendaele, Belgium.)

construction industry. A pallet of unfired clay bricks was brought back from Flanders, slaked down and reconstituted into plastic clay. This clay was used to model a large portrait sculpture, which became the centrepiece of the exhibition. The portrait took the form of an 'everyman', an assemblage of features from soldiers from both sides of the conflict, and was based on photographs of individual soldiers sourced in the Memorial Museum Passchendaele 1917 archives (Figure 16.7).

Each section of the portrait was modelled on a named soldier, from the host of nations who fought at Passchendaele. For example, the eyes were those of

Private Bernard Johann te Loken, 7th Reserve Infantry Regiment, Germany; the nose and moustache were modelled on Major Harry Moorhouse, the Kings Own Yorkshire Light Infantry; the left shoulder was from Captain Georges Guynemer, Combat Group 12, the French Air Force. The intention was to highlight the shared experience of conflict at Passchendaele, between soldiers of all ranks and nationalities. Unlike the *Resonate* head (which was unfired and left to dry, shrink and crack apart during the British Ceramics Biennial exhibition) this portrait was fired in its individual 'identikit' sections and then assembled after the firing to form a permanent memorial.

Although the large terracotta portrait was the centrepiece of the exhibition, there were other important elements that also engaged with the materiality of the battle. Three vitrines contained objects representing the main combatants – the United Kingdom (plus Australia, Canada and New Zealand), France and Germany – and examined the emotive resonance of material objects from a curatorial perspective. Each vitrine contained excavated battlefield artefacts and items of popular culture, from the collections of the Memorial Museum Passchendaele 1917 and from private collections. These included pianola rolls, romantic song postcards and objects that bore poignant, personal associations: a pair of eyeglasses, a penknife, a harmonica, a cigarette lighter, a wristwatch, a toothbrush. The similarity of the objects in each of these installations deliberately emphasized the communal experience of soldiers from both sides of the conflict.

Passchendaele: Mud and Memory extended and refined the public participation model first developed for *Resonance*, this time working with museum visitors and volunteers to directly engage with the materiality of the First World War battlefield. Regular public workshops on site at the National Memorial Arboretum made use of a handling collection of excavated First World War objects, and participants were assisted to make drawings of the artefacts and then to print the drawings onto water-slide transfer paper using a laser printer. They were then able to print these drawings onto facsimile NACB (Navy and Army Canteen Board) plates,[10] as an installation of 108 plates around the walls of the exhibition space. The laser printer uses a toner containing iron oxide, which fires to the colour of rusted iron, making a material connection to many of the original rusted and oxidized artefacts. In a similar way to the *Column* piece in *Resonance*, the installation of whitewares was gradually populated with drawings as more workshops were completed during the exhibition. This was a significant advance in the public-participation model, as the volunteers were able to complete the decoration of the plates themselves, rather than simply design the artwork for the ceramic transfers.

The *Passchendaele: Mud and Memory* exhibition was shown at the National Memorial Arboretum during the centenary of the battle, from 31 July to 10 November 2017. The portrait was exhibited again at Bury Art Museum in October 2018 and then travelled 'home' to the Memorial Museum Passchendaele

FIGURE 16.8 Stephen Dixon and project volunteers, *Passchendaele: Mud and Memory* (2017). Facsimile NACB plate. (© Stephen Dixon. Photographer Johnny Magee. Medium: transfer printed earthenware. Dimensions: 27-cm diameter. Location: Manchester Metropolitan University.)

1917 where it was exhibited from February to May 2019, adjacent to the Commonwealth War Grave Commission display. Responding to this location, the installation of plates was reworked, adding poignant and personal epitaphs[11] taken from headstones in Commonwealth War Grave Commission cemeteries in France and Belgium (Jones 2007). These epitaphs give a fascinating insight into the attitudes of ordinary people immediately following the armistice (Figure 16.8). Many are patriotic and signal their pride in the contribution made by their loved ones, but others are openly critical of the war and the sacrifice their relatives had made:

IF THIS IS VICTORY, THEN
LET GOD STOP ALL WARS
HIS LOVING MOTHER[12]

Others are simply heartbreaking; the title of this chapter is taken from one of these epitaphs:

ADIEU DEAR LAD
WHAT NEED OF TEARS
OR FEARS FOR YOU[13]

The objects and artworks in *Passchendaele: Mud and Memory* exploited the significant and specific congruences of time, place and material to create a physical encounter with the excavated personal artefacts of soldiers from both sides of the conflict. The project adopted the methodological strategies of *congruence* (the use of resonant and symbolic objects as the components of a visual narrative which makes connections across time and place) and *encounter* (a confrontation with personal objects and named individuals) to directly engage the audience. The portrait was permanently sited in the visitor centre at Tyne Cot Commonwealth War Graves Cemetery, Passchendaele in January 2020.

Refugee Tales

A further Voices of War and Peace community engagement award enabled Dixon and Magee to develop a multi-media commemorative project in collaboration with project partners The Clay Foundation. *Refugee Tales* (2017–2019) compared and contrasted the parallel experiences of First Word War Belgian refugees with contemporary refugees and asylum seekers in the United Kingdom.

An estimated 250,000 Belgian refugees fled to the United Kingdom following Germany's invasion of Belgium at the beginning of the war (Calahan 1982). Many arrived traumatized and destitute, disembarking from small boats at channel ports in southern England in huge numbers (16,000 in one day at Folkestone on 14 October 1914). They were dispersed across the country to individual family homes and charitable institutions and initially were warmly received; supporting the 'plucky Belgians' was regarded as a patriotic duty. By the end of the war, however, four years of hardship had turned public opinion against such widespread acts of charity, and a parliamentary Repatriation Committee was set up to expedite the return of the refugees to Belgium.

Dixon and Magee engaged refugees and asylum seekers from the Burslem Jubilee Group in Stoke-on-Trent as active co-producers, to co-create a collection of objects and artworks that examined narratives of identity, displacement and refuge. The central premise of the project was based on the impossibility of gaining first-hand insight into the experience of First World War Belgian refugees, now long dead, and that a parallel insight might be gained from the lived experience of a group of contemporary refugees and asylum seekers.

These came from a variety of nations and locations, from Syria, Iraq, Iran, Libya and North Africa to South America. Their first-hand knowledge of displacement and marginalization was initially expressed through hands-on

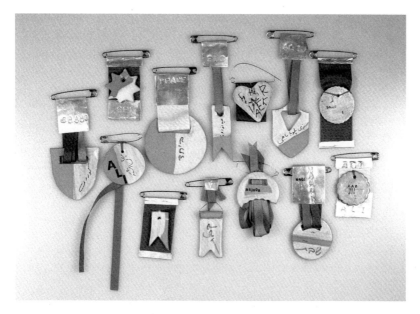

FIGURE 16.9   Stephen Dixon, Johnny Magee and project volunteers, *Medals for Peace* (2015). (© Johnny Magee. Medium: ceramic and mixed media. Dimensions: variable, 8–16 cm high × 4–7 cm wide. Location: Manchester Metropolitan University.)

object-making workshops. These involved responding to historic artefacts relating to Belgian refugees of the First World War, specifically 'support the Belgians' fund-raising badges, medals and postcards, as well as the commemorative peace medals that were minted throughout the United Kingdom at the end of the war. The asylum seekers were particularly keen to focus on commemorating *peace* as opposed to *war* and made their own medals using ceramic, metal and textiles, under the creative direction of Jo Ayre and Elle Simms (Figure 16.9). The workshops resulted in the installation *Medals for Peace*, which was shown as part of the 2017 British Ceramics Biennial. The medals workshops had a positive effect on the participants' sense of worth and well-being, as they were empowered and were given agency as co-creators of the installation.

In parallel sessions, the asylum seekers also took part in creative writing workshops with writer Barry Taylor, producing a collaborative prose poem which captured their experience of conflict, displacement and refuge:

Home
A knock on the door – the neighbour with a dish to end our fast.
Grand-father's house. No work today – we eat, and talk, and watch the
  young ones dancing.
Bright karaoke laughter. Coke in a cold, glinting glass. White pomegranate flesh, and the blood-red seeds.

A roomful of noise and voices. Mother the centre, stirring, handing out
jobs. The youngest bounces across with a fistful of fresh-ground pepper.
A text pings in – a shell's made a mess of the school field. Fetching them
home early through silent streets.
The plates the family ate from, smashed and scattered.

The journey
Hungry, sleepless, the black cold lorry juddering screeching the endless
length of Europe. Roaring black night container, fear cold hungry pain
in every joint, long hours to go and no more money. All taken.
Long way, hard way, lost way.
The pain fills you up, like salt spooned into a glass of water, again and
again. Sometimes you have to pour it out.
Arrived
The smell of our three-times-brewed coffee – filling a Frankfurt basement,
Vienna stairwells, up through the floor of the boy's new room in Stoke.
Remembering is hard.
Green trees, green parks. The rain. I struggled with going from place to place.
I was very new. The rain was new. The sun comes sometimes.
Warmth. New friends. We learn and work the clay, share food. There is
safety here, and hope, and kindness.
The clay is soft, and accepts new shapes – a cup, a plate, a knife, a brooch
with a space for our names. It goes into the fire and hardens. Strong
then, good to use, but breakable. Take care.

The poem was displayed on a scrolling screen alongside the medals for Peace in
the British Ceramics Biennial exhibition and became the catalyst for a further
development of the project. More public workshops were undertaken, in which
the refugees' original hand-written texts were enlarged and made into A4-size
clay letters. These were cast in plaster of Paris to create an alphabet of letter
moulds, which were in turn used to recreate the prose poem on a massive scale.
Additional funding from Manchester Metropolitan University enabled Dixon
and Magee to film the lines of the poem laid out in liminal and lyrical landscape
settings, using drone camera technology. The result was the artist film *Breakable*
(2019) which combined footage from the workshops with film of the poetic
text, and a voice-over by Ayad, one of the refugees (Figure 16.10). The film was
screened at the *Legacies of the First World War Festival* at Midlands Art Centre in
Birmingham,[14] where it challenged audience perceptions of the experiences of
refugees, both historical and contemporary.

Reflections

Reflecting on this body of work, it is clear to see how the artists' roles evolved over
the five projects, and how public participation gradually gained in importance.

FIGURE 16.10 Stephen Dixon, Johnny Magee and project volunteers, *Breakable* (2019. Screen grab from the film. (© Stephen Dixon and Johnny Magee. Photographer Johnny Magee.)

Resonance began as a curatorial commission, with the potential for an additional element of community participation, following a conventional model whereby the public work sits outside of, or at best alongside, the artists' work. However, the collaborative artwork *Column* became a central element of the touring exhibition and established an iterative method based on repeated public workshops that resulted in commemorative objects which in turn contributed to the evolving artwork. This strategy was revisited and built upon in *Passchendaele: Mud and Memory*, where the participants were able to contribute to the artwork by both drawing, printing and transferring their designs onto the installation of facsimile plates. *Resonate* took this further still, by involving volunteers and visitors at all levels and stages of the memorial-making process, from the making of forget-me-nots and the construction of the monumental clay head to the application of floral and written tributes to the installation. And most significantly, the evolution in methodology culminated in *The Lost Boys* and *Refugee Tales*, where participation with a particularly relevant group of participants was at the heart of both projects.

Further reflection, based on the response and feedback from participants and audiences, has revealed some important themes and strategies for further development in future commemorative projects:

- A strong **narrative** was seen as crucial to engaging an audience, and additional textual information was important in contextualizing the artworks.
- **Materiality**, the emotive power of objects to capture the imagination, was an effective strategy, particularly when related to items of popular culture, such as crested china and its connection to *The Beautiful Game*.

- Materiality can also provoke **empathy**, which allows the audience to make an emotive connection with historic individuals' personal possessions and objects of daily use.
- And **lyricality**, in poetry, prose and film, can add another layer of emotive engagement, taking an artwork beyond the realm of hard facts and historical statistics and into the realm of human imagination.

Notes

1 *Resonance: reflections on the Great War through artwork inspired by Staffordshire collections* toured to the Museum of Cannock Chase; Staffordshire County Museum; The Ancient High House; The Potteries Museum and Art Gallery; Brampton Museum; Gladstone Museum and Wedgwood Museum, from March 2015 to April 2016.
2 Also used to great effect by Peter Jackson in the film *They Shall Not Grow Old* (2018).
3 One striking example of this is a crested China piece titled *To Berlin!* which depicts a British Tommy driving a steamroller over the Kaiser.
4 Recently rediscovered in the Staffordshire County Council archives.
5 The members of the public who took part in the workshops were able to collect their commemorative mugs from the relevant host venue at the end of the tour.
6 Based on Jerome Kern's music for the song, *They Didn't Believe Me* (1914). (From the musical *The Girl from Utah*.)
7 This is a direct quote from one of the labels attached to the sculpture, taken from a BBC TV news report (BBC Midlands Today 2015).
8 Lithophanes make use of the translucency of porcelain and bone china to create images by imprinting a relief image into the clay. After firing the image is revelled when illuminated, due to the differential thickness of clay within the imprinted area.
9 The Military Service Act of January 1916 stated that single men aged 18–40 were eligible for military service, though the upper age limit was raised to 51 by the end of the war.
10 These drawings were printed onto Dudsons white-ware using Fotocal transfer paper and a black and white laser photocopier.
11 The relatives of fallen soldiers were invited by the Commonwealth War Graves Commission to add their own personal epitaphs to the base of the headstone. This was subject to a maximum of 66 characters, and a fee of three and a half pence per letter. (The fee was later withdrawn.)
12 Private Frank Hitchin, 59th Battalion, Machine Gun Corps. Grove Town Cemetery, Meaulte, near Albert (Jones 2007: 91).
13 Private Leslie Andrew Sheffield, 17th Battalion, Australian Infantry. Delville Wood Cemetery, Longueval (Jones 2007: 67).
14 *Legacies of the First World War Festival: Diversity*, Hosted by the Arts & Humanities Research Council WW1 Engagement Centres at the Midlands Arts Centre, Birmingham, 22 and 23 March 2019.

References

BBC Midlands Today. (2015) [Television] BBC, 18.30, 11 November.
Brown, M. and S. Seaton. (2001) *Christmas Truce, the Western Front 1914*. London: Pan Macmillan.
Calahan, P. (1982) *Belgian Refugee Relief in England during the Great War*. New York and London: Garland Publishing.

Cook, H. (1970) *The North Staffordshire Regiment (The Prince of Wales's Own)*. London: Leo Cooper.

Jones, T. (2007) *On Fame's Eternal Camping Ground: A Study of First World War Epitaphs in the British Cemeteries of the Western Front*. Pinner, Middlesex: T.G. Jones.

MacDonald, L. (1993) *They Called It Passchendaele: The Story of the Third Battle of Ypres and of the Men Who Fought in It*. London: Penguin.

Southall, R. (1982) *Take Me Back to Dear Old Blighty: the First World War Through the Eyes of the Heraldic China Manufacturers*. Horndean: Milestone Publications.

Van Emden, R. (2012) *Boy Soldiers of the Great War*. London: Bloomsbury.

17

CONTESTED MEMORIES

Exhibiting the Great War in the Ulster Museum, Belfast

Siobhán Doyle

Introduction

The history of Northern Ireland is highly contested. It is also marked with tragedy and suffering, especially during the politically motivated violence, commonly referred to as The Troubles, which took place between 1969 and 1998 and resulted in over 3,500 deaths. Divisions in Northern Irish society have in many ways rendered the past problematic and contested, which has caused a reluctance to commemorate conflict, including the Great War, in its museums. This chapter offers an outline of this reluctance in relation to the Ulster Museum in Belfast, formerly a municipal museum and now a national cultural institution. In a consideration of the display history of the museum with regard to the Great War, this chapter explains how the political redefinition of Northern Ireland paired with significant anniversaries of political events has sparked a new willingness by the Ulster Museum to engage with the contested memory of conflict.

Through a critical examination of the 'Remembering 1916: Your Stories' exhibition held in 2016, I explain how the Ulster Museum presents the Great War through a local perspective. The first days of the Battle of the Somme in 1916 have particular resonance in Northern Ireland as the 36th (Ulster) Division led the Allied troops' attack of the German lines on 1 July 1916 with some 2,000 Ulster men dying on that day (Bryan 2014: 296). The importance of the first days of the Battle of the Somme and the battle's relationship with Ulster identity is carefully examined by analysing the displays of a soldier's bloodstained pocketbook, a photograph of an anonymous casualty and an artwork by James P. Beadle. The mobilization of these images and artefacts in the display demonstrate the multifaceted modes of representing the Great War in the complex political post-conflict society of Northern Ireland.

DOI: 10.4324/9781003263531-21

Ulster Museum and Difficult Histories in Northern Ireland

While the roots of the Ulster Museum can be traced deep into the nineteenth century, it was 1929 that saw the first section of what was then known as the Belfast Museum building opened in the Botanic Gardens, a municipal park south of the city centre and immediately adjoining Queen's University Belfast (Deane 1902: 31). The Museum Act (Northern Ireland) 1961 established the Ulster Museum as a national museum charged with the responsibility of serving all the people of Northern Ireland. Despite the Troubles breaking out in Northern Ireland in 1968 and threatening progress, the Ulster Museum opened its new extension in 1972 and represented 'one of the most significant social and cultural developments to have taken place in Northern Ireland', with the facilities provided equalling if not surpassing those of similar multi-discipline museums in Britain and Western Europe (McCutcheon 1980: 75). The museum was subject to various organizational and governmental changes in the 1990s and early 2000s.[1] Today it is managed by National Museums Northern Ireland (NMNI), who also oversee the Ulster Folk and Transport Museum, Ulster American Folk Park and Armagh County Museum.

The mission of the Ulster Museum is to tell 'the unique human story of this part of Ireland' (National Museums Northern Ireland 2020). As a result of its contemporary collecting policy, the Ulster Museum represents the only public collection of international contemporary ceramics in Ireland, as well as some 40 years of contemporary art in Northern Ireland (NMNI 2015: 7). Historically, the collections of NMNI, which are estimated to be in the region of 1.4 million items, have grown on the site-based framework and are multidisciplinary, diverse and span all time periods, referencing Northern Ireland within and to the wider world (NMNI 2015: 6). These collections are classified within six broad and complementary subject areas of the museum's collections: Art, Emigration, Folk Life and Agriculture, Human History, Transport, Industry and Technology and Natural Sciences.

With regard to collecting and exhibiting conflict in NMNI and the Ulster Museum, Karine Bigand remarks how a 'general avoidance of representing conflictual history [...] could be observed at least until the early 2000s' (Bigand 2017: 43). This was true of historical episodes, such as the 1690s Williamite/Jacobite war and the Famine in the 1840s, but even truer of modern conflict such as the Great War and more recent conflict in Northern Ireland. Further to this, Andrew Sawyer maintains that Northern Ireland's difficult past may be the reason for an absence of policy guidance for its museums, relatively low expenditure and impoverished collections (Sawyer 2011: 625).

There have been several initiatives in addressing Northern Ireland's difficult history and the general reluctance to engage with the subject of conflict. The Consultative Group on the Past, for example, was established by the Northern Ireland Assembly in 2007 to find a way 'to deal fairly with the outstanding legacy of the past without it dominating the future' (Consultative Group on the

Past 2018: 23). The cross-community project 'Healing Through Remembering' surveyed collections of conflict-related artefacts by collaborating with Queen's University Belfast (Healing Through Remembering 2008). Although these initiatives were set up to encourage engagement with more recent conflict particular to Northern Ireland, their existence has impacted upon museological approaches to other conflicts and allowed for a reconsideration of the 1916 Rising and its place in Northern Irish museums as 'an event critical to the history of the island' (Crooke 2015: 194).

In 2009, the Connection and Division project was established with the aims 'to collect material relating to the period 1910–1930 and the impact of the border on those communities...that will help to make links between places, people, events and objects' (Cultural Consulting Network and Heritage Lottery Fund 2009). It also has a wider benefit than simply the project itself, fostering a greater knowledge of the other museums and their future plans. Supported by the National Lottery through the Heritage Lottery Fund, the innovative partnership between Fermanagh County Museum Service, the Inniskillings Museum and Derry Heritage and Museum Service, in collaboration with the University of Ulster/Academy for Irish Cultural Heritages, enabled the three partnership museums to acquire works relating to the period. With a focus on Home Rule, the Great War, 1916 Rising, War of Independence, partition and the Irish Civil War, this initiative allowed for the purchase of artefacts, extensive research, new learning resources and activities, interactive exhibitions and displays. The Connection and Division project marked a willingness amongst museums in Northern Ireland to engage with non-traditional stories, to challenge perceptions of the period and add 'critical mass' to their existing holdings (Crooke 2015: 201).

1916 and Commemorating the Great War in Northern Ireland

1916, the third year of the Great War, saw huge engagements and heavy losses at the Somme, Verdun and Jutland, as both sides sought to strike a decisive blow and end the conflict. In Ireland, while the majority of the public were supportive of the war effort, a small but significant minority were interested in a struggle closer to home as was evidenced on Monday, 24 April, when the 1916 Easter Rising began (National Library of Ireland 2019). Although the Rising was a failure, it has remained a landmark in modern Irish history and of particular importance in Republican rhetoric 'in order to continually reiterate Republicans' opposition to a Unionist history of Northern Ireland' (Graff-McRae 2010: 86). In the context of Northern Ireland, the Battle of the Somme is a 'predominantly Unionist commemorative event' and is often 'used as a symbol of Ulster's commitment to the British Empire' (Higgins 2017: 849). The events of 1916 have since been at the crux of the opposition between Republican and Unionist historical narratives. Previous commemorations of conflict in Northern Ireland had a significant political impact, especially the 50th anniversary of the Rising and the Somme in 1966, which Coleman and Bryan view as having affect upon the emergence of the Troubles two years later (Coleman and Bryan 2015). Importantly, the centenary of both conflicts coincides, giving even more relevance to this particular commemorative context.

While the National Museum of Ireland in Dublin was relatively swift in exhibiting memorabilia from the conflicts of the early twentieth century, with its first exhibition of relics of the Rising in 1932, the Ulster Museum did not act as promptly. It was not until 1941, in the midst of the Second World War, that the Ulster Museum staged art exhibitions such as 'War Artists', directly arising out of the war situation (Nesbitt 1979: 40). 1943 saw a highly successful exhibition on the post-conflict future of Belfast, in which ten architects outlined their visions for a remodelled city (Woodward 2015:136). Thomas Cauvin contends that the Ulster Museum becoming a national institution in the 1960s modified its exhibiting policy and provided new sorts of displays, with the multiplication of commemorative exhibitions accompanied by a change in topics addressed along with the history of politics and wars becoming much more important (Cauvin 2012: 96–97).

The museum exhibited more comprehensive displays of military nature, with one held in 1964 to mark the 50th and 25th anniversaries of the two world wars, the other in 1966 to mark the 50th anniversary of the Battle of the Somme (Nesbitt 1979: 56). The 'Somme Anniversary Exhibition' ran from 1 July to 31 August 1966 and featured a 'small' display of medals, badges, uniforms, weapons and documents, with particular reference made to the part played by the Ulster Division (Seaby 1966: 9). The exhibition provided heroic Unionist narratives of the Great War and the Museum report stressed that 'the theme of the exhibition was particularly the part played by the 36th (Ulster) Division in the initial attack on 1 and 2 July 1916' (Ulster Museum 1966: 17). The 36th Ulster Division suffered over 2,000 fatalities on 1 July 1916 and these deaths gained a powerful political meaning, especially in Northern Ireland, as they brought about a shared trauma (Orr 2014: 20–21).

This emphasis on the association between Ulster and the 36th Division was what Cauvin describes as 'the traditional mark of a political discourse that excluded Catholics from the Ulster past, marking a new role of the museum in representing the whole province of Ulster' (Cauvin 2012: 99). The exhibition emphasized heroic narratives of the Battle of the Somme by dedicating an entire panel to 'some stories of outstanding heroism of individuals'.[2] Further, any artefact that did not focus on the 36th Ulster Division was removed by Noel Nesbitt – the librarian in charge of the display and of the local history collections, resulting in the detriment of the 16th or the 10th Irish Divisions who also fought in 1916 but which were mostly composed of Catholics (Cauvin 2012: 99). [3] This exclusion is an example of what Guy Beiner attains as the memory of the Somme being dominated by Ulster Protestants and explicitly excluding Catholics from the commemorative process (Beiner 2007). In other words, the Ulster Museum created commemorative barriers by presenting heroic narratives of one particular collective in the Great War during its jubilee exhibition.

The outbreak of political violence in Northern Ireland in 1968 diminished public interest in commemorating modern conflict in the Ulster Museum. John Turpin describes how historical events that were 'once safely commemorated' in Northern Ireland had then become 'all too contemporary and real' (Turpin 2007: 111). The prospect of creating exhibitions commemorating conflict proved so problematic that virtually none were constructed from the 1960s until the 1990s. The temporary exhibition in 1966 remains the only instance where the Great War was subject to a dedicated, singular exhibition within the Ulster Museum.

A Centenary Exhibition

The centrepiece of NMNI's First World War centenary programme was the exhibition 'Remembering 1916: Your Stories'. It was produced in conjunction with the *Living Legacies 1914–18* First World War Engagement Centre and Queen's University Belfast. Co-production was a defining characteristic of this exhibition, which featured a selection of objects identified during community collecting roadshows staged across Northern Ireland over the two years leading up to the exhibition. The temporary exhibition was on show for 12 months, opening in April 2016 alongside a programme of events, workshops, screenings, tours and lectures. 'Remembering 1916: Your Stories' marked a new focus in commemorating conflict at the Ulster Museum. No longer segregating conflict, the exhibition team set out to break down historical barriers by approaching 1916 as a tumultuous year, where the Great War and the Easter Rising are displayed alongside one another for the first time. The objective is to offer a representative overview of the iconic events of 1916 by considering the impact of war and revolution on society as a whole. The exhibition located in Room 13, comprised two audiovisual displays, one video-based display (without audio), one interactive touchscreen table, text panels, reproduced images and six floor-standing display cases. These displays were grouped into four main sections: 'War and Society', 'The Easter Rising', 'Battle of the Somme' and 'Legacy'.

The choice of the Battle of the Somme in particular to encompass an entire display case in the exhibition is no doubt due to the significance of this event in the historical discourse of Northern Ireland. Thomas Hennessey remarked that 'if any one event in the Great War might be selected as the moment which symbolised the psychological partition of Ulster Unionism from the rest of the island, it was probably the impact of the Battle of the Somme' (Hennessey 1998: 198). Furthermore, the exploits of the 36th (Ulster) Division at the Somme in July 1916 became the foundational narrative of the new Northern Irish state (Evershed 2015: 27). Crucial to constructing these historical narratives and shaping memories of the Somme were photographs, which provided a means to view and imaginatively connect with wartime experiences.

FIGURE 17.1 The view towards the German lines on 1 July 1916, with casualty in foreground. Jim Maultsaid. (© National Museums NI, Collection Ulster Museum.)

Photography plays a particular role in the exhibition as photographs are not only stand-alone artefacts in the displays, but are also reproduced on a large scale and used as backdrops to the four large display cases. The large-scale photograph in the background of the 'Battle of the Somme' display case captures the German lines during the advance on the first day of the battle but due to the size of the artefacts presented, most of the photograph is obscured. Crucially, the only element of the image that is not obscured by an artefact or display text is a casualty lying in the foreground (Figure 17.1). In a discussion of war photography, Susan Sontag contends that injured bodies are the frankest representations of war and indicates that images may be too terrible and need to be suppressed in the name of propriety or of patriotism (Sontag 2003: 55–57). The photograph displayed is candid, but the realities of conflict and human mortality inherent in the image are associated with an anonymous soldier, rather than a named individual.

Many aspects of the first day of the battle on 1 July 1916 throughout the exhibition emphasize the role of local Ulster men and their sacrifice. One of these is Private Adam Stewart, a member of the 10th Royal Iniskilling Fusiliers from Derry who was killed in action on that first day. Located in the centre of the exhibition space are two table top display cases, one of which features pages

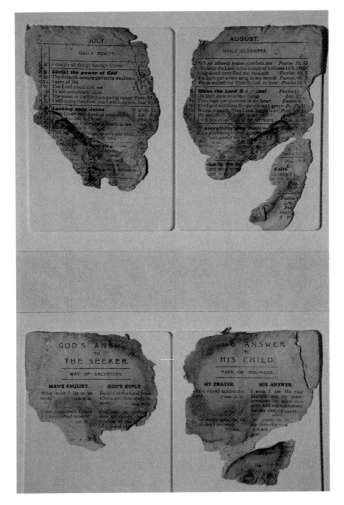

FIGURE 17.2 Bloodstained pocketbook belonging to Private Adam Stewart. (© National Museums NI.)

from Stewart's bloodstained pocket book and the next of kin memorial plaque of another soldier who died during the first days of the Somme (Figure 17.2). The arrangement of the pristine bronze plaque in the centre of the table-top display case creates a juxtaposition with the fragile, dismembered condition of the ten pages from the pocket book, which have become creased, torn, stained and dog-eared, possibly as a result of Stewart's blood spilling onto them as 'changes in the moisture content' can cause such damage (Conservation Register 2019).

The bloodstained pages detached from the pocket book had 'a powerful impact' on visitors to the exhibition, many of whom singled out the artefact in self-completion questionnaires (National Museums Northern Ireland 2016: 10). Visitors describe this artefact as 'emotional', 'a sad strangely beautiful object' and 'particularly powerful as it helps portray the human aspect of war' (National Museums Northern Ireland 2016: 10). The pocket book and specifically the bloodstains that are visible represent what Patrizia Violi states as a direct link with the past that is activated by the indexicality of the objects present at the time of the event being commemorated (Violi 2012: 39). This indexicality, Violi expands, is signified by traces of the past that are endowed with a direct, causal connection with the particular embodied instance that, at a particular time, produced them (Violi 2012: 39). In this instance, the blood that Stewart shed because of being caught in shellfire during the Battle of the Somme maintains, so to speak, an embodied memory of the actual event that caused the marks of indexicality.[4]

Despite the visible traces of use in the bloodstained pages in the display case positioned in the middle of the exhibition space, their indexical agency is contradicted by the unblemished contents of the other display cases. The thematic narratives of the large display cases are illustrated using uniforms, weapons and other items of equipment. The uniforms such as the German medic uniform in the 'War and Society' display case is in pristine condition with no visible scuffs or traces of use (Figure 17.3). Similarly, the documents, medals and badges in the displays are also practically unblemished and in excellent condition. In fact, the only other items with visible traces of use during conflict in the entire exhibition are in the display of objects recovered from the Somme battlefields. The entrenching tool, pieces of shrapnel and cartridge cases are displayed in a rusty

FIGURE 17.3 'War and Society' display case in *Remembering 1916: Your Stories* exhibition, Ulster Museum (2016). (© National Museums NI.)

condition, which prevents them from being considered in purely aesthetic terms. The lack of artefacts with visible traces of use or indexicality of conflict ensures that the displays are somewhat sanitized and avoid any visually obvious reflection on the devastation of war. This approach to display adheres to Ralf Raths' cautioning that the overt display of violence can actually have a detrimental effect on the learning process if it delivers a shock to the visitor (Raths 2013).

An Iconic Painting

Displayed in the 'Legacy' section is a print of James Prinsep Barnes Beadle's artwork *The Battle of the Somme – Attack of the Ulster Division*. This 'academic battle picture' shows the first wave of troops from the 5th Battalion Royal Irish Rifles, a section of the Ulster Division advancing on the German reserve lines, having already breached the first line of defence (Malvern 2004: 67) (Figure 17.4). In the period between the advance itself and the public unveiling of the painting in Belfast in July 1918, there was no visual image to assist the public in imagining what had happened to the Ulster Division on the slopes north of Thiepval, making the artwork an important record of the Great War (Switzer 2007: 99).

Many descriptions of the painting emphasize the depiction of a young officer who is the main central figure in the painting. The display text in 'Remembering 1916: Your Stories' reads:

> One of 1,000 signed prints of a painting by J P Beadle that were produced and sold to raise money for the UVF Patriotic Fund, the UVF Hospital for Limbless Soldiers and the Ulster Prisoners of War Fund. The scene depicts troops from the 5th Battalion Royal Irish Rifles, a section of the

FIGURE 17.4 *The Battle of the Somme – The Attack of the Ulster Division*. J.P. Beadle (1916). (© National Museums NI, Collection Ulster Museum.)

Ulster Division, being led over the top by Lieutenant Francis Bodenham Thornley during the Battle of the Somme. Lt. Thornley was wounded and advised Beadle on the composition of the painting during his recovery. The original painting was presented to the Belfast Corporation in 1918 and hangs in Belfast City Hall.

The display text accompanying the print focuses on the provenance of the print, composition of the original painting and Thornely's recovery after leading the troops. In failing to mention the 5,482 casualties sustained by the Division during the action and highlighting Thornely's role, the display masks the real consequences of the event in order to coincide with the overall optimistic narrative of the 'Legacy' display.

The artist focuses on the most successful phase of 36th Ulster Division's attack on 1 July 1916 and, despite his application of 'illustrative realism' to this exceptionally violent scene, death is not much in evidence. One of the 'bombers' spearheading the advance with bags of hand grenades is shown in the act of being wounded or killed and, almost hidden at the bottom left, a clearly dead German soldier lies in the captured first line trench. Given that the print is displayed in the 'Legacy' section as the exhibition moves to a post-war narrative, a depiction of the enemy soldier in this humanized, fragile way is deemed appropriate. This curatorial strategy of displaying the enemy in distress is implemented here because, firstly, the enemy is no longer a threat and secondly because visitors can comprehend that the enemy suffered during conflict, which influences a more empathetic approach (Bogumil et al 2015: 45). Furthermore, Beadle's painting is an artistic representation of the conflict that understates the physical strains of war for the Allies and indicates the bravery of Thornely and his comrades.

The artwork had a strong Ulster connection from the outset. Beadle's decision to depict the Ulster Division may have been due to his family association with the area as his wife was a daughter of Mr J.A.M. Cope of Drumilly, County Armagh, and his cousin Lieutenant-Colonel McNamara was fatally wounded on 1 July 1916, leading the 1st Royal Irish Rifles at Ovillers-la-Boisselle on the Somme (Belfast Telegraph 1934: 7). Even before the first anniversary of the events it depicted, a committee of prominent Unionists purchased the painting and donated it to the City of Belfast in 1918 (Switzer 2007: 100). The Ulster Volunteer Force (UVF) were 'most anxious' to assist in making a profit for war charities by the sale of engravings of the picture (*Belfast Newsletter* 1918: 2). A committee chaired by politician and former Major in the 4th Battalion of Royal Inniskilling Fusiliers Sir James Stronge was appointed to oversee the reproduction and sale of 1,000 copies of the painting, with the profits allocated to three charities (Blair 2016: 207–208). Beadle spent a great deal of time in arranging for these reproductions, as well as signing 250 of the artist's proofs free of charge (*Belfast Newsletter* 1918: 2). Sales were 'disappointing' and the committee distributed the remainder of them to ex-servicemen's clubs on the condition that 'they would frame them and hang them in a prominent position'.[5]

Despite the lack of commercial interest in the officially produced prints, over time the image has entered the realm of popular visual memory of the Great War and has become 'the dominant visual representation of the Battle of the Somme in Northern Ireland' (Switzer 2007: 99). The focus on Thornely and his recovery in the Ulster Museum display correlates with the themes in the 'Legacy' section: reconciliation, survival and hope in a post-conflict society. The memory of the soldiers who did not survive the advance seeks room within the hero worship of Thornely that colours the confident narrative of the 'Legacy' display.

Narratives of Reconciliation

1916 has become part of the political and cultural identity of Northern Ireland and during the past 100 years, the events of this period have been marked in different ways. The 'Legacy' display case aims to materialize the public memory of both the Rising and the Somme by displaying medals, commemorative memorabilia and photographs of memorials, murals and commemorative events. The use of large-scale colour photographs in the background of the case moves the narrative to a more contemporary interpretation of events and informs visitors that this case differs from the other three in the exhibition (Figure 17.5). The introductory text of this section uses the present tense, as opposed to the past tense as used in the other display cases. By positioning the narrative in the present, the exhibit infers a lived experience and invites visitors to connect with the content. The subject of the text also moves from the objective to the personal collective pronoun by using terms such as 'our homes', 'our political and cultural identity' and 'our present and future'. This is an example of what Jenny Kidd

FIGURE 17.5 'Legacy' display case in *Remembering 1916: Your Stories* exhibition, Ulster Museum (2016). (© National Museums NI.)

acknowledges as museums becoming sites of identity construction for collective and personal memories in the present as opposed to merely sites for exploration of identities past (Kidd 2014: 3–4).

An emphasis on (re)conciliation in the 'Legacy' section is evident through the inclusion of photographs of Sinn Féin's participation in commemorating the Somme at Belfast City Hall in 2008 and Queen Elizabeth II's visit to the Garden of Remembrance in 2011, which Edward Madigan describes as 'a truly meaningful gesture of conciliation' (Madigan 2013: 2). Belfast's strong tradition of commemorative murals is represented by images of a nationalist mural on Beechmount Avenue depicting an armed Volunteer in front of the GPO with a tricolour background. A photograph of a Unionist mural on Thiepval Street portraying a Great War soldier beside the crest of the 36th Ulster Division and a portrait of Unionist leader Edward Carson surrounded by commemorative poppies is also presented in the displayed image.

The photographs of these murals embody the contemporary artistic legacy of the Rising and the Great War in the city and further emphasize the community aspects of commemoration within the exhibition. Given that such murals are 'the public representation of community separation', in the form of 'public symbolic displays', these images have been carefully selected so as to avoid any religious signifiers, which are often a common characteristic of murals in Belfast (Arts Council Northern Ireland 2016). The five photographs in the 'Legacy' case positioned together take the form of a mural itself as it articulates current issues and historical concerns into a single visual statement by combining a retrospective collage of images which have become iconic and which have been taken from different media.

Conclusion

The Ulster Museum has, for a long period, provided Unionist interpretations of the past and focused on a politicized version of the Battle of the Somme as the key event in Ulster's early twentieth century history. The merging of the Great War and the 1916 Easter Rising into one exhibition for the centenary marked a milestone in the Ulster Museum's commemorative history. Given the strong Ulster connection and depth of the museum and community collections in representing the Somme, the narrative focuses upon commemorating local individuals, as demonstrated in the display of Private Adam Stewart's bloodstained pocketbook and Beadle's artwork *The Battle of the Somme – Attack of the Ulster Division* (1916). The 'Legacy' display case further strengthens the local significance of the conflict and aligns the Great War and its commemoration with contemporary politics and narratives of reconciliation in Northern Ireland.

Dominic Bryan acknowledges how commemorations of the Somme have been closely allied to the Unionist tradition but since the Good Friday Agreement in 1998, an intensified process of commemoration has developed, one that is more inclusive and powerful now that the Irish government have become participants in official remembering processes (Bryan 2014: 296–309). The 'Remembering

1916: Your Stories' exhibition reveals how the political redefinition of Northern Ireland paired with significant anniversaries sparked a new willingness to present narratives of conflict through display, which can be a meaningful practice. Considering the complex historical, societal and institutional dynamics in Northern Ireland, the centenary exhibition at the Ulster Museum marks a significant transformation in commemorative traditions, especially in light of the institution's previous avoidance of mounting exhibitions on the subject of conflict. Furthermore, there is a public interest for acknowledging the Great War as pivotal for understanding contemporary politics in Northern Ireland. The reconfiguration of commemorative boundaries in the Ulster Museum speaks today of a more tolerant and inclusive political attitude to the memory of the events of 1916 and the Great War.

Acknowledgements

Thanks you to Dr Niamh Ann Kelly and Dr Tim Stott (Technological University Dublin) for their advice and comments. Thanks are also due to Stephen Weir (NMNI) for his help with image copyrights. The photographs are by kind permission of NMNI.

Notes

1 In 1998, the Ulster Museum came under the aegis of the umbrella organization Museums and Galleries of Northern Ireland (MAGNI), whose funding came principally from the Department of Culture, Arts and Leisure. MAGNI was established under the *Museums and Galleries (Northern Ireland) Order* (1998) and merged four long established museums: Ulster Museum, Ulster Folk and Transport Museum, Ulster American Folk Park and Armagh County Museum. In 2006, National Museums Northern Ireland took over from MAGNI in overseeing these museums.
2 Texts and panels from the 1966 exhibition, *The Battle of the Somme*, National Museums Northern Ireland Archives, Cultra.
3 While the 36th (Ulster) Division was made up of members of the Ulster Volunteer Force, mostly Protestants and against the Home Rule, other Irish fought in the 10th (Irish) and 16th (Irish) Divisions. They were mostly members of the National Volunteers, Catholics and in favour of the Home Rule.
4 See also the parallel popularity of a bloodstained jacket displayed in IWM London's First World War Galleries (Cornish 2017: 25).
5 Ulster Unionist Council Somme Sub Committee: Entry on 8 September 1921 and 5 November 1923, D/1327/15/1, Public Records Office Northern Ireland, Belfast.

References

Arts Council Northern Ireland. (2016) *Evaluation of the Re-imaging Communities Programme: A Report to the Arts Council of Northern Ireland.* http://www.artscouncil-ni.org/images/uploads/publications-documents/BPttA_Final_Programme_Evaluation.pdf. Accessed 17 January 2020.
———. (2009) *Evaluation of the Re-imaging Communities Programme: A Report to the Arts Council of Northern Ireland.* Lisburn: Arts Council Northern Ireland.

Beiner, G. (2007) Between trauma and triumphalism: The Easter Rising, the Somme, and the Crux of Deep Memory in Modern Ireland. *Journal of British Studies* 46 (2):366–389.

Belfast Newsletter. (1918) The Ulster Division: Memento of the Somme Battle: Painting Unveiled in Belfast. 2 July.

Belfast Telegraph. (1934) A Famous Picture: Ulster Division Charge: Exhibit in Council Chamber. 2 July.

Bigand, K. (2017) The role of museums in dealing with the legacy of the troubles in Northern Ireland. *RISE – Review of Irish Studies in Europe, 2017, Memory and Trauma in Post-Agreement Northern Ireland* 1 (2):40–53.

Blair, W. (2016) Myth, Memory and Material Culture: Remembering 1916 at the Ulster Museum. In R.S. Grayson and F. McGarry (eds.), *Remembering 1916: The Easter Rising, the Somme and the Politics of Memory in Ireland*, pp 194–216. Cambridge: Cambridge University Press. https://books.google.ie/books?id=fGbiCwAAQBAJ.

Bogumil, Z., J. Wawrzyniak,, T. Buchen, C. Ganzer and M. Senina (2015) *The Enemy on Display: The Second World War in Eastern European Museums*. New York: Berghahn Books.

Bryan, D. (2014) Forget 1690, Remember the Somme: Ulster Loyalist Battles in the Twenty-first Century. In O. Frawley (ed.), *Memory Ireland Volume 3: The Famine and the Troubles*, pp 293–309. New York: Syracuse University Press.

Cauvin, T. (2012) *National Museums and the Mobilization of History: Commemorative Exhibitions of Anglo-Irish Conflicts in Ireland and Northern Ireland (1921–2006)*. PhD diss., European University Institute. https://cadmus.eui.eu/handle/1814/24601.

Coleman, M. and D. Bryan. (2015) *Northern Ireland's 2016: Approaching the contested commemoration of the Easter Rising and the Battle of the Somme, Northern Ireland Assembly*. http://www.niassembly.gov.uk/globalassets/documents/raise/knowledge_exchange/briefing_papers/series5/bryan-coleman-.pdf. Accessed 28 January 2019.

Consultative Group on the Past. (2018) *Report of the Consultative Group on the Past*. http://cain.ulst.ac.uk/victims/docs/consultative_group/cgp_230109_report.pdf. Accessed 13 January 2020.

Conservation Register. (2019) *Care and Conservation of Books*. http://conservationregister.com/downloads/books.pdf. Accessed 13 January 2020.

Cornish, P. (2017) Sensing War: Concept and Space in Imperial War Museums' First World War Galleries. In N.J. Saunders and P. Cornish (eds.), *Modern Conflict and the Senses*, pp 13–28. London: Routledge.

Crooke, E. (2015) A Story of Absence and Recovery: The Easter Rising in Museums in Northern Ireland. In L. Godson and J. Brück (eds.), *Making 1916: Material and Visual Culture of the 1916 Rising*, pp 194–202. Liverpool: Liverpool University Press.

Cultural Consulting Network and Heritage Lottery Fund. (2009) *Collecting Cultures Programme Evaluation Year One 2009*. https://www.heritagefund.org.uk/sites/default/files/media/research/collecting_cultures_evaluation_year_01.pdf. Accessed 17 January 2020.

Deane, A. (1902) Ireland's First Museum. In, *Guide to Belfast and the Counties of Down and Antrim by the Belfast Naturalists' Field Club*. Belfast: Linen Hall Press.

Evershed, J. (2015) From Past Conflict to Shared Future?: Commemoration, peacebuilding and the politics of Loyalism during Northern Ireland's 'Decade of Centenaries'. *International Political Anthropology* 8 (2):25–42.

Graff-McRae, R. (2010) *Remembering and Forgetting 1916: Commemoration and Conflict in Post-Peace Process Ireland*. Dublin/Portland (OR): Irish Academic Press.

Healing Through Remembering. (2008) *Artefacts Audit: A report of the material culture of the conflict in and about Northern Ireland*. http://web-previews.com/healingthroughremembering/wp-content/uploads/2015/11/HTR_Artefacts_Audit.pdf. Accessed 8 August 2018.

Hennessey, T. (1998) *Dividing Ireland: World War I and Partition*. London: Routledge.

Higgins, R. (2017) Commemoration and the Irish Revolution. In J. Crowley, D.Ó. Drisceoil, M. Murphy and J. Borgonovo (eds.), *Atlas of the Irish Revolution*, pp 848–856. Cork: Cork University Press.

Kidd, J. (2014) Introduction: Challenging History in the Museum. In J. Kidd, S. Cairns, A. Drago, A. Ryall and M. Stearn (eds.), *Challenging History in the Museum: International Perspectives*, pp 1–17. Surrey/Burlington: Ashgate.

Madigan, E. (2013) Introduction. In J. Horne and E. Madigan (eds.), *Towards Commemoration: Ireland in War and Revolution 1912–1923*, pp 1–8. Dublin: Royal Irish Academy.

Malvern, S. (2004) *Modern Art, Britain and the Great War*. New Haven/London: Yale University Press.

McCutcheon, W.A. (1980). The Ulster Museum. *The Canadian Journal of Irish Studies* 6 (2): 74–78.

National Library of Ireland. (2019) *World War I in Ireland 1914–1918*. National Library of Ireland. http://www.nli.ie/wwi/. Accessed 13 January 2020.

National Museums Northern Ireland. (2015) *Collections Development Policy*. Belfast: National Museums Northern Ireland.

National Museums Northern Ireland. (2016) *Evaluation of Remembering 1916: Your Stories, Ulster Museum, Belfast, 2016*. Belfast: National Museums Northern Ireland.

National Museums Northern Ireland. (2020) *About National Museums NI*. https://www. nmni.com/Corporate-information/About-us.aspx. Accessed 13 January 2020.

Nesbitt, N. (1979) *A Museum in Belfast: A History of the Ulster Museum and its Predecessors*. Belfast: Ulster Museum.

Orr, P. (2014) Remembering the Somme. In D. MacBride (ed.), *Remembering 1916: Challenges for Today: The Easter Rising, the Battle of the Somme and the First World War*, pp 20–25. Belfast: Community Relations Council and Heritage Lottery Fund.

Raths, Ralf. (2013) From Technical Showroom to Full-fledged Museum: The German Tank Museum Munster. In W. Muchitsch (ed.) *Does War Belong in Museums?: The Representation of Violence in Exhibitions*, pp 83–98. Bielefeld: Transcript Verlag.

Sawyer, A. (2011) National Museums in Northern Ireland. In P. Aronsson and G. Elgenius (eds.), *Building National Museums in Europe 1750–2010, Conference Proceedings from EuNaMus, European National Museums: Identity, Politics, the Uses of the Past and the European Citizen, Bologna 28–30 April 2011, EuNaMus report no. 1*, pp 625–652. Linköping: Linköping University Press.

Seaby, W.A. (1966) Somme Exhibition. *Irish Times: March* 3: 9.

Sontag, S. (2003) *Regarding the Pain of Others*. London: Penguin.

Switzer, C. (2007) *Unionists and Great War Commemoration in the north of Ireland 1914–1939: People, Places and Politics*. Dublin/Portland (OR): Irish Academic Press.

Turpin, J. (2007) Monumental Commemoration of the Fallen in Ireland, North and South, 1920–60. *New Hibernia Review* 11 (4): 107–119.

Ulster Museum. (1966) *Ulster Museum Annual Report 1966–1967*. Belfast: Ulster Museum.

Ulster Unionist Council Somme Sub Committee: Entry on September 8, 1921 and November 5, 1923. D/1327/15/1, Public Records Office Northern Ireland, Belfast.

Violi, P. (2012) Trauma site museums and politics of memory: Tuol Sleng, Villa Grimaldi and the Bologna Ustica Museum. *Theory, Culture & Society* 29 (1):36–75.

Woodward, G. (2015) *Culture, Northern Ireland and the Second World War*. Oxford: Oxford University Press.

18

THE PREDICAMENT OF MATERIAL CULTURE

In situ legacies of the Isonzo Front after the First World War centenary (2014–2018)

Boštjan Kravanja

The past three decades have seen a tremendous progress in heritagization of the legacies of the Great War's Isonzo Front in the Soča Valley, Slovenia. Its *in situ* remains, such as fortifications, trenches, shelters, caverns and military roads, have been turned into a big thematic landscape, which was upgraded with memorial structures during the all-European marking of the First World War centenary (2014–2018). Managed by a group of local enthusiasts, a well-promoted heritage brand – the *Walk of Peace from the Alps to Adriatic* – was created on the basis of these remains (Walk of Peace 2017; and see Cimprić, this volume).

Interpretation and presentation of these legacies resulted in a great increase in knowledge about the Isonzo Front. Numerous thematic exhibitions that followed the initial exhibition cycle of nations involved in the Isonzo Front discussed different aspects of life during the First World War in Slovenia.[1] Themes such as life in the hinterlands, the political role of women, the role of animals on the front, photographic collections, diaries, the life of residents in exile and reconstruction after the war were presented. An important orientation of these carefully considered public representations was a sensitive and contextual approach towards different people who suffered because of the First World War (Svoljšak 1993).

Local heritage managers were, here as elsewhere (Gegner and Ziino 2012: 4), the final arbiters of the process that integrated the place itself into these changing structures of heritage interpretation. They were aware that the Isonzo Front heritage will require continued support by national and supranational structures, as has been the case since the 2000s (Clarke et al 2017; Kravanja 2018a). But they were equally aware that the Walk of Peace has much potential to develop independently, because the local stakeholders have always been motivated to integrate the story of the Isonzo Front into the wider tourism development that correspondingly also started in the Soča Valley in the 2000s.

DOI: 10.4324/9781003263531-22

In this long-term process of heritagization of the Isonzo Front, amateur collectors of military artefacts, heritage associations and individual enthusiasts of the First World War can be considered as founding fathers of this project (during the early 1990s). Their enthusiasm, knowledge and work are still important in the maintenance of the front's material legacies today. However, as the project has grown, a new generation of stakeholders appeared and the older one changed, as the evolving contexts of heritage and tourism trends demanded new approaches and flexibility, such as common European values, cultural tourism, heritage marketing, difficult contents and the popularity of authentic legacies *in situ*.

The engagement with the Isonzo Front that had been the norm among the older generation of stakeholders – often focused on wartime events specific to the locality or founded upon an interest in the military equipment of the era – was gradually superseded by an engagement that promoted commemoration of the victims and a cosmopolitan 'agonistic mode of remembering' the First World War (Cento-Bull and Hansen 2016). However, the narrative that had grown out of the hobbies and military-historical passions of the original stakeholders survived within the heritage structures and was indeed further nourished in their small military heritage sites and amateur collections of military equipment. These materials, therefore, supported a sort of 'cannonball history' (Sutton 2012: 113) that could not be omitted from the Isonzo Front heritage narrative, but adjusted to the new circumstances that used the marking of the centenary of the First World War for promotion of the common European identity.

As the Walk of Peace was firmly set into the complex networks that established these conceptual and cultural orders of European solidarity, a gap emerged between the physical places and their social construction within local frameworks. This gap can be described with Foucauldian heterotopia, a concept that 'reflects on how potentially regulative these collective modes and practices are' (Meijer-van Mensch 2017: 25).[2] A potential unwanted result of this heterotopic gap is therefore the consolidation of material culture in a 'unified space', a 'homogeneous "monster"'(ibid.) that suppresses the subjectivity, creativity, passion, inspiration and enthusiasm of different stakeholders, amateur associations and collectors instead of being inspired by them (Meijer-van Mensch 2017: 26–27).

It is in the nature of this 'unified' space to inexorably contextualize all of the local heritage relative to the overarching precepts that it promotes. However, it also gives birth to a set of discourses between it and 'excluded' spaces, such as private collections of war objects, open-air museums on wartime sites and war-related tourist attractions. The dynamics of the heterotopic gap between the forthright military culture of the Isonzo Front conflict landscape and the consciously humanistic, scholarly and politically aware public representations that form the officially approved norm have yet to be fully analysed. The predicament of material culture in the title of this chapter refers to the field of management and entrepreneurship of the Isonzo Front heritage, where the ways of overcoming the above dichotomy have been explored through maintenance, invention and giving meaning to its material legacies.

Locally specific narrative about events on the Isonzo Front

The locally specific narrative refers to the history of events that happened in this area during the 888 days of the Isonzo Front's existence. The front was formed in May 1915, when Italy declared war against Austro-Hungarian Empire and was superseded in November 1917, when the Austro-Hungarian and German forces pushed the Italian army back 170 kilometres west to the Piave River. This battle, the Twelfth Offensive, today also known as the 'breakthrough at Caporetto', the 'miracle at Caporetto' (Koren 2015: 17–19) or even 'the greatest highland battle in the human history' (cited in Kravanja 2014: 93), has persisted as one of the guiding threads since the beginnings the Isonzo Front heritagization in the 1990s. It is symbolized in the logo of the Kobarid Museum of the First World War, founded in Kobarid, the Slovenian name for the Italian *Caporetto* in 1990.

The story of this battle that newly defined the identity of Kobarid (Kravanja 2014: 102–103) also facilitated the town's tourism development, which started in an organized way 10 years after the establishment of the museum. However, the locally specific narrative about the Isonzo Front does not consist only of its key 1917 battle, but points also to the extraordinariness of the First World War in this mountainous region. It demands local expertise that had already started to develop in the 1980s, when the first modern collectors of military artefacts appeared in the Upper Soča Valley.

Today, the old amateur collectors are still considered as local experts, not only on the material remains of the Isonzo Front, but on its topography. They are the founding fathers of the Isonzo Front heritage, from whom the curators of the Kobarid Museum learned much as they began their work. But, of course, the latter drew upon a wider range of sources for their representation of the Battle of Caporetto. Official documents, photographs, cartographic materials and more were obtained from different archives and other war museums in the wider region (see note 1). The battle has been the museum's headline story since its establishment,[3] but was never emphasized in its interpretation of the Isonzo Front, which rather highlighted the tragedy of ordinary men and their personal stories. The sheer brutality of war (and the battle) was used to convey the emotional antiwar message and not to glorify any of its aspects.

This humanized, but not demilitarized, way of presenting war brought the museum swift recognition: apart from receiving the highest Slovenian museum award in 1992, the museum was nominated for the European Museum of the Year in 1993 and the Council of Europe Museum Prize for 1993. At the awarding ceremony in Strasbourg the representative of The European Museum of the Year Award Committee Friedrich Waidacher, said:

> In the course of my professional career, I visited hundreds of museums, among them war museums. Kobarid was the first one where I could not find the slightest trace of chauvinism, bias, or glorification. Its display is deeply touching. It takes its visitors by their hearts and souls and conveys

a message which cannot be disseminated too often and too loud: war is insanity, crime, it only generates victims.

(Kobarid Museum 2018)

Indeed, the front claimed the lives of about 3,00,000 soldiers of more than 20 nationalities, which were brought to the front from different parts of the Austro-Hungarian Empire, Germany and Italy (Slovenian Press Agency 2015–2020; Klavora 2016: 134). It also deeply affected the civilian population: many residents of nearby towns and villages were evacuated to various parts of the Austro-Hungarian Empire and Italy (Sedmak 1997: 91–92). Finally, the front also profoundly changed the landscape of the Soča Valley; its consequences were inscribed into the valley as different 'layers of conflict landscapes' throughout the twentieth century until today, when its neatly arranged and promoted legacies serve the purposes of remembering, connecting and educating (see Saunders et al 2013).

Due to this complexity of the whole story, the local military operations and events could only ever be a small part of it. However, the Twelfth Offensive was not an ordinary battle, but a multilayered and widespread operation that has always inspired local historians, amateur collectors, First World War enthusiasts, military experts and also numerous visitors to the museum.[4] Incidentally, the establishment of the museum at Kobarid helped cement the identity of the Twelfth Battle of the Isonzo as the 'Battle of Caporetto'. While it had long been known as such in Italy and the Anglophone world, German and Austro-Hungarian military documents always emphasized the breakthroughs made at Tolmin and Bovec and not at Kobarid (Dovjak 2018; Torkar and Kuhar 2018). Thus the museum altered both the identity of the town and, to an extent, the historiography of the Isonzo Front.

Cosmopolitan and commemorative narrative about the meaning of the Isonzo Front

Ten years after the Kobarid Museum was founded, a sister institution named the Walk of Peace in the Soča Region Foundation was established. The Foundation was meant to become the scientific centre for Isonzo Front heritage and the umbrella manager of its well-preserved legacies in the surrounding mountains. Its establishment was extensively supported by the Slovenian state and European cross-border programmes (Kravanja 2018a). The Foundation coordinated restoration and arrangement of military infrastructures, cemeteries, sacral objects, ossuaries and memorials. Over subsequent years, it added commemorative parks and monuments to these sites (see Klavora 2016). In 2015, the 100-kilometre Walk of Peace of the Upper Soča Valley was extended to create a 300-kilometre Walk of Peace from the Alps to the Adriatic (see Čimpric, this volume). The trail became a thematic landscape with 15 outdoor museums on both sides of the former Slovenian-Italian border and a host of memorial infrastructures that were built primarily for commemorative use (Testen and Koren 2015: 193).

The Foundation also bound the Isonzo Front heritage into the institutional landscape of numerous heritage-related organizations and associations that had developed into a vast network in the preceding 20 years. Apart from local and cross-border programmes and projects, this network included national and European interests (Clarke et al 2017) as well as many scientific and humanistic endeavours. An emphasis on the First World War suffering of soldiers and residents was part of the scholarly narratives of historians, professional museum curators and national institutions that helped establish this renewed engagement with the Isonzo Front's heritage (Svoljšak 1993). The First World War also became a prominent subject for military scholars, political scientists, archaeologists and anthropologists (Hudales and Roženbergar 2017; Jezernik and Fikfak 2018; Košir 2014; Saunders et al 2013; Torkar and Kuhar 2018).

With the Foundation, the multifaceted and many-layered legacies of the Isonzo Front were prepared for the marking of the First World War centenary (2014–2018), when dozens of commemoration events, conferences, exhibitions, opening ceremonies, diplomatic meetings and news items were prepared and organized. In the context of these activities, the approaches, meanings, and public presentations of the First World War were firmly aimed at spreading the peace message through the practices of 'engineered and orchestrated remembrance' (Seaton 2018) (Figure 18.1).

FIGURE 18.1 *The Dance of Life and Death* by Slovenian painter Rudi Španzl was unveiled at the Memorial on Cerje hill on a ceremony with high State officials on 25 November 2017. In media coverage, the picture was sometimes dubbed the 'Slovenian Guernica'. (© Author 2017.)

A benefit of this commemorative narrative is that the heritage has so far successfully avoided the curse of becoming the milieu of 'dark tourism' or 'thanatourism' (see Baldwin and Sharpley 2009; Light 2017; Seaton 2018; cf. Clarke et al 2017). Because of its deep symbolic message, this heritage is valued as 'dissonant' or 'difficult', rather than 'dark' (Light 2017: 294). On the debit-side, however, the great expansion of tourist activity arising from the centenary has put increased pressure on the often fragile legacies of the war.

Today, the full package of the Isonzo Front heritage includes all kinds of representations of the front, which seek to fulfill the needs of as many audience-segments as possible, as well as the needs of the local population. There was also an opportunity for various new stakeholders to enter the field and engage in tourism entrepreneurship, something which has brought to the surface more trivial and spectacular aspects of the front's landscape. The lure of increasing tourist traffic meant that the interpretation and sense-making of the Isonzo Front became more flexible, even if its humanized perspective still prevails in its public image.

The military technology narrative of the Isonzo Front

As stated above, the technological side of the First World War warfare has always been an important part of the institutional presentation of the Isonzo Front. Battlefields were presented in a scholarly manner, trenches were cleaned, restored and preserved, and outdoor museums were established on the front lines (see Koren 2015). Specialized tourist guides were educated and trained for the Isonzo Front heritage and a new documentation-information centre was established next to the Kobarid Museum with an exhibition hall (Figure 18.2). Over two decades, the legacies of the Isonzo Front simultaneously received scholarly attention, were internationally promoted and, importantly, were adapted to the Soča Valley's recreational and leisure tourism.

Within this framework, the narrative of the achievements of military technology and the formation of the front lines in the demanding mountainous environment was the most interesting part of the story for the occasional visitors. The weapons, military equipment and technological evolution that so importantly marked the emergence of twentieth-century industrialized warfare (Saunders 2004: 5–6) were either presented indirectly within the guided tours of the Foundation or directly by amateur associations and collectors.

The marking of the centenary gave this stream of development further impetus; many events were organized on a weekly basis and small initiatives started to mushroom at lower levels. Heritage events were organized in villages, small local exhibitions were held and new information signposts were placed at different war-related spots. Within this omnipresent bustle of the centenary, the First World War became a promising resource for local entrepreneurship.[5] Furthermore, the curators of the Kobarid Museum and the Walk of Peace Foundation could not resist contributing their share.

FIGURE 18.2   A sign board in front of the Pot Miru/Walk of Peace Foundation centre in Kobarid promoting its services. (© Author 2018.)

On 17 September 2017, the Kobarid Museum organized a re-enactment of the 'Battle of Caporetto' in cooperation with the Walk of Peace and the Municipality of Tolmin at Mount Kolovrat near Kobarid. This spectacular presentation, marking the centenary of the beginning of the Twelfth Offensive (24 October, 1917), was explicitly conceived as a martial spectacular (Figure 18.3). It involved about 200 actors from associations across Europe with experience in this kind of event. The 'battle' included pyrotechnic effects, simulated explosions, artillery fire, an air raid (cancelled due to fog), a portable flamethrower and more such elements that made the event as 'authentic' as possible. The event was in general well received by its audience, with the only objection being that the location of the re-enactment was an actual battlefield a century previously. Critics claimed that,

FIGURE 18.3 An advertisement for re-enactment of the Battle of Kobarid at the centenary of the breakthrough at Kobarid. The short description of the event says: 'Demonstration of the armed conflict on the original battlefield of the Isonzo Front with a rich complementary programme'. (© Cultural Historical Association Triglav.)

as many soldiers had died on that battlefield, in a symbolic sense, the re-enactment was performed on their graves (Košir et al 2019: 104).

The world of amateur collectors

By opening their collections to the public in the mid-2000s, amateur collectors were recognized as important co-creators of the modern Isonzo Front heritage. Today, 18 of them are promoted within the Walk of Peace exhibition hall as an additional or optional attraction for visitors interested in the front (Koren 2015: 205). These collections were also inventoried by the Tolmin Museum and, as a result, became a sort of convenient, multi-site common depot for professional curators, who occasionally incorporated artefacts from these collections into their own museums' public exhibits.

The requirements of tourism have also brought amateur collectors onto an (often international) stage as spokespersons and proponents of the material authenticity of war legacies. Their role within this framework was to complement the master story with brutal 'hard evidence' of the weapons and to highlight the technological side of First World War warfare. In this way, the Foundation could distance itself from the 'vulgar' brutality of war and cultivate an interpretation of the war that accorded with the generally accepted standards of European commemoration. Meanwhile the collectors bore the task of satisfying tourists' desire for a more exciting and spectacular stimulus.

Even before they were incorporated into these unifying heritage and tourism frameworks, and received specific roles within them, amateur collectors were

FIGURE 18.4   A handmade lifting weight in the amateur collection – *The Paths of Retreat at Kobarid 1917* – situated near the Italian ossuary above Kobarid. (© Author 2018.)

in constant interaction with their local surroundings. They built their own net-works and channels, through which they communicated with artefacts and with the knowledge that they acquired from them. Many of them also turned their interest away from weapons to small personal items of soldiers, which had more potential for imagining the experience of war. Nevertheless, their collections have always been heterogeneous and usually arranged according to the national armies that fought on the Isonzo Front. These items were primarily attractive to collectors because of their variable materiality. They were different from the artefacts of the local community's past (rural) life also in terms of their quantity. Some of these items repeatedly sparked discussions among collectors about their manufacture, use and functioning (Figure 18.4).

Amateur collecting became problematic in the late 2000s, when metal detec-tors became more accessible and started to be widely (ab)used by the local pop-ulation and by 'detector tourists' from abroad. These 'new' collectors were soon condemned as 'looters' of national archaeological heritage and the authorities started to pursue them.[6] In comparison to the older generation of collectors and their children (and now even grandchildren), the newcomers also used different communication channels, for the availability of information was much greater and the world of collectors more organized internationally.

In light of this, war artefacts started to increasingly move through international trade, different exhibitions and among different collections (Saunders 2010: 27–30;

Saunders et al 2013: 47). Items started to vanish due to the antiquities market. Last but not least, for the younger amateur collectors who combined their hobby with recreation and hiking, even the simple rush of adrenaline that accompanies the signal of the metal detector was sufficient encouragement to continue their activity. In common with this new generation of amateur collectors, other war-enthusiasts – frequently organizing themselves in small associations – displayed a similar level of detachment from official institutional structures, as the following two cases show.

'Association 1313' and 'Rommel's site'

The 13 members of the Association 1313 started to collect Isonzo Front material and explore its sites in the mountains as early as the 1980s. In the 2000s, they arranged an outdoor museum on the hill of Ravelnik (formerly an Austro-Hungarian military position near the town of Bovec), where all of the typical appurtenances of the First World War, such as caverns, an observation post, a machine gun nest, a hospital and more, are presented. But unlike at other outdoor museums of the Walk of Peace, conservation principles were not strictly followed at Ravelnik: elements were added to the site, fortifications strengthened with concrete, barracks artificially built and so on.[7]

The members of the Association 1313 guide through the site wearing uniforms (Figures 18.5 and 18.6). Excursions for schoolchildren from different parts

FIGURE 18.5 Miloš Domevšček, president of the Association 1313. He is pointing out a shell-hole, in his role as guide at the open-air museum Ravelnik. (© Author.)

FIGURE 18.6   Miloš Domevšček as curator of his private collection at his home in Bovec. (© Author.)

of Slovenia are offered and many different groups book them for this comfortable and short open-air experience. The members of the Association 1313 also established a folk theatre group and specialize in presenting the everyday life of soldiers on the Isonzo Front. Their predominantly humorous sketches are performed in original uniforms of all nationalities that were involved at the front. They also attract considerable media attention and often act as photo models in tourism promotion brochures of the region.

The Association 1313 trivialize the dissonance and difficulty of the Isonzo Front heritage. As the oldest self-sufficient heritage association, its members appear as a kind of curiosity in the eyes of managers of the Walk of Peace. But they manage to maintain an existence within the new framing of the Isonzo Front heritage. Their sketches performed in replica uniforms can claim to be of educational value, with their light-hearted approach being loved by schoolchildren and tourists alike. Nevertheless they have rarely been invited to participate in officially organized commemorative events.

The case of Erwin Rommel's site is different. The initiative for presenting Rommel's role in the battle of Kobarid came from the local community of the village of Jevšček, where Rommel and his men spent the night between 25 and 26 October 1917. The next day they conquered Mount Matajur above Kobarid. Twenty years later, Rommel described that night and the conquest in his book *Infantry Attacks* (Rommel 2009 [1937]) which, along with diaries and other archival sources, served for reconstruction of this event *in situ*. The authentic homestead, where Rommel planned the attack and a small trench near the village was arranged with the help of the Kobarid Museum. A memorial plaque was placed on the house's front wall and was unveiled for the centenary of the beginning of the Twelfth Offensive. The site also became part of the Walk of Peace in 2018 (see Brgolič homestead 2018; Rommel's site 2018).

Soon after Rommel appeared on the map of the Isonzo Front heritage, a controversy emerged about presenting the famous 'Desert Fox' within its framework. To some, his role in the battle was no more notable than that of many other German officers who – in accordance with the doctrine of mission-command (*Auftragstaktik*) – had to take their own decisions for achieving their military goals (see note 4) (Potočnik 2021). However, to the local supporters, Rommel seemed a suitable figure for creating an interesting local attraction. Because of the risk of giving an impression that the Walk of Peace mythologizes a mass killer and a well-known supporter of Italian fascism in this region during his Nazi times (Močnik 2017), the managers of the Foundation hesitated to include this site for a long time. There are of course different levels of 'inclusion'. The presence of 'Rommel's Encampment' on the webpage of the Foundation falls well short of full endorsement, and it is not highlighted in the latter's education and tourism programmes.

The owner of the Brgolič homestead was the main motivator of this project. He was similar to the amateur collectors in that he was not a professional curator, but differed in that he was a newcomer. He wanted to be independent and self-sufficient in presenting the site, but at the same time to have it promoted by official institutions. As the marking of the centenary triggered the restoration and touristic exploitation of ever more wartime sites, Rommel's Encampment may function as a precedent for their integration into the already crowded brand of the Walk of Peace.

Conclusion

With the pan-European marking of the centenary of the First World War, the former Isonzo Front became a place of 'engineered and orchestrated remembrance' (Seaton 2018), was simultaneously mobilized for state-level diplomacy (Clarke et al 2017) and adapted to recreational tourism (Kravanja 2014). In this chapter, we have seen how the heterotopic gap between the European commemorative framework of its overall presentation and its 'other spaces' (Foucault 1984) have been changing and shifting in the last 30 years. Two basic narratives of the Isonzo Front have been discussed: that of its military history and technology and that concerning its humanistic, democratized and commemorative meaning.

In many instances, the two approaches towards presentation on the Isonzo Front have been mutually compatible. Especially in practices of maintenance and development of its material culture, both approaches were complementary and created the heritage brand of the Walk of Peace, which was adapted to leisure tourism practices as an educational approach to the Soča Valley destination. The top-down imposition of pan-European commemorative principles impregnated the image of the Isonzo Front with notions of peace and commemoration of its victims, while the presentation of military and material legacies was – to a certain extent – left to amateur collectors and enthusiasts.

However, the creation of a 'unified' space that, besides coordinating diverse war-related commemoration practices, also defined the role of the local stake-holders, made the relationship between the two narratives not always an easy one. The predicament of material culture, therefore, emerged out of the heter-otopic gap between the empirical order of things and their interpretation (see note 2). Publicly funded institutions supported local initiatives, small amateur projects and alternative presentations of the Isonzo Front heritage; especially if these activities were carried out by early enthusiasts and amateur collectors, regarded, as we have seen, as the founding fathers of this heritage. But the cente-nary also brought new initiatives that were, in addition to the existing group of amateurs, motivated by an entrepreneurial and commercial spirit. The growing crowd of events and initiatives has brought about a re-evaluation of military remains in the region and foregrounded the difficulty and dissonance of adapting such a heritage for tourism and hospitality.

By the time these new initiatives began to press for inclusion within the ambit of the Walk of Peace, the latter project was effectively complete, and its dis-plays of military structures and technology were both sufficient and adjusted to a pan-European framework of meaning-making. This did not prevent the further development of these new sites and attractions in accordance with the preferences of their 'owners'. Meanwhile strategic questions regarding the future development of the Walk of Peace continued to revolve around the relationship between the heritage 'brand' that had been established and the exigencies of (potentially 'dark') tourism (Light 2017).

Nogués Pedregal (2008: 141) rightly stated that 'tourism is one of the names of power'. Its discourse can enter into public justification of any cultural pro-duction, almost like an amorphous fog. As such, it creates complexity, which for umbrella institutions is not exactly a desirable thing. Accordingly, these institu-tions either act as simplifiers of an otherwise vivid and rich cultural product or lose themselves in an increasing heterogeneity of too many local initiatives and search for their own independent path of branding that is based on cooperation with similar institutions from elsewhere.

According to other development streams of the Soča Valley (Kravanja 2014), the umbrella institutions of the Isonzo Front heritage tried to integrate as much as possible of the local cultural production into their framework and make it suitable for wider (inter)national orders and their intended audiences. However, the flurry of activity that followed the success of the Walk of Peace during the marking of the centenary was a powerful process. In searching for entrepreneur-ial opportunities, it once again pushed the military aspect of the Isonzo Front heritage to the fore.

In this sense, the creation of a transferable heritage brand that was promoted on international heritage stages was a parallel process, by which the Foundation distanced itself from decision-making on the local levels. If the domain of interest groups, individual initiatives, amateur collectors and, last but not least, the local community as a whole, became a self-sufficient stakeholder, then the Walk of Peace Foundation might have become a stranger in its own home. But if the integration of this cultural production into the official heritage brand continues, then the emerging gap between the two narratives will remain concentrated on the question of material legacies of the Isonzo Front.

Acknowledgements

The chapter is a result of the national research projects *Heritage of the First World War: Representations and Reinterpretations* (Slovenian Research Agency, 2016–2018) and *Young entrepreneurs in times of uncertainty and accelerated optimism: An ethnological study of entrepreneurship and ethics of young people in modern-day Slovenia* (Slovenian Research Agency, 2019–2022). The main argument of the chapter is derived from research published in Kravanja (2018b). I am grateful to the employees of the Kobarid Museum and the Walk of Peace Foundation, amateur collectors and other enthusiasts for their cooperation in the research.

Notes

1 These first exhibitions took place in the Kobarid Museum of the First World War and gave an opportunity to the nations of the Austro-Hungarian and Italian army to present their part on the Isonzo Front. With them, the museum obtained additional documentation about the Isonzo Front, especially from archives in Vienna and Budapest.

2 Michel Foucault used the notion of hetorotopia in two different (con)texts. In his famous lecture about 'other spaces' (Foucault 1984), he defined six principles (or types) of heterotopias that include places of life crisis and transitions, cemeteries, gardens, museums, libraries, colonies, etc. The function of these places is mainly to localize different utopias and reflect other surrounding or distant sites (24). In the second context (Foucault 2002: preface), heterotopia is a space that creates a gap between empirical order of things and its interpretation. In this sense, the empirical order of things becomes open to changes, reinterpretations and 'related to a series of variables or defined by separate systems of coherences [...]' (Foucault 2002: xxii).

3 A detailed presentation of the Battle of Caporetto/Kobarid is still present in the museum's introductory multivision projection and further explained in a large model that is placed in one of its exhibition halls.

4 In terms of military doctrine, this one-and-only attack of the Austro-Hungarian army on the Isonzo Front is interesting because it introduced a so-called 'mission command' (Germ. *Auftragstaktik*) into the fighting. According to this command, the subordinate commanders had to achieve a military goal independendly, with their own initiatives, decision-making, tactics and manoeuvring. Today, mission command is widespread in military doctrine, but its origins, importantly, were introduced by the German army on the Isonzo Front (Dovjak 2018; Torkar and Kuhar 2018).

5 Especially in gastronomy. Different 'authentic' First World War menus and dishes were introduced. Amongst other things, public places were decorated with First World War aesthetics, a new collection was opened to the public on a prestigious location near the Italian ossuary above Kobarid, and new thematic guided tours were introduced by tourist agencies online.

6 The tension between collectors and authorities intensified with the new Heritage Protection Act in 2008. Article 3 of this act newly defined archaeological heritage, in which arms, ammunition and other military materials, vehicles and vessels or their parts that had been under the ground or water for at least 50 years were included. With this act, the collection of war-related materials became strictly forbidden, and the act also interfered with the existing private collections.

7 For example, the Outdoor Museum Kolovrat above Kobarid (the Italian defence line) and the Park of Peace at Mt. Sabotin above Gorica (an Austro-Hungarian bridgehead siezed by Italians in August 1916) have many artificial elements too. Among other reasons, educational and touristic purposes prevailed over a strict conservation approach because these sites were accessible for cars and buses.

References

Baldwin, F. and R. Sharpley. (2009) Battlefield Tourism: Bringing Organized Violence Back to Life. In R. Sharpley and P.R. Stone (eds.), *The Darker Side of Travel: The Theory and Practice of Dark Tourism*, pp 186–206. Bristol, Buffalo and Toronto: Channel View Publications.

Brgolič homestead. (2018) Battle of Caporetto: Erwin Rommel on Brgolič Homestead. Website: https://rommel-isonzo.com/eng.html

Cento-Bull, A. and H.L. Hansen. (2016) On agonistic memory. *Memory Studies* 9 (4): 390–404.

Clarke, D., A. Cento-Bull and M. Deganutti. (2017) Soft power and dark heritage: Multiple potentialities. *International Journal of Cultural Policy* 23 (6):660–674.

Dovjak, R. (2018) 'V 12. soški ofenzivi so se postavljali doktrinarni temelji sodobnega kopenskega vojskovanja'. Website: https://www.rtvslo.si/prva-svetovna-vojna/v-12-soski-ofenzivi-so-se-postavljali-doktrinarni-temelji-sodobnega-kopenskega-bojevanja/469261

Foucault, M. (1984) Of other spaces. *Diacritics* 16 (1):22–27.

———. (2002) *The Order of Things: An Archaeology of Human Sciences*. London and New York: Routledge.

Gegner, M. and B. Ziino. (2012) Introduction: The heritage of war: Agency, contingency, identity. In M. Gegner and B. Ziino (eds.), *The Heritage of War*, pp 1–15. London and New York: Routledge.

Hudales, J. and T. Roženbergar (eds.) (2017) *Collecting and collections in times of war or political and social change: COMCOL annual conference, Celje 2014*. Ljubljana: ZZFF.

Jezernik, B. and J. Fikfak. (2018) Cultural heritage of the Great War. *Traditiones* 47 (1):7–32.

Klavora, M. (2016) Pot miru od Alp do Jadrana in dediščina soške fronte. *Glasnik Slovenskega etnološkega društva* 56 (3–4):134–136.

Kobarid Museum. (2018) Awards. Website: https://www.kobariski-muzej.si/en/museum/201802121741285002/awards/

Koren, T. (2015) *The Walk of Peace from the Alps to the Adriatic: A guide along the Isonzo Front*, 2nd ed. Kobarid: Ustanova Fundacija Poti miru v Posočju.

Košir, U. (2014) Arheologija in prva svetovna vojna. *Apokalipsa* 185–186:102–128.

Košir, U., N.J. Saunders, M. Črešnar and G. Rutar. (2019) Between Tourism and Oblivion: Rombon and Kolovrat – Conflict Landscapes on the Soča Front, 1915–2017. In U. Košir, M. Črešnar and D. Mlekuž (eds.), *Rediscovering the Great War: Archaeology and Enduring Legacies on the Soča and Eastern Fronts*, pp 90–108. London: Routledge.

Kravanja, B. (2014) Selling and sharing culture: On relations between cultural heritage, nature conservation and tourism development institutions in the Upper Soča Valley, Slovenia. *Narodna umjetnost* 51 (1):89–112.

————. (2018a) Dediščina soške fronte kot izhodišče za razmislek o sodobnih pristopih k dediščinski politiki. *Etnolog* 28:105–122.

————. (2018b) Learning by collecting: Amateur collectors and their shifting positions in the Isonzo Front heritagization and tourism adaptation. *Folklore* 73:95–116.

Light, D. (2017) Progress in dark tourism and thanatourism research: An uneasy relationship with heritage tourism. *Tourism Management* 61:275–301.

Meijer-van Mensch, L. (2017) Profiling and reflecting on collections and collecting. In J. Hudales and T. Roženbergar (eds.), *Collecting and Collections in Times of War or Political and Zocial Change: COMCOL Annual Conference, Celje 2014*, pp 19–27. Ljubljana: ZZFF.

Nogués Pedregal, A.M. (2008) A Contextual Approach to Power Relation between Tourism and Development. In P. Burns and M. Novelli (eds.), *Tourism Development. Growth, Myths and Inequalities*, pp 141–158. Wallingford: CABI.

Potočnik, A.J. (2021) Controversy in the Julian Alps: Erwin Rommel, Landscape, and 12th Battle of the Soča/Isonzo. In N.J. Saunders and P. Cornish (eds.), *Conflict Landscapes: Materiality and Meaning in Contested Places*, pp 85–106. London: Routledge.

Rommel, E. (2009) [1937] *Infantry Attacks*. Minneapolis: Zenith Press.

Rommel's site. (2018) Erwin Rommel at Caporetto 1917: Battle for Cragonza. Website: https://www.youtube.com/watch?v=9D7D7kZHZ9g

Močnik, B. (2017) Rommel teh krajev ni osvobajal, ampak je prišel le izpolnit svojo nalogo. An Interview with a historian Blaž Torkar. Newspaper *Delo: Sobotna priloga*, 20 October:14–15.

Saunders, N.J. (2004) Material culture and conflict: The Great War, 1914–2003. In N.J. Saunders (ed.), *Matters of Conflict: Material Culture, Memory and the First World War*, pp 5–25. London and New York: Routledge

————. (2010) *Killing Time: Archaeology and the First World War*. Stroud: The History Press.

Saunders, N.J., N. Faulkner, U. Košir, M. Črešnar and S. Thomas. (2013) Conflict landscapes of the Soča/Isonzo Front, 1915–2013: Archaeological–anthropological evaluation of the Soča Valley, Slovenia. *Arheo* 30: 47–66.

Seaton, T. (2018) Encountering Engineered and Orchestrated Remembrance: A Situational Model of Dark Tourism and Its History. In P.R. Stone, R. Hartman, T. Seaton, R. Sharpley and L. White (eds.), *The Palgrave Handbook of Dark Tourism Studies*, pp 9–31. London: Palgrave Macmillan.

Sedmak, D. (1997) Prva svetovna vojna. In Z. Likar, A. Raspet and Ž. Cimprič (eds.), *Kobarid*, pp 85–118. Kobarid: Kobariški muzej.

Slovenian Press Agency. (2015–2020) Soška fronta v številkah. Website: https://www.sta.si/soska-fronta/v-stevilkah

Sutton, R.K. (2012) Commemorating the American Civil War in National Park Service Battlefields. In M. Gegner and B. Ziino (eds.), *The Heritage of War*, pp 108–124. London and New York: Routledge.

Svoljšak, P. (1993) Prva svetovna vojna in Slovenci. *Zgodovinski časopis*. 47 (4):547–562.

Testen, P. and T. Koren. (2015) Učilnica na prostem – Primer *Poti miru*. *Prispevki za novejšo zgodovino* 55 (2):183–198.

Torkar, B. and M. Kuhar. (2018) *Zadnja bitka na Soči 1917*. Celovec: Mohorjeva družba.

Walk of Peace. (2017) About the foundation. Website: http://www.potmiru.si/eng/the-walk-of-peace-from-the-alps-to-the-adriatic

Afterword

COMMEMORATING THE FIRST WORLD WAR TODAY

The In Flanders Fields Museum, Ypres, Belgium

Dominiek Dendooven

To commemorate

Commemoration is the core business of In Flanders Fields Museum. It is what my colleagues and I devote ourselves to every day, and often into the night. It's also something we think about a lot together: what we commemorate, how we commemorate and why we commemorate.

There is a difference between remembering, remembrance and commemoration.[1] First and foremost, remembering is an individual and contemplative act: evoking something from the past in our minds. Remembrance is remembering collectively. It is a meaningful, yet still passive act. Commemorating, however, is much more than just remembering. It is remembering with a certain purpose: to evoke events or facts from the past together, and this is in relation to the way in which that past has formed various identities. By commemorating that particular past, we affirm collective values for today. We do not commemorate just anything. What we commemorate is the result of a choice in which political or other social forces play a role, but also something practical such as the available budget. Every commemoration has a voluntary aspect, but in a democracy such as ours, that choice cannot be completely arbitrary, nor can it be completely at odds with either the historical knowledge of the moment or the way we see the world today. Contrary to remembrance, commemoration must be meaningful for the present: it is remembering with an important active, even activist element. In contrast to remembrance, therefore, commemoration is not merely contemplative, but also operative: it does something and calls for something to be done in the world (Figure 19.1).

At In Flanders Fields Museum, this activist element was there from the beginning. When, in the mid-1990s, the Ypres city council decided that the rather traditional Ypres Salient Memorial Museum (what's in a name!) needed to

DOI: 10.4324/9781003263531-23

FIGURE 19.1 A display on commemoration at In Flanders Fields Museum. (© Author.)

professionalize and transform into the In Flanders Fields Museum, the additional assignment was to propagate the idea of 'Ypres, City of Peace'. In the words of the museum-co-ordinator Piet Chielens, 'This museum... has grown from a kind-hearted region that is still trying to make sense of the fact that it was once a hell, and in which a message has been deeply engraved' (Chielens 1998: 31). Those who would visit the new museum should, it was thought, be more inclined to the idea of peace afterwards. Actually, this should be a matter of course: after all, every good war museum should show what war does to people. And if it does that in a positive and effective way, then only the most wicked visitor will leave with the belief that war is a good idea. But the city of Ypres went one step further: at the same time as the In Flanders Fields Museum was being constituted, a Peace Fund was set up to support peace initiatives and award an Ypres Peace Prize every three years. Today, there is a Peace and Development Department within the town administration. Its activities are coordinated with those of the museum. The idea is not simply to look at the past for its own sake, but also to do good for today and tomorrow.

Cosmopolitan commemoration

For a long time, it was assumed that there were mainly two types of commemoration: the antagonistic and the cosmopolitan. Antagonistic commemoration practices are related to monumental heritage (such as war memorials) and a canonical version of history, as well as a black-and-white division of the historical characters into good and bad. It is also based on a festive, glorifying or nostalgic style of storytelling in which 'heroes' often take centre stage. It is the classic us-against-them rhetoric in which, consciously or unconsciously, hostile thinking is perpetuated. The cosmopolitan or ethical way of remembrance, on the other hand, emphasizes the human suffering caused by atrocities and violations of human rights in the past. Rather than 'us' versus 'them', good and evil are represented in more abstract terms. The narrative is characterized by contemplation, regret and mourning, and the emphasis in this mode of remembrance is on the victims. If we want to translate this theory to the First World War in a somewhat simplistic way, it means that in the antagonistic discourse, the Allies (or one's own nation) are the good guys, and the Germans (or the other nation) the bad. In a cosmopolitan narrative about the First World War, there is another contradiction: ordinary people (civilians or soldiers) are 'all victims', misled by their officers, politicians and other powers-that-be.

It is clear that In Flanders Fields Museum, from its inception in 1998, has embedded itself in that cosmopolitan discourse. Since the aim was to show what war does to people, the emphasis was on how the First World War was experienced by those who lived it without too much distinction according to nationality, gender, or status. After all, such issues make little difference when it comes to how it felt to be in no man's land and liable to lose one's life any moment or what it was like to lose an arm or a leg. At In Flanders Fields Museum #1 (1998–2011), the visitor was offered a large collection of the most individual emotions, with victimization as the common thread. Occasionally we were criticized for 'not saying clearly enough who started the war, who won the war and what the stakes of the war were'. Our answer was always that this was sufficiently discussed elsewhere, for example in other war museums.

Inclusive commemoration

In addition, In Flanders Fields Museum tried and is trying to be as inclusive as possible in its way of commemorating the First World War. By this I mean that the museum wanted to integrate ever more forgotten groups into the existing Great War narrative. For example, since the museum's second major temporary exhibition in 2004, we have been paying ample attention to Belgian refugees (Figure 19.2). Despite the fact that up to a quarter of Belgians were estimated to have fled the country in October 1914, it is a subject neglected by historiography and to which only one doctoral thesis has so far been devoted. In my own research, publications and exhibitions, I have focused on the non-European presence in Europe during

FIGURE 19.2 The display dedicated to refugees at In Flanders Fields Museum. (© Author.)

the First World War. Once again, we are talking about hundreds of thousands of individuals whose presence and contribution had until recently been either completely forgotten or deliberately written out, and who are now happily and justifiably re-integrated in our view of the Great War. Other forgotten groups that we are trying to give a voice to in commemoration include the civilian victims of the First World War (Figure 19.3) and the tens of thousands of 'Zivil-Arbeiter' (Belgian and French civilians employed as forced labourers by the German Occupying forces) who are accounted for almost nowhere else.

An important question is why are such groups not, or hardly, remembered? I think the answer is quite simple: they are not 'heroes' but rather 'losers'. They have no place in a national and nationalist discourses, so they are not officially commemorated. There are few heroic stories to be told about refugees, colonial workers, forced labourers, personnel in munitions factories and so on. They cannot set an example and we do not wish to identify with them. This is a worldwide phenomenon – simply compare the number of scholarly studies dedicated to combat troops with those dedicated to the much less 'heroic' support units behind the lines, estimated in the First World War to make up a third to half of the rank and file (if not more) (McGrath 2007: 11–16).

What and how we commemorate is a political choice and this became clear, for example, in 2015–2016 at the start of the so-called refugee crisis when Europe was confronted with hundreds of thousands of refugees crossing the

FIGURE 19.3   The display dedicated to the ordeal of civilian populations in occupied Belgium at In Flanders Fields Museum. (© Author.)

Mediterranean, and all the human tragedies this entailed. In Flanders Fields Museum wanted to make a comparison between 'our' refugees during the First World War and those of today. Never before did we receive so much hate mail. Most of the criticism voiced in these mails was devoid of rational elements and could be categorized as emotional, even aggressive outbursts. It seemed that for many people the idea that our ancestors would even be compared to today's desperate refugees was unbearable. The chairperson of one of Belgium's leading political parties even managed to claim that the comparison with the world wars was not valid 'because we now don't know how long this will take' (as if people in 1914 and 1940 did).

Agonistic commemoration

The Belgian political scientist and philosopher Chantal Mouffe pointed out in her publications of the last 15 years that the cosmopolitan way of commemorating has certainly not supplanted antagonistic thinking (Mouffe 2005, 2012). On the contrary, she even sees the recent rise of populism and the extreme right as a consequence of the pernicious desire for consensus that just misses fundamental contradictions. That is why Anna Cento Bull and Hans Lauge Hansen advocated a third form of commemoration, which they call agonistic. (Cento Bull and Hansen 2016: 399–400). This is contemplative but also seeks dialogue. It is based on a multitude of politicized representations of the past. In doing so, it recognizes the existence of a wide variety of different civil and political emotions and takes into account different forms of collective and individual 'agency' (acting). It is therefore a method of remembrance that does not claim to possess the truth, but rather seeks nuance. Once again translated into the First World War, this means, among other things, avoiding generalizations: not all British/Belgian/German/... soldiers are de facto heroes; not all British/Belgian/German/... soldiers are de facto victims, ...

In Flanders Fields Museum took Mouffe's criticism and especially the plea for a 'third way' in commemoration to heart. This is also desperately needed: while a lot of good things happened during the recent centenary of the First World War, there are numerous signs that the exclusive, antagonistic commemoration is back. In 2018, for example, the Sir John Monash Centre opened in Villers-Bretonneux, France, which celebrates and praises the Australian Army uncritically during the First World War. In my country, the project to make the graves of Belgian soldiers who had been repatriated to their hometown cemeteries recognizable is called 'Our Forgotten Heroes' and the sign to mark their graves bears the inscription 'Pro Patria'. And what about the steep rise of the phenomenon of re-enactment, which involves dressing up as a soldier and re-enacting war (and even imitating gas attacks). Re-enactment is pretentious (for one imagines that it is even possible to put oneself in the shoes of a soldier at that time), deceitful (for some things like being terrified or injured can never be imitated) and is de facto antagonistic (for one puts on the uniform, i.e. one explicitly identifies oneself with this or that party fighting against the other).

In Flanders Fields Museum tries to counterbalance these, in its view, evil tendencies by dealing with the war past in an even more nuanced way. On the one hand by working even more inclusively, thus involving even more (forgotten) voices in the commemoration of war, thus demonstrating the multitude of experiences and counteracting simplified black/white thinking. On the other hand, we also need to have an eye in that multitude of voices for phenomena that 'don't appeal to us' such as nationalism, hero worship and the attraction that the military exercises on many. There is no point in denying the existence of such feelings, so it is better to frame them and place them in context than to try and conceal or minimize them. This antagonistic remembrance is not easy because it is sometimes counterintuitive. It is necessary, however: only in this way can we really enter into dialogue.

Museums of loaded themes

In Flanders Fields Museum is by no means the only museum that commemorates and critically self-reflects on the way it does so. For some time, now there has been a collaboration between various 'museums of loaded themes' in Belgian

Flanders. Besides IFFM, these include the Kazerne Dossin in Mechelen, the Museum Dr Guislain in Ghent, the Red Star Line Museum in Antwerp, and recently joined by the well-known AfricaMuseum in Tervuren. What these museums have in common is that the subjects they deal with (war, holocaust and human rights, psychiatry, emigration, colonialism) hold up a mirror to today's society and force it to self-reflect. Therefore, the way in which these subjects are commemorated easily leads to contestation. A case in point are the events related to the Dossin Kazerne at the end of 2019 and beginning of 2020. The partly politicized management board of this museum of holocaust and human rights had banned an award ceremony for a well-known Middle East specialist because she was also known to be a critic of Israel's occupation policy. In protest at the ban and the infringement on their freedom of action, the director, some of the leading staff and most members of the scientific committee resigned.

What few members of the public question is the raison d'être of our institutions. After all, we all agree that there is a need for commemoration. However, who exactly is to be commemorated, what exactly is to be commemorated (in other words, what the emphasis should be on), how it is to be commemorated and, above all, for what purpose it is to be commemorated, that is the stakes of debate, of a battle of ideas. Commemoration is not simply remembering. Commemoration is about the values we want to uphold in our society. Commemoration therefore also serves to guide today's society. In other words, it is looking to the past to work for the future.

Note

1 In my mother tongue, Dutch, there is a clear difference between 'herinnering' and 'herdenking'. The former is usually translated as memory, the second as remembrance or commemoration. The former one is introspective, the latter activist. In Dutch both come from verbs: herinnering is from herinneren = to remember ; herdenking is from herdenken = to commemorate. There is even more to it as her-inneren is literally 'to re-inner' and her-denken is literally 'to re-think about'. And that makes the difference much clearer between the two. For this English text, I have opted to use the word 'remembrance' for (passively) remembering collectively and commemoration for a more active form of remembrance.

References

Cento Bull, A. and H.L. Hansen. (2016) On agonistic memory. *Memory Studies* 9 (4): 390–404.

Chielens, P. (1998) The story of the museum. In *In Flanders Fields Museum Guide*, pp 26–31. Ypres: In Flanders Fields Museum.

McGrath, J. (2007) *The Other End of the Spear: The Tooth-to-Tail Ratio (T3R) in Modern Military Operations*. Fort Leavenworth: Combat Studies Institute Press.

Mouffe, C. (2005) *On the Political*. London: Routledge.

———. (2012) An agonistic approach to the future of Europe. *New Literary History* 43 (4): 629–640.

Index